THE HOLY YEAR OF JUBILEE

THE OPENING OF THE HOLY DOOR AT ST. PETER'S.
Reproduced from a drawing of Pietro Gagliardi.

THE HOLY YEAR

OF

JUBILEE

AN ACCOUNT OF THE HISTORY AND CEREMONIAL OF THE ROMAN JUBILEE

BY

HERBERT THURSTON, S.J.

ILLUSTRATED FROM CONTEMPORARY ENGRAVINGS AND OTHER SOURCES

THE NEWMAN PRESS

WESTMINSTER, MARYLAND

1949

Nihil Obstat.

SYDNEY F. SMITH, S.J.,

CENSOR DEPUTATUS.

Imprimatur.

HERBERTUS CARD. VAUGHAN,

ARCHIEP. WESTMONAST.

September 15, 1900.

Lithographed By

WICKLAND - NALLEY INC.

Westminster, Md.

Printed in the United States of America

O Roma nobilis, orbis et domina,
Cunctarum urbium excellentissima,
Roseo martyrum sanguine rubea,
Albis et virginum liliis candida:
Salutem dicimus tibi per omnia,
Te benedicimus: salve per secula.

Petre tu prepotens cœlorum claviger,
Vota precantium exaudi jugiter.
Cum bis sex tribuum sederis arbiter,
Factus placabilis judica leniter;
Teque petentibus nunc temporaliter
Ferto suffragia misericorditer.

O Paule suscipe nostra precamina,
Cuius philosophos vicit industria.
Factus economus in domo regia
Divini muneris appone fercula,
Ut, quæ repleverit te Sapientia,
Ipsa nos repleat tua per dogmata.

Hymn discovered by G. B. Niebuhr in Vatican MS. 3227 of the eleventh century and assigned by him to the seventh century; but cf. Traube, *Abhandlungen der Philosoph.-Philolog. Classe der K. Bayerischen Akademie der Wissenschaften*, vol. xix. p. 301 (1892).

PREFACE

The comprehensive account of the Roman Jubilee which is presented to the public in the following pages has developed considerably since its first inception. It was originally intended to be no more than a compilation from well-known authorities—a compilation for which the writer of this preface proposed only to discharge the functions of editor. The difficulties, however, of adapting for modern readers the language and ideas of the older Jubilee manuals were soon found to be insuperable. Accordingly, the book which has resulted has grown in scope, and is practically an original work. At the same time, it has not been written entirely by one hand, and the responsibility indicated by the attribution upon the title page must be understood in some portions to represent revision rather than direct authorship.

Upon one point of some little interest the conclusions of the writer are at variance with those commonly received. Historians of every school, from Bonanni and Zaccaria down to Gregorovius, have hitherto been agreed in attributing the introduction of the Holy Door ceremonial to Pope Alexander VI. in the year 1500. So universally has this opinion been accepted that certain early specimens of papal medals, otherwise open to no suspicion, have been pronounced forgeries, simply because they contained some reference to the Holy Door at a date prior to the Jubilee of Alexander.[1] The evidence now for the first time[2] brought together is sufficient, I think, to show that the view just mentioned is quite untenable. Unfortunately, many of the facts have

---

[1] See pp. 40-43.

[2] Since chapter ii. was written and in type, attention has been drawn in two different periodicals to a portion of this evidence, viz.. in the *Zeitschrift für Katholische Theologie*, 1900, p. 174, by Dr. N. Paulus, and in the *Civiltà Cattolica* for February the 17th, 1900. Several other early references, besides those cited in these articles, will be found in the present volume, pp. 35-39, 151-153, 179-181, and Appendix C, pp. 405-406.

only come to hand while the book was in the press. Chapter ii. was originally written in a much less confident tone than I should now feel justified in assuming, and it has perhaps suffered somewhat in coherence from the alterations made in proof. Moreover, there are further details bearing on the subject which it has only been found possible to introduce in an Appendix.

In other matters the book does not present any notably original views. Most readers will probably be surprised at the amount of interest which seems to have been elicited in this country by the Holy Year of 1700, an interest which is conspicuously illustrated by the title of George Farquhar's comedy.[1] It is also probably the first time[2] that any connected account has been given of what may be called the English Jubilee, which, curiously enough, dates back, it seems, to the days of Cardinal Stephen Langton, and may, by a rather strained interpretation, be held to have anticipated the first Roman Jubilee of Boniface VIII. in 1300. The higher standards of culture and humanity which prevailed in Rome during the seventeenth and eighteenth centuries, as compared with the other countries of Europe, are also a matter which appears worthy of more attention than it has commonly received. The question of the hospitals and charitable institutions of Italy could not, however, consistently with the scope of the volume, have been developed at greater length.

It has not been at all the writer's wish to make the book controversial, nor has his first intention been to consult the devotional needs of his fellow-Catholics. It seemed desirable, however, for the sake of completeness, to include some account of the practical aspects of the Jubilee, and to enter a protest against the serious misunderstanding of the phrase *a pœna et culpa* which has prompted sundry attacks on the Catholic system of Indulgences. It is easy for those who have no interest in such matters to pass over the contents of chapters viii. and ix. In the former of these chapters has been incorporated the greater part of an article on "the Jubilee Indulgence *a pœna et culpa*," for permission to reproduce which the author wishes to express his gratitude to the editor of the *Dublin Review*.

---

[1] See pp. 113 *seq.*

[2] I am far from wishing to underrate my obligations to Dr. Brigstocke Sheppard's preface to the third volume of *Literæ Cantuarienses*, but he seems to have overlooked certain aspects of the subject, and his book is not accessible to the majority of readers.

A word of explanation ought to be added with regard to some of the illustrations which, from an artistic point of view, are not particularly pleasing. Several of them are taken from a set of Jubilee broadsides at the British Museum, and these being both exceedingly rough in their original execution, and having further suffered from the rough usage of centuries, offered exceptional difficulties in reproduction. It seemed better, however, to leave them in their primitive crudity than to have them re-drawn. In one or two cases the author has thought he might be pardoned if in illustration of contemporary Italian manners he introduced subjects whose connection with the Jubilee is comparatively remote. The references to the Cardinals' coaches on pp. 90-92, and to travelling in Italy, pp. 280-282, may be cited as instances in point.

In one passage[1] the author regrets to find that he has quoted, as belonging to the sixth century, a stanza of a hymn written by Father Faber in the nineteenth. He can only plead in excuse that he was betrayed by an oversight in the, as a rule, most adequate and trustworthy translation of the Roman Breviary by the Marquis of Bute. In the first edition of that work is printed Father Faber's translation of the famous hymn, *Decora lux æternitatis*, attributed to Elpidia, the wife of Boethius, and assigned in the Breviary for the feast of SS. Peter and Paul. Lord Bute has not noticed that the stanza beginning—

For thou alone art worth them all

is not represented by anything in the original, but is an addition of Father Faber's. Another much more inexcusable error is contained in the reference made to Professor Rudolph Lanciani on p. 140, where that distinguished antiquary is described as a non-Catholic writer. Unfortunately the author discovered his mistake too late to correct it in his proper place, and he can now do no more than offer to Professor Lanciani his most sincere apologies.

The author's thanks are due to many persons who have kindly helped him in answering questions or procuring photographs, and more especially to one friend who has compiled materials for several of the chapters, who has prepared the index, and rendered many more services than could be easily specified here.

HERBERT THURSTON, S.J.

---

[1] P. 163.

TABLE OF CONTENTS

LIST OF ILLUSTRATIONS

THE HOLY YEAR OF JUBILEE

CHAPTER I

The Beginnings of the Jubilee

The Bull of promulgation proclaiming "the Universal Jubilee of the Holy Year" was published by his Holiness Pope Leo XIII. on Ascension Day, 1899. In this document the aged Pontiff, addressing himself to the faithful of Christ throughout the world, introduces his announcement of the Jubilee with the following impressive words:—

"The century which, by God's favour, we have ourselves lived through almost from its commencement is drawing rapidly to a close. Gladly, then, and in conformity with the custom of past ages, we have determined to publish a decree which may be a source of salvation to Christian peoples, and may, as it were, mark the last step of the solicitude with which we have exercised the supreme pontificate. We refer to the Great Jubilee long ago made part of Christian custom and sanctioned by the forethought of our predecessors. In the speech and the tradition of our fathers it has come to be known as the Holy Year, and the name is justified both by the extraordinary sacred ceremonies with which it is accustomed to be celebrated, and especially by the more abundant help which it affords for the correction of morals, and for that renewal of mind and heart which leads to holiness."

Seventy-five years before, little Joachim Pecci, then a boy of fifteen. who had for just a fortnight been frequenting the classes of the Jesuit Fathers in the Collegio Romano, wrote in a letter to his father, Count Lodovico Pecci—

"I was so pleased to hear from Uncle Anthony of the trip which you are thinking of making to Rome as soon as you can get away. I beg and implore of you to come, so that the 'Holy Year' may be some distraction to you in your grief and loneliness, and may bring with it at least a little change of scene."[1]

This letter, which is still preserved, is dated the 15th of December, 1824, ten days before the solemn opening of the only "Anno Santo" which has been held in the nineteenth century. Poor little Joachim's mother, the Countess Anna Pecci, had then been but a few months dead, and the father was still in the first grief of his bereavement. Whether Count Lodovico came to Rome in time for the opening of the Jubilee there is nothing to tell us, but the impression left upon his son's mind by the scenes of that year 1825 has never been effaced. It is thus that Pope Leo XIII. continues in the Bull of promulgation for the present Holy Year—

"We Ourselves were witness in Our youth how helpful to salvation was the last Jubilee decreed in solemn form during the pontificate of Leo XII., at a time when Rome was the greatest and safest theatre for public acts of religion. We remember and We ever seem to see in Our mind's eye the crowds of pilgrims, the multitudes who in processional order went from church to church—the holiest in Christendom; the apostolic men who preached in the public streets, the most sacred places in the city resounding with the praises of God, and the Pontiff with his College of Cardinals setting an example of piety and charity before the eyes of all. From the memory of those times the mind is recalled with some bitterness to the sad reality of the present day. For demonstrations of which We speak, and which, when carried out without hindrance in the full light of the city, are accustomed wonderfully to foster and arouse the

[1] Boyer d'Agen, *La Jeunesse de Leon XIII.*, p. 226.

piety of the people, there is now in the changed state of Rome either no opportunity of organising them, or the permission depends on a will other than Our own."

In the case of Pius IX. the feeling to which these last words give expression was so deep, that in 1875, when the blow of the occupation of Rome was still recent, he could not bring himself to invite his devoted sons to visit the city in which he had once been Sovereign, but in which he now lived a prisoner. An extraordinary Jubilee[1] was proclaimed for the world at large, but no pilgrimage was prescribed to the tombs of the Apostles, and the solemn opening of the Holy Door did not take place. So again at the beginning of 1850 the Pope was an exile in Gaeta, and the revolution of the previous year had put to flight all thought of a universal pilgrimage to the Holy City. Hence it has happened that the ceremonial of the Porta Santa had not been enacted since 1825, and that the holy gates had remained closed for three-quarters of a century when the present Jubilee was proclaimed. Possibly of all the crowds who assisted at the function of last Christmas Eve there was no one save the Sovereign Pontiff himself who had ever crossed the threshold of the Porta Santa before.

Before we make any attempt to discuss the origin of the

[1] Three extraordinary Jubilees, those of 1879, 1881, and 1886, have been held in the present pontificate alone. So far as regards the Indulgences granted, they are to all intents and purposes the same as those offered to the faithful in an ordinary Jubilee, when extended to all Christendom at the expiration of the Jubilee year itself. Furthermore, they are almost invariably attended by the communication of increased powers to ordinary confessors, while the conditions of the pilgrimage to Rome and the visits to the greater Basilicas are replaced by visits to local churches and by fasting and almsgiving. As the name implies, extraordinary Jubilees are not attached to any fixed intervals of time. They are granted, for instance, at the coronation of a Pope or for some special occasion, and they last for just so long or short a space as the Pope may choose to decide. Perhaps we should reckon among the ordinary Jubilees certain plenary Indulgences which are granted in accordance with a fixed law and are attended by special privileges, *e.g.*, the Jubilee to be gained at Compostella when the feast of St. James falls on a Sunday, the Jubilee at Puy en Velay when the feast of the Annunciation falls on Good Friday, the Jubilee of Lyons when the feast of St. John Baptist, the patron of the city, coincides with Corpus Christi. Cf. *Études*, Nov., 1899, p. 433.

Christian Jubilee it may be worth while to note, although it hardly needs saying, that both the word and the idea are borrowed from what we find in the Old Law recorded in the Book of Leviticus. The word Jubilee in its stricter sense denotes, of course, a period of fifty years, and the number fifty is arrived at, not through any decimal system of numeration as being the half of a century, but simply because it is the numeral which follows next after seven complete sevens. The same principle, we may remark, has given the Jewish Pentecost—the "fiftieth-day" feast—with its Christian analogue best known to us as Whit Sunday. The Jews were to number seven weeks of years, *i.e.*, forty-nine years, and the fiftieth was the year of Jubilee. The earth was to lie fallow, land and houses in the open country were to return to their original owners or their heirs, and slaves recovered their freedom. It is in imitation of this Old Testament prototype that the Christian Church also has established its Jubilee proclaiming from time to time "a year of remission" from the penal consequences of sin. In its origin, the Jubilee could only be gained by a visit to Rome, but in return for this pious pilgrimage, then an undertaking of great difficulty and danger, the successors of St. Peter, in whose hands resides the authority to bind and to loose, bestowed upon the pilgrim, duly confessed and contrite, a complete remission from all the temporal punishment due to his sins. Inasmuch as with this remission of penalties there were also included special privileges by which certain confessors were empowered to give absolution for almost any class of sins, however grievous, which otherwise were reserved to the Holy See, the Jubilee Indulgence and others of similar amplitude became popularly known as remissions from guilt and punishment *a culpa et a pœna*, a phrase which afterwards caused difficulty, but which cannot conveniently be discussed in this place. Certain other conditions —in particular, the praying during a specified number of days in the greater Churches of Rome—were also indicated, and in the course of time, when the actual visit to the Eternal City came on some occasions to be dispensed with, this pilgrimage was often compensated for by the giving of alms for the crusade against the Turks, or for the rebuilding of this or that Church or Basilica.

The first Jubilee of which we have clear record was proclaimed by Pope Boniface VIII. in the year 1300. It was intended by him to be celebrated every hundred years, and he seems to have framed his Bull upon the presumption that some such celebration, with special privileges and Indulgences to pilgrims visiting Rome, had existed in Rome from time immemorial, although it was frankly admitted that no written record of these celebrations was any longer to be found. When the middle of the fourteenth century was reached, Clement VI. was earnestly besought by the people of Rome to proclaim another Jubilee, this time a true Jubilee as occurring after a fifty years' interval. Clement VI., who was then residing at Avignon, consented, and the Jubilee was held at Rome in 1350 by the Cardinal Annibaldo, his delegate. Then came the great schism which followed almost immediately upon the return of the successor of St. Peter to the city of the Apostles. A rival papacy to the true line of Popes in Rome was set up in the dominions of the French king. It was not unnatural that Gregory XI., as well as Urban VI. and Boniface IX. who succeeded him, should wish to rally Christians round the genuine Pope and the true centre of Christendom. A Jubilee was accordingly proclaimed by the first, and as he did not live to see its opening, was eventually held by the last-named in 1390; and on the grounds that the allotted span of human life was short, and that comparatively few could hope to enjoy the benefits of a Jubilee which was celebrated but once in two generations, the term was further reduced to the period of thirty-three years, which was the third part of a century, and was also believed to correspond with the lifetime of our Blessed Saviour. One Jubilee was held in conformity with this arrangement—that of 1423—under Pope Martin V. shortly after the healing of the schism; but in 1450 the older and more natural period of fifty years again asserted itself, to be replaced in accordance with the decrees of Paul II. and Sixtus IV. with a twenty-five years' Jubilee, so that every generation of Christians might normally hope to see during the time of their manhood the occurrence of at least one such holy year of pardon. I have touched in this way upon six Jubilees. From 1475, when this arrangement first came into force, the celebrations succeeded each other uninterruptedly every twenty-five years, and that of 1775, in the beginning of the pontificate of Pius VI., was the eighteenth.

During the first months of the year 1800, however, the Holy See was vacant, the world was at the feet of Napoleon, and the new Pope, Pius VII., elected at Venice, did not come to Rome until July. Hence the nineteenth Jubilee was deferred until 1825,[1] when its opening ceremonies were witnessed, amongst others, by the present Pope, and by Cardinal Wiseman, who was then a subdeacon. The latter has left us an account of the ceremony, which we shall have occasion to quote in a subsequent chapter.

But we must turn now to the beginnings of the Jubilee, so far as our historical records enable us to trace them. Few Popes have suffered more from the detraction of unscrupulous calumniators than Pope Boniface VIII., to whom, by common consent, the institution of the Anno Santo is attributed. It may readily be conceded that he was a man who exhibited conspicuous faults of character; it is also probable that he overstepped the bounds both of moderation and of strict right in his energetic efforts to vindicate for the Holy See a supremacy over temporal rulers. But yet his motives were far from unworthy, and the more grievous acts that have been laid to his charge are simply the invention of unscrupulous calumny. Nothing, as Cardinal Wiseman has long ago shown,[2] could be more recklessly mendacious than the account of Boniface to be found in most

[1] It would seem that a Jubilee Bull was drafted in the year 1800 in spite of the delay caused by the election of the new Pope. The state of political events in Europe, however, prevented its ever being published. See Hilgers, *Das Goldene Jahr*, p. 10.

[2] *Essays*, vol. iii., Pope Boniface VIII.

popular histories, notably in the *Italian Republics* of Sismondi. The fierce and inflamed political passions of the time in which Boniface lived, the incredible freedom of speech in days when libel laws were unknown, the heedlessness as to scandal where there were no Protestants to be scandalised, together with the comparative impossibility, before telegraphs and newspapers had come into existence, of controlling and verifying malicious rumours,—all these things have borne hard upon many medieval reputations, and not least of all upon the character of the Popes. Boniface VIII. in particular has suffered from the often-renewed attacks of Dante, his contemporary, who belonged to a hostile political faction, and who, like most other poets, is not conspicuous for sobriety of language where he believed himself to be aggrieved. But even Dante was softened at the picture of that venerable old man of eighty-six unflinchingly facing his enemies and offering himself, unappalled, for martyrdom. "Open the doors," cried Boniface, as the rough soldiers of William of Nogaret advanced to assault his palace at Anagni; "here am I, ready to suffer martyrdom for the Church of God. As I am taken, like Christ, by treachery, so will I die as Pope." Dante re-echoes the spirit of the words when he tells us—

> Lo! the flower de luce
> Enters Alagna! in his Vicar, Christ
> Himself a captive and His mockery
> Acted again! Lo! to His holy lips
> The vinegar and gall once more applied!
> And betwixt living robbers doomed to bleed.[1]

This is not the conduct of a man who, if his enemies were to be believed, soon after committed suicide in despair, refusing the Sacraments. In fact it may be said that all modern historians of any note, even the most anti-papal in their sympathies, have

[1] Veggio in Alagna entrar lo fiordaliso
E nel vicario suo Cristo esser catto.
Veggiolo un' altra volta esser deriso;
Veggio rinnovellar l'aceto e'l fele,
E tra vivi ladroni essere anciso.
—*Purgatorio*, canto xx.

given up the Boniface of the Ghibelline legend.[1] "Thou didst enter fraudulently, thou hast ruled tyrannically, thou shalt die in misery,"[2] was the pretended prophecy of the Abbot Joachim's "Pope Book," really a piece of political pamphleteering, as pamphleteering was understood in the Middle Ages, and composed some time after the event. But the falsehood of the first[3] and the third clause has long been demonstrated; it is only the second which in any sense remains matter for debate. As to this, the summary of Boniface's character by Cardinal Wiseman in one of the most famous of his Essays, already referred to, expresses in substance the truth, and it has found important confirmation in the researches of Abbot Tosti and in those of other writers still more recent—

---

[1] On Boniface VIII. and the references made to him in the course of the *Divina Commedia* the reader may be referred to the articles "Bonifacio VIII. ed un celebre commentatore di Dante" in the *Civiltà Cattolica* for 1899, in answer to Scartazzini.

[2] Fraudulenter intrasti, potenter regnasti, gemens morieris"—this is the form in which it appears in the last line of the reproduction opposite, which is taken from the beautifully illuminated Harleian MS., 1340, at the British Museum. It is also cited in the chronicles in this form, "He shall creep in as a fox, he shall reign as a lion, he shall die like a dog."

[3] Nothing could more clearly show the innocence of Boniface as to the charge of treacherously supplanting his predecessor Pope St. Celestine and inducing him to resign the tiara by false representations than the attitude of Cardinal Stefaneschi towards both of them. While in his writings he constantly proclaims Celestine (Peter de Murrone) a Saint, and extols his holiness to the skies, he is an equally devoted and earnest admirer of Boniface, clearly showing his conviction that Celestine was destitute of those practical qualities which are needed in the ruler of the Universal Church. Stefaneschi was not, as has been wrongly stated, the nephew of Boniface, but he was his friend, and must have known both him and Celestine intimately. So the canonist Joannes Andreas says of Celestine, "Erat unum pecus, de mane faciebat gratiam, et de sero auferebat et alii conferebat." Karl Wenck, *Clemens V. und Heinrich VII.*, p. 143, and Grisar in the *Zeitschrift für Katholische Theologie*, 1883, p. 587. With regard to his own intimate knowledge of Boniface, Stefaneschi observes, "Hinc scito, qui noscere desideras, hunc quidem esse qui ex veridica re, veluti præsens, videns, ministrans, palpans et audiens, notusque Pontifici, quin Pontificibus carus, impactam compegit metrisque refudit historiam ; Dominum Jacobum nomine, cognomento Cajetanum, Diaconum Cardinalem St. Georgii ad Velum Aureum." Cf. Andrea de Angeli, *Jacopo Stefaneschi e il suo "Opus Metricum,"* p. 396. De Angeli also agrees that he was not a nephew of Boniface (*ibid.* p. 388).

DOMINUS BENEDICTUS GAIETANUS. QUI ET BONIFATIUS VIII. PAPA.

Ecce homo de Scariothis progenie occultum principatum habens, qui agnus ruit neromate regnans, morieris desolatus. Abbreviabuntur ei dies illi qui totus mundus tyrampnis terribilis conturbatur. Gallum ferit aquilam deplumat. Gallus et aquila ejus superflua auferent; potestatem columba non timebit ramum portans olive, et in petre foraminibus nidificans cuius securitas est in angelo testamenti quid tantum affectans babilonicum principatum quem obtinere non poteris; contra justum vinculis alligabit.

Fraudulenter intrasti, potenter regnasti, gemens morieris.

A PAGE OF JOACHIM'S "POPE BOOK."
(Harleian MS., 1340.)

"Accustomed as we have been to read and hear so much to the disadvantage of this Pope, we naturally required some cause, however slight, to turn our attention towards a more particular examination of such grievous charges. The pencil of Giotto must claim the merit, such as it is. The portrait of Boniface by him, in the Lateran Basilica, so different in character from the representations of modern history, awakened in our minds a peculiar interest regarding him, and led us to the examination of several popular assertions affecting his moral and ecclesiastical conduct. He soon appeared to us in a new light: as a Pontiff who began his reign with most glorious promise and closed it amid sad calamities; who devoted through it all the energies of a great mind, cultivated by profound learning, and matured by long experience in the most delicate ecclesiastical affairs, to the attainment of a truly noble end; and who, throughout his career, displayed many great virtues, and could plead in extenuation of his faults the convulsed state of public affairs, the rudeness of his times, and the faithless, violent character of many among those with whom he had to deal. These circumstances, working upon a mind naturally upright and inflexible, led to a sternness of manner and a severity of conduct which, when viewed through the feelings of modern times, may appear extreme, and almost

BONIFACE VIII. PROCLAIMING THE JUBILEE.

From painting of Giotto, in the Lateran.

unjustifiable. But after studying the conduct of this great Pope, after searching through the pages of his most hostile historians, we are satisfied that this is the only point on which even a plausible charge can be brought against him—a charge which has been much exaggerated, and which the considerations first enumerated must sufficiently repel, or in great part extenuate."

We may supplement this judgment of the English cardinal, which perhaps inclines to over-leniency, by the verdict of a distinguished French historian of our own days, who will not be suspected of any pro-clerical bias. M. Felix Rocquain, in his more recent work, *La Cour de Rome et l'esprit de Réforme avant Luther*, speaks perhaps a little less favourably of Boniface than in his earlier book, *La Papauté au Moyen Age.* Still, there is nothing to cancel or revoke the following words, which he published in 1881, seemingly after a careful study of Abbot Tosti's *Life of Boniface*:—

"The enemies of this Pope," says M. Rocquain, "have attributed to him all vices and made him guilty of every crime. It is the part of historical justice to clear his reputation of the foul imputations which have undeservedly been cast upon it, the whole odium of which must fall rather upon those who have accused him. Head of the Church at an epoch of degeneration, he was, no doubt, betrayed at times into that indulgence for lax principles which is characteristic of periods of decadence. But more than once he displayed a greatness of character to which it is impossible to shut one's eyes."[1]

This, then, is the Pontiff to whom we owe, if not the origin, at least the first definite recognition and promulgation of the Christian Jubilee of the Holy Year. The story of how this came about has been told in detail by the Cardinal Stefaneschi,[2] whom we have just mentioned, and from his pages we may summarise as much of the narrative as falls in with our present purpose.

---

[1] Rocquain, *La Papauté au Moyen Age*, p. 232.

[2] *De Anno Jubileo*, printed in the *Bibliotheca Patrum* of La Bigne, vol. vi. p. 536. Paris, 1610.

On Christmas Eve, in the year 1299, a vast congregation assembled in the Basilica of St. Peter's for vespers. The congregation was not exclusively Roman. A large number of strangers were present, who had been attracted to Rome, it seems, by a report that great Indulgences could be gained by all who visited the tombs of Sts. Peter and Paul during the course of the ensuing twelvemonth. The reports took various and fantastic forms, but they were consistent in asserting that an Indulgence of some kind or other could be gained at some time not specified during the opening year of the next century. Some said that a plenary Indulgence was offered to all who prayed at the tombs of the Apostles on the first of January; others asserted that the same Indulgence was available upon any day of the year; and others again limited the grant to a hundred days, but supposed that it might be repeated every day of the year for all who daily said a prayer at the shrines of the two great Apostles and patrons of the Holy City. During the week the number of pilgrims increased; the different reports as to what Indulgence could be gained became more numerous and conflicting; the tombs of the Apostles were hourly besieged by a growing throng of worshippers, and the streets were so crowded that, as an early writer expresses it, "It was scarcely possible to walk through the city, vast and large though it was."[1]

Meanwhile the Pope, whenever he chanced to visit St. Peter's, saw his Basilica filled with worshippers; he heard what had induced so many to flock to his capital, was delighted at the piety and religious devotion of the faithful, but took no immediate step either to check it or to encourage it. Even in those early days the Roman Court seems to have possessed in perfection the art of waiting, and it was not till the second Sunday after the Epiphany, 17th January, 1300,[2] when the Sudarium[3]

[1] Platina, *De Vitis Pontif.*

[2] Hefele, *Conciliengeschichte*, says this took place on the feast of St. Veronica, 4th February.

[3] The Sudarium of St. Veronica is the handkerchief with which she is believed to have wiped the face of our Lord, when with some other holy women she met Him on His way to Mount Calvary (Luke xxiii. 27). Our Lord returned the handkerchief with the impression of His countenance upon it.

of St. Veronica was exposed to public veneration, that the Pope, on his way to the Basilica, chanced to meet an old man of one hundred and seven years, a Savoyard, who was being carried to the church in the arms of two or three of his sons. Touched at such a sight, the Pope summoned father and children to his presence, and before several cardinals inquired of the old man his reason for undertaking such a journey at so advanced an age. "I remember," said the aged pilgrim, in reply to his Holiness, "that at the beginning of the last century my father who was a labourer, came to Rome and dwelt here as long as his means lasted, in order to gain the Indulgence. He bade me not to forget to come at the beginning of the next century, if I should live so long, which he did not think I should do." Whereupon he was asked what Indulgence he hoped to gain by coming to Rome. "A hundred days' Indulgence every day of the year," he replied. This report was confirmed by two other men, both centenarians, from the diocese of Beauvais. Aged pilgrims from different parts of Italy gave evidence of a similar tradition. The Pope was interested in these stories, and commissioned some of the cardinals to examine the ancient records, and collect what oral testimony they could as to the belief of the faithful regarding the spiritual favours they expected to obtain by coming to Rome in the opening year of a new century. The result of the inquiry proved the existence of a general belief that an Indulgence of some kind was to be gained, but no written document in support of it could be discovered. Unwilling that his flock should be deprived of what they had put themselves to great inconvenience to obtain, the Pope, on the 22nd of February, issued the following Bull:—

"Boniface, Bishop, Servant of the Servants of God.

"For the perpetual remembrance of the thing.

"The trustworthy tradition of our ancestors affirms that great remissions and Indulgences for sins are granted to those who visit in this city the venerable Basilica of the Prince of the Apostles. Wherefore We who, according to the dignity of our office, desire, and ought to procure, the salvation of each, holding all and each of these remissions and Indulgences to be authentic, do, by our apostolic authority, confirm and approve the same, and even grant afresh and sanction them by this our present writing. In order that the blessed Apostles Peter and Paul may be the more honoured as their Basilicas in this city shall be the more devoutly frequented by the faithful, and that the faithful themselves may feel that they have been replenished by an abundance of spiritual favours in approaching their tombs, We, confiding in the mercy of Almighty God, in the merits and power of these His Apostles, in the counsel of our brethren, and in the plenitude of the apostolic authority, grant to all who, being truly penitent, and confessing their sins, shall reverently visit these Basilicas in the present year 1300, which commenced with the festival of the Nativity of our Lord Jesus Christ which has just been celebrated, and to all who being truly penitent, shall confess their sins, and shall approach these Basilicas each succeeding hundredth year, not only a full and copious, but the most full pardon of all their sins. We determine that whatever persons wish to gain these Indulgences granted by us must, if they be inhabitants of Rome, visit these same Basilicas for thirty days, either successively or at intervals, at least once a day; if they be foreigners or strangers, they must in like manner visit the Basilicas for fifteen days. Nevertheless, each one will merit more, and will the more efficaciously gain the Indulgence as he visits the Basilicas more frequently and more devoutly. Let no man, therefore, dare to infringe or impugn this our rescript of confirmation, approval, renewal, grant, and decree. And if any one presumes to assail it, let him know that he will incur the indignation of Almighty God and of the blessed Apostles Peter and Paul.

"Given at St. Peter's, Rome, February 22, 1300, in the sixth year of our pontificate."

It will be noticed that the word jubilee is not anywhere mentioned in the papal Bull, and that the usage of which tradition spoke is not stated to be connected with the first year of the century. But we know from the very title of

Stefaneschi's treatise[1] that the name was familiar at that epoch, and one finds in the thirteenth century such events celebrated as the jubilee of the translation of St. Thomas of Canterbury, and, of course, the jubilee of a monk's religious profession. In itself there is nothing improbable about the existence of a vague popular tradition which supposed exceptional privileges to be attached to a pilgrimage to Rome in the hundredth year. The coming of the year 1000, as is well known, excited consternation all over Europe, and the centennial year may well have come in for a share of the curious beliefs and superstitions which centred in the millennium.

Again, it is quite conceivable that some surviving memory still persisted among the people of the old Roman secular jubilee of pagan times, of which we have an abiding monument in Horace's *Carmen Sœculare.* Any such belief was likely to transfer itself to the Christian commemoration, when the point of departure in the reckoning changed from the Foundation of the City to the Birth of Christ. It must be frankly confessed, however, that there is very little positive evidence to support these conjectures. Pilgrimages to Rome, no doubt, are recorded in the centennial years, but then they are frequently recorded in other years which are not centennial. On the other hand, curiously enough, the one real testimony that can be quoted for the existence of any Jubilee in Rome prior to that of Boniface belongs to a year which was not centennial, and which cannot in any way be accounted for on Jubilee principles. It is in a German monastic chronicle best known as that of Alberic of Three Fountains, that under the year 1208 (not 1200, be it noted) we find this brief remark—

"It is said that this year (1208) was celebrated as the fiftieth year, or the year of jubilee and remission in the Roman Court."

Now, although there is no doubt that the chronicle of Three

---

[1] The title prefixed to his work by Card. Stefaneschi himself was *De Centesimo seu Jubileo Anno Liber ;* and of the papal Bull, when it was published, he writes, "Ea incerta jubilei luce jubilans populus," etc. La Bigne, *Bibliotheca Patrum*, vol. vi. p. 539 (Paris, 1610).

Fountains has been interpolated, its latest editor is satisfied that the interpolations were certainly introduced before the year 1295,[1] and we may regard the selection of such a date as 1208 as telling distinctly against the supposition that the entry could have been made after the proclamation of Boniface's Jubilee, coinciding with the century. Though this evidence stands alone, it proves—and such adversaries as Mr. Lea do not dispute the validity of the proof—that the conception of a jubilee year, or year of remission, was current in the minds of men before the time of Boniface, and was connected with the Court of Rome. How far it is to be traced back, and why it is entered under such a date as 1208, must probably remain a mystery. It may be noticed, however, that this gain of eight years reduces notably the difficulty of believing that any of the old men who attended the Jubilee of 1300 would have been children at the time when the previous great Indulgence was granted, and it seems also that this date would fit in very well with what our English scholar, Giraldus Cambrensis, tells us of a visit which he himself paid to Rome, for purely devotional purposes, about this time. He does not speak of any concourse of people, but he does seem to imply the existence of certain special privileges then offered to pilgrims, though these Indulgences were calculated on a scale vastly more moderate than that which came subsequently to prevail.[2]

Be that as it may, it would not seem that the appeal to tradition had very much to do with the promulgation of the first Jubilee. Cardinal Stefaneschi admits, as we have already seen, that the papal archives were searched, but without result, for any trace of such an usage. Indeed, a careful study of the Bull

---

[1] Pertz, *Monumenta Germaniæ*, SS. vol. xxiii. p. 889. Cf. Preface by Paul Scheffer Boichorst, *ibid.* p. 648. Attention seems to have first been called to this passage of Alberic by F. Zaccaria, *Trattato dell' Anno Santo*, Rome, 1775.

[2] See Giraldus Cambrensis, *Opera* (Rolls Series), vol. i. p. 137. Giraldus remained in Rome from Epiphany until Low Sunday, visiting all the shrines, attending all the stations, and given up almost entirely to works of devotion. He accounted himself fortunate in having gained in sum, at the end of all this, 100 years' Indulgence.

issued by Boniface shows that it does not, as might at first sight be expected from the words *antiquorum fida relatio,* make appeal to any definite centennial or Jubilee Indulgence of the past, but only to the notorious fact that special remissions were accorded at all times to pilgrims to Rome. From Stefaneschi's whole narrative, as well as from the Bull, it seems plain that the institution of the Jubilee was in no sense premeditated.

As to the considerations which weighed with the Pontiff in publishing his Bull, no adequate reason appears for doubting that he really had mainly at heart the spiritual welfare of the Roman people and of the faithful of Christ in general. This need not exclude some admixture of less exalted motives, but even these last bore a distinct relation to what, under the circumstances of the times, Boniface understood to be the cause of God. Without accepting as final the verdict of the French historian already quoted, there is much that is worthy of consideration in the following remarks:—

"Historians differ as to the motives which influenced Boniface in instituting the Jubilee. Some have maintained that he desired by this means to bring to Rome the riches of Christendom. The offerings of the faithful were in fact so numerous that in the Basilica of St. Paul clerics were occupied night and day in collecting the money cast at the foot of the altar of the Apostle. It has also been said, and with more reason, that Boniface, seeing that faith was growing cold, hoped to reanimate it by the unaccustomed spectacle of the Church's splendours. He may also have flattered himself that by enhancing the prestige of the Holy See he would be able more authoritatively to impose peace on Europe, and to unite Christian nations in a crusade against the infidel—a project which to the last he never relinquished. Again, it is not impossible that, knowing the preparations made in September, 1299, by the Khan of Tartary, in concert with the King of Armenia, against the Sultan of Egypt, he wished to make some effort on his side in the cause of the Holy Land. At any rate it is certain that in the very year of the Jubilee, on the receipt of the news of a victory gained by the Tartars—a victory speedily rendered inoperative by subsequent defeat—he urged the Sovereigns of the West to unite their forces to those of the conquerors in order to regain possession of the holy places, and with this object levied a tithe on the whole of Christendom.

"Added to this there may have been a further consideration to which this Pontiff was not likely to be insensible. Boniface, who had only just succeeded in triumphing over the Colonnas, had learned, not without alarm, that they had escaped from the city where they were imprisoned. He may have feared that they meant to recommence their hostile manœuvres, and have thought that by appearing before the world in all the splendour of his dignity, he might be able to dispel the doubts fomented by these men as to the lawfulness of his own title to occupy the See of Peter." [1]

There is, moreover, much probability in M. Rocquain's suggestion that in some incidents of the rather theatrical conduct of Boniface, the aged Pontiff was under the influence of Cardinal d'Acquasparta. The resemblance at any rate between the scene of the two swords and the discourse of the Cardinal just named is certainly very striking. The Cardinal had preached a sermon about the spiritual and the temporal sword by which the Pope might enforce his authority over all princes who resisted him, and shortly afterwards we hear of Boniface having two swords borne before him and proclaiming aloud, "Lo, here are two swords. Look, Peter, upon thy successor, and do Thou behold Thy vicar, O Saviour Christ."[2] It is hard to believe that such a coincidence can have been purely accidental.

But whatever may be thought of the motives or conduct of the Pope in proclaiming the Jubilee, there can be no question as to the deep religious impression which the spectacle produced upon all who witnessed it. From every country the pilgrims streamed to Rome, not only from France and Germany, but from the far North and from the East, rich and poor, young and old, sound and infirm, men and women. The roads of Italy were

---

[1] Felix Rocquain, *La Cour de Rome*, vol. ii. pp. 289, 290.

[2] Kervyn de Lettenhove, *L'ordre de Citeaux et la Lutte de Boniface VIII. et de Philippe le Bel.* Migne P.L. 185, p. 1902.

safe; pilgrims of all nations were allowed to come and go unhindered. Vast as was the concourse, and though an inundation of the Tiber at one moment threatened famine, there was no disturbance, thanks mainly to the exertions of Pope Boniface and of the magistracy of Rome. "It was a wonderful spectacle," wrote the Florentine merchant and chronicler, Giovanni Villani. "There were continually upwards of 100,000 pilgrims in the city, without counting those that each day came and went, and yet all were cared for and abundantly supplied with provisions, both men and horses, and all this in the best order, without disturbance or conflict." "The crowd of men and women," records the chronicler of Asti, "was stupendous. I saw it with my own eyes, for I spent fourteen days in the city. There was abundance of flesh, fish, and oats to be purchased in the market. Hay was very dear, and so also was lodging, so that my bed and stabling for my horse, without fodder, cost me every day a grosso tournois. As I rode away from Rome on Christmas Eve, I found the roads encumbered with a multitude of pilgrims which no man could count, and amongst the Romans it was said that more than two millions of men and women had come to the city in all. Over and over again I saw both men and women trodden under foot in the press, and I myself more than once was hard bestead to escape the same danger."

Very touching also are the descriptions preserved for us of the behaviour of the pilgrims. They came in pilgrim garb, or in the national dress of the countries to which they belonged, on foot, on horseback, in waggons, bringing with them those that were exhausted and sick, and laden with their baggage. There were aged men there a hundred years old, led by their children, and there were youths who carried father or mother to Rome on their shoulders. They spoke in the dialects of many lands, but they sang the litanies in the one only language of the Church, and all their eager desires were directed to one and the same object. While yet afar off, when they caught a glimpse of the towers of the Holy City across the broad Campagna, they broke into joyous shouts of "Roma, Roma," like sailors who, after a long voyage, sight the land once more. Then they threw themselves on their knees for a while, and rose up with the inspiring cry, "Saints Peter and Paul, graciously hear us." At the gates their countrymen or acquaintances received them to conduct them to their lodging, but first of all they made their way to St. Peter's, to climb upon their knees the steps of the ante-court, and they did not attend to their own bodily needs until they had thrown themselves down in rapture before the tomb of the Apostles.

It affords a curious illustration of contemporary Roman manners to learn from Stefaneschi, who evidently records the circumstance as something quite out of the common, that even young unmarried girls were allowed to make the visit to the two Basilicas. "During the day, in protection of their virginal modesty, they remained at home, shielded from the rude gaze of the men, but at night, under the safe escort of matrons, they sallied forth to visit the Churches of the Apostles." [1]

Whether Dante himself undertook a pilgrimage to Rome during any part of the year 1300 does not seem quite certain. What we know of his official occupation at Florence, and of the fierce hostility with which he regarded Pope Boniface, would incline to a negative answer, but he has none the less a reference to the regulations made for preserving order in the throng, which seems hardly to come naturally from any one but an eye-witness—

> E'en thus the Romans, when the year returns
> Of jubilee, with better speed to rid
> The thronging multitudes, their means devise
> For such as pass the bridge; that on one side
> All front toward the Castle, and approach
> St. Peter's fane, on the other towards the mount. [2]

There is in the *Purgatorio* another reference to this great occasion, which has attracted the attention of Dante students because it supplies a useful clue to the correct dating of the poem.

---

[1] "Nec defuere innuptæ, die ob virginitatis pudorem domi virorum aspectibus obtectæ, nocte sub fida matronarum custodia ad sacras Principum ædes migrantes." —Stefaneschi, *De Jubileo*, p. 538.

[2] Cary's Dante, *Inferno*, canto xviii.

He represents the souls during that year of grace as carried into Purgatory, ferried by the angel of God across the waters—

> These three months past indeed
> He whoso chose to enter with free leave
> Hath taken.[1]

In spite of the difficulty of feeding such huge crowds, the commissariat problem seems, on the whole, to have been successfully solved. For the first three months there was an abundance of provisions, but then fears began to be entertained that the supply of food would run short, especially as it was thought that, even if there was sufficient corn, there would be a deficit of mills and ovens. In reality, there was enough corn, and extra precautions were taken by bidding the inhabitants of the neighbouring towns to supply bread ready made, whilst the country people brought in whatever fruit and vegetables they could spare. Fortunately the harvest was good, the wine presses flowed with a generous vintage, and although things became dearer in October, this in no way affected the people's devotion.

Two points only does it seem desirable to emphasise before we conclude our account of the Jubilee of Boniface VIII. In the first place, no one who reads Stefaneschi's narrative can feel any doubt of the really spiritual character of the whole institution. The pilgrimage to Rome was not a trip or jaunt—an outing—but a true incentive to piety, in which the absolute necessity of contrition of heart as a condition of gaining the Indulgence was never for a moment lost sight of. Besides his prose work, Stefaneschi also composed a short poem on the subject of the Jubilee, and there, putting into verse the conditions of the Bull, he insists—

> All crime is washed away,
> Not merely fully, but in fullest sense,[2]
> When bounteous grace extends to every fault
> Entire forgiveness. Only let those rash men,
> Who have defiled God's image in their souls,
> With true compunction manifest their sins
> And pray for pardon.

---

[1] *Purgatorio,* canto ii., Cary.

[2] Non solum plenam et largiorem imo plenissimam omnium veniam peccatorum. —Bull *Antiquorum.*

So again in one of the German chronicles printed in Pertz, *Monumenta Germaniæ*, there is given a contemporary exposition of Boniface's Bull *Antiquorum* by a Roman canonist, who had evidently been asked to explain what this new and unheard-of Indulgence might mean. The exposition amounts to hardly more than a paraphrase of the Bull, but the writer does introduce a reference to the Jubilee, or Year of Remission of the

BASILICA OF S. PAOLO FUORI LE MURE, to which a visit was enjoined in the Jubilee Bull of Boniface VIII. Restored since the fire of 1823.

Old Law, and he insists, like the Pope, that these Indulgences were granted only to those *vere penitentibus et confessis* who were truly penitent and who had made their confession. The point is, in reality, one that hardly needs noticing save for the assertion so often made, that such clauses were mere formalities, buried away under a cloud of verbiage and attended to by no one.

The other matter to which allusion has just been made is the question of the alms of the pilgrims. The phrase of the chronicler Ventura, who describes, obviously with some rhetorical exaggeration, the two clerks standing day and night by the altar of St. Paul's and gathering in countless sums of money *with rakes*, has remained firmly impressed upon the minds of the assailants of Roman Indulgences. But here also a reference to the narrative of Cardinal Stefaneschi helps to set the matter in its true light. The offerings so described were not gifts of the rich, pieces of gold and silver, but contributions of the very poor made in the smallest coin then current. Again, they were purely voluntary, and in no way made a condition for the gaining of the Indulgence. Neither were the churches of Rome show-places where a fee was required from visitors, and where a verger was employed to hurry them from altar to altar. What is more, although some 50,000 gold florins were received in all at the two Basilicas of St. Peter and St. Paul, Stefaneschi informs us that this was not much more than double the sum offered in ordinary years,[1] and we learn both from him and from other writers that the money was spent either directly or indirectly upon the fabric of the Roman churches, and in making proper provision for the clergy connected with them. In any case, no portion of these alms seems to have found its way into the papal treasury.

The first Jubilee was not specially remarkable for the dignity of those who visited Rome to take part in the celebrations. Charles Martel, of the House of Anjou, the son of the King of Naples, was there, attracted probably by the hope of inducing the Pope to favour his claim to the throne of Hungary. So also Charles of Valois, the brother of Philip the Fair, had come with equally interested motives, desiring to make himself master of Constantinople and Emperor of the East. In neither case does Boniface seem to have done much to further their cause. On the other hand, the most interesting to us of all the deputations was undoubtedly that which, according to Tosti, was sent by the Guelf party, now dominant in Florence. To emphasise in some sort the equality which the democratic city claimed with the crowned

[1] Cf. Tosti, *Storia di Bonifazio VIII.*, vol. ii. p. 288.

heads of Europe the personages composing the embassy appeared in the character of different monarchs. Thus, Varmilio Alfano represented the Emperor of the West, Simon dei Rossi the Emperor of the East, Musciatto Franzese the King of France, Ugolino de' Cerchi the King of England, Romero Frighinello the King of Bohemia, Guicciardo Bastaro the great Cham of Tartary, and so on. The embassy was most splendidly equipped and mounted, the envoys being of course attired in the costumes appropriate to their assumed characters. A cavalcade of five hundred horsemen escorted them on their way.[1]

Who the Ugolino de' Cerchi was who represented the King of England, we have no means of learning. Could he by any possibility be identical with the Ugolino of whose visit to the Jubilee a strangely interesting testimony existed at Florence in the seventeenth century in the shape of an inscription in the Via della Fogna? The inscription may be thus translated—

"For the perpetual memory of the fact. Be it plainly known to all who look upon this slab, how Almighty God, in the year of our Lord Jesus Christ MDCCC. conferred a special boon upon the Christians. For His Sepulchre, which had been in the possession of the Saracens, was recovered by the Tartars and given back to the Christians. And the same year, since a solemn remission of all sins, to wit, both of guilt and of penalty (solemnis remissio omnium peccatorum, videlicet, culparum et pænarum), was granted by Pope Boniface to all who visited Rome, many—both Christians and Tartars—came to Rome for the aforesaid Indulgence; *and there went thither also Ugolino and his wife.*"

The last words in italics are written in Italian. There is another contemporary inscription referring to the Jubilee in the

[1] Tosti, *Storia di Bonifazio VIII.*, vol. ii. p. 73. Tosti does not seem to have noticed the account of this embassy given by St. Antoninus of Florence in his *Chronicle.* The Saint states that Boniface said in reference to it, "For the glory of the name of Florence I declare that the Florentines will form another factor in the ruling of the world."—*Chronicon* (Lyons, 1586), part iii. p. 240.

Cathedral at Siena. The rude leonine hexameters may fairly be represented by some such jingle as the following:—

At Rome each hundredth year
  Occurs the Jubilee;
Sins are washed clear,
  The penitent set free.
  Pope Boniface made this decree.[1]

Most important of all the memorials of the first Jubilee year must not be forgotten Giotto's painting of Pope Boniface, still preserved in the Lateran. A rough outline of it is reproduced on p. 10. It is generally supposed to represent Boniface in the act of promulgating the Jubilee. The mat-shaped trappings which hang down on either side, and which appear almost to be part of the vestments of the two ecclesiastics, display the wavy bend which were the arms of Boniface (Benedict Gaetano), and from which, in the pseudo-prophecy of Malachy, he is described by the motto *Ex Undarum Benedictione* (from the benediction of the waves).

When the time appointed for the Jubilee terminated with the Christmas Eve of 1300, Boniface was asked to extend the period further until Easter. He allowed some extension for the benefit of those who had already begun to fulfil the conditions, but the Jubilee proper closed with the Christmas Eve, as originally arranged. This practice of beginning the Jubilee with Christmas Day and not with the new year is still observed, and is an interesting survival of the old custom of dating from the Nativity of our Lord instead of from the kalends of January. One of the early books, which deals with the history of Indulgences, affords an interesting illustration of the general prevalence of the same usage in the time of Alexander VI. It is a work undertaken by a certain Stephanus ex Nottis, in view of the Jubilee of 1500, and the author has printed at intervals throughout the exact dates at which, as the work progressed, he resumed his task of writing it. Disregarding the prefatory matter, which

[1] Annus centenus Romæ semper est jubilenus,
Omnia laxantur, cui penitet ista donantur,
Hæc decrevit Bonifacius et roboravit.

was a later addition, we find at the top of the first page: "In nomine Domine Jesu Christi; die 3 Novembris, 1498. Hic liber est defensivus a crudeli morbo desperationis et ductivus in vitam æternam."[1]

On the 25th September, 1499, "at 23 o'clock," he was about half-way through, the last sentences of the text were written down on the 16th January, 1500, at the second hour of the night, and on the 18th of January he began the dedication and table of contents, the whole being completed at 20 o'clock (about 1.30 p.m.) on 26th January, 1500. "Laus Deo," adds the writer. Unfortunately the work took nearly ten months to print, and it only came from the press on 1st December, 1500, when the Jubilee was all but over. As he was nearing the end of his treatise, we find abundant time-notes which mark his rate of progress. He seems to have got through a good section on 24th December, 1499, then he took two days' holiday (he was writing, we may note, in Milan), and the next entry is on 27th December, in this form: "The 27th day of December at the beginning of the year one thousand five hundred, beginning from the feast of the Nativity of our Lord Jesus Christ in that year, to wit, 1500." I may add that Burchard in his *Diario* also makes the change from 1499 to 1500, as he passes from the 24th to 25th of December, Christmas Day being thus reckoned, even as it was by Christians in the early centuries, the first day of the new year.

If we may judge from the scanty notices in our own monastic chronicles, the Jubilee of Boniface VIII. attracted little attention in England. It is expressly remarked by one of the Italian writers, who has left an account of this Jubilee, that few Englishmen were found among the pilgrims. On the other hand, we are told by Stefaneschi that the prudence of the Northern peoples was much commended, "who, waiting for a season of the year when the climate in Rome is somewhat similar to the cold in their own country, came at the end of

[1] "This book is a protection against the cruel disease of despair, and a guide to eternal life."

autumn and the beginning of winter." One fact we know which may have interfered to some extent with the free passage to Rome of English gentleman and distinguished ecclesiastics. King Edward I. had strictly forbidden that money or plate should be conveyed out of the kingdom; the result was that any person of note who wished to journey abroad was practically reduced to asking the king's permission if he wished to travel in any comfort. We have still in existence the writs issued by the king to the Bishop of Winchester and others, who were declared to be going across the seas on the king's business, and dispensing them from the law just referred to forbidding the exportation of specie.

CHAPTER II

The Porta Santa

In the course of the last chapter we have more than once had occasion to mention the Porta Santa or Holy Door, and before we go further the questions may not unnaturally be asked, "What is the Holy Door? and what is its precise connection with the opening of the Jubilee?" The second of these questions broaches a somewhat puzzling historical problem, and will require a longer discussion. The first, without anticipating the full description of the ceremonies reserved for a subsequent chapter, may be conveniently answered by a short quotation from Cardinal Wiseman's *Four Last Popes* already referred to.

It can hardly be necessary to repeat that this opening of the Porta Santa by Leo XII. in 1825 was the last occasion before the present year upon which the ceremony was carried out.

"The visitor to Rome may easily have noticed that, of the five great doors opening from the porch into the church (of St. Peter's), the one nearest to the palace is walled up, and has a gilt metal cross upon it, much worn by the lips of pilgrims. On inquiry he will be told that it is the *Porta Santa*, or 'Holy Gate,' like the 'King's Gate' at Jerusalem, never to be opened except for most special entrance.

"Only during the year of Jubilee is this gate unclosed, and it is for the purpose of opening it, as symbolical of the commencement of the Jubilee, that the Pope has descended to the vestibule. The immense church is empty, for the doors have been kept closed all day; an innumerable multitude, beginning with royal princes and descending to the poorest pilgrims from Southern

Italy, eagerly wait in the portico and on the steps without. After preliminary prayers from Scripture singularly apt, the Pope goes down from his throne, and, armed with a silver hammer, strikes the wall in the doorway, which, having been

The Portico of St. Peter's, in which takes place the ceremony of opening the Holy Door, which is seen on the right. In the distance the Statue of Charlemagne, erected for the Jubilee of 1725.

cut round from the jambs and lintel, falls at once inwards, and is cleared away in a moment by the active *sanpietrini*.[1]

"The Pope then, bareheaded and torch in hand, enters the door, and is followed by the Cardinals and his other attendants to the high altar, where the First Vespers of Christmas Day are chanted as usual. Well does the ceremonial of that day remain

[1] These are a body of workmen of "every arm," retained in regular pay by St. Peter's, and wearing a particular dress. They keep the church in its perfect repair and beautiful condition almost without external help. Their activity and intelligence are quite remarkable.

impressed on my memory, and one little incident is coupled with it. Among the earliest to pass, with every sign of reverence and devotion, through the Holy Gate, I remember seeing with emotion the first clergyman who in our times had abandoned dignity and ease as the price of his conversion. He was surrounded, or followed, by his family in this pilgrim's act, as he had been followed by them in his 'pilgrimage of grace.' Such a person was rare in those days, and indeed singular; we little thought how our eyes might become accustomed, one day, to the sight of many like him."[1]

Such is, in brief, the function which has been carried out in the opening of the Holy Door since the beginning of the sixteenth century. But now comes the question, how did this ceremony originate, and what is its connection with the granting of the great Jubilee Indulgence at the beginning of the Anno Santo? According to a view which for a long time past has been generally accepted, the whole rite was the invention of John Burchard, the famous master of ceremonies to Pope Alexander VI., and was never used in any form before the Jubilee celebrated by that Pontiff in the year 1500. This theory may be substantially correct, and it is not precisely the object of the present chapter to prove it to be untenable, but there are, as we shall see, the strongest reasons for doubting, and in any case it is certain that the central idea of the throwing open of the gates, as symbolical of the outpouring of God's mercy, was of much older date, and did not originate in a pontificate of such evil name as that of Alexander VI.

But let us first see, in Burchard's own diary, what that famous ecclesiastic himself has to say upon the matter. His account amounts to this—

In the third week of Advent, 1499, the Pope summoned the ordinary Penitentiaries to hold counsel with him at St. Peter's, in order to decide upon the conditions of the Indulgence, the faculties to be granted, and other measures to be taken in view of the approaching Jubilee. The Pope wished them to think

[1] Cardinal Wiseman's *Recollections of the Four Last Popes*, pp. 270, 271.

these matters over, and then to make their report to him. On Wednesday, 18th December, the Pope came down to St. Peter's in the afternoon to hear what had been resolved upon, and "then," says Burchard, "I took the opportunity to show his Holiness the place in the chapel of St. Veronica which the Canons of the Basilica declare to be the so-called golden door which was wont to be opened by the Sovereign Pontiffs upon each *hundredth* [1] year of the Jubilee, which I had also frequently heard said and maintained in common talk (*in vulgo*). His Holiness was of opinion that it ought to be opened in the same way at the time of the inauguration of the Jubilee, and he gave directions to have blocks of marble arranged and cut for the adorning of the said door to such height and width as the contour of the door showed on the inside, giving orders also that the walls in front and at the side of the said chapel should be entirely removed, that the people might pass through more freely." [2]

Then Burchard tells us that the Pope further gave directions for the appointment of four religious men, two of whom should patrol the Basilica by day and the other two by night, to see that no impropriety took place, since the golden gate was not to be closed either day or night during the whole of the coming year of Jubilee, and that the same was to be observed in the other three Basilicas.[3]

"Orders were likewise given to Thomas Matarati, the master mason, to have the surface of the wall picked away within the contour of the golden door so as to leave a thickness of only four or five fingers' breadth, but without on any account breaking a hole right through, so that when his Holiness at the hour of vespers on the above-mentioned Vigil of the Nativity should lay hand upon it, it might fall easily and without delay, leaving free entrance to all.

"When all these arrangements had been made, he, the Pope,

---

[1] Quæ singulo centesimo jubilei anno consuevit per summos pontifices aperiri.

[2] *Diarium* (ed. Thuasne), vol. ii. p. 582.

[3] *Ibid.* p. 583.

returned to the palace, and the said master mason set to work upon the charge entrusted to him for the adornment of the door . . . and then it was discovered[1] that there had never been any door at all in this place, but that the wall was solid and even, built into the other part of the wall on either side. There had only been an altar in that place which we thought was a doorway. But since the populace had this idea, I was unwilling to disturb them in their belief, which could only foster devotion."

Again, when speaking of the ceremonies at the opening of the Jubilee in St. Peter's, Burchard describes how the three Cardinals-delegate were commissioned "to open the golden doors" at the other three Basilicas. Whereupon Burchard remarks, "I gave to his lordship the Archbishop of Ragusa a copy of the versicles and prayer (which he, Burchard, had arranged for the occasion) for his own information and guidance as to how he was to proceed in the opening of the golden door of the Basilica of St. Paul; but neither the abbot nor the monks had any idea which was the golden door in the said Basilica; accordingly, he opened, as he afterwards informed me, three doors in the front of the church which had been walled up, rather, as I conceive, to keep out the bad air than for any other reason. But this is a matter of little moment, for the unlearned are saved by faith alone;[2] but it seemed to me ridiculous that

[1] Thuasne (ii. p. 583) prints *co-opertam*, an obvious blunder for *compertum*.

[2] "*Quia sola fides salvat rusticum.*" Burchard clearly means that the credulity of simple people is meritorious, and that it does not much matter whether what they believe is objectively correct. As long as the populace visited the church with the good intention of gaining the Indulgence and fulfilling the conditions, it was quite immaterial whether the door by which they entered was really that which tradition prescribed. It is not a little ridiculous that M. Thuasne, the editor of Burchard, should convert this innocent observation into a cynical profession of infidelity. "Cette remarque de Burchard," he says, "donne la note exacte du scepticisme des prélats romains qui exploitaient le culte d'un dieu auquel ils ne croyaient pas." It is quite possible that some of the Roman prelates of the days of Alexander VI. had not very much faith in Christianity, but there is nothing whatever to suggest such an inference in the above-quoted words of Burchard.

all the religious of the said monastery should remain in ignorance of a point so important."[1]

It seems clear, from these last words, that Burchard was himself a firm believer in the tradition of the golden door. He would never have embarked upon this elaborate mystification, recording all the details in his diary as he does, if he had known quite well all the time that there was no tradition of any golden door beyond what he himself had invented. We may take the existence of some such vague rumour as certain; the whole difficulty lies in deciding how far the rumour had any foundation in fact. It is important to notice that the alleged golden door in the chapel of St. Veronica at St. Peter's was supposed to have been opened only in the Jubilee of the *hundredth* year. Such, at least, was the view of Alexander VI., and he not only introduced into his Bull of 20th December the statement that he intended to open the door of St. Peter's, which was accustomed to be opened in the Jubilee of the hundredth year,[2] but he made Burchard add the word *centesimus* in the prayer drawn up for the occasion, together with a reference to the supposed practice of opening such a door. That Burchard himself would have insisted upon the fact that this ceremony was attached to the hundredth year celebration is not quite so clear. It is curious that Philip Bonanni, who had access to the MSS., in quoting Burchard's remark about the Veronica Chapel omits the word *centesimus*.[3] Still it appears in Thuasne's text, and two manuscript copies of Burchard in the British Museum undoubtedly contain it.[4] On the other hand, we know that no formal Jubilee

[1] Burchard's *Diarium*, vol. ii. p. 600.

[2] "Quo tempore (*i.e.*, the first vespers of the Nativity) portam dicte Basilice Beati Petri *centesimo* quoque anno jubilei pro majore fidelium devotione aperiri solitam adstantibus venerabilium fratrum nostrorum sancte Romane Ecclesie cardinalium collegio et maxima prelatorum, cleri, et populi multitudine, propriis manibus aperiemus, faciemusque aperiri alias basilicas S. Pauli ac Lateranensis et Beate Marie Majoris de dicta Urbe ecclesiarum portas etiam de more anno jubilei aperiri consuetas."—Burchard, ii. p. 586. Be it noted that Burchard does not state that the "golden door" of the Lateran was only opened in the hundredth year.

[3] Bonanni, *Numismata Pontificum*, i. p. 125.

[4] MS. Ad. 8437, fol. 310 r°, and MS. Ad. 26805, fol. 198 v°.

had been celebrated at Rome in the last centesimal year, 1400. The pilgrims, indeed, had come mostly from the countries which recognised the authority of the Anti-Pope, and Boniface IX., as we shall see later on, had accorded them a gracious reception, but no Jubilee Bull seems to have been published, and it is most unlikely that any such solemn function would have been enacted as that of the "golden door." Again, the hundredth year before that (1300) had been the occasion of the first promulgation of the great Jubilee Indulgence, and it is quite inconsistent with the circumstances of that promulgation, as already related, and with the silence of Stefaneschi and the chroniclers, that any unwalling ceremony should then have taken place. It therefore seems natural to suppose that the Roman tradition of the "golden door of the hundredth year" was a fiction, and that there never had been seen before the time of Burchard any ceremony like the walling or unwalling of such a door with masonry.

When we come to ask, however, whether there is any foundation earlier than the sixteenth century for the association of the Jubilee Indulgence with the ceremony of the opening of a door, we are on very different ground. Leaving for a moment out of account all questions of symbolism, and also the scriptural allusions which might easily suggest such a function, we may turn first to one or two coincidences which rest upon certain evidence and which are sufficiently striking. Amongst those who came to Rome for the second great Jubilee, celebrated in 1350, fifty years after that of Boniface VIII., was a certain famous canonist, Albericus a Rosate. He tells us in one of the articles of his great Dictionary or Lexicon of Canon and Civil Law how, "together with his wife and three children, he was present, by God's favour, at the aforesaid Indulgence (of 1350), and all of them, by the mercy of God, returned safe home again." Alberic gives in full the authentic Bull of Clement VI. promulgating the Jubilee, as it may now be read in Raynaldus, but he adds also a second document about which he remarks, "With regard to the aforesaid Indulgence there was another form which came into my hands. Whether it is really a papal document or not I am unable to say, but it is a fine piece of work, and so I append it here." The supposed Bull gives an account of the coming of a deputation to Clement from Rome to ask for the reduction of the Jubilee interval from a hundred years to fifty. "And because," says the Pope, "the envoys had a long story to tell, we gave instructions that a Consistory should be summoned on the morrow, but in the night-time preceding the Consistory there appeared to us in a vision a certain venerable personage bearing two keys in his hand, who addressed to us the following words, '*Open the door*, and from it send forth a fire by which the whole world may be warmed and enlightened'; and on the following day we said a Mass of our Lady, for the intention that if the vision were really from God it might appear a second time, but if it were a fancy or illusion that it might vanish for good and all. After making this prayer, however, we beheld the vision again on the following night," etc.

What is more, another text of the same spurious Bull, printed by Amort, and taken, as he says, *ex codice manuscripto Bibliothecæ Pollinganæ*, makes the suggestion of this *aperi ostium* still more explicit. "We knelt down," the Pope is represented as saying of himself, "baring our knees and raising our hands to heaven, and then we opened and unbarred for sinners the holy gate of paradise in the following terms."[1] Nothing could be more natural than that such language should be remembered and should produce its effect when any sort of ceremonial was devised for the opening of the Jubilee. Moreover, although there is no likelihood that this Bull is authentic, it is certainly of contemporary date, and many of its details are of curious interest as manifesting the feeling of the times.

[1] Genibus flexis ac denudatis et manibus compositis versus cœlum aperuimus peccatoribus sanctam portam paradisi et reseravimus per hunc modum. Amort, *De Origine Indulgentiarum*, Venice, 1738, p. 70. It is curious that the MS. which Amort used gives the reading "aperi os tuum," instead of "aperi ostium," but the latter is confirmed indirectly by the chronicle of Meaux and other early references.

In any case, the document became widely known. A summary of it may be found in the Chronicle of the English Cistercian Abbey of Meaux, in Yorkshire,[1] where it is coupled with an extremely unpleasant account of the life of Clement VI., its reputed author. Although the summary is short, the words of the vision, "*Aperi ostium*—open the door," etc., are retained.

The next piece of evidence is still more striking. It is found in the "Dialogue concerning the Year of Jubilee," written in anticipation of the Jubilee of 1450 by the jurist, Felix Hämmerlin. The writer's tone is sneering and disaffected,[2] and fully prepares one for the more open attack on the papacy which he published on returning to the same topic in his *Recapitulatio* shortly afterwards. But the character of Hämmerlin's opinions is for the moment immaterial. We are concerned here only with his allusion to the "golden door."

Quoting the Gospel of St. Mark, one of the two interlocutors in the Dialogue remarks—"Enter ye by the narrow gate, because broad is the gate and spacious is the way that leadeth to destruction, and many there are that enter by it, but narrow is the gate and strait is the way that leadeth to life, and few there are that find it. Now, of this gate we will make a most fitting application to the golden gate of Rome, which will be opened[3] in the celebration of our Jubilee at St. John Lateran, and the Basilica of St. Peter, the prince of the Apostles, at the present time, seeing that for fifty years it had stood most securely walled up."

---

[1] *Chronicon Monasterii de Melsa*, vol. iii. p. 88.

[2] Dr. Pastor, strange to say, has expressed a comparatively favourable estimate of Hämmerlin's *Dyalogus de Anno Jubileo.* See *Geschichte der Päpste*, vol. i. p. 423.

[3] *Dyalogus de Anno Jubileo*, printed at Basle in 1497, sig. P2, v°. The important words are—"Ad hanc igitur portam faciemus applicationem congruissimam ad Romæ portam auream, quæ aperietur in nostræ jubilationis solemnitate apud S. Joannem Lateranensem et beati Petri principis apostolorum basilicam pro nunc prout per quinquaqinta annos steterat muris firmissimis obstructa."

Taken in connection with Burchard's plain statement that there "was a place in the Chapel of St. Veronica at St. Peter's which the canons of the Basilica declare to be the golden door, as it is called, which it was the custom for the Popes to open every hundredth year of the Jubilee," this passage of Hämmerlin must be admitted to be not a little remarkable. One point is clear—it cannot possibly be a later interpolation suggested by the ceremony instituted in the Jubilee of Alexander VI. The very book in which we now read the words, a collection of Hämmerlin's various opuscula, was printed two or three years before that Jubilee took place. We must conclude that the only reasonable explanation of this remarkable coincidence is that there really was, as Burchard says there was, a popular tradition among the Romans on the subject, though Hämmerlin seems to have heard that the door was opened in the fiftieth year, and Burchard only in the hundredth.

The existence of a tradition need not, of course, establish the truth of the fact. How many such traditions about subterranean passages connecting one place with another are we familiar with here in England, and how rarely do they prove correct upon actual exploration? Or again, how definitely was the story of Pope Joan, which the wildest no-popery pamphleteer would not now dream of defending, connected by the populace with certain objects and sites in medieval Rome? It might even conceivably have been maintained that the language of Hämmerlin was only figurative, and that the "golden door" was a sarcasm levelled at the very considerable sum of money which a Jubilee was bound to realise for the papal treasury. If this were so, it would also be conceivable that the tractate of Hämmerlin, being understood literally by Burchard and others, had itself originated the tradition. Still, however easy it may be to suppose that the phrase *aperi ostium*—in other words, "make use of the keys"—of Clement's spurious Bull is intended as a mere metaphor, it is more difficult to conceive that the explicit mention of both the Lateran and St. Peter's and "the gate which for fifty years had stood closed with the most solid walls" could merely have been a literary conceit[1] of the writer's, the more so that, if the memory had survived of any Jubilee, it should rather have been that of Martin V. in 1423,[2] than the very shadowy and dubious celebration of 1400. Bishop Rutilius Benzonius, in his voluminous work on the Jubilee, further states that St. Antoninus of Florence, who lived some time before Alexander VI., makes mention in his Chronicle of the ceremony of opening the Holy Door. Unfortunately, Benzonius gives no reference, and the present writer, in spite of a prolonged search, has been unable to find any such passage. But with the example of Hämmerlin before us, it would be rash to conclude that the bishop's statement is erroneous.

But whatever doubt may be felt as to this testimony of St. Antoninus of Florence,[3] the existence, and even the unwalling of the golden door at the Lateran, are proved beyond question by evidence which has only come to the writer's knowledge since the first draft of this chapter was in type. We may notice in the first place a passage in the fifteenth-century work entitled *Reliquiæ Rhomanæ Urbis atque Indulgentiæ.* In this may be read the following clear statement:—"Also in the said Church of the Lateran is a certain door which is called the

[1] At the same time the phrases to any one who studies the argument of the Treatise will not seem so pointless, regarding it as a mere metaphor, as it might seem at first sight. Hämmerlin makes a difficulty of the fact that the Jubilee Indulgence, being so important a means of salvation, is not always available. "Now, therefore," he says half sarcastically, "our opportunity has come at last; the golden door is open after it has been shut as tight as tight can be for fifty years."

[2] Hämmerlin, in his later *Recapitulatio*, shows his knowledge of Pope Martin V.'s Jubilee, but he seems to assign it to the wrong year, and to attribute to him the reduction to twenty-five years. The Pope, he says, ought to reduce the interval of the Jubilee non tantum ad centum prout fecit Bonifacius VIII., et non tantum ad quinquaginta prout ipsum jubileum abbreviaverat Clemens VI., et non tantum ad vigintiquinque prout moderaverat Martinus V. quinimo ad viginti vel decem vel per singulos annos, etc.—*Ibid.* sig. 95, v°.

[3] It seems not improbable that this statement, if made by St. Antoninus, is to be found in his *Decisio Consiliaris super Dubio Producto de Indulgenciis.* This scarce tract treats, it is said, of the pardon of the "Golden Year." But the book is inaccessible to me.

golden door. This is opened in the Jubilee year. There every man who is penitent has all his sins forgiven; that is to say, so far as regards punishment and guilt."[1] This testimony, however, it might be objected, like that of Hämmerlin, is of German origin, and cannot be entirely depended upon as evidence of a Roman tradition. But no such exception can be taken to the statement of the Florentine merchant, Giovanni Rucellai, who himself went to the Jubilee of 1450 and has left us a description of the Holy City as he saw it.[2] He describes the principal Basilicas and other shrines in order; and in his notice of the Church of St. John Lateran, speaking of the five doors by which it may be entered, he remarks—"Of these five doors, there is one which is always walled up except during the Jubilee year, when it is broken down at Christmas, when the Jubilee commences. The devotion which the populace has for the bricks and mortar of which it is composed is such that, at the unwalling, the fragments[3] are immediately carried off by the crowd, and the foreigners (*gli oltremontani*) take them home as so many sacred relics. It is said that the face of our Lord Jesus Christ, which is placed in the tribune of the High Altar of that church, passed through that door; and out of devotion every one who gains the Indulgence passes through that door, which is walled up again as soon as the Jubilee is ended."[4]

---

[1] "Item in dicta ecclesia lateranensi est quædam porta quæ dicitur aurea porta et ista aperitur in anno jubileo ibi quilibet (*sic*) penitenti remittuntur omnia peccata scilicet a parte pena et culpa" (*sic*).—*Reliquiæ*, col. 10. The book (see Hain, 13855), according to Mr. Proctor, was printed by Johann Amorbach at Basel. It is not dated, but to judge from the types used it must be reckoned among the earliest productions of that printer, *i.e.*, of about the year 1483.

[2] This evidence is further confirmed by the German *Rombüchlein*, a block-book, printed about 1475, or perhaps earlier, to which attention has lately been directed by Dr. Paulus, *Zeitschrift f. k. Theologie*, xxiv. p. 174. In this medieval guide-book an account is given not only of the Lateran "gulden phort," but also of that in the Vatican chapel of St. Veronica.

[3] This devotion to the fragments of masonry is often spoken of, and will frequently come under notice in the course of this little work.

[4] Guiseppe Marcotti, *Il Giubileo dell' anno* 1450, in *Archivio di Storia Patria*, iv. p. 569, 570.

Let us pass on, however, to another source of evidence which suggests not less strongly than the last the existence of some long-standing association of the Jubilee in the popular mind with the opening of a door.[1] In spite of the difficulties which beset the study of the medals attributed to some of the fifteenth-century Popes, the inquiry is a singularly interesting one, and seems to lead to fairly certain results. The principal embarrassment is caused by the circulation among collectors of a large number of "reconstructions," medals not fabricated for any definitely fraudulent purpose, but struck or cast by skilful artists in the sixteenth and seventeeth centuries in commemoration of the past, and often in such a way as to reproduce the characteristics of the work of the early die-sinkers. Upon this ground a whole set of medals purporting to represent fifteenth-century Popes in the act of unwalling the Holy Door must at once be rejected as spurious. They have been suggested by the frequent recurrence of this theme in the Jubilee medals of later ages, and Bonanni and Venuti, with other learned numismatists, were no doubt justified in their day in taking the mere occurrence of this subject in any medal of the fifteenth century as a sure proof of its spuriousness. In one or two cases we have even the signature of the sixteenth century artist adorning the exergue of what professes to be a fifteenth-century medal. Famous among these reconstructions is the supposed Jubilee medal of Boniface VIII., a representation of which is given opposite. On the obverse of the medal we have the portrait of Boniface in a tiara with a triple circlet;[2] on the reverse a doorway with a bust or face of our Saviour above it, and two candles burning on either side. Around it runs the legend IVSTI INTRABVNT PER EAM.[3] Although the medal is really old, and

---

[1] *De Anno Sancto Jubilei*, Venetiis, 1599, p. 469; P. Bonanni, S.J., *Numismata Pontificum*, vol. i. p. 98 (1699); R. Venuti, *Numismata Pontificum Romanorum Præstantiora*, p. 12. Rome, 1743.

[2] It seems probable that Boniface introduced the third crown of the tiara, but no contemporary representation of him exists in which the third crown is clearly defined. See Müntz.

[3] Through it the just shall enter.

dates probably from the early part of the sixteenth century, it certainly is not as old as the time of Boniface, and the head of the Pope belongs to a well-known series of reconstructions.

The same reverse is also found with the head of Clement VI., Boniface IX., of Martin V., and other Popes. On the other hand, it seems probable that there is a genuine medal of Martin V. with this same device, *justi intrabunt per eam.* Venuti[1] seems satisfied that a medal of this nature which he had seen was no reconstruction, and he is at pains to explain that the Holy Face

SPURIOUS JUBILEE MEDAL OF BONIFACE VIII.
obv. BONIFACIVS VIII. PONT. M. *rev.* IVSTI INTRABVNT PER EAM.

between the two candlesticks was used as a device by the confraternity of the Sancta Sanctorum at the Lateran This does not sufficiently explain either the doorway or the legend. It seems much more probable that the early artists were right in treating it as a Jubilee medal and in reconstructing other Jubilee medals on this model. In fact, it is impossible not to connect this medal with the fifteenth-century legend that the miraculous image of our Saviour at the Lateran was brought by angels through the Golden Door.

Still more interesting is the medal of Sixtus IV., reproduced on the next page. Like most early specimens it is cast, not struck.

[1] Venuti, *Numismata Pontificum Romanorum Præstantiora*, p. 4, must clearly have had before him something quite different from the later type of the same medal, the spuriousness of which can be recognised at a glance.

On the obverse we have a portrait of Sixtus with the words *Sixtus IIII. Pon. M. Ano. Jubileii* (*sic*). The reverse shows a door inserted in a wall of masonry, the Pope, wearing the tiara, is knocking upon it with a hammer, two ecclesiastics attend upon him, one of whom raises his cope. Around the margin runs the legend, *Gloriosa dicta sunt de te Civitas Dei* (Glorious things are said of thee, O City of God—Ps. lxxxvi.). This medal, which

JUBILEE MEDAL OF SIXTUS IV.
obv. SIXTVS IIII. PON. M. ANO · IVBILEII.
rev. GLORIOSA · DICTA · SVNT · DE · TE · CIVITAS · DEI.

professes to have been cast for the Jubilee of Sixtus IV. (1475), twenty-five years before the opening of the "Golden Door" by Alexander VI., is in many ways remarkable. In the first place several of the best authorities,[1] overlooking, it seems, the suspicious character of the subject depicted on the reverse, include it unhesitatingly among the genuine medals. The opinion of the British Museum experts may be quoted on the same side. So far as the execution of the medal goes, there is, they consider, no ground for doubting its authenticity.[2] Let us add that the

[1] *e.g.*, Armand, *Les Médailleurs Italiens*, vol. ii. p. 62; C. Lenormant, *Trésor de Numismatique*, *Médailles d'Italie*, vol. i. plate xxiv. n. 5; Molinet, *Numismata*, p. 20. Though Venuti pronounces it spurious it is clear that he had not himself seen it, for his account of the lettering is quite inaccurate.

[2] The writer is greatly indebted to Mr. Grüber and the other officials of the Department of Coins for their kindness in examining these medals and answering his inquiries.

head of Sixtus on the obverse of the medal bears a close resemblance in treatment and workmanship to that found in another medal of the same Pontiff representing St. Francis and St. Antony crowning the Pope, the genuineness of which last is attested by its having been discovered in his tomb.

But what of the scene on the reverse, apparently representing the opening of the Holy Door? We must remember, in the first place, that even if we admitted the medal to be a reconstruction the difficulty would hardly be lessened. The treatment of the subject in the Sixtine medal does not follow the tradition of the sixteenth century. As a matter of fact we possess a reconstructed medal representing the opening of the Porta Santa attributed to this Pope and this same Jubilee. It bears the name of the artist, G. Palladio, well known for his reconstructions, and it is to be found both cast and struck. But this medal is of quite a different type from that which we are considering, and closely follows the ordinary sixteenth-century models.

The point is important, and even at the risk of wearying the reader, it seems worth while to show how the medal depicted above differs from the ordinary treatment of the scene at the Holy Door current in the sixteenth century. First, the door in the Sixtine medal shows no signs of masonry; it might well be a wooden door; on the other hand, in the wall adjacent the masonry is carefully indicated. Secondly, whereas all the sixteenth-century medals show the stones of the doorway half-broken down under the Pontiff's blows,[1] in the Sixtine medal the doorway is intact. Thirdly, all the sixteenth-century medals and reconstructions show the Pontiff armed with a long-handled pick, the point towards the door; in the Sixtine medal he holds an ordinary hammer. Lastly, it may be remarked that the number of the figures in the Sixtine medal is very much less, their grouping different, and the legend, *Gloriosa dicta sunt de te*, etc., absolutely

[1] This is the case even when the scene at the Holy Door is only introduced in miniature as a decoration of the orphrey of a cope. See, for example, the Jubilee medal of Paul III. on page 52.

unique. It seems to follow from this, that the supposition that the medal under discussion is merely a later reconstruction becomes extremely improbable.

None the less it would perhaps be rash to draw the inference that the ceremony of the unwalling the gate was carried out by the Roman Pontiff himself in the time of Sixtus IV. as it was in the Jubilee of Alexander VI. The Sixtine medal lends itself as readily to a figurative as to a literal interpretation, though it may very possibly have been understood literally

Penitents Kneeling before the Bishop at the Church Door.
From the Giunta Pontificale of 1520.

by Burchard, and even have suggested to him the idea of the picturesque ceremony which he afterwards organised. The idea of the Supreme Pontiff knocking at or beating in a door with a hammer may appear to us now sufficiently far-fetched, but there was much to suggest it to liturgical minds at the close of the Middle Ages. In the first place, the whole penitential discipline of the Church for a thousand years had been built upon the idea of penance as an exclusion from the holy place, or shutting out from the sacred mysteries. Although this penitential discipline had been greatly relaxed, its ceremonies might still be witnessed in the cathedral churches of each diocese during Lent, on Ash Wednesday and Maundy Thursday. Some of the quaint woodcuts contained in the Giunta Pontifical of 1520 will help to make this clear; in nearly all of them the church door is conspicuous. First, on Ash Wednesday, the penitents, barefoot, bareheaded, and clothed in sackcloth, await the bishop just outside the entrance to the church. He comes to them from the altar, puts ashes upon their foreheads, blesses their hair shirts, and finally leads them to the door after reminding them by a short address, so at least the rubric prescribes, that Adam was expelled from Paradise on account of his sins, and that in like manner they are to be banished for a while from the house of God. Then as this old Pontifical quaintly directs, "Let him put them outside the church, saying with tears, 'Behold, we cast you out to-day from the threshold of Holy Mother Church on account of your sins and iniquities. May Almighty God make you to return with the fruits of penance. Amen.'"

Before the re-admission of the Penitents.
From the Giunta Pontificale of 1520.

After this the bishop addresses them in a final exhortation while they kneel outside the porch; and then, upon his returning to the choir, the doors of the church are shut in their face.[1]

On the other hand, on the re-admission of the penitents on Maundy Thursday, this rite is reversed. The penitents assemble and kneel outside the church door while the bishop and his clergy within recite the litanies and other prayers. Then the bishop comes down to the entrance, and the archdeacon makes himself the spokesman and advocate of the penitents, until at

---

[1] "Valvæ ecclesiæ ante oculos eorum clauduntur," p. 176. Pontificale Secundum Ritum Sacrosanctæ Romanæ Ecclesiæ. Venice, per Lucam Antonium de Giunta, 1520.

length the bishop, with many exhortations and much chanting, leads them up the church by the hand and restores them finally to the communion of the faithful. It is interesting to note the rubric in the last stage of this long ceremony, "*Ultimo dat eis indulgentiam prout sibi placuerit*"; finally he grants them an Indulgence as he may think well.

The pictures belonging to it will be intelligible without further explanation.

Neither was the reconciliation of penitents the only rite into which the church door entered prominently. In the order of baptism, both for infants and adults, and in the "benedictio mulieris post partum," popularly known as "churching," the recipient is first met outside the church door and, after certain exorcisms or prayers, is led into the church clasping the end of the priest's stole. So again in the course of the procession of palms on Palm Sunday there is a ceremonial fiction by which the returning procession find the church door closed against them; and after knocking thereat with the foot of the processional cross, and the singing of appropriate antiphons, are finally admitted by those within. What is not quite so familiar is the ceremony which forms part of the rite of the dedication of a church, the picture belonging to which is here reproduced from the Giunta Pontifical. In this case the bishop three times makes the circuit of the building with his attendants, and at the end of each circuit knocks at the closed door with his pastoral staff, saying, "Lift up your gates, ye princes, and ye eternal gates be lifted up, and the King of Glory will enter." To which

THE BISHOP LEADING THE PENITENTS INTO THE CHURCH.
From the Giunta Pontificale of 1520.

the deacon and others within the building reply, "Who is this King of Glory?" The bishop answers, "The Lord powerful and mighty, the Lord mighty in battle." It is only at the third summons, to which the words "Open, open" are added, that those within unbar the door, and the bishop enters first, saying, *Pax huic domui*—"Peace be to this house."

But an even closer parallel, when we regard its immediate connection with a famous plenary Indulgence, is the ceremonial used, seemingly from an early date, at the Church of the Por-

CEREMONY OF THE DEDICATION OF A CHURCH.
From the Giunta Pontificale.

tiuncula, near Assisi, on the evening of the 1st of August. M. Paul Sabatier, who previously regarded the grant of this Indulgence as apocryphal, has now entirely retracted his opinion.[1] He has

[1] M. Sabatier's frank admission that the concession of the Portiuncula Indulgence was after all really obtained by St. Francis from Pope Honorius III., is the more remarkable on account of the very strong language formerly used by him in maintaining the contrary opinion. "It would be tedious," he then said, "to refer even briefly to the difficulties, contradictions, and impossibilities of this story." And again: "Begun in a misapprehension, it ends by imposing itself upon the Church, which to-day guarantees it with its infallible authority, and yet in its origin it was a veritable cry of revolt against the decisions of Rome."—*Life of S. Francis*, pp. 444-448. Mr. H. C. Lea, of course, in his *History of Confession and Indulgences*, iii. p. 238, goes even further than M. Sabatier. He remarks, "To appreciate fully the audacity of the Franciscans

satisfied himself from the best of evidence that multitudes came to the Portiuncula to gain this Indulgence during the greater part of the thirteenth century, and, of course, continuously afterwards. As the Indulgence for visiting the little church could only be gained on the one day alone, crowds used to assemble for hours or even days beforehand. The door of the church had to be kept closed until the proper hour arrived, and then with much ceremony the door was opened and the throng outside were allowed to enter.[1] It would seem that there was a popular belief that no one could validly gain the Indulgence until the priest first crossed the threshold, holding in his hand the document in which St. Francis had written down the privilege, a document which was solemnly brought from Assisi for the purpose. So great was the crush on the occasion of this opening, that we hear of many people losing their lives in the attempt to gain admittance, and precautionary measures were taken to lessen the danger by erecting barricades to keep off the crowd. It is not easy to ascertain the precise nature of the ceremony in the earlier ages. There is no probability that the door of the little church was ever walled up, but that some kind of formal opening was looked upon as essentially connected with the Indulgence may be gathered from the phrase *aperire ecclesiam*, which occurs more than once in early documents referring to the Portiuncula.[2]

From all these analogies we infer that no kind of opening ceremony would more naturally have suggested itself on occasion of an Indulgence, of which the visiting of a church was the essential condition, than the knocking at or the solemn opening

---

in claiming this Indulgence and framing the legend in its support, we must bear in mind how wholly foreign to the ideal of St. Francis would have been the endeavour to bring crowds of pilgrims to the little church he loved so well." Strange as it may seem, it is nevertheless a fact, as the evidence quoted in M. Sabatier's recent article abundantly proves.

[1] Cf. Bonanni, *Numismata Pontificum Romanorum*, vol. i. p. 128.

[2] See those quoted in M. P. Sabatier's article in the *Revue Historique*, 1896. Cf. B. de Amanatis' *Constitutiones Clementis V.* (c. 1388), fol. 225 b. "Nam habent ex more singulis annis die prima Augusti hora vesperarum vel circa aperire dictam ecclesiam, asserentes," etc.

of a door. Moreover, before the time of Alexander VI., it is clear from the account of the Florentine merchant quoted above that there took place in 1450 an unwalling of the Golden Door, at any rate, at the Lateran. Whether it was performed by the Pope himself, whether it was observed at any other Basilica, and whether it was repeated in 1475, is not certain. There is nothing in the expressions used by Burchard to negative these suggestions. If this be true, the fact would explain the medal *justi intrabunt per eam,* and also perhaps that of Sixtus IV.,[1] while the origin of the tradition of the walled-up "Golden Door" would itself become much more intelligible. In any case, we may fairly adopt the conclusion already stated by Dr. Pastor, that the ceremonial framed by Alexander VI. and Burchard was not so much a new invention as a development of observances long familiar.[2]

Those who have paid most attention to the ritual practices of early ages will probably be the most ready to allow that, while few ceremonies have ever been devised with any conscious intention of symbolising mystical truth, there has been a very remarkable "survival of the fittest," allowing some to fall into desuetude and retaining others which appealed more forcibly to the devotional feeling of the faithful. This law certainly seems to hold in the case of the opening of the Holy Door. The ideas suggested by that ceremony are in singular harmony with many expressions of Holy Scripture, long identified by usage with the Unity of the Church and the Power of the Keys. It would take us beyond the scope of this little book to dwell upon the symbolism which this ceremony has suggested to many pious minds, but we may notice that the papal Jubilee medals, many of which are reproduced in these pages, form an interesting commentary upon the devotional thoughts to which the opening

[1] It should be remembered that the Pope never uses a crozier, though he sometimes, as now in this particular ceremony, holds a long-handled cross. It is possible, then, that a hammer may have been used by the Pope in the time of Pope Sixtus IV. to *knock at* the door, where a bishop would have knocked with the foot of his crozier.

[2] Pastor, *Geschichte der Päpste,* vol. iii., third edition, p. 508.

of the Holy Door has given rise. Very touching and appropriate is that of Clement VIII., in which the sheep are brought by the Vicar of Christ to the door of the fold, while we read in the

Reverse of Two Jubilee Medals of Clement VIII., 1600.

legend the words of Psalm xcix., *Introite in exultatione*—"Go in before His presence in exceeding great joy" (or jubilee). Another medal of the same Pontiff shows us the pilgrims kneeling before the Holy Door, behind which is seated Christ our Lord, His hand raised in benediction, and with the legend, "I will refresh you."

Medal struck by Benvenuto Cellini in 1534.
VT · BIBAT · POPVLVS ·

So it would seem that a famous medal originally designed by Benvenuto Cellini to commemorate the hydraulic works undertaken by Pope Clement VII. at Orvieto, and representing Moses striking the rock, with the legend, *Ut bibat populus*—"That the people may drink"—was afterwards adapted to the idea of the opening of the Holy Door.[1] The Pontiff striking the Porta Santa with the golden hammer was to be looked upon as calling forth the living streams of grace and pardon from the

[1] A medal of this type with the head of Paul III. on the obverse is in the collection of Stonyhurst College, but I have not met with it elsewhere.

rock, which is Christ. At any rate this conception was introduced into the beautiful specimen of goldsmith's work preserved in the Munich Museum, and attributed, but perhaps incorrectly,[1] to Benvenuto Cellini. It is the Jubilee hammer used in the opening of the Holy Door by Julius III. in 1550, which will be found reproduced, by the kind permission of Messrs. Plon, Nourrit et Cie, on p. 85. On one side we have the tiara and arms of the Pontiff, on the other a medallion of Moses striking the rock. Under each subject is a short inscription—

JULIUS III PONT. MAX. JOB ILÆUM VIII CON DIDIT FE LICITER	PERCUS SIT PE TRAM ET FLUX ERUNT AQUÆ

"Julius III., Supreme Pontiff, happily inaugurated the eighth Jubilee," and beneath the subject of Moses, "He struck the rock and the waters flowed"—the waters, of course, being the waters of grace and pardon.

Very similar is the idea in the beautiful "Ganymede" medal of Paul III. (see next page), which has not always been recognised as designed for this Jubilee. Whatever the first intention may have been, the obverse of the later medals, where on the orphrey of the papal cope the Pope is represented in the act of breaking down the door, shows that they were undoubtedly struck for the Holy Year. The punning[2] Greek legend,

ΦΕΡΝΗ ΖΗΝΟΣ ΕΥΡΑΙΝΕΙ,

"The Farnesian (or the dowry of Jove) pours water," seems

[1] See M. Eugène Plon, *Benvenuto Cellini, Orfévre, Médailleur, Sculpteur*, p. 315.

[2] ΦΕΡΝΗ ΖΗΝΟΣ (dowry or gift of Jove) would have been pronounced Fairnezenos, which sounds very like a Latinised form of the name Farnese. The designer of the medal was a Greek, Alessandro Croate.

clearly to allude to the life-giving streams with which the Farnese Pope, in the character of the cup-bearer of the gods, is watering the drooping plants. The lilies are probably introduced by preference

"Ganymede" Medal of Paul III.—ΦΕΡΝΗ · ΖΗΝΟΣ · ΕΥΡΑΙΝΕΙ.

as identified with the Farnese coat-of-arms and as emphasising the punning legend. The somewhat pagan tone of the whole conception was quite in the style of the period, in which such a man as Benvenuto Cellini still set the fashion in art. One of the early medals of this same Pontiff bears on the obverse the inscription,

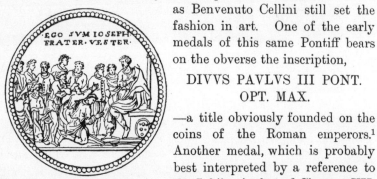

Medal struck for Clement VII. by Giovanni Bernardi. EGO · SVM · JOSEPH · FRATER · VESTER.

DIVVS PAVLVS III PONT. OPT. MAX.

—a title obviously founded on the coins of the Roman emperors.[1] Another medal, which is probably best interpreted by a reference to the Jubilee, is that of Clement VII. with the inscription, *Ego sum Joseph frater vester*—"I am Joseph your brother"—and a representation of Joseph receiving his brethren. The Pope belonged to the family of the Medici, and his Florentine fellow-citizens made pilgrimage to Rome to find him

[1] It is worth noticing that this style was quite commonly adopted by other European sovereigns at the same period. It was a mere classicism and meant nothing, *e.g.*, *Divi Fredericus Pater et Maximilianus Filius, Imperatores Rom.*

exalted in dignity and bestowing spiritual treasures upon his brethren. An interesting medal, or rather coin,[1] more certainly belonging to the same Jubilee, represents the scene of the Nativity —the Jubilee, it will be remembered, always opens on Christmas Eve—with the legend, *Hodie salus facta est Mundo*—"On this day salvation has come to the world." On the reverse we have the Pontiff with a long-handled pick-axe breaking through the Holy Door, while St. Peter with the key unlocks the gate of heaven above, the legend reading, *Apertæ sunt et portæ cœli*— "The gates of heaven are open too." In other medals we find

Jubilee Coin of Clement VII., 1525.
obv. HODIE · SALVS · FACTA · EST · MUNDO.
rev. APERTÆ · SVNT · ET · PORTÆ · CŒLI.

such inscriptions as *Laudent in portis opera ejus*—"Let His works praise Him at the gates";[2] *Domus Dei et porta cœli*—"The house of God and the gate of heaven";[3] *Aperi eis thesaurum tuum*— "Open to them Thy treasure (the fountain of water)";[4] *Per me si quis introierit salvabitur*—"Whosoever shall enter through Me shall be saved";[5] and so on. Some special medals have been struck for the indiction of the Jubilee, one in particular, in 1724, by

[1] See Cinagli, *Le Monete de' Papi*, p. 96; Venuti, *Numismata Romanorum Pontificum*, p. 370.

[2] Prov. xxxi. 31.

[3] Gen. xxviii. 17.

[4] Num. xx. 6.

[5] John x. 9. In this medal of Benedict XIII. Christ and a group of pilgrims are represented as standing before the Holy Door.

Benedict XIII., representing a female figure with a chalice and a cross, and bearing the legend, *Haurietis in gaudio de fontibus salutis*—"Ye shall draw water in joy from the fountains of salvation,"[1] and another, reproduced below, depicts the Vatican palace with the she-wolf and Romulus and Remus in the foreground encircled by the inscription *Fluent ad eum omnes gentes*—"All nations shall stream to Him."[2] But the symbolism of the door is that which, more than all others, is connected with the

REVERSE OF TWO JUBILEE MEDALS OF CLEMENT X., 1675.
On the left, Indiction Medal, FLVENT · AD · EVM · OMNES · GENTES. On the right, Closing of the Holy Door, BENEDIXIT · FILIIS · IN · TE.

Jubilee, and it is, or was, once familiar to the thought of every Roman. The story runs that when a new theatre was built in Rome in the time of Benedict XIV. (it must be remembered that such institutions were always looked askance at and barely tolerated in the papal city), the Pope yielded to his curiosity so far as to visit the building when completed, before it was opened to the public. Whereupon some wag chalked up over the entrance by which the Pontiff had gained admittance the words, PORTA SANTA, INDULGENTIA PLENARIA—"The Holy Door, Plenary Indulgence."

[1] Isa. xii. 3.
[2] *Ibid.* ii. 2.

CHAPTER III

The Holy Year in its Earlier History

THE second Jubilee was celebrated by Clement VI. in 1350. Early in the century Clement V. had removed the papal Court to Avignon, and to this city an embassy, consisting of eighteen members of noble Roman families, was sent on the accession of Clement VI. in 1342, supplicating him to return to Rome and also to celebrate another Jubilee. As a motive for granting the latter request, the Pontiff was asked to remember the brevity of human life and the very small number of persons who could profit by a Jubilee celebrated only once in a hundred years. The prayers of the ambassadors are said to have been enforced by a letter of St. Bridget of Sweden, in whose revelations we read that by the command of God she wrote to communicate to Clement the following message:—"I have raised thee above all others in honour; arise, then, and make peace between the Kings of France and England, and afterwards return to Italy to announce the year of salvation and divine charity."

The poet Petrarch, accompanied by Cola di Rienzo,[1] also went to France to endeavour to persuade the Pope to bring back the papal Court to Rome, and to shorten the interval between the Jubilees. Petrarch addressed a poetical epistle to Clement,[2] beginning—

Spes mihi longa nimis, pater O sanctissime patrum.

[1] Papencordt, *Cola di Rienzo e il suo Tempo*, pp. 65 and 324, considers that there were two embassies, one in 1342 and the second in 1343. Rienzo, in his opinion, was a member of the second embassy, Petrarch of the first.

[2] *Epistolarum Carmine Scriptarum*, liber ii. ep. 5.

What follows is a rough translation of that portion of the poem which more directly concerns our present purpose—

With other boons, this I devoutly pray,
That henceforth quicklier may cycle round
The sacred and all-salutary year,
That sickness easy remedy may find,
And sin, nigh hope of pardon: that when storms
Lash the fierce waves, we shipwrecked mariners
May find near harbourage, lest to far shores
Struggling in vain we perish in the surf.
For who dare hope to pass the extremest mark
Of mortal life, or tell an hundred years,
Since in the twinkling of an eye our day is spent?
Wherefore, more quickly bring that season round
Which washes clean the world's iniquity,
Pardons the guilty, breaks the captive's chains;—
Nor strange my prayer, nor alien to God's writ.

There is no foundation for the suggestion which has been made,[1] that the Pope was induced to institute this Jubilee by the pestilence (the "black death") which devastated Rome, like the rest of Europe, in the years 1348-49. The Bull *Unigenitus* proclaiming the Jubilee was issued in 1343, and the motives which weighed with the Pontiff are clearly stated in the text. After setting forth reasons drawn from Holy Scripture why the fiftieth year should be thus honoured, the Pope goes on—"Considering also the prayers of our people of Rome who, by special and solemn embassies, humbly supplicate us,[2] as in the case of Moses and Aaron of old, in the name of all the faithful saying: O Lord, open to them Thy treasure, the fountain of living water. . . . We wishing that as many souls as possible should participate in this Indulgence, and recognising that from the brevity of human life but few survive until the century, by the advice of our brothers, the Cardinals of Holy Church, have decided for the above and other reasons that the

[1] By Gonzalo de Illescas in his *Historia Pontifical*.

[2] *Attendentes et clamorem peculiaris populi nostri Romani videlicet hoc humiliter supplicantis . . . et dicentis. "Domine aperi eis thesaurum tuum fontem aquæ vivæ."*—Num. xx. 6. These last words are noteworthy for their connection with the symbolism spoken of in the last chapter.

term of the said concession of Indulgence shall be reduced to fifty years."

The Pope despatched copies of this constitution to many patriarchs, archbishops, and bishops, ordering them to publish it in their respective dioceses. He also sent Cardinal Annibaldo Gaetani Ceccano, Bishop of Frascati, as his legate to Rome conferring on him the fullest powers in everything that concerned the celebration of the Jubilee.

At the Jubilee of 1350 we are told that the concourse of people was so great that between Christmas, 1349, when it commenced, and the following Easter 1,200,000 persons visited the Holy City. The author of the *Life of Rienzo* remarks—"In that year (1350) all Christendom flocked to Rome to gain the Indulgence."[1] So also the Italian chronicler, Matteo Villano, writes—"On the Feast of the Nativity, 1349, the Holy Indulgence commenced for all those who went on pilgrimage to Rome, visiting, as ordered by Holy Church, the Basilicas of St. Peter, St. John Lateran, and St. Paul without the walls,[2] to which pardon men and women of all sorts and conditions ran in great and incredible numbers (there had recently been great mortality from the pestilence of 1348, which, indeed, still raged in many places), and they made the pilgrimage with great devotion and humility, bearing with much patience bodily discomforts of all kinds, arising from extreme cold, frost, snow, inundations, rough and broken roads, and insufficient shelter. Germans and Hungarians in multitudes passed the night in the open air herding together and making great fires to lessen the cold. The hosts at the inns were too busy—not, indeed, to provide bread, wine, etc., but to take the money that was offered for them. To number the crowds was impossible, but it was estimated that from

---

[1] Walsingham, *Historia Anglicana*, the Chronicon de Melsa, and some other English chronicles, take notice of the Jubilee. But Edward III. put all possible obstacles in the way of intending English pilgrims for fear money should be taken out of the country, and but few Englishmen went to Rome.

[2] Clement VI. added the visit to St. John Lateran to the two prescribed at the previous Jubilee. The visit to St. Mary Major was afterwards enjoined by Gregory XI. See further in chap. v. on the visits to the Basilicas.

Christmas to Easter there were constantly at Rome from ten to twelve hundred thousand people, and at Ascension and Pentecost eight hundred thousand. The numbers diminished as the summer advanced, partly on account of the heat, partly because of the labours of the harvest; but a great multitude remained. The visits to the three churches, when we take into account the going and returning to the place where each person lodged, involved on the average a journey of eleven miles.[1] The roads were so crowded that all the pilgrims, whether they travelled on foot or on horseback, went very slowly."[2]

The Volto Santo or Sudario, the napkin believed to have been offered to our Saviour by St. Veronica, and to have retained the impression of His sacred countenance, was shown at St. Peter's on every Sunday and Feast day, at which time the multitudes who thronged the church were so great that many were suffocated or trampled to death. It is curious to note how deep a feeling of devotion the exposition of this relic—the authenticity of which is, unfortunately, more than doubtful—would seem to have evoked. The spurious but contemporary document quoted by Alberic a Rosate,[3] and purporting to be a Jubilee Bull of Clement VI., represents the veneration of the Volto Santo as the climax of the whole pilgrimage, and, indeed, it even implies that to receive the blessing given with the Sudario was one of the necessary conditions for gaining the Indulgence. Hence we are hardly surprised to notice that the deep impression made upon the pilgrim, when after months of toil and hardship he found himself at last regarding the imprint of those sacred features, is commemorated in one of the most beautiful sonnets of Petrarch.

> The palmer bent, with locks of silver grey,
> Quits the sweet spot where he has passed his years,
> Quits his poor family, whose anxious fears
> Paint the loved father fainting on his way;
> And trembling on his aged limbs slow borne,

---

[1] See further on this distance in chap. v.

[2] Villani, lib. i. cap. 55.

[3] See above p. 34.

In these last days that close his earthly course,
He in his soul's strong purpose finds new force.
Though weak with age, though by long travel worn:
Thus reaching Rome, led on by pious love,
He seeks the image of that Saviour Lord
Whom soon he hopes to meet in bliss above:
So, oft in other forms I seek to trace
Some charm, that to my heart may yet afford
A faint resemblance of thy matchless grace.[1]--DACRE.

The crystal case, adorned with ornaments of silver-gilt in which the Sudarium is still enclosed, was given in this Jubilee year by three Venetian nobles—Nicolo Valentini, Bandino de' Garzonibus, and Franceschino in Glostro.[2]

There is no record of any large number of distinguished visitors. St. Bridget of Sweden was then residing in Rome. Petrarch himself was hardly to be counted a stranger in the Holy City. The most notable person who came from afar was Ludovic, King of Hungary, who daily made the round of the Basilicas on foot, and who, before he left, offered 4000 gold crowns at the altar of St. Peter's.

But the Jubilee did something, nevertheless, to secure peace and a measure of prosperity for the afflicted city. The following passage from Mrs. Oliphant's *Makers of Rome* gives a striking picture of the temporal benefits it brought in its train. It should be remembered that Rome was just at this time in the throes of the disturbances created by the revolt of the great tribune Cola di Rienzo.

"Many and great had been its troubles in those seven years.

---

[1] Movesi'l vecchierel canuto, e bianco
Dal dolce loco ov' ha sua età fornita,
E dalla famigliuola sbigottita,
Che vede il caro padre venir manco:
Indi traendo poi l'antico fianco
Per l'estreme giornate di sua vita.
Quanto più può, col buon voler s'aita
Rotto dagli anni, e dal cammino stanco;
E viene a Roma segueudo'l desio
Per mirar la Sembianza di Colui
Ch'ancor lassù nel ciel vedere spera.—*Sonnet xiv.*

[2] Cancellieri, *De Secretariis*, t. ii.

It had fallen back into the old hands—an Orsini and a Colonna, a Colonna and an Orsini. There had been a temporary lull in the year of the Jubilee (1350), when all the world flocked to

CASTLE OF ST. ANGELO DURING A SOLEMN PAPAL CAVALCADE.
A segment of Falda's engraving of the "Possesso."

Rome to obtain the Indulgence, and to have their sins washed away in the full stream of papal forgiveness. It is said that Rienzi himself made his way stealthily back to share in that Indulgence, but without making himself known; and the interest of the citizens was so much involved in peace, and it was so essential to keep a certain rule of order and self-restraint on account of the many guests who brought money to the city, that there was a temporary lull of its troubles. The town was no more than a great inn from Easter to Christmas, and wealth, which has always a soothing and quieting influence, poured into the pockets of the citizens, fully occupied as they were by the care of their guests, and by the continual ceremonials and sacred functions of those busy days. The Jubilee brought not only masses of pious pilgrims from every part of the world, but innumerable law-suits — cases of conscience and of secular disputes—to be settled by the busy Cardinal who sat instead of the Pope, hearing daily what every applicant might have to say. There had been a new temporary bridge built in order to provide for the pressure of the crowd, and avoid that block of the old bridge of St. Angelo, which Dante describes in the *Inferno*, when the mass of pilgrims coming and going broke down one of the arches. Other large, if hasty, labours of preparation were also in hand.

"The Capitol had to be repaired and old churches furbished up, and every scrap of drapery and tapestry which was to be had employed to make the city fine. So that for one year at least there had been no thought but to put the best possible face on things, to quench internal disorders for the moment, and make all kinds of temporary arrangements for comfort and accommodation, as is often done in a family when important visitors force a salutary self-denial upon all; so that there were a hundred inducements to preserve a front of good behaviour and fit decorum before the world."[1]

The appeal made by St. Catherine of Siena to Gregory XI., who ascended the papal throne in 1370, to restore the Apostolic See to Rome, proved more efficacious than that which St. Bridget had formerly addressed to Clement VI. for the same object. Gregory returned from the Babylonian exile at Avignon in January, 1377. He had already, in 1373, issued a Constitution

[1] *The Makers of Modern Rome*, pp. 399, 400.

Salvator Noster, in which he decreed that for the future, in order to obtain the Jubilee Indulgence, it would be necessary to add a visit to the Basilica of St. Mary Major over and above the visits to be made to St. Peter's, St. Paul's, and St. John Lateran. Gregory XI. only lived one year after his return to Rome, and to him succeeded Urban VI. in 1378. In 1389 Urban, considering, as St. Antoninus of Florence relates, that the term of human existence was even shorter now than formerly, and that many men no longer attained the age of fifty,[1] published the Constitution *Salvator Noster*, in which he shortened the interval between the Jubilees to thirty-three years, the third part of a century, in honour of the number of years our Lord lived on earth. According to some writers, Gregory XI. first conceived this idea, but was prevented by death from putting it into execution. The letter sent by Boniface IX. to the King of Portugal,[2] granting him and his Queen participation in the Jubilee Indulgence without leaving their kingdom, upon condition that they gave the money which the journey would have cost towards the restoration of the churches of Rome,[3] establishes the fact that it was Urban VI. who instituted the shorter term for the celebration of the Holy Year, though death also prevented him, as it had done his predecessor, from actually inaugurating the next Jubilee. This was finally held under his successor, Boniface IX., in 1390.

We must not forget that at this period the Great Schism was at its height, and that France, Spain, and Catalonia all acknowledged the Anti-Pope Clement VII. It is therefore not surprising to learn that the number of persons who visited Rome in 1390 was considerably less than at the previous Jubilees. At the same time, Theodoricus de Niem, one of the Pope's secretaries,

---

[1] *Chronicon*, p. 3, tit. ii. cap. 2.

[2] A similar letter was also sent to Richard II. of England and his Queen, Anne of Bohemia.

[3] *Urbanus VI. statuit ut universi Christi fideles vere pœnitentes et confessi, qui in Anno Domini 1390 instante nunc futuro et deinceps perpetuis temporibus de XXXIII. annis in XXXIII. annos, Apostolorum Petri et Pauli Basilicas de Urbe et Lateranensem et St. Mariæ Majoris Ecclesias visitassent, etc.*

and an eye-witness, assures us that great crowds of pilgrims flocked in from the countries which remained faithful to the rightful Pope.[1] We are also told[2] that the desire of beholding the Supreme Pontiff again in his ancient see contributed something towards attracting pilgrims to Rome in this year.

Only ten years after this, *i.e.*, in 1400, it is stated by some authorities that the same Pope, Boniface IX., celebrated another Jubilee, though as no Bull was issued concerning it,[3] the fact may be considered as very questionable. Nevertheless, according to Theodoricus de Niem and others, a number of Frenchmen made their way to Rome for the century year, France having at this juncture withdrawn her obedience from the Anti-Pope Benedict XIII. A pestilence was raging in Italy, and the roads were infested with brigands, rendering the journey perilous to life and property; nevertheless, a throng of devout pilgrims presented themselves in the city just as if peace and safety reigned supreme. Bohemia at the same epoch seems to have enjoyed a Jubilee of its own, since the King Wenceslaus IV., who had been deposed by the College of Electors on account of his many crimes (conspicuous among which was the murder of St. John Nepomucene), professed repentance and besought the Pope to grant to the city of Prague the Indulgences hitherto reserved for Rome alone.

From the scanty details which have been handed down to us of the next Jubilee under Martin V., it has been sometimes inferred either that but few pilgrims came to Rome on this occasion, or even that no pilgrimage took place at all.

---

[1] *Innumerabiles peregrini toto illo anno postquam incepit Jubileus præsertim de Alemania, Hungaria, Polonia, Boemia, Anglia, et aliis Regnis et Provinciis quae fuerunt de obedientia Urbani, ad Urbem venerunt unde et maxima offertoria Ecclesiis et Basilicis Urbis per visitatores data fuerunt.*—Theodoricus de Niem, *Storia della Scisma di Occidente*, lib. i. cap. 68.

[2] Torsellino, *Storia Lauretana*, lib. i. cap. 21.

[3] It may be noted that the inscription upon the Jubilee hammer of Julius III. (see chap. ii. p. 51) reckons the celebration of 1550 as the *eighth* Jubilee. This seems to take account neither of the supposed Great Pardon of 1400, nor of that which took place under Martin V. in 1423.

Gregorovius, among modern writers, makes no mention of it; Platina, Volterrano, and some other of the older chroniclers are equally silent; but the explicit testimony of Niccola della Tuccia leaves no room for doubt that a Jubilee really was celebrated by Martin. Dr. Pastor, in the latest edition of his *History*, observes that since writing the first volume in 1885 three additional witnesses to the fact have come to his knowledge. These are—*A de Tummullis* in the *Notabilia temporum* (p. 37), and the unpublished *Cronaca* of Fra Francesco di Andrea; while the third piece of evidence is furnished by a papal Brief addressed to the Duke of Lithuania, granting the Jubilee Indulgence to himself and fifteen councillors.[1] Various years have been assigned for this Jubilee, but Dr. Pastor considers that usually given, viz., 1423, to be alone correct. In contradiction to the idea that this Jubilee was but poorly attended, the humanist Poggio complains in one of his letters that "Rome was inundated by Barbarians," meaning by this term non-Italians, who had thronged there for the Jubilee and "had filled the whole city with dirt and confusion."[2] The chronicle of Viterbo also speaks of the great number of "Ultramontanes who had hastened to Rome to gain the Jubilee Indulgence."[3]

One other reference to this Jubilee may be quoted from an English source. The chronicler of St. Albans,[4] under the year 1423, gives a long account of the journey of their abbot to Italy to attend the Council of Sienna, and to obtain certain privileges for the monastery at the papal Court. Abbot John was duly present at the Council, but finding little doing there he determined to push on to Rome, "as it seemed a favourable time for such a visit, on account of the Jubilee ("in Jubileo tunc instante").[5] It is a curious fact, however, that in the full

[1] *Archiv. für Œsterreich. Gesch.*, lii. 204-205.

[2] *Epist. Poggii*, ed. Torelli, i. 86.

[3] Niccola della Tuccia, *Cronaca*, 52.

[4] Joannes Amundesham, *Annales*, vol. l. p. 143 *seq.*

[5] "Cœpit ad mentem reducere qualiter pro tunc se tempus obtulit opportunum quo, in Jubilæo tunc instante, posset pro salute animæ et limina visitare Apostolica," etc., p. 143.

account of the abbot's subsequent proceedings in Rome, the Jubilee is not once mentioned or even alluded to. On the contrary, in a very severe illness of which the English monk nearly died, the Pope sent him a special plenary Indulgence. This the abbot mentions in such terms as would seem to imply that he could hardly have realised that he was entitled to a plenary remission of sins on account of his pilgrimage to Rome in the Anno Santo.

From a pontifical letter of the year 1423, which is printed in Raynaldus' *Annales Ecclesiastici*,[1] it appears that Martin V. addressed a reproof to the Archbishop of Canterbury for having arrogated to himself powers which belong to the Holy Father alone, inasmuch as during the reign of Henry VI. the archbishop proclaimed an Indulgence in England like that of the Holy Year, granting to those pilgrims who should visit Canterbury Cathedral the same remission of penance as was to be obtained at Rome during the Jubilee time.

The next Jubilee, that of 1450, in the reign of Nicholas V., was a very famous one, and it passed all previous record in the solemnity of its observances and the numbers who attended it. In his Bull of the 19th January, 1449, Nicholas had abrogated the regulation of Urban VI. as to the time of celebrating the great Indulgence, and reverted to the longer interval of half a century determined by Clement VI.

The "Golden Year" opened on Christmas Day, 1449, and an immense concourse of pilgrims flocked to Rome from every country in Europe. An eye-witness[2] compared the bands of pilgrims to the flight of starlings or the march of myriads of ants. Æneas Sylvius Piccolomini[3] estimates that 40,000 people entered Rome daily. Christoforo a Soldo, the Brescian chronicler, says—"A greater crowd of Christians was never

---

[1] Vol. xxvii. p. 573. See chap. x., and Creighton, *History of the Papacy*, ii. p. 25.

[2] Manetti, J., *Vita di Nicolai V.*, p. 924. See Pastor, vol. ii. p. 77 (English edition). The whole of the account of this and the following Jubilee is based upon that of Pastor.

[3] *Historia Friderici III.*, p. 172.

known to hasten to any Jubilee—kings, dukes, marquises, counts, and knights; in short, people of all ranks in Christendom daily arrived in such multitudes in Rome that there were millions in the city. And this continued for the whole year excepting in the summer, on account of the plague, which carried off innumerable victims. But almost as soon as it abated in the cold season the influx again commenced."[1]

The canonisation of St. Bernardine of Sienna on Whitsunday, the 24th May,[2] was one of the great events of the Jubilee.[3] St. Peter's was splendidly decorated for the occasion. A lofty throne was erected for the Pope, who was surrounded by all the cardinals then in Rome, as well as by many archbishops and bishops. Every detail of the rite of canonisation was carried out with the greatest solemnity and splendour, the Pope himself pronouncing the panegyric of the saint. Two hundred wax lights were kept burning, and the whole expenses amounted to 7000 ducats, which were defrayed by the towns of Sienna and Apulia.[4] According to the *Cronaca di Bologna* there were present fourteen cardinals, twenty-four bishops, and more than 2000 Frati of the Observance, these latter all being entertained at the Pope's expense.

Numbers of pilgrims were lodged at the Convent of the Ara Cœli, among them being the Spaniard Didacus, afterwards canonised. The immense numbers who went on pilgrimage to Rome, especially during the Jubilee years, were the occasion of many foundations there for the reception of the sick and travel-worn. The origin of the German Hostelry of Our Lady at the Campo Santo, near St. Peter's, has been assigned to the Jubilee of 1300; this is uncertain, but it dates probably from the fourteenth century. A second German hospital, that of the "Anima," was founded in the Jubilee year of 1350. In the Jubilee of 1450 Alfonso Paradinas, Bishop of Rodrigo, erected a Spanish hospital

---

1 *Ist. Bresc.*, 867.
2 Pastor, vol. ii. p. 81.
3 Vittorelli, Historia de' Giubilei Pontificii, p. 292.
4 Niccola della Tuccia, 214.

which, together with its church, was dedicated to St. James. We shall see later on the confraternities also, and in particular the arch-confraternity of the Holy Trinity, founded by S. Philip Neri, giving help and shelter to needy pilgrims, especially in the years of Jubilee.

The Roman chronicler Paolo di Benedetto di Cola dello Mastro has left a very vivid and naive picture of this Jubilee of 1450. A few passages may be quoted here.[1]

"I recollect," he says, "that even in the beginning of the Christmas month a great many people came to Rome for the Jubilee. The pilgrims had to visit the four principal churches—the Romans for a whole month, the Italians for fourteen days, and the Ultramontanes for eight. Such a crowd of pilgrims came all at once to Rome that the mills and bakeries were quite insufficient to provide bread for them. And the number of pilgrims daily increased, wherefore the Pope ordered the handkerchief of St. Veronica to be exposed every Sunday, and the heads of the Apostles Saints Peter and Paul every Saturday; the other relics in all the Roman churches were always exposed. The Pope solemnly gave his benediction at St. Peter's every Sunday. As the unceasing influx of the faithful made the want of the most necessary means of subsistence to be more and more pressing, the Pope granted a plenary Indulgence to each pilgrim on condition of contrite confession and of visits to the churches on three days. This great concourse of pilgrims continued from Christmas through the whole month of January, and then diminished so considerably that the innkeepers were discontented, and every one thought it was at an end, when, in the middle of Lent, such a great multitude of pilgrims again appeared, that in the fine weather all the vineyards were filled with them, and they could not find sleeping-place elsewhere. In Holy Week the throngs coming from St. Peter's, or going there, were so enormous that they were crossing the bridge over the Tiber until the second or third hour of the night. The crowd was here so

[1] *Cronache Romane*, pp. 16-20. See Manni, pp. 63-66; also Pastor, vol. ii. We have in part availed ourselves of the translation of the "*Cronaca*" there given.

great that the soldiers of St. Angelo, together with other young men—I was often there myself (says Paolo)—had often to hasten to the spot, and clear a passage through the throng with sticks in order to prevent serious accidents. At night many of the poor pilgrims were to be seen sleeping beneath the porticos, while others wandered about in search of missing fathers, sons, or companions, so that it was pitiful to see them. And this went on till the Feast of the Ascension, when the multitude of pilgrims again diminished because the plague came to Rome. Many people then died, many, more particularly, of the pilgrims; all the hospitals and churches were full of the sick and dying, and they were to be seen in the infected streets falling down like dogs. Of those who with great difficulty, scorched with heat and covered with dust, departed from Rome, multitudes fell a sacrifice to the terrible pestilence, and graves were to be seen all along the roads even in Tuscany and Lombardy."[1] Manni tells us that the officials in charge of the hospital of Sta. Maria Nuova in Florence showed great charity to the pilgrims who fell sick in the roads, sending out mules and muleteers, as far even as Sienna, to bring in all those whom they found ill to the hospital, where they were carefully tended. The Pope himself left Rome for Fabriano, but returned in September, when with the colder weather the pestilence ceased and the pilgrims again poured in. To quote our chronicler[2] once more—"So many people came to Rome that the city could not contain the strangers, although every house became an hotel. Pilgrims begged, for the love of God, to be taken in, but it was not possible. They had to spend the nights out of doors. Many perished from cold; it was dreadful to see them. Still such multitudes thronged together that the city was actually starving. Every Sunday numerous pilgrims left Rome, but by the following Saturday all the houses were again fully occupied. If you wanted to go to St. Peter's, it was impossible to reach it on account of the masses of men that filled the streets. St. Paul's,

[1] *Cronache Romane*, p. 74.

[2] Paolo dello Mastro, *Cronache Rom.*, p. 18.

St. John Lateran, and St. Maria Maggiore were crowded with worshippers. All Rome was packed so full that one could not go through the streets. When the Pope gave his solemn blessing, all the open spaces in the neighbourhood of St. Peter's, even the surrounding vineyards, from which the Loggia of the benediction could be seen, were densely packed with pilgrims, but those who could not see him were more numerous than those who could, and this continued until Christmas."

In the crowds that flocked to Rome this year were included many distinguished visitors. There were saints and sinners, secular princes and ecclesiastics, humanists, and those whom the humanists called barbarians. Amongst the first class may be mentioned the celebrated St. John Capistran, also St. Jacopo della Marca, and the Spanish friar St. Didacus, or Diego.[1] The ecclesiastics could hardly be numbered, but few attracted so much attention as James, Archbishop of Treves, who came accompanied by 150 knights. Among the secular princes who also made the pilgrimage were Duke Albert of Austria, the brother of the Emperor; William, Earl of Douglas; and several German potentates.[2] But a terrible occurrence took place on the 19th December,[3] when an unusually dense crowd had assembled at St. Peter's to venerate the *Santo Sudario.* At about four o'clock in the afternoon the Pope sent word that benediction would not be given that day, and the people hurried home by the bridge of St. Angelo. Some horses and mules took fright, and a block ensued. Many pilgrims were pushed down, trampled under foot, or fell into the Tiber. The castellan of St. Angelo caused the gates of the bridge to be closed to prevent others entering, but the fatal crush lasted for an hour. The dead were carried into the Church of San Celso. "I myself carried twelve dead bodies," writes the chronicler

---

[1] Manni, pp. 60, 61.

[2] The safe-conduct issued by Henry VI. to William, Earl of Douglas, and his suite to pass through Calais is still preserved. See *Calendar of Documents relating to Scotland*, vol. iv. No. 1229.

[3] Manni, p. 62, and the *Cronache Rom.*, p. 18, say the 18th, but this is an error. See Pastor, vol. ii. p. 96 n.

Paolo dello Mastro, "and it was pitiful to see there one hundred and seventy-two corpses; the weeping and lamenting of those who found fathers, mothers, sons, and brothers among the dead resounded in the streets *usque ad mediam noctem.* Truly, it was misery to see the poor people, with candles in their hands, looking through the rows of dead who lay there." At midnight, by the Pope's orders, one hundred and twenty-eight were carried to the Campo Santo, near St. Peter's, where they were left all Sunday for identification. The remainder of the bodies were brought to Sta. Maria della Minerva, or buried in St. Celso. "Their garments were given in charge to Benedetto, my father," says Paolo, "and put in one part of the church, and many *quærebant suos*—many searching those clothes, learned their loss."[1] The Pope was deeply distressed at this appalling catastrophe, and, to guard against future accidents, had a row of houses in front of the bridge cleared away so as to form an open space. Two chapels, dedicated respectively to St. Mary Magdalene and the Holy Innocents, were erected at the entrance of the bridge, and Mass was said daily for the souls of the victims. Clement VII. replaced these chapels by the statues of the Holy Apostles which now stand there.

Large sums of money were brought as offerings by the pilgrims, and we learn that money was scarce at this time, because "it all flowed into Rome for the Jubilee." Nicholas V. used the resources thus obtained partly in rebuilding the public edifices, partly in the promotion of art and learning; but the poor were not forgotten in the distribution of his wealth.[2] Early in the following year the Pope, generally at the request of their respective sovereigns, despatched legates to certain foreign countries, to extend the Jubilee Indulgence to the faithful who were unable to visit Rome.[3] The conditions usually enjoined

---

[1] Another account of this accident is contained in an anonymous diary at the British Museum.—MS. Addit. 8434, fol. 29.

[2] Manetti, *Chronica di Perugia*, 924 *seq.* See Manni, pp. 70-72. Müntz, *Les Arts à la Cour des Papes*, Nicholas V., pp. 68 and 92.

[3] Further details are given in Noethen, *Geschichte aller Jubeljahre*, p. 63.

were a visit, or series of visits, to the cathedral of the Diocese, and an alms to be offered there for a specified intention. Cardinal Nicholas of Cusa was one of these legates, a most holy prelate, who by his labours and preaching throughout Germany did much towards reforming the abuses which were then rife in the Church.

No one who reads the account of his preaching of the Jubilee in Pastor or Janssen can doubt of the great moral good produced by this opportunity of grace. "He looked," says Pastor, "on the work of ecclesiastical reform as one of purification and renovation, not of ruin and destruction, and believed that man must not deform what is holy, but rather be himself transformed thereby. And, therefore, first of all and above all, he was a reformer in his own person. His life was a mirror of every Christian and sacerdotal virtue. Justly persuaded that it is the duty of those who hold the chief places in the Church to exercise the office of preachers, he everywhere proclaimed the Word of God to both clergy and laity, and his practice accorded with his preaching. His example was even more powerful than his sermons. Detesting all vanity, he journeyed modestly on his mule, accompanied only by a few Romans, and scarcely to be recognised, save by the silver cross which the Pope had given him, and which was mounted on a staff and carried before him. On arriving in any town his first visit was to the church, where he fervently implored the blessing of Heaven on the work he had taken in hand. Many princes and rich men brought him splendid presents, but he kept his hands pure from all gifts. Among his companions was the holy and learned Carthusian, Dionysius van Leewis, a man filled with the most ardent zeal for the renovation of monastic life."[1]

It seems doubtful whether we possess any authentic medals for the Jubilee of Nicholas V. Those that are commonly seen are unquestionably reconstructions, but there is much to suggest that for one or two of these there was some genuine prototype,

[1] Pastor, *Popes* (English translation), vol. ii. pp. 107, 108.

a few rare specimens of which may still be extant. The representation of the Holy Door with the glory above it seems to allude to a legend about the Golden Gate of St. John Lateran that was undoubtedly current in that age.[1] This bears the inscription ALMA ROMA; and the same words are found in certain coins of Nicholas V. bearing the imprint ANNO JUBILEI, the authenticity of which is not disputed.[2]

After the space we have devoted to this celebrated Jubilee we may pass somewhat more rapidly over the following celebrations, which now recur at shorter intervals.

Paul II., in a Bull, *Ineffabilis Providentia,* dated 19th April, 1470, decreed that the Jubilee of the Anno Santo should be celebrated every twenty-five years, beginning from the first vespers of Christmas Eve and ending on the same day in the year following. In this Bull, *Ineffabilis Providentia,* after recapitulating the decrees of former Popes concerning the Jubilee, the Pontiff observes that "the thought of all that the Church had suffered from schism at two different periods, and of all that it had cost her to end it; the terror which had settled upon Western Christendom when, by the fall of Constantinople, the Turks gained a footing in Europe; the alarming outbreaks of pestilence, and finally the havoc which ceaseless wars had wrought in the moral life of the Western kingdoms, led men to turn their eyes to Heaven, and showed that in order to arrest the chastening hand of Almighty God it was needful that all should tread the paths of penance."[3]

Paul II. died in 1471, but Sixtus IV., who succeeded him, confirmed his decision that every twenty-fifth year should be a year of Jubilee, and by a further Bull of 29th August, 1473, abrogated all other Indulgences and Faculties during the Jubilee year; this practice, now introduced by Sixtus for the first time, was followed by succeeding Popes.[4]

---

[1] See the German *Romb√ºchlein* of 1472 (?), fol. 28 v°.

[2] Cinagli, *Le Monete de' Papi*, p. 49.

[3] Pastor, vol. iv. p. 117. See also for this Bull, Vittorelli, pp. 310, 311.

[4] Manni, p. 76. Cf. N. Paulus in *Zeitschrift f. K. Theologie*, vol. xxiv. p. 177.

As the time for the Jubilee approached, the Pope set about various improvements in the city of Rome.[1] Chief among these improvements was the rebuilding from its foundations the old bridge of the Janiculum—long called by the Romans the *Ponte Rotto,* from its ruinous condition. It was afterwards known as the Ponte Sisto. The Pope, with the cardinals and several prelates, solemnly laid the foundation stone in April, 1473, and

FONTANA DI TREVI FURTHER RESTORED AND EMBELLISHED BY BENEDICT XIV.
From an engraving, c. 1840.

this "most durable and solid" bridge was finished in time for the use of the pilgrims in the Jubilee year.

An anonymous diary amongst the manuscripts at the British Museum tells us that the foundation stone of the Ponte Sisto was laid upon the 29th of April, 1473. "Behind the stone," says the writer, "the Pope deposited certain gold medals bearing his own effigy, and on top of these he had the bridge built."[2] It

[1] Vittorelli, p. 324, and Manni, p. 77.

[2] "Dietro a quella pietra mise il Papa certe medaglie d'oro con la sua testa e dopo fece edificare quel Ponte."—MS. Ad. 8434, fol. 45 (an abstract of Infessura ?).

does not seem quite likely that these medals would have been designed for the purpose, with a representation of the finished bridge, but it is, of course, possible that this was done. In any case, an authentic medal of this Pope is in existence, which shows the Ponte Sisto with the Tiber running beneath it. It bears the legend CURA RERUM PUBLICARUM.

Another work also of great public utility was finished this year. The Aqueduct conducting the Acqua Vergine to Rome, which had been almost stopped up, was cleared out and lengthened from the Quirinal to the Fontana di Trevi.[1]

The cardinals emulated the Pope in their endeavours to improve and embellish their city.[2] There remained hardly a church in Rome which was not renovated during the Jubilee year. Another good work undertaken at this time was the restoration of the Hospital of Santo Spirito, in expectation of the pilgrims who would need its shelter. Furthermore, in 1475 was laid the foundation stone of the new church at the Hospice of the *Campo Santo al Vaticano.* The number of the Jubilee pilgrims does not seem to have equalled the expectations that had been entertained. Ciacconius says that the wars in France, Burgundy, Germany, Hungary, Poland, Spain, and elsewhere interfered notably with the influx of visitors to Rome, though other writers[3] maintain that the concourse was very great, notwithstanding these and other drawbacks. At any rate, at Easter the pilgrims swarmed in the city. One of the ambassadors gives 200,000 as the number present when the Pope solemnly blessed the people on Ascension Day. This, no doubt, is an exaggerated estimate, but the report of this eye-witness fully establishes the fact that the concourse was immense.[4]

---

[1] Platina, *Sixtus IV.*, p. 1064.

[2] Vittorelli, 324.

[3] Giulio Roseo, *Libri del Centesimo del Cardinale de S. Giorgio;* and Gonzalo d'Illercas, *Storia Pontifical.* See Zaccaria, p. 65, n. 1, who thinks Ciacconius the more reliable authority.

[4] Pastor, vol. iv. p. 281.

The royal visitors during this Jubilee included Ferrante of Naples,[1] Queen Dorothea of Denmark, Nicholas of Ujlak, who had been made King of Bosnia; Anthony of Burgundy; and, lastly, Charlotte of Lusignan, the deposed Queen of Cyprus.

The Jubilee year ended unpropitiously. In November the Tiber rose and overflowed a great part of the city, so that pilgrims visiting St. Paul's without the walls had to go in boats. The mud and dampness of the flooded quarters brought pestilence and malaria; the roads had also become unsafe, and the influx of pilgrims naturally fell off. Under these circumstances the Pope commanded that the Jubilee should be held at Bologna during 1476, from the 1st May till the end of the year, granting the plenary Indulgence to all who should visit the four principal churches in that city. Participation in the benefits of the Jubilee was also granted to other countries—to Scotland among the number—in most cases with the condition that the Jubilee alms should be devoted to the defence of Christendom against the Turks.

With the pontificate of Sixtus IV. the medallic illustrations of the Jubilee become more prominent. Even in 1470 the Bull by which Paul II. reduced the period to twenty-five years was commemorated in a medal of considerable size and of curious oval shape.[2] It bears, together with the effigy of Paul II., the inscription—

PAULO VENETO PAPA II. ANNO
PVBLICATIONIS IVBILAEI ROMA.

---

[1] A curious statement concerning Ferrante's visit is made in Infessura and in the diary to which reference was made above. The object of this shifty potentate in coming to Rome was much more political than religious. He surveyed the city with the eye of a military commander, and he told Sixtus IV., says our diarist, that he would never be the true sovereign of Rome until he cleared away the porches of the houses, which projected into the narrow streets, together with the "mignani," seemingly the overhanging balconies and gable windows. With such thoroughfares, said Ferrante, the women in the houses might put to flight an army. Sixtus is reported to have taken this advice, setting to work at once to pull down the porches and the "mignani," upon the pretence of paving the streets and beautifying the city.—M.S. Ad. 8434, fols. 46, 47.

[2] Lenormant, *Trésor de Numismatique*, Médailles d'Italie, 1 Pl. xxiv.

Under Sixtus himself we have a singularly interesting specimen described by Armand [1] as a medal, but by Cinagli [2] as a coin—a dubloon of the value of fourteen zecchini. It is in any case a magnificent gold piece. On the obverse is shown the figure of Jesus Christ entrusting His flock to St. Peter, with the inscription, PETRE PASCE OVES MEAS, SIXTUS IV. PONT. MAX. AN. JUBILEI. On the reverse we see the disciples in a boat, and Jesus as He walks upon the waters stretching out His hand to St. Peter. The legend is, DOMINE ADJUVA NOS: MODICÆ FIDEI QUARE DUBITASTI. This beautiful coin measures 59 millimetres —more than two and a quarter inches—in diameter. Six other coins of the same Pontiff bearing the words AN. IVBELEO are enumerated by Cinagli. The medals strictly so called belonging to this Jubilee are generally considered to be restorations, but good reason has been shown in the last chapter for thinking at least one of them genuine. Of the others there is much to suggest that the medal inscribed CITA APERITIO BREVES ÆTERNAT DIES is founded on some authentic model.

The Jubilee held in 1500 by Alexander VI. has hitherto been supposed to be the first in which the ceremonies were introduced of the solemn opening and closing of the Porta Santa. These ceremonies will be described at some length in a subsequent chapter, and they may be passed over here.

Alexander caused the Holy Year to be published three times —on the 12th April, 1498; [3] on the 28th March, 1499, being Holy Thursday; and finally on the 22nd December of the same year, the formal proclamation by heralds on this last occasion being preceded and followed by a blast of trumpets, after the

[1] *Les Médailleurs Italiens*, vol. ii. p. 62.

[2] Cinagli, *Monete*, p. 60. A representation of it is given in Van Mieris, *Histori der Nederlandsch Forsten*, vol. i. p. 128.

[3] In this Bull *Consueverunt Romani Pontifices* notice was given of the suspension of all Indulgences not only during the Jubilee year, but from Low Sunday, 1498, *i.e.*, for nearly two years before the beginning of the Jubilee. This regulation naturally caused a good deal of dissatisfaction, which was not disguised even by so devout a Catholic as Geiler of Kaisersberg. See Paulus in *Zeitschrift f. K. Theologie*, vol. xxiv. p. 177; but cf. Pastor, *Geschichte der Päpste* (third edition), iii. 506.

manner recorded in the Old Testament in the case of the Israelitish Jubilees.

The road leading from the Castle of St. Angelo to the Vatican Basilica being very narrow, Alexander caused a wider and more commodious thoroughfare to be made for the convenience of the

CARDINAL'S WALKING DRESS IN THE TIME OF ALEXANDER VI.
From Bonanni.

pilgrims. This road, at first called the Alexandrian, after the Pope, is the same as that now known as the *Borgo Nuovo.* Julius II. had the street paved. During the three days preceding the opening of the Jubilee all the bells in Rome were ordered to be rung as for a festival. This custom, for the first time introduced by Alexander VI., has remained in force during succeeding Jubilees. The Pope also forbade those cardinals who were in Rome to quit the city under heavy penalties, as he wished them to add splendour to the ceremonial of both ecclesiastical and civil functions. Great multitudes came to this Jubilee, and Alexander extended it till the Epiphany of the following year, being twelve days longer than usual, to show some little favour to late comers. Moroni[1] states that among the pilgrims in 1500 were many French, Germans, and Bohemians, recently converted from the heresies of John Huss and reconciled to the Holy See.

Alexander VI. was the first Pope who extended the Jubilee during the following year to the whole of Christendom, despatching legates to the different European nations for the purpose of proclaiming the Indulgence. We have already seen Nicholas V. granting this privilege to some few countries, and it has also frequently been conceded to princes and others who had specially petitioned for the favour; but it was after this Jubilee of 1500 that the custom was introduced which now prevails universally, thus enabling all the faithful who, from one cause or another, cannot visit the Eternal City, to share, nevertheless, in the benefits of the Holy Year.

It may be interesting to give here some few extracts from an old English version of the Bull extending the Jubilee in 1501. It is headed—"The Articles of the Holy Jubilee of full remission and great joy granted to the realm of England, Wales, Ireland, Gernesey, and Garnesey (*sic*), and other places under the subjection of our Sovereign Lord King Henry the Seventh, to be distributed according to the true meaning of our Holy Father unto the King's subjects by the hands of his dear and well-beloved William Butts in the University of Cambridge." The Bull, which is of considerable length, after setting forth that the Jubilee privileges are renewed thus for the sake of those who, through sickness, poverty, and other causes, were hindered from coming to Rome in 1500, and also that the Pope might have aid and support in the struggle against the Turks, extends the

[1] P. 116.

Jubilee "First (to) our Sovereign Lord King Henry the Seventh, with all his progeny, all archbishops, bishops, . . . and all other Christian people, both men and women, whatever degree or condition soever they be of, . . . dwelling . . . under the domination of our said Sovereign Lord the King, . . . who, . . . truly confessed and contrite, shall visit such churches as shall be assigned to be visited by the right reverend Father in God, Jasper Pon, protho-notary and doctor of divinity of our said holy father, the Pope's ambassador, and in this Holy Jubilee commissary, . . . and there put into the chest for the intent ordained such sum or gratuity of money, gold or silver, as is limited and taxed here following in the last end of this paper, to be spent for the defence of our faith, shall have the same indulgence, pardon," etc., . . . "as if they had gone personally to Rome . . ." Confessors appointed by Jasper Pon shall have the same privileges as those at Rome enjoyed during the Jubilee, and may commute all vows for alms. Various stipulations and conditions are laid down, and then comes the "Tax what every man shall put into the chest that will receive this great grace of their Jubilee." A regular tariff follows, proportioned to the income of the person, beginning with those who have £2000, or above, who must pay for themselves, their wives and children, £3 6s. 8d., and ending with those whose incomes do not amount to £20, who are to pay ". . . as it shall please them of their devotion." Finally, we have "The Articles of the Bull of dispensation with Simony, Usury, and of Goods wrongfully kept reserved to the commissary only."

The said commissary also had power to create doctors in both laws, as if he were create in any university.[1]

[1] *Letters and Papers illustrative of the Reigns of Richard III. and Henry VII.* Gairdner, Rolls Series, vol. ii. p. 93 *seq.* [MS. *Cott. Cleop.*, E. iii. f. 157, modern copy.]

CHAPTER IV

THE JUBILEE OF MODERN TIMES

WITH the Holy Year of Clement VII. in 1525 we may consider that the history of the Jubilee enters upon a new phase. Luther had delivered his first attack upon the Indulgence system and its abuses in the autumn of 1517, and since then events had moved rapidly. Long before this many of the more earnest and religious minded of the prelates at the Roman Court had shown their disapproval of the way in which Indulgences were turned to profit for dubiously spiritual ends. Backed by the criticism of the Reformers, and by the defection from the Holy See of so large a part of Germany, their arguments at last began to have weight; and although another Jubilee was still to pass before the Council of Trent would denounce, in its twenty-fifth session, those "evil gains for the obtaining of Indulgences whence a most prolific cause of abuses amongst Christians has been derived," the papal Court began to show signs of much greater vigilance in cutting off the avenues of any unworthy greed of money. It must not be supposed that no vigorous action had been taken in reforming abuses of this nature before the sixteenth century. The fourth council of Lateran and the decree of Clement IV., included in the *Corpus Juris*, not to speak of numberless provincial synods,[1] had condemned the dishonest proceedings of the pardoners in terms which left nothing to be desired, while there never had been any lack of conscientious prelates and earnest preachers

[1] A useful list of such conciliar decrees is given in Lea, *History of Confession and Indulgences*, vol. iii. p. 287. It does not, however, pretend to be exhaustive.

who had used the opportunities afforded them by the various Jubilees and great Indulgences simply, as they were intended to be used, to foster devotion and to draw sinners to repentance and amendment of life.

No one who reads the account of Cardinal Nicholas de Cusa's labours, already referred to, could hesitate for a moment to believe that the Jubilee Indulgence, which he as papal Legate was commissioned to administer, was a real source of moral reformation in Germany. Moreover, as long as we confine ourselves strictly to the ordinary papal Jubilees there is very little evidence indeed that any great abuses had crept in, even when things were at their worst. It is true that when the Jubilee of 1500 was extended to the world at large, the alms which were offered by the faithful in compliance with the conditions prescribed seem in comparatively few cases to have found their way ultimately to their legitimate destination, *i.e.*, the war fund for hostilities against the Turks. The temporal princes in whose dominions the Indulgence was preached secured for themselves a large commission out of the proceeds even when, as happened in more than one case, they did not appropriate the whole. Worst of all, Cæsar Borgia, the son of the Pope, seems to have taken forcible possession of all the Jubilee alms he could lay hands on, and to have squandered them amongst the soldiers who fought his campaigns.[1] But even at this date there can be no question about the great moral renovation which resulted from the labours of Cardinal Peraudi, the commissary for the Jubilee in Germany.[2] Of the earlier Crusade Indulgence of 1490 Peraudi, whose conscientiousness and moral integrity are not disputed, himself declares that hundreds of thousands of souls in Germany, which were previously in imminent danger of eternal ruin, have been brought back into the way of salvation, as those commissaries, preachers, and confessors very well know who have been concerned in this undertaking.

---

[1] Pastor, *Geschichte*, third edition, iii. p. 513.

[2] *Ibid.* note 4.

Johann von Paltz, the author of the *Celifodina*, who was also one of the preachers, states that many more and greater sinners have been converted at the time of the Indulgence than had been known for many years before. "At ordinary seasons men will not come to sermons, but the fame of the Indulgence attracts them, and an earnest preacher can do more good in a short time than otherwise he would do in the space of twenty years." And this is not intrinsically improbable, for Peraudi, the papal Legate, had, as Paltz tells us, taken great pains to gather round him the most learned, the most famous, and the most devout preachers in the whole country. So again, the Archbishop of Cologne, Hermann von Hessen, writing to the Chapter of Utrecht in 1503, expressed his belief that "many thousands of souls had been saved by the late Jubilee."[1]

But with all this we need not be afraid of confessing that there was something which rather shocked the better feeling of Catholics in the system of offerings and fees and compositions, according to a regular tariff, with which even the Jubilee Indulgence had by degrees become identified. It is a relief to be able to record that with the Holy Year of Clement VII. all practices which could suggest any suspicion of interested motives in the concession of Indulgences by the Head of the Church were finally put a stop to. It is true that the giving of alms is still commonly enjoined among the conditions of a Jubilee Indulgence,[2] but neither the amount nor the object are specified, and the treasury of the Holy See is not usually benefited in any way by the liberality of the faithful.

The conditions under which the Jubilee of 1525 was celebrated were decidedly unfavourable. There was pestilence at home, and war was raging almost everywhere abroad. Nevertheless, Clement VII. did all in his power to draw pilgrims to Rome.

---

[1] See the article "Johann von Paltz über Ablass und Reue," by Dr. N. Paulus, in the *Zeitschrift für Katholische Theologie*, 1899, p. 59.

[2] This is true primarily of the "extraordinary" Jubilees, in which the Indulgence can be gained without a journey to Rome. In the case of the ordinary Jubilees the labour involved in visiting the churches is accounted a sufficient motive in itself for granting the Indulgence.

He had been elected Pope on the 19th November, 1523, after the short pontificate of Adrian VI., but he deferred the ceremony of the "taking possession" (*i.e.*, of the Lateran Basilica) until this year, when it was carried out with great pomp towards the end of April. On the 1st May, after the pontifical Mass in the same Basilica, the Pope proclaimed the league formed against the Turks between Charles V. (King of Spain), the King of England (Henry VIII.), and Mantua, granting the plenary Indulgence of the Jubilee to those present, and giving the papal benediction, as it was usually given, from the *loggia* of the Vatican on the Feast of SS. Peter and Paul.

The scorn of the Reformers at the proclamation of the Jubilee of 1525 found vent in a set of satirical verses, more than once reprinted in Germany. A copy of this curious little book is in the British Museum library. The first stanza, which practically serves the purpose of a title-page, may be thus translated without grave injustice to the original—

OF THE JUBILEE YEAR.
This booklet tells, 'tis plain to see,
How men keep twofold Jubilee;
The one is that of Christ our Lord,
The other what the Popes accord.
Who wisely reads this book at home,
Will not for pardon run to Rome.[1]

The distinction between Christ's Jubilee and the Pope's Jubilee emphasised by the writer is that the Pope's Jubilee is costly, and can only be gained at Rome; Christ's Jubilee is given everywhere gratis to every one who repents.

In Jhesu Christi Jubel Jar
Der sünder würt verzygen gar,
Er sey gleich wo er sey uff erden
Darff nit zü Rom ein bilger werden.

---

[1] VON DEM JUBEL JAR.
Diss büchlin sagt gar offenbar
Von zwifeltigen Jubel Jar
Das ein des herren Jhesu Christ
Das ander des Bapsts Jarmarck ist
Welcher diss büchlin recht besicht
Der laufft gen Rom umb Ablass nicht.

Cf. Panzer, *Annalen ii.* 395.

The Jubilee medals of Clement VII. are not numerous. One of the most interesting of the pieces struck on this occasion, though included amongst the *Numismata* by Bonanni, is in reality a coin and has been described above in chap. ii.

While Clement VII.'s Jubilee medals are not specially remarkable, he was, as we learn from Benvenuto Cellini, greatly interested in the art of die-sinking. This taste was shared by his successor, Paul III. (Farnese), and in preparation for the Jubilee which he hoped to celebrate in 1550 the latter Pontiff caused a number of admirable medals to be struck, amongst others, the beautiful "Ganymede" medal, already referred to. Death, however, intervened to prevent his presiding at the opening of the *Porta Santa*, and some of the dies were used for the medals of his successor.

From November, 1549, till the 7th February in the following year, the See was vacant, consequently the Jubilee did not begin till the 24th February, on which day the new Pope, Julius III., opened the Holy Gate with the accustomed ceremonies. This Jubilee is specially interesting on account of the presence in the city of so many holy men afterwards canonised. One of these was the Duke of Gandia, venerated by posterity as St. Francis Borgia, who came to Rome from Spain at the head of thirty knights. He had just resigned his possessions to his son in order to enter the Society of Jesus, and we are told that the Pope, in giving him a most cordial welcome, remarked that if other princes would imitate his virtues the Church would enter upon a fresh term of existence.[1] The Pontiff was also pleased to accede to the request of St. Ignatius Loyola, the founder of the Society, that the benefits of the Jubilee might be extended both to the army of the Emperor Charles V., then warring against the famous Corsair, Draguto Rais, and also to the newly-converted peoples of the East Indies, Brazil, and the Congo.

This Holy Year witnessed the two solemn functions of the coronation of the Pope and the "taking possession," which

[1] Ribadeneyra, *Vida del P. Francisco de Borgia*, Madrid, 1592, pp. 54, 55.

last was carried out with much pomp on the 24th June, the procession entering the Lateran Basilica by the Holy Gate.[1] On account of the accession of a new Supreme Pontiff an unusually large number of ambassadors and other great personages came to Rome during this year, while the closing of the Porta Santa was postponed until the Feast of the Epiphany, as the vacancy

JUBILEE HAMMER USED BY JULIUS III., ATTRIBUTED TO BENVENUTO CELLINI.
For a detailed description see above p. 51.
Reproduced by permission of Messrs. Plon, Nourrit et Cie.

of the Holy See had prevented the Jubilee beginning at the ordinary time. The Arch-Confraternity of the Holy Trinity, founded by St. Philip Neri some sixteen months previously, undertook on this occasion the pious work of caring for and sheltering the poorer pilgrims. The number thus helped

---

[1] Moroni, p. 120. The coronation of Julius III. took place on 22nd February, 1550; for some reason the "*possesso*" was deferred till June.

was very large, but it bore no proportion to the multitudes which, in ages to come, were to benefit by this charitable institution.[1]

We have now arrived at the Jubilee of Gregory XIII. in 1575—"a Jubilee," writes Zaccaria,[2] "of which Rome had hitherto not seen the equal." Even as early as 1573 the Pope commenced preparing for it, and every precaution was taken that nothing might be wanting to add to the splendour of the celebration, or to ensure the comfort of the pilgrims.

An inundation of the Tiber in 1557 had ruined half the bridge now called Santa Maria, but formerly known as the Palatine bridge. The Romans had endeavoured to rebuild it of wood in 1561, but had not succeeded. Gregory XIII., at a cost of about 54,000 scudi, commenced the new bridge in 1574, and it was finished the following year. He also caused great stores of provisions to be laid in, and erected a public granary in the Baths of Diocletian. During the Holy Year itself he had the portico of Sta. Maria Maggiore raised at great expense, and also widened the street leading from that Basilica to the Lateran, in order to lessen the discomfort and danger arising from the crowds of pilgrims passing along it. The Jubilee was proclaimed for the first time on the 20th May, 1574, being Ascension Day. The practice then introduced has been followed ever since, and the first solemn promulgation now always takes place on the Ascension Day of the preceding year. According to the account of this ceremony, as given by Manni,[3] "When Gregory was at the great door of the Vatican Basilica, in the *Sedia Gestatoria*, proceeding to the High Mass, Cesare Glorieri, secretary of briefs, presented the Bull at the feet of his Holiness, and then by his order gave it to the master of ceremonies, Francesco Mocante, who, vested in a cotta, read it in a loud voice in Latin from one pulpit, while from another pulpit it was read by a Cantor in

[1] See ch. viii. for fuller information about the Arch-Confraternity of the Holy Trinity.

[2] P. 80.

[3] P. 130.

Italian. The Governor of Rome, with many clerics of the Apostolic Chamber and other Court officials and a great number of people, were present in the Great Portico to assist at the function. The proceedings ended with a blast of trumpets and the beating of drums. High Mass followed, and when the sub-deacon had finished singing the Epistle of the day, which is the narrative of the Ascension as read in the Acts of the Apostles, a salvo of artillery was discharged in the piazza outside. After dinner the Cursors affixed the Decretal in the usual places, and it was published in Italian all through the city to the sound of trumpets, as has been done ever since in the successive Holy Years." We may compare this account with the following passage from a description of the scene translated into English a century later:—

"At the approach of the Jubilee the Popes of Rome cause the bill of Jubilee to be published with a great deal of pomp and magnificence. This ceremony is always performed on Ascension Day in the great portal of St. Peter's Church in the Vatican, where for this purpose are placed two rich chairs, from whence the ministers chosen by his Holiness read, with a very loud and distinct voice, the Brief or Bull of the Jubilee in Italian. After this publication four several copies of the said Bull are affixed to the east, south, west, and north corners of the city of Rome, as it was practised in Pope Urban VIII.'s time, who, in the year 1624, upon Ascension Day, which then fell upon the 16th of May, appeared in person in the Church of St. Peter's and commanded Signor Don Austin Durando to read the before-mentioned Brief in presence of some of the clerks of the Apostolic Chamber, and some other officers, but neither any of the canons of St. Peter assisted at the ceremony. The Sunday next following, the said Bull was likewise published in the same manner in the other churches, where, according to ancient custom, they are used to open the Holy Gate.

"This being done, briefs or letters are despatched to all the patriarchs, primates, archbishops, bishops, and other superiors of all the provinces in the kingdom, to notify the celebration of the Jubilee, and to exhort the prelates to be more than ordinarily zealous in their duty to instruct, either themselves or by their ministers, the flocks committed to their care, by which means they may qualify themselves to obtain the happy effects of the approaching Jubilee, just as the Jubilee instituted by Moses according to God's order was published before the seventh month to the sound of trumpets."[1]

The Jubilee of 1575 was published the second time on 19th December, being the fourth Sunday in Advent, with ceremonies resembling those of Ascension Day. At the opening function of this Jubilee it was estimated that about 300,000 spectators were present in the piazza of St. Peter's, besides those who assisted at the opening the gates of the other Basilicas. So great was the crush that the guards were powerless to keep back the people, and about 200 persons pushed their way through the Holy Gate before the Pope had himself crossed the threshold, a thing which was contrary to all order and precedent. Many were injured in the crowd, and six, or, according to other accounts, eight, unfortunate victims were suffocated.

Connected with this overcrowding of the thoroughfares, one regulation made by Pope Gregory for the Jubilee year, which is alluded to by nearly all writers on the subject, is sufficiently curious to deserve rather more than a mere reference. In the still unpublished Latin diary of the papal master of ceremonies of that date we read the following passage. The quaintness of the extract must serve as an apology for its length[2]:—

"On this same day the most illustrious and reverend cardinals rode to the palace on horseback in pontifical state, (*pontificaliter*) according to ancient and long-established custom,

[1] "A true and exact account of all the ceremonies observed by the Church of Rome at the opening, during the progress, and at the conclusion of the next approaching Jubilee in the year 1700. Taken and translated into English from the Latin original printed at Rome. By order of the Pope."—*Somers's Tracts.* Ed., W. Scott. Vol. ix. p. 580 *seq.*

[2] The diary of Mucantius may be found in a manuscript at the British Museum, Ad. 26811.

by the Pope's express command. This custom for some years past had been dying out on account of the convenience of

CARDINAL ON HORSEBACK IN A SOLEMN PROCESSION. From Bonanni. The arms on the trappings show that the cardinal represented was of the Barberini family.

coaches to such an extent that hardly more than one or two cardinals were left to keep up this laudable practice, amongst whom Cardinal Orsini observed it invariably whenever he was not prevented by foul weather, and Cardinals Farnese and Medici also were faithful to the same, though not so consistently. Finally, as I have said, on the approach of the year of Jubilee our most holy Lord, in view of the expected confluence of all nations to the city, revived the ancient usage and commanded it to be adhered to. We remember that Pope Pius IV. also made the same regulation a few years ago, being indignant that the public order and the splendid ceremonial of the Roman Court should be set aside for private convenience. On that occasion, also, the cardinals complied with the order for a time, but soon afterwards, being attracted by the commodity of these vehicles, they gradually ceased to pay attention to it, while the Popes connived at their negligence. Hence it will be the duty of our most holy Lord and his successors to see that this laudable custom, which is closely connected with the ceremonial state and due honour of the Holy See, be not again suffered to fall into desuetude, and, in my opinion, this would be most effectually secured if the free toleration of so many vehicles were either entirely abolished or were kept under strict control by ordaining that no cardinal should have the right to keep more than a single coach, or should use it at any time when he is bound to appear in state. Such a regulation would not only conduce to win respect for his high dignity, but would promote the general convenience of the citizens and residents, seeing that now, whenever any one of the more wealthy or distinguished cardinals goes abroad, he is attended by such a crowd of coaches that the roads are obstructed for all other passengers, and these are compelled, sorely against their will, to await the passage of the long train of vehicles. Moreover, if a solemn festival be anywhere held, or if there be a confluence of people on occasion of any public rejoicing or spectacle, or the funeral procession of some cardinal or dignitary, whatever the cause may be, the roads and open spaces are so packed with the crowd of vehicles that it becomes impossible for foot passengers to move along; nay, even the public ceremonies and processions are interfered with, to the great inconvenience and scandal of all, sometimes even with danger to life."[1]

The writer goes on to recommend that private persons should be forbidden to use coaches altogether on account of the spirit of luxury and extravagance which this new fashion had introduced. He complains that the total number of such vehicles in Rome now amounted to more than two thousand, and he adds that if

A CARDINAL'S COACH IN ROME AT THE CLOSE OF THE SIXTEENTH CENTURY.
From a contemporary print.

they could all be piled up in one bonfire and burnt it would be a good riddance, as well as a most acceptable sacrifice to God.

To any one who examines the extraordinarily cumbrous and unwieldy construction depicted in the contemporary engraving of Bertellius reproduced above, it will be difficult to understand the "commodity" which made these vehicles so fashionable. The coach seems to have been almost as large as a brewer's dray. The cardinal sat perched up behind with an effect which

[1] MS. Ad. 26811, fol. 120, v°.

reminds us of the raised poop in the ships of the same period. The cardinal's attendants, at a lower level, occupy the middle of the vehicle, and are seen looking out of the open doors. The coach is, of course, innocent of springs; and when one remembers the too probable condition of the roadway in the streets of Rome, far from suggesting any notion of comfort, it would seem to have been a veritable engine of torture. None the less, fashion inexorably prescribed the use of a carriage, and even St. Charles Borromeo is reported to have said that in Rome two things were necessary—"to love God and to keep a carriage."[1] In many of the engravings of the period may be seen representations of crowds in the open spaces of the city assisting at some religious procession or function. Almost invariably we find them dotted with what look like the white tilts of a number of country carts.[2] (See, for example, p. 359, and the representation of the Lateran on p. 94.) These are, in truth, the coaches of the cardinals and the aristocracy; and the abundant allusions in contemporary literature are detailed enough to prove that the engravings give no false impression of this curious feature of Roman life.

In spite, however, of what might seem a mark of effeminacy and deterioration, there can be no doubt that the general moral tone of the people of Rome, and in particular of the Roman ecclesiastics, at the Jubilee of 1575, and, indeed, from this time forward, stood very high. The Venetian Ambassador Tiepolo is an impartial witness not likely to be deterred by any thought of edification from sending a faithful report to his Government. In a despatch written the year after the Jubilee the Ambassador says—

"Gregory XIII., though less severe than Pius V., does as well. He takes great care of the churches, builds and restores several,

[1] Hübner, *Sixtus the Fifth* (Eng. trans.), ii. p. 95.

[2] In the case of the cardinal's coaches, these coverings will have been made of rich red velvet, gilt and sometimes, apparently, glazed. Montaigne in his account of Rome speaks of some contrivance by which fashionable people looked out of the roof of their coaches, and quotes the remark of a contemporary who said that the Romans turned their carriages into astrolabes.

and promotes, with the help of the clergy, the great work of reform. It is fortunate that two Pontiffs of such irreproachable lives should have succeeded one another, for by their example every one has become, or appears to have become, better. The cardinals and prelates often say Mass, live quietly, their household likewise, and the whole town leads a better and incomparably more Christian existence, so that the affairs of Rome, from a religious point of view, are in a good condition, and not far short of that state of perfection which human weakness allows of our attaining. The throng in the churches on the occasion of this Holy Year just past, not only composed of Roman inhabitants but of people belonging to all parts of Italy and of various foreign nationalities, was immense. Whole populations from the villages and even towns of the pontifical states came to the holy city. Three and four thousand were seen travelling together. One hospital, that of the Trinità dei Monti, where poor pilgrims were harboured for three days, lodged and fed 250,000 people with an admirable order, and without ever wanting more than what money had been collected in alms for this purpose."[1]

This Jubilee undoubtedly drew an extraordinary number of pilgrims to Rome. Muratori does not discredit the report that 300,000 persons were present at the opening of the Holy Door, and that there were probably not fewer on any one day than 100,000 strangers in the city drawn thither by their devotion. There were pilgrims from Armenia, Arabia, and Syria; there were many princes from Germany, and with them Alessandro Farnese, Prince of Parma, Paolo Orsini, Duke of Bracciano, Ernest of Bavaria, and others. The Pope gave the impulse to this great movement of devotion, and it was furthered with singular zeal by the cardinals; but, undoubtedly, the two persons to whom were mainly due the great success and fruit of this Jubilee were St. Charles Borromeo and St. Philip Neri. They both rendered personal service in the Confraternity of the Pilgrims which, as we have seen, had been founded by St. Philip in 1548.

[1] Hübner, *Sixtus the Fifth*, i. p. 86.

St. Charles gave twenty-five crowns a month to the confraternity; and Philip, by his influence and example, drew thither a number of prelates and religious desirous to take part in this charitable work. Muratori[1] relates that from Christmas, 1574, to May,

Sixtus V. Blessing the People from the Loggia of the Lateran.
From a contemporary engraving in the British Museum.

1575, the confraternity had afforded food and shelter to 96,848 pilgrims. Theiner, in the second volume of his "Annals," quotes a contemporary writer,[2] who states that the officials of the confraternity had promised the Pope that they would lodge and feed 600 pilgrims daily; but, as the writer of the diary

[1] So also Vittorelli, Manni, and Zaccaria.
[2] Mucantius, *Diar. Cœrem.*

continues, "since the work was of God it grew so much that the 600 soon increased to more than 6000, and during the year the said confraternity provided food and lodging for 144,263 pilgrims, besides 21,000 during their sickness and convalescence. And these were provided with all things needful to them, some for three days, some five, and those who came from beyond the mountains for ten days. And many nobles and gentlemen, moved by this example, received numerous pilgrims into their houses and ministered to them in like manner." There are letters still extant of St. Charles Borromeo, written from Rome during the Jubilee to various persons in his diocese of Milan, mentioning his visits to the churches and his being present at the opening of the Holy Gate. We have also a letter from Gregory XIII. to St. Charles, authorising him to leave his diocese to come to Rome on this occasion.[1] The Pope, it seems, specially wished St. Charles to be at Rome for the opening ceremony,[2] in order that he might consult with him about many things relating to the Jubilee.

Many of the pilgrims came in procession from various parts of Italy—from Tuscany, Lombardy, the Romagna, etc.—some of them being accompanied by their bishops, who wished to make the pilgrimage together with their flocks. Manni tells us that the citizens of Terni, Macerata, and other places entered Rome in symbolical processions. Those from S. Gennesio della Marca represented the triumph of the Church, some of their number personating the penitents of Nineveh, others the prophets, others the apostles, evangelists, etc., having in their midst a triumphal car. The citizens of Pisa, headed by their magistrates, and clothed in sackcloth, came to obtain absolution from the excommunication laid on them by Gregory IX. in 1227: when in the strife between Guelf and Ghibelline, Pisa had espoused the cause of the Emperor Frederick and borne arms against the Holy See.

---

[1] Sala, *Documenti circa la Vita di San Carlo Borromeo*, vol. i. p. 294, and vol. iii. pp. 560 *seq.*

[2] Sala, *Biografia di S. Carlo Borromeo*, p. 56.

But the Pope was not unmindful of those of the faithful who were unable to visit Rome, and especially he remembered the unhappy condition of English Catholics at the period. Vittorelli[1] says—"Gregory, beholding with compassionate eyes and paternal clemency the tribulations and trials of the English Catholics, both within and without that most noble kingdom, granted to them that not being able to come to Rome, by piously visiting four churches in whatever place they might be, or three, or two, or one, if they could do no more, for fifteen days, and devoutly supplicating God, etc., etc. . . . And to those who were in England or elsewhere where the public worship of God according to the Catholic rites of the Holy Roman Church was not permitted, . . . he conceded the same benefits, provided they carried out what was prescribed them by a prudent confessor, according to the estate and condition of each. . . . And to those who could not resort to a confessor, he desired that with true contrition of heart they should devoutly recite the Rosary or Crown of the Blessed Virgin fifteen times; and also conceded that whatever confessor, secular or regular, they had access to might absolve even in cases reserved to the Holy See. This Brief, *Sub Annulo Piscatoris*, was issued at Rome on 30th March, 1575."

The Jubilees of the seventeenth century may be dismissed with comparative brevity; not that the interest in them was waning, or that they attracted a less concourse of pilgrims, but that their character as purely religious celebrations was now so thoroughly appreciated that there is little to diversify the uniform and somewhat monotonous record of the multitudes which thronged the churches; the seemingly endless processions of pilgrims through the streets; the edifying example of Popes, cardinals, and prelates; the splendour of the papal ceremonial; the crowds around the confessionals; and the marvellous charity displayed by the people of Rome in welcoming their fellow-Christians from far and near. The example of such men as

---

[1] P. 394. See also Manni, p. 148.

St. Philip Neri and St. Charles Borromeo had left an ineffaceable impression. Their zeal and charity were recognised as the ideal to which all earnest ecclesiastics endeavoured to conform their lives, and no one who impartially examines the evidence of contemporary records can hesitate to affirm that the spectacle of what they witnessed in *Roma la Santa,* as at this epoch it was popularly called, made a deep moral impression upon the vast majority of the pilgrims who flocked to the Jubilees.

For the proclamation of the Jubilee of 1600, which took place as before on the Ascension Day of the preceding year, Clement VIII. had a special medal struck, representing the Pontiff upon his throne, with two cardinals beside him, listening to the reading of the Bull of indiction, while two trumpeters stand in advance with their trumpets to their lips, a detail meant to recall the analogy to the Jubilee in the Old Law.[1] Zaccaria tells us that "the good old Pope"[2] left nothing undone which could help to make the Holy Year an occasion of edification to the faithful. To this end he appointed two congregations of cardinals—one to attend to the spiritual, the other to the temporal matters connected with the celebration. Clement himself was so deeply moved by feelings of devotion that he wept during the ceremony of opening the Holy Door. He caused a commodious lodging to be prepared in the Borgo for the reception of foreign bishops and other ecclesiastics visiting Rome, each of whom was to be entertained for ten consecutive days. A table was prepared in the Gregorian Gallery, which was always ready to dine nine guests (this being the number of

Medal of Clement VIII.
Commemorating Proclamation of the Jubilee of 1600.

---

[1] Leviticus, ch. xxv. v. 9.

[2] *Il buon vecchio Pontefice,* p. 90. See also Noethen, *Geschichte aller Jubeljahre,* p. 122.

years of Clement's pontificate), the same kind of food being served to them as to the Pope himself. The latter also had twelve pilgrims to dine with him every day in honour of the twelve Apostles. He also gave fifty scudi every week to the Confraternity of the Holy Trinity, besides other alms, estimated to reach the sum of 7025 scudi. The Pope also himself distributed personally about 300,000 scudi in alms during the year. On account of the Pope's illness, the opening of the Holy Gate had to be postponed till the 31st December; the Jubilee Indulgence, however, began on Christmas Eve as usual. We are told that this Holy Year was kept with singular devotion. The theatres remained closed, the carnival and other public diversions were forbidden, and even private entertainments were but few in number; in short, it was a prolonged Lent. Numerous confraternities came from the papal and adjacent States. Those from Ginnesio della Marca, as at the last Jubilee, entered in symbolical procession. This time the mysteries of the Old and New Testament were represented, *e.g.*, the obedience of Abraham, Jacob's ladder (!), Judith carrying the head of Holofernes, Jonah as a penitent, etc. None the less, we are told that the pilgrims went barefoot, with hands joined, and with cast-down looks, while others again were disciplining themselves.[1] Those who came in August made the visits to the Basilicas by night, on account of the intense heat in the daytime. It is again stated that overwhelming numbers flocked to Rome for this Jubilee. Without reckoning those who were received in the various monasteries and private houses, as well as in the hospices established by the Germans, Spaniards, and others for pilgrims from the countries they represented, the Confraternity of the Holy Trinity alone sheltered 500,000 people. Contemporaries computed the total number of visitors to Rome during this Holy Year at three millions, and on Easter Day it was estimated that the city contained 200,000 souls.

On the other hand, Cardinal Valerio, who was in a better position to know the truth, seems to adopt a much lower figure.

[1] Manni, *Storia dell' Anno Santo*, p. 124.

The unsatisfactory character of all such calculations, however, is curiously illustrated by a remark which occurs in Zerola's work *De Jubileo.* Speaking of the Great Jubilee of 1575, he complains "that very few Englishmen and hardly any Scotch, Saxons, Bohemians, Frenchmen, and Germans came to Rome to profit by this time of spiritual gain," and he adds (he was writing seemingly at the beginning of 1600), "if Almighty God does not by His Divine Clemency provide otherwise, there will again be extremely few in the present year."[1]

We are told that many conversions were made, among them

Reverse of Two Jubilee Medals of Clement VIII.; one at the beginning of the Jubilee, INTROITE IN EXULTATIONE; the other representing the Pope walling up the Holy Door at its close, ABSOLUTO ANNO JUBILEI.

being that of Stephen Calvin, who, seemingly in virtue of his relationship to the arch-heretic of Geneva, was baptized by the Pope himself, and by him protected until he entered the order of Discalced Carmelites, where he afterwards made a holy death.

It may be noticed that such a writer as Mr. H. C. Lea, in his *History of Confession and Indulgences,* does not seem to dispute the reality of the deep religious impressions which the scenes of the Jubilee at this date produced upon the pilgrims. "Many heretics," he writes, "who had been attracted by curiosity were converted at the sight of the popular enthusiasm, and the humble zeal of Clement VIII. in washing the feet of pilgrims,

[1] Zerola, *De Jubileo,* bk. i. chap. 9.

and his assiduity in celebrating Mass and in personally hearing confessions—four hundred converts in all, according to some accounts, but Valerio gives the more probable number of fifty. It is evident from his recital that the population was wrought to a pitch of religious delirium not unlike that of a prolonged camp meeting, but all the fiercer from the infectious enthusiasm of so vast a multitude crowded together."[1]

Among the more noteworthy names met with at this Jubilee are those of Camillus de Lellis and of Andrew Avellino, both of whom have since been canonised. The two Cardinals Baronius and Bellarmine, who also played a conspicuous part in connection with the same celebration, were hardly less eminent for their virtues. With regard to the last named, Cardinal Bentivoglio relates in his memoirs[2] that during the Holy Year the Pope, Clement VIII., was desirous of hearing the Word of God more frequently, and to that end caused sermons to be preached in his presence by the most celebrated preachers of the time. The three discourses which gave him the most pleasure were those which he heard delivered in his private chapel by the Cardinals Baronius, Antoniano, and Bellarmine.[3] A letter of the latter Cardinal to the Bishop of Verdun, written this year (1600), is still extant, in which he expresses the wish that the bishop could visit Rome, in order to take part in the celebrations.[4] "Would that," he writes, "I might have the consolation of meeting your illustrious lordship here in Rome, especially during this Holy Year of Jubilee, that I might converse with you, embrace you, visit the holy places in your company, that we might together wash the feet of Christ, represented to us in the pilgrims who come here in crowds, and that we might, in waiting upon these same pilgrims, serve our Redeemer as He sits at table; for these are the offices which are continually performed with the utmost devotion by the Vicar of Christ himself, by the Cardinals also

[1] Vol. iii. p. 217.
[2] *Memorie del Card. Bentivoglio*, lib. ii. pp. 158, 159.
[3] Père Couderc, S.J., *Le Vénérable Cardinal Bellarmin*, vol. i. p. 293.
[4] Quoted by Manni, p. 174.

and other prelates, and with no less humility even by secular princes."

The Pope, being indisposed at the Christmas of 1600, the ceremony of closing the Holy Gate was postponed till the 13th January, 1601, the octave day of the Epiphany.

The twelfth Holy Year was celebrated by Urban VIII. in 1625. The Bull of proclamation, *Omnes gentes plaudite manibus*, was published on Ascension Day (May 16), 1624. In the enumeration of the four Basilicas made in it, we find for the first time the Lateran mentioned before the Vatican. At this Jubilee, while suspending all other Indulgences except those of the Holy Year, the Pope also excepted the Portiuncula Indulgence. The Holy Gate was opened on Christmas Eve by Urban, in the presence, among others, of Ladislaus, Prince of Poland, who had recently arrived in Rome, and who on Christmas night received the insignia of the Consecrated Sword and Cap at the Pope's hands. In the beginning of the new year visits to the Basilica of Sta. Maria in Trastevere were substituted for those to St. Paul without the walls, partly on account of an inundation of the Tiber, and partly also from fear of the pestilence which then prevailed in Italy. The Basilica of St. Paul's was reopened in November, when the pestilence ceased; but both from this cause, and also on account of the troubled state of the times, a much smaller number of pilgrims came to Rome. A contemporary writer, Giacinte Gigli, says—"During the whole of the Holy Year few people came from foreign countries, on account of a sudden outbreak of war, which was kindled in Italy, the Kings of France and England, the Duke of Savoy, and the Republic of Venice being leagued against the King of Spain, because the Valtelline district in Switzerland, in the possession of the Spaniards, was seized by the French, and a war ensued which roused all Italy to take arms."[1] At the same time a respectable number of pilgrims were present during the year, and special provision was made by the Cardinal Francesco Barberini, nephew of the Pope, for those

[1] Zaccaria, pp. 97, 98.

who came from Ireland, Scotland, and Greece. All these found a commodious lodging prepared for their reception, and were entertained at the Cardinal's expense. The canonisation of St. Elizabeth, Queen of Portugal, and the beatification of Andrew Avellino and Felix Cantalice, added to the solemnity of the Holy Year. Several conversions are also recorded, among them those af Gabriel Besin, Prince of Transylvania; Vincent Bajon, a Calvinist; and others. The Holy Gate of the Vatican Basilica was closed by Urban VIII. on Christmas Eve with the usual ceremonial.

There has never yet been an instance of one Pope celebrating two ordinary Jubilees,[1] and there has only been one example of two successive Jubilees being celebrated by two successive Popes. This took place in the pontificate of Innocent X. (Pamphili), who was the immediate successor of Urban VIII. Innocent, like his predecessors, made extensive preparations in anticipation of the Holy Year. He restored the Lateran Basilica, adorning the edifice with costly marbles, and he not only prepared a lodging for "Ultramontane" bishops and ecclesiastics, but also one for poor Italian priests, where they were hospitably entertained. Imitating the example of Gregory XIII. and Clement VIII., the Pope forbade the usual carnival plays and diversions to take place in 1650, and the money thus saved was spent in enriching and rendering more elaborate the decorations of the churches in which was held the exposition of the "*Quarant' Ore.*"

The civil dissensions in France, and the war raging between that country and Spain, together with the alarm awakened throughout Italy by the extensive military preparations of the latter power, gave reasonable cause to fear that the number of pilgrims would fall far short of the record of previous years. But this alarm does not seem to have been justified. At any

---

[1] The case of Boniface IX. does not constitute any proper exception. Even if the celebration of 1400 ought to be counted a true Jubilee, which is very improbable, it was separated from its predecessor by an interval of only ten years.

rate the diarist Gigli records that they flocked in from nearly all the countries in Europe, and that there was a much larger influx of strangers than in the time of Urban VIII. In confirmation of this may be quoted the fact that the Confraternity of the Holy Trinity lodged 334,453 pilgrims during these twelve months. A society of ladies was organised, having at their head Donna Olympia Maidalchini, the Pope's sister-in-law, who was Prioress of the Hospice

DORMITORY FOR MALE PILGRIMS AT THE HOSPICE OF THE HOLY TRINITY.
From a scarce Jubilee print of 1650, at the British Museum.

of the Holy Trinity, in order to collect alms. The society numbered forty-two ladies, being three for each of the fourteen regions of the city, and the offerings collected by them amounted to the sum of 16,582 scudi, which were given to the above-mentioned hospice for the entertainment of pilgrims, to which the Pope contributed 11,944 scudi. A bronze statue of Innocent, bearing an inscription, was erected in token of gratitude by the Confraternity. An interesting account of this Jubilee has been left us by an eye-witness, a Protestant, one John Ernest Schmieden,[1] in the form of a letter written by him to Menard, Comte de Beaumont, in Paris. He speaks of Rome as being "a little world in itself, multitudes from almost all parts of the globe coming and going continually." He describes in some detail the celebration of the "*Quarant' Ore*" at

CARDINAL IN WALKING DRESS, c. 1650.
From Bonanni.

St. Peter's and at the Basilica of San Lorenzo and at the Jesuits' Church, and seems to have specially admired the decorations of the latter, where the Blessed Sacrament was exposed in an elaborate "teatro" made to represent Solomon's Temple.[2] The

---

[1] *De Jubileo Romano, Anno 1650.* Amsterdam, 1653.

[2] *Romæ Microcosmus et omnium gentium ac plagarum ferè orbis ad stationes Jubileei, promiscua et obstupenda multitudo*, pp. 46, 47. Cf. 53-55.

devotion shown by the Pope and Cardinals and the Holy Week ceremonies also gave him great edification.[1] Cardinal Lante in particular, an old man of ninety and Dean of the Sacred College, seems to have distinguished himself by the piety and zeal which he displayed at this Jubilee,[2] during which many conversions took place. The Pope closed the Holy Gate on Christmas Eve.

As we proceed in this rapid survey of the series of Holy Years, we find each successive Pope rivalling his predecessors in the preparations undertaken to ensure the success of the Jubilee. Clement X. in making provision for that of 1675 was, if possible, more energetic than former Pontiffs. The churches were adorned and restored, public works for the improvement of the city were undertaken, and that the spiritual edifice might not be neglected, an edict was issued relative to the tonsure and dress of the clergy, to ensure that they also should be in keeping with the religious but festive appearance of the city. Provision was also made as in former years for the hospitable entertainment of foreign ecclesiastics and the poorer clergy of Italy. The faithful showed a corresponding eagerness on their part to avail themselves of the spiritual favours placed within their reach. Two hundred thousand people are said to have witnessed the opening of the Holy Gate by the Pope, many foreign princes being among the number. The Dukes of Brunswick and Baden and other German potentates were present, also ambassadors from Louis XIV., King of France, and the Venetian Republic. There were royal ladies also, chief among whom was Queen Christina of Sweden, who had abdicated the throne in 1653 and renounced the Lutheran heresy. For all these distinguished visitors ornamental lodges or grand stands had been erected in the portico of St. Peter's, and the ceremony which ensued seems to have produced a profound impression.

Amongst other scraps of gossip current at the time we are

---

[1] *Intervenire vestitu, ac squallore pœnitentium, Eminentissimi, Oratores, Principes, Præsules . . . denique lente incedere flagellantes, velato capite, pectus pedesque nudi.*

[2] Zaccaria, p. 108, and Moroni, vol. ii. p. 129.

told that Queen Christina invited some gentlemen, among whom were two English Protestants, to occupy places in the stand allotted to her. One of the Englishmen, on the arrival of the Pope, neglected to kneel like the rest. Christina perceiving this, ordered the offender to go down upon his knees, and as he still

Fountain in the Piazza of St. Peter's, completed by Clement X. for the Jubilee of 1675.

delayed to comply, she rebuked him in such terms as to compel his obedience, "though whether from fear or from compunction," says the chronicler, "I know not."[1]

The beatification of St. John of the Cross, together with

---

[1] Ruffiero Caetano, *Le Memorie de l'anno Santo 1675*, etc. Rome, 1691. Manni also (p. 212) mentions the incident.

that of Francis Solano, a Franciscan, and of the nineteen martyrs of Gorcum, were among the noticeable events of this year. Bossuet is said to have made it the occasion of writing his devout and edifying *Méditations pour le Temps du Jubilé,* which were first printed in 1696. The famous Jesuit Bourdaloue also delivered a discourse on the observance of the Jubilee, which has obtained a lasting reputation, not merely as a piece of oratory, but also because Benedict XIV. expressly referred to it in his constitution setting forth the solemnisation of the Holy Year of 1750.[1] The number of pilgrims in 1675 was estimated at 1,400,000, of whom 280,496 were received at the Hospice of the Holy Trinity. Towards the support of these the Pope gave to the arch-confraternity the sum of 6000 scudi, which in ordinary years would have been expended on the carnival amusements, and we hear that he raised a subsidy of 1500 scudi from the Jews. Large sums also were collected by the Roman ladies as at the last Jubilee, and the Holy Father himself, together with the Queen of Sweden, contributed liberally to the funds of the hospice. Many conversions, both of heretics and others, are said to have been made, among them that of a Turkish family—husband, wife, and son. The Pope was particularly gracious to one "robust and hearty"[2] old pilgrim from Mantua one hundred and nine years of age, permitting him twice to kiss the feet, and bestowing on him all the Indulgences and also some gold medals. The Holy Year terminated as usual on Christmas Eve with the ceremony of the walling up of the Holy Door.

One slight memorial of the echoes awakened in Protestant England by the proclamation of the Jubilee of 1675 may be found in a broadside of that date, a reduced facsimile of which may be seen on the next page. A copy is preserved in the British Museum. The bulk of the document consists of a sort of ballad in doggerel verse, but the heading runs as follows:—

---

[1] Noethen, *Geschichte aller Jubeljahre*, p. 139.

[2] Manni, *Istoria degli Anni Santi*, p. 215.

The Popes Great Year of Iubilee.

OR, The Catholicks Encouragement for the Entertainment of Popery.

With an Account of an Eminent Mart or Fair, which is to be kept by his Holineſs, where all ſorts of Indulgencies, pardons, Remiſsions, Relicks, Traſh, and Trumperies, are to be expoſed to Sale, and may be had for ready mony at any time of the day; With the uſual ceremonies thereunto appertaining.

Therefore ſuch ſons as are deſirous to imbrace the kind proffers of their holy Mother; are adviſed in the nick of time to, come all away Tune is, Have at all.

BROADSIDE.

From the Percy Collection at the British Museum.

THE POPE'S GREAT YEAR OF JUBILEE

OR THE CATHOLICKS ENCOURAGEMENT FOR THE ENTERTAINMENT OF POPERY

With an account of an eminent Mart or Fair, which is to be kept by his Holiness, where all sorts of Indulgencies, Pardons, Remissions, Relicks, Trash and Trumperies are to be exposed to sale, and may be had for ready money at any time of the day; with the usual ceremonies thereunto appertaining.

Therefore such sons as are desirous to imbrace the kind proffers of their holy Mother; are advised in the nick of time to, "Come all away."

Tune is, Have at all.

To give an idea of the nature of the poem itself the following two stanzas will amply suffice:—

For now with you I shall be free,
This is the year of Jubilee,
When all are welcome to their charge,
For we our coffers shall enlarge,
  Good wares we proffer every day,
Which you may try before you buy,
  Come all away, come all away.

Pardons, and indulgencies,
Relicks and such rarities,
If you but ready money bring,
You shall not want for any thing.
  Our Holy Father, we'll obey,
And serve you all, both great and small,
  Come all away, come all away.

The interest which English Protestants took in the Roman Jubilee was curiously accentuated, as we shall shortly see, on occasion of the next celebration, that of 1700. An excellent account of the Jubilee observances was translated from the Latin and published in London. Seeing that the description there given belongs rather to the seventeenth than the eighteenth century, an extract from this interesting pamphlet may fitly be introduced here:—

"We must also take a short view of those transactions which are performed in the City of Rome to obtain the happy end of the Jubilee. As those who hope to reap the fruits of a plenary Indulgence must qualify themselves for it by many acts of charity, a true penitence, and other good works, so I must needs tire the reader's patience if I should pretend to give an exact account of those who flock from all parts to Rome, to make their confessions and appear before the highest tribunal of penitence. It will suffice to say that both day and night all the churches of that great city are filled up with innumerable multitudes of people, who offer up their prayers in the presence of God Almighty. I may say it without vanity, that there is no street, no, not so much as a by-lane, in this vast city, which, being formerly the capital empire of the world, is now the capital of God's Kingdom upon earth, where you may not see most evident marks of an unfeigned piety; here you meet those who make it their whole business to give alms to the poor with so much profusion, that you cannot imagine otherwise but that they are giving away all they have the better to follow Christ; others you may observe to bestow most of their time and substance in giving a good reception to those pilgrims, who come from all the corners of Christendom, to partake of the happy effects of the Jubilee. You will meet, as well in the streets as in the churches, vast numbers of both sexes, who, touched with remorse for their past crimes, appear in miserable dress and a most abjected posture; some are clad in long, coarse gowns, others covered only with sackcloth, some cover their hands and faces with ashes, others knock their breasts with their fists; many there are who tear the flesh all over their bodies by the violence of the discipline; and, to be short, there is scarcely any kind of mortification invented to give satisfaction to, and appease, God's anger, which you see not put in practice at that time.

"Neither must you imagine that those exercises are performed by private persons only; no, you will see whole fraternities and congregations, composed of a considerable number, who, all animated by the same spirit, strive to excite one another to the performance of them by their mutual examples. Thus you may behold entire chapters and colleges of canons, and other societies, enter in procession the City of Rome; nay, whole parishes with their curates at the head of them, who leave their habitations to pay their adoration to the Lord and His Son Jesus Christ in that church, where, as it may be said, God has erected His tabernacle, and honoured it with His particular protection, and which claims a prerogative before others, by the death of the chief of the Apostles and his fellow-sufferer. With this kind of people you see all the streets and other public places of this vast city crowded, going in procession from one church to the other, some singing, others sighing and shedding tears. For whilst some are busy in singing the litanies and psalms appointed for that purpose, others offer their prayers with their eyes fastened to the ground, and when they approach the churches, especially that of St. Peter, you may see many of them crawling upon the ground to the foot of the altar, where they continue for a considerable time in saying their prayers. These and such like

REVERSE OF JUBILEE MEDAL AND JUBILEE COIN OF CLEMENT X.
The medal represents the opening of the Holy Door, with the legend DOMVS DEI ET PORTA COELI. The coin shows the pilgrims passing through the Holy Door, with the words DEDI CORAM TE OSTIVM APERTVM. The arms below are those of Monsignor E. B. Costaguti, Master of the Papal Mint.

devotions are practised at Rome throughout the course of the whole Jubilee."[1]

The Holy Year for which this little volume was published in England was proclaimed, as usual, on the Ascension Day of 1699. The reigning Pope, Innocent XII., amongst other preliminary measures, appointed a congregation of cardinals to draw up an instruction for its due celebration, which was eventually sent to the patriarchs, bishops, and other ordinaries throughout the Christian world. The instruction contained certain regulations concerning the deportment and behaviour of the pilgrims and others during the Jubilee time. For instance, the women were enjoined to be modestly and soberly attired, under penalty of

[1] Somers's Tracts, vol. ix.

being precluded from taking part in the processions or from being received at the hospices. At these latter places men and women were to be lodged in different parts of the building, and were to be visited daily by a priest. All pilgrims were to make a general confession before commencing the visits to the Basilicas. On their way to the churches they were to recite the Rosary and sing hymns, and not endeavour to get the foremost places. Conductors of processions were to be at least fifty years old and of unimpeachable reputation, showing a good example to the other pilgrims by their frequent visits to the churches and reception of the Sacraments.

When the time came for opening the Holy Gate the Pope was unfortunately ill, as was also Cardinal Cibo, Dean of the Sacred College; the function was therefore performed by the French Cardinal Bouillon, the Sub-Dean, who was Bishop of Porto.

Among those present at St. Peter's was Maria Casimira, widow of John Sobieski, King of Poland, with her three sons. The Duke of Parma and Placentia and the Grand Duke of Tuscany were also in Rome later on in the year. The latter, who came at Whitsuntide, was made an honorary canon of the Vatican, that he might have the privilege of handling the sacred relics of the Holy Cross, the Lance, and the Volto Santo. We are told that one of the most touching spectacles of this celebration was that afforded by the children of Rome, who, by reason of their tender years, were permitted to fulfil the conditions of the Jubilee Indulgence by one visit to St. Peter's. On the 12th of July the children from the region of the Borgo came in procession, clad in the penitential garb of pilgrims, and accompanied by their parents, to visit the Basilica and to offer up their prayers at the Tomb of the Holy Apostles for the health of the Pope, who was then seriously ill and nearing his end. The example was afterwards followed by the children from the other regions of Rome.[1]

Innocent XII. died in the September of the year, at the

[1] Manni, p. 230.

advanced age of eighty, and it was not until November the 23rd that the Cardinals agreed on his successor, Cardinal Albani, who took the name of Clement XI. An inundation of the Tiber which took place shortly after his election caused him to substitute a visit to Sta. Maria in Trastevere instead of that to St. Paul's, as Urban VIII. had also done under similar circumstances. The Pope ordered boats to be kept moored in the water near the bridge of St. Angelo in case of accidents; and the precaution was not needless, many persons being pushed down and falling from the bridge, owing to the crush of carriages and pilgrims. Notice was published on the 4th Sunday in Advent that the Jubilee Indulgence might be gained by visiting the Lateran Basilica between the first and second vespers on St. Thomas's day. The number of persons availing themselves of this dispensation was so great that all the churches in Rome could not hold them, and confessions were heard in the open air, while communion was given in the Lateran until a late hour in the afternoon. During this year 299,697 pilgrims were received by the Confraternity of the Holy Trinity, and about 32,293 at the other hospices.

The Jubilee of 1700, as already noticed, seems to have attracted more attention in England than any other Holy Year either before or since. For some not very intelligible reason—probably it was connected with the interest taken by the Tories in the movements of the exiled James II. and his relations with the Holy See—a large number of young men of fashion appear to have started off for Rome to witness the opening and other papal functions. George Farquhar, the dramatist, introduced the subject into a comedy which was entitled *A Trip to the Jubilee,* and which was performed with great success at Drury Lane. One of the actors, Harry Norris, was so appreciated in his part that he was afterwards familiarly known by the name of Jubilee Dicky. In the Epilogue occur the lines—

But from side-box we dread a dreadful doom,
All the good-natured beaux are gone to Rome.[1]

[1] There can be little doubt that the word was intended to be pronounced *room.* This was clearly the usage in Shakespeare's day, and it seems to have lasted down to the time of our grandfathers.

The play brings before us a curious anticipation of a phraseology of which we all got heartily sick two years since. "O gemini!" one of the characters exclaims, "my Jubilee pistols"; or again, "Murdered my brother! O crimini! my Jubilee brother!" "Gone with my clothes, my fine Jubilee clothes." "Now that I'm elder brother, I'll court and swear, and rant and rake, and go to the Jubilee with the best of them!" and so on. But beyond the name and a few such satirical touches the Jubilee really plays no part in the action of the drama.

The following account, written to Mr. Pepys by his nephew, J. Jackson, who was one of these fashionable pilgrims, will be read with interest:—

"Rome, Dec. 25, 1699.

". . . We made our entry here on Tuesday last, about 23 o'clock, and were soon after deafened with the jangling of all the bells of the town, which for several days, morning and evening, had proclaimed the approach of the Holy Year. Our first visit was, as you may imagine, to St. Peter's, to see the preparations for the great solemnity, where we found them busy in building the scaffolds about the *Porta Santa,* which is a lesser door on the right hand entering within the Portico. . . . Part of these scaffolds were destined for the Queen of Poland and her suite, part for the Ambassadors, and part for the Ladies, Roman and Foreign, and a separate one, the most remote, for the Gentlemen Strangers, where not above 100, I am sure, could see well. The seats for the Cardinals and Bishops, etc., assisting, were on the area, where also a good number of persons of the first quality were admitted. But with all this I entertained but very little hope of seeing what I had come so far to see, till encouraged by Father Mansfield, Doctor of the College of English Jesuits here, . . . he having an interest with the two Prelates appointed for the placing of strangers; by which means, in short, and force of crowding, Mr. Martin and I have had the good fortune to see all the minutest parts of this solemn ceremony, the whole process of which falling within my notice was this:

"The morning, being yesterday the 24th, was ushered in by

the jangling of bells I have mentioned; soldiers, like those of our Trained-Band, were placed in different quarters of the town to prevent disorders, and chiefly in the Piazza of St. Peter's, where were the Swiss Halberdiers, in red and yellow, and a troop of horse, in armour, drawn up.

"About 16 o'clock we got into our places, and about 23 began the procession from the Vatican, through the corridor into the Piazza, and so into the Portico, drums beating, etc., all the while. First came the Choristers and the officiating Priests, with tapers in their hands, singing; then the Bishops; and last of all, the Cardinals in their Pontificalibus; the Cardinal de Bouillon, appointed by the Pope to perform this office in his stead, by reason of his extreme illness, closing the whole, and being distinguished from the rest by a mitre of rich gold stuff, the others being of white damask.

Cardinal Bouillon.
From the Jubilee Medal of 1700.

"After a short office with some singing, neither of which could be well distinguished, the Cardinal advanced to the Holy Door, the guns of Castell St. Angelo were discharged, and he knocked thrice with a silver hammer on a small cross of brass, fixed in the mortar of the door, pausing a few minutes between each stroke, whilst some words were repeated. Having given the last stroke, he retired a little, and down fell the door, which made no small dust, being of brick, plaistered on both sides, and kept together by a frame of wood round, and supported on the inside with props, which, being taken away, it fell into a case set to receive it, for its more ready removal; the Cardinals, etc., entering afterwards to sing vespers, and the people by degrees following in most astonishing crowds. There was a throne, with six palls prepared for the Pope, of crimson velvet, close by the door, but he not being there no use was made of it. The scaffold was hung with tapestry and crimson damask, with stripes of golden galoon, as are also all the pilasters of St. Peter's and some other of the churches in the city.

"In the meantime, others of the Cardinals, etc., in cavalcade, went to the Campidoglio, and there divided to go to the other churches, to open each of their Holy Gates also; but of this I saw nothing. . . .

"I afterwards saw the Cardinals' supper, in the Vatican Palace, which both for form and substance was very singular, and from hence went to the midnight devotions at St. Lorenzo, where I heard most ravishing music suited to the occasion. . . . The crowd still continues at St. Peter's so great with pilgrims going in at the Holy Gate upon their knees that I have not yet been able to make my way through it; but I have got a piece of the ruin of it, which will serve in the meantime to support my devotion."[1]

There is a curious little French book, published in London in the year 1700, written seemingly by one of the refugee Huguenots, many of whom at that time had come to England. It is entitled *Traité du Jubilé Romain*, and, like the other books already noticed, it bears indirect witness to the great amount of attention which the Jubilee was then receiving in England. The author, a certain J. Cailloüé, dedicates it to Lord Somers, at that time Lord Chancellor, and he mentions incidentally in his dedication that this nobleman had already had dedicated to him two other sermons or treatises which had been printed on the subject in English.

One of them is presumably to be identified with a tract in the Bodleian Library, entitled *The Year of Jubilee, or the time for the Restitution of all Things, being a discourse occasioned by the much talked of Mock Jubilee celebrated at Rome this*

[1] *Correspondence of Samuel Pepys*, vol. v. pp. 378-380. Letter from his nephew, J. Jackson.

year 1700. The first sentence gives a sufficient idea of the spirit in which it was written. "Every one," says the writer, "at present is talking of the Jubilee; and at the rate that they are spirited, some discourse of it from their superstitious apprehension of it, others from their learning, others from the letter of scripture, etc."

Another English publication which bears witness to the interest the subject had aroused is a little book entitled *A Pilgrimage to the Grand Jubilee* (London, 1700). It is a very scurrilous narrative of a visit paid to Rome in that year by an Englishman, seemingly an apostate Catholic. The book was reprinted at least twice, with a slightly altered title,[1] and was rendered still more objectionable by the addition of a number of licentious anecdotes. The testimony of this writer, however, may be accepted without suspicion as long as he is merely describing the concourse of pilgrims and the enthusiasm which the occasion evoked. From this point of view the following passage is interesting:—

"In our passage thither we found the roads were filled with numerous crowds of travellers, pilgrims, poor priests, and a continued train of sunburnt, sad, weather-beaten sinners of both sexes, crawling along the highways in such despicable apparel that nothing, sure, but the mercy of an Infinite Being could think such a parcel of contemptible wretches worth notice. Had I not known the occasion that called them together in these numbers, instead of believing 'em to be Christians going to the Jubilee, I should have took 'em by their looks and garb to have been infidel Indians moving towards grand Paw-Waw. All ranks and qualities were so promiscuously mingled, that they seemed to me like the original of Michael Angelo's 'Resurrection,' and that the whole world was jogging on in disorder towards a general tribunal—bishops in coaches, poor priests on foot, gentlemen on horses, beaus upon mules, pilgrims upon asses; and thus

---

[1] *The Travels of an English Gentleman to Rome*, by A. F. (London, 1718); and *A Trip to the Jubilee* (London, 1749).

they moved on higgle-de-piggle-de, like Don Quevedo's revel rout when they were running headlong to the Devil."[1]

Again, after reaching his destination, the writer remarks—

"The innumerable concourse of strangers that are come hither upon the account of the Jubilee is so incredibly great, that the country adjacent is scarce able to supply 'em with provisions; and the poorer sort are almost ready to petition the Pope to feed 'em by a miracle, which I fear, if once tried, would prove but lean fare, to the great grumbling of the multitude, who, like a parcel of French Protestants at a Spitalfields chandler's, are ready to go together by the ears about who shall be first served. The pilgrims, only, that flock to this city are so very numerous, that from the opening of the Holy Gate to the 5th instant (*i.e.*, from 24th December to 5th January) it is computed above 100,000 have visited the four churches appointed for gaining the Indulgences of the Holy Year, besides other strangers, whose number is not much less, so that the whole town is thronged like a Bartholomew Fair in the height of their revels."[2]

This evidence, and the other facts already quoted concerning the celebration of 1700, are the more worthy of attention, because Mr. Lea has asserted in his *History of Indulgences* that after the Holy Years of 1575 and 1600, which last he regards as the "high-water mark" of the success of the Jubilee, the tide of popularity turned, and that during the seventeenth and eighteenth centuries we remark "a gradual falling off in numbers and zeal." Mr. Lea is no doubt right in saying that there was a reduction in the offerings of the pilgrims; and as he professes to believe that the Jubilee was regarded by the Roman ecclesiastics in absolutely no other light than as a money-making speculation, the later Jubilees, from this point of view, may no doubt be described as less successful. This, however, is not the place to discuss the mercenary motives so constantly imputed to the Holy See in connection with this subject. It will be sufficient

[1] *A Pilgrimage to the Jubilee*, pp. 84, 85.
[2] Pp. 112, 113.

to have pointed out how few signs were to be seen in the Jubilee of 1700 of any falling off in popular devotion.

Another indirect confirmation of the same conclusion is furnished in a curious little book published by that very shifty personage, the numismatist Nicholas Chevallier, of Amsterdam. It is entitled *Le Jubilé de l'An 1700 Publié par la Bulle d'Innocent XII.*[1] The treatise is a polemical tract of the ordinary no-Popery type directed against papal Jubilees, but its distinctive feature consists in an elaborate account, illustrated with engravings, of a number of satirical medals, which the author alleges to have been struck on the occasion of this Holy Year. There seems good reason to suppose that the whole account is a fabrication, and that no such medals ever existed; but whether they be imaginary or not, the mere fact that the supposition could be made with any plausibility is an evidence of the prominent place which the Roman Jubilee was then occupying in men's minds. Some of these medals which the author professes to describe are seemingly serious, others are openly satirical. Belonging to the former class we have medals with such legends as VENIT VENIA, VENITE, or EN PIUS ALCIDES, ATLANTE FESSO, ANNO ABSOLUTO 1700, referring to the Pope; or, again, UNO ICTU PANDIT OLYMPUM, ANNO JUBILATORIO 1700.[2] The openly satirical medals, however, are in the majority, and as a single specimen of a large selection, reference may be made to one which is engraved by Chevallier, and which from its size is made particularly prominent. On the obverse the Pope, wearing a tiara, stands before a tub marked *Onguent pour la Brulure du Purgatoire* (ointment for the burns of purgatory). Round the field runs the legend VAINES ESPÈRANCES, and in the exergue the words *Le jubilé à présent se gagne par argent.* The reverse exhibits an ape in front of the Holy Door, crowned with the tiara and holding a hammer. A crowd of people stand behind him. The legend reads, VOUS EN PAYFREZ LA FOLIE, and beneath, UN SINGE AMUSE BIEN LES SOTS.

---

[1] A copy exists in the Bodleian Library, but none seems to be found in the British Museum.

[2] P. 115. None of these medals seem to be known to the British Museum experts.

A number of these probably bogus medals are aimed at the French Cardinal Bouillon, who, as we have seen, in consequence of the Pope's illness, supplied his place in performing the opening ceremony at St. Peter's. The Cardinal's descent from Godfrey de Bouillon, his nationality, his personal characteristics are all alluded to. It would be tedious to give details, but a reference may be made to one which is there fully engraved, and in which the Pope is represented in bed, handing over his powers to Bouillon. Two hexameter lines adorn the exergue—

> Scande gradum Sedana domus populusque per ævum
> Sentiat unguento dextram ; sic lilia crescunt.[1]

The rest are in much the same style.

This year 1700 was the only occasion on which a Cardinal has supplied the Pope's place in *opening* the Holy Door in St. Peter's. Beside the ordinary papal Jubilee medals, one or more medals of large size were struck in honour of the Cardinal, seemingly by French artists. The portrait on the obverse of these is accompanied only by the Cardinal's name, EMMANUEL THEOD. CARD. BULLIONIUS.[2] On the reverse is represented the scene at the opening of the Holy Door. The Cardinal in cope and mitre holds in his hand the golden hammer, other ecclesiastics attend him, and to the left are seen his cross-bearer, and pilgrims prostrating themselves. The medal bears a legend which is certainly a very ingenious if not felicitous application of scripture. Referring to the Cardinal's Christian name it reads, APERITE PORTAS QUONIAM EMMANUEL.[3] This is taken from the Vulgate of the Book of Judith (xiii. 13), *aperite portas quoniam nobiscum Deus* (open the gates for God is with us)—*Emmanuel* and *Nobiscum Deus* being regarded as synonymous.

---

[1] The point is not entirely clear at first sight. The *Sedana domus* refers to the title of Bouillon's father, who was prince of Sedan. The *Sentiat unguento dextram* seems to insinuate something about greasing the Cardinal's palm.

[2] See *Trésor de Numismatique* (Médailles Françaises), Pl. xxxiv. n. 6. M. Lenormant says it is signed SVZAN DIT. REY. F. In the original of the medal reproduced opposite the signature clearly reads DUBUT F.

[3] Open the gates for it is Emmanuel.

The sixteenth Jubilee was celebrated by Benedict XIII. in 1725. As usual, we are told that the function of opening the Holy Door was performed by the Pope with even more than the accustomed pomp and solemnity. The spectators included the Crown Prince of Bavaria, and his brother, Duke Ferdinand. Notwithstanding the great inclemency of the season, many foreigners came to Rome. By the liberality of Charles VI., Emperor of Austria, from the beginning of Lent an allowance of half a florin a day each was made to fifty pilgrims to enable them to profit by the Jubilee and visit the churches, under the guidance of some of the Roman religious. As the year wore on the number of visitors increased. Among them was the widow of the Grand Duke of Tuscany, a Bavarian princess; and in her train came the poet Stefano Perfetti, who, at the request of the Grand Duchess, was by the Pope's order crowned with laurel at the Campidoglio on the 23rd of May. This distinction had not been bestowed on any poet since Petrarch received the laurel crown in 1341.

Reverse of Jubilee Medal of Cardinal Bouillon.

In order to lend additional solemnity to the functions of the Holy Year, Benedict held a Provincial Council in April and May, which brought a large number of prelates to Rome. The beatification of six of the seven founders of the Servite Order also took place in this year; B. Alessio Falconieri, the seventh founder, having already been raised to the altar by Clement XI. The Pope showed himself zealous in every sort of good work. Not only did he prohibit all masquerades and other licentious amusements during the carnival time, but he forbade under heavy penalties every sort of gambling, especially the Genoese lottery. During this season he himself retired to the Dominican Monastery on Monte Mario to make a Retreat.

Among other preparations for the Jubilee made in this pontificate, we may mention particularly the erection of an equestrian statue of Charlemagne in the portico of St. Peter's. It was designed to match the statue of Constantine, by Bernini, which had been standing close beside the Holy Door for nearly a century. This statue of Charlemagne, by A. Cornacchini, was erected at the other extremity of the portico, and it may be

Jubilee Medal of Benedict XIII.
Commemorating the erection of the Statue of Charlemagne.

distinguished in the photograph reproduced on p. 29 above. This new embellishment of the principal scene of the Jubilee ceremonies was commemorated in a very beautiful medal, designed by Hamerani. The inscription reads, CAROLO MAGNO ROMANÆ ECCLESIÆ VINDICI ANNO JUBILEI MDCCXXV.

Benedict XIV. began his preparations for the Jubilee of 1750 as early as February in the preceding year. He sent a circular letter to all the bishops in the papal States, in which he urged on them (1) the duty of seeing that all the churches in their respective dioceses were clean and in good repair; and (2) the need of reform in the music used at the divine services. This was in future to be of a more severe and less florid type; the music commonly heard being, the Pope said, more fitted for the theatre than for the worship of God. Further, in a secret consistory of cardinals held in March, the Pontiff reminded them of the approaching Holy Year, and exhorted them to restore and beautify their titular churches and such others as might be under their care. This he had himself already done in the case of several of the principal churches of Rome. The Jubilee Bull was issued on the 17th of May, and the indefatigable Pontiff followed it up by another circular letter, this time addressed to the various European sovereigns, exhorting them to maintain peace and to facilitate the coming of their subjects to Rome to participate in the benefits of the Jubilee. Moroni[1] says that the French Government made a difficulty about receiving this letter because the King, Louis XV., was not expressly named in it as was the Emperor of Austria, Francis I.

It would be a great mistake to suppose that either in this or in previous Jubilees the Roman Pontiffs had made provision only for the bodily comfort of the crowds that flocked to the Indulgence, and had no regard for the proper preparation of their souls. The discernment of the more judicious among the clergy, and the experience gradually accumulated as years rolled by, had brought the conviction that, if the Holy Year was really to be a season of grace and spiritual renovation, it was necessary that the good seed should be sown beforehand. The custom, therefore, had by degrees been introduced of giving missions among the people and exhorting them to repentance, not only during the Jubilee itself, but in the months which immediately preceded it. In this particular year Pope Benedict XIV. not only took the keenest personal interest in bringing every influence to bear which could enkindle the devotion of his people, but he also himself set a conspicuous example. He was not content with attending many of the sermons which he had caused to be preached in the city, but immediately before the Christmas Eve on which the opening ceremony of the Jubilee took place, he withdrew from public life to make the spiritual

[1] Vol. ii. p. 137.

exercises of St. Ignatius for ten days under the direction of the Jesuit Father Duranti, one of the penitentiaries of St. Peter's. That this thoroughgoing preparation for the season of grace was not confined to Rome alone we may learn from certain incidents recorded in the life of St. Alphonsus Liguori. We are there told that "at the opening of the Jubilee in 1750" Mgr. de Novelles invited Alphonsus to give a mission at Sarno, which is in the Neapolitan territory. "The sight of the holy man," the biographer continues, "clad in an old mantle mended in a thousand places, with a cassock in the same condition, was itself a sermon, for all in Sarno knew his noble birth and were confounded to see him clothed like a beggar." The effects of the mission were marvellous, and, what is more, they were lasting. We are assured on grave authority that "for ten years after this the taverns in Sarno were quite deserted." When Alphonsus had finished the mission in this town, in which he was aided by fourteen missionaries, "he commenced preaching throughout the diocese. Everywhere grace triumphed, sin was banished, and piety re-established."[1]

In Rome itself it was the holy Franciscan friar, canonised in our own times and known as St. Leonard of Port Maurice, who produced the most profound impression. The life of the saint, by Fra Giuseppe Maria di Masserano, gives the following details:—

"Having ended the missions in Sabina, St. Leonard received a summons to Rome from the Pope, Benedict XIV., in order that he might prepare the people for the Jubilee which was to be celebrated the following year. He was appointed to preach successively in the provinces and in the city, which he did with so much zeal and fervour to an immense assemblage of people of all ranks, and succeeded in making so deep an impression on the minds of all who heard him, that Rome became quite a different place in consequence of the reformation of morals. It would fill many volumes to give an account of all he did for the salvation of souls. The first crusade against vice was begun in the Piazza

[1] Tannoja, *Life of St. Alphonsus Liguori*, Eng. trans., vol. ii. pp. 16, 17.

Navona, where the concourse was so numerous that every one was astonished, especially at the last sermon, which was attended by all the nobles of Rome, and not only was that spacious square filled, but also all the streets that led to it.

"This mission lasted a fortnight, and the Holy Pontiff himself came four times to hear him; and as it was his custom, before beginning his sermon, to expose the Blessed Sacrament and to give benediction at the end, the Pope himself one evening elected to discharge this sacred function, and on every other evening one or other of the cardinals officiated, some twenty of whom continually attended the mission. Blessed Leonard always gave first a meditation on the Blessed Sacrament; and after the sermon on the last day, the Holy Pontiff, who had remained to hear it, accompanied by the cardinals, ascended an open gallery and gave the papal benediction to the countless multitude assembled below, and so ended the first of these most salutary devotions and exercises. But that which caused the greatest astonishment in this mission was the fact that those who could not approach near enough to hear the voice and distinguish the words of the holy missionary, no sooner perceived him on the platform than they began to weep and express their compunction, and very soon, throughout the crowd, nothing was heard but weeping and lamentations. Although it was in August—the hottest season—gentlemen and ladies of the highest distinction took their station in the Piazza, and remained there, exposed to the burning heat of the sun, from the beginning to the end of the sermon, thinking nothing of what they endured, from the time the man of God appeared; a sign from him was sufficient to cause the most perfect silence, so that you would hardly suppose there was a living person in that immense crowd. The other missions were given in the square of Sta. Maria in Trastevere, and Sta. Maria Sopra Minerva, and were also honoured by the presence of the Holy Father. To conceive the fruits that resulted from these missions, it is sufficient to say that, although Rome was full of churches and confessors, they had to remain from morning to night hearing the confessions of the people who crowded round the church doors even before daybreak."[1]

With regard to the Jubilee itself, for which these missions served as a preparation, there is not much which seems specially worthy of remark. All accounts agree that it was very numerously attended, and that the devout bearing of the pilgrims was most edifying. The Confraternity of the Holy Trinity alone entertained 194,832 persons. From many Italian towns came collective pilgrimages; one of the most remarkable being that headed by the Bishop of Spoleto. The church bells were rung, and a salute was fired, as he entered Rome accompanied by his

Jubilee Medal of Benedict XIV.

canons and by many of his people, while twenty-four gentlemen of the noblest families in Spoleto rode before him bearing torches. The bishop and his attendants were all attired in pilgrim's dress. The Jubilee medal above, which represents a crowd of pilgrims passing through the Holy Door with their staves and tall lanterns and covered processional crosses, would seem to commemorate some such solemn entry. It bears the legend, *introite portas ejus.* Finally, it may be remarked that one is a little startled in reading an Italian account of the opening of the Holy Door at the Jubilee of 1750 to learn that "there assisted at the ceremony, in a special lodge or grand stand magnificently decorated, His Majesty the King of Great Britain." It needs an effort to remind one's self that under this designation we must

[1] *Life of St. Leonard*, pp. 131-133.

recognise James Francis Edward, the Old Pretender, whose younger son, Henry Benedict, best known as the Cardinal of York, afterwards struck medals bearing his own effigy in his cardinal's robes, and with a legend which styled him Henry IX., King of Great Britain and Ireland.[1]

The next Jubilee, that of 1775, was proclaimed by Clement XIV. in 1774. Following the example of his predecessors, he issued directions as to the care and adornment of the churches, and he also caused missions to be preached in four different places, at some of the exercises of which he was himself present. Clement, however, died on September the 22nd, and it was on Pius VI., his successor, elected February the 15th, 1775, that the duty devolved of carrying out the arrangements made for the Holy Year. Owing to the long vacancy of the See the Holy Door was not opened by the new Pope until February the 26th. The crowds who came to Rome this year are still declared, as so often before, to have exceeded all previous record. The Hospice of the Holy Trinity received and lodged for three days 130,390 people, and during Holy Week alone 95,038 were accommodated. Many families lent rooms and beds to the confraternity for the accommodation of pilgrims. On the 30th November Pius VI., with great pomp, took solemn possession of the Lateran, entering by the Holy Gate, and not, as is generally the case at such "*possessi*," by the principal entrance. Among the personages of high rank who were in Rome at this time we may mention the Duke of Gloucester, brother of our King George III.; the Archduke Maximilian of Austria, brother of the Emperor Joseph II.; Charles Theodore, the Elector Palatine of the Rhine; and the Margrave of Anspach and Bayreuth, nephew of the King of Prussia. Pius VI. closed the Holy Gate with the accustomed rites on Christmas Eve, but the Jubilee lasted till the end of December. It was extended to other countries for six months in the following year, 1776. There is a little booklet still extant relative to this extension of the Jubilee in England and the

[1] It is only fair to note that the legend on the reverse was, "Gratia Dei sed non Voluntate Hominum."

English colonies.[1] Of the Jubilee of 1775 it is stated that D'Alembert considered it to have retarded the Revolution for twenty years, while Voltaire is said to have declared that, another such Jubilee, and it would be all over with philosophy.[2]

Before taking leave of this, the last Jubilee of the eighteenth century, it may be interesting to make a couple of citations from the very entertaining description of Rome at this epoch left by Dr. John Moore, the father of the hero of Corunna. Though he was by no means Catholic in his sympathies his prejudices were very honest ones. He was present at the ceremony of the closing of the Holy Door by Pius VI., and he has left the following account of it:—

"There is one door into the Church of St. Peter's, which is called the Holy Door. This is always walled up, except on this distinguished year; and even then no person is permitted to enter by it but in the humblest posture. The pilgrims and many others prefer crawling into the church on their knees by this door, to walking in in the usual way by any other. I was present at the shutting up of this Holy Door. The Pope, being seated on a raised seat or kind of throne, surrounded by cardinals and other ecclesiastics, an anthem was sung, accompanied by all sorts of musical instruments. During the performance his Holiness descended from the throne with a golden trowel in his hand, placed the first brick, and applied some mortar; he then returned to his seat, and the door was instantly built up by more expert, though less hallowed, workmen; and will remain as it is now till the beginning of the nineteenth century, when it will be again opened by the Pope then in being with the same solemnity that it has now been shut. Though his Holiness places but a single brick, yet it is very remarkable that this never fails to communicate its influence in such a rapid and powerful manner

[1] *Instructions and Directions for gaining the Grand Jubilee of the Holy Year, celebrated at Rome anno 1775, and extended to the Universal Church anno 1776, by His Holiness Pius VI.* London: Printed by J. P. Coghlan, in Duke Street, Grosvenor Square.

[2] Noethen, *Geschichte aller Jubeljahre*, p. 167. Unfortunately, Noethen gives no references.

that within about an hour, or at most an hour and a half, all the other bricks which form the wall of the Holy Door acquire an equal degree of sanctity with that placed by the Pope's own hands. The common people and pilgrims are well acquainted with this wonderful effect. At the beginning of this Jubilee year, when the late wall was thrown down, men, women, and children scrambled and fought for the fragments of the bricks and mortar with the same eagerness which less enlightened mobs display on days of public rejoicing, when handsful of money are thrown among them. I have been often assured that those pieces of brick, besides their sanctity, have also the virtue of curing many of the most obstinate diseases; and if newspapers were permitted at Rome there is not the least reason to doubt that those cures would be attested publicly by the patients in a manner as satisfactory and convincing as are the cures performed daily by the pills, powders, drops, and balsams advertised in the London newspapers.

"After the shutting of the Holy Door Mass was celebrated at midnight, and the ceremony was attended by vast multitudes of people. For my own part I suspended my curiosity till next day, which was Christmas Day, when I returned again to St. Peter's Church and saw the Pope perform Mass on that solemn occasion."[1]

Having begun to quote Dr. Moore, the following remarks upon the personal character of Pope Pius VI. are too interesting to be passed over:—

"Pius the Sixth performs all the religious functions of his office in the most solemn manner, not only on public and extraordinary occasions, but also in the most common acts of devotion. I happened lately to be at St. Peter's Church when there was scarcely any other body there. While I lounged from chapel to chapel, looking at the sculpture and paintings, the Pope entered with a very few attendants. When he came to the statue of St. Peter he was not satisfied with bowing, which is the

---

[1] Moore, *View of Society and Manners in Italy*, vol. ii. pp. 40-42.

usual mark of respect shown to that image; or with kneeling, which is performed by more zealous persons; or with kissing the foot, which I formerly imagined concluded the climax of devotion; he bowed, he knelt, he kissed the foot, and then he rubbed his brow and his whole head with every mark of humility, fervour, and adoration, upon the sacred stump. It is no more, one-half of the foot having been long since worn away by the lips of the pious; and if the example of his Holiness is universally imitated, nothing but a miracle can prevent the leg, thigh, and other parts from meeting with the same fate. This uncommon appearance of zeal in the Pope is not imputed to hypocrisy or to policy, but is supposed to proceed entirely from a conviction of the efficacy of those holy frictions, an opinion which has given people a much higher idea of the strength of his faith than of his understanding. This being jubilee year, he may possibly think a greater appearance of devotion necessary now than at any other time.[1]

The sincerity of the writer from his point of view is made obvious in this passage, and so also is the sincerity of the Pontiff. But surely one does not measure the understanding of a lover by the more or less of fervour with which he kisses his mistress' portrait, nor condemn the soldier for the almost childish marks of devotion he may pay to his colours. It is interesting to remark that the only time Pius IX. left the precincts of the Vatican after the occupation of Rome was to pay a visit to the statue of the Prince of the Apostles in St. Peter's during what should have been the Jubilee year of 1875, just one hundred years after the scene just described. The reader will possibly recall the touching picture of Pius IX. standing in silent prayer with his head bowed and resting upon the foot of St. Peter's statue, which is familiar from many engravings.

We pass now to the nineteenth and last in the series of Jubilees, the only Holy Year celebrated in the nineteenth

---

[1] *A View of Society and Manners in Italy*, etc., by John Moore, M.D. London, 1783, vol. ii. pp. 34, 35.

century. The Jubilee which should have been held in 1800 did not take place. Pius VI. had died in exile in the preceding autumn, and the pontificate of his successor, Pius VII., was too full of misfortune and calamities to permit him to celebrate a Holy Year. Pius VII. died in 1823, and was succeeded by Leo XII. (Cardinal Hannibal della Genga). In the face of much opposition, both from his own ministers and the representatives of foreign Powers, the Pope resolved to celebrate the Jubilee in 1825. On Ascension Day, 1824, the Bull of proclamation was issued, and preparations were immediately begun. Missions were preached, not only in the churches, but in the public squares. In the Piazza Navona 15,000 persons are said to have been present, when, on the 15th August, the Pope closed these services by his benediction. In addition to this spiritual preparation, material improvements were not forgotten. Churches, oratories, etc., were restored and beautified; often, as in the case of the greater and older Basilicas, at very considerable expense.

Preparation was also made for the accommodation of the large number of pilgrims expected, and, as heretofore, the Confraternity of the Holy Trinity took a large part of this duty on themselves. We are told that during the month of November 38,844 persons, besides 350 members of branch confraternities, were lodged and fed for three days.

Leo XII. opened the Holy Gate of St. Peter's on 24th December. Those who were present at the ceremony included Maria Teresa, widow of Victor Emmanuel IV., King of Sardinia, with her daughters, and the Infant of Spain, Charles Louis, with his consort, Maria Teresa. Francis I., King of the two Sicilies, and his wife, were also at Rome later in the year. Several servants of God were beatified, amongst others St. Alphonsus Rodriguez, of the Society of Jesus. The great and beneficial improvement in the state of the country about Rome may be traced to this Jubilee. The Pope was determined that the roads should be safe for the poor pilgrims, and, in concert with the neighbouring States, took such active measures that brigandage was, for the time being, completely suppressed.[1]

The Holy Year terminated as usual by the closing of the Holy Gate on Christmas Eve, and a triduum was held, by the Pope's command, from the 26th to the 28th December, in thanksgiving for the benefits received during the Jubilee.

We have already quoted, on an earlier page, the record of the deep impression left upon the mind of the present Pope by the edifying scenes which he witnessed in his boyhood[2] during the Jubilee of 1825, and we shall also have occasion to refer again to Cardinal Wiseman's admirable description of the practical working of the Confraternity of the Trinità. For the present, we may conclude this chapter by an extract from the same writer's account of the singular interest shown by Leo XII. in all the observances of the Holy Year—

"The Holy Father was the soul of all this work. To see him, and carry back his blessing, was of course one of the most highly-coveted privileges of a pilgrimage to Rome. Hence he had repeatedly to show himself to the crowds and bless them. They were instructed to hold up whatever they wished to have blessed; and certainly scarcely ever did Rome present a more motley crowd, arrayed in every variety of costume, from the sober, and almost clerical, dress of German peasants, to the rainbow hues of the Abruzzi or Campania. But the Pope manifested his hearty sympathy in his Jubilee by a more remarkable proof than these. He daily served in his own palace twelve pilgrims at table, and his biographer tells us that he continued this practice throughout his reign. To his accompanying them I well remember being an eye-witness. For one of such delicate health and feeble frame it was no slight undertaking to walk from the Vatican to the Chiesa Nuova; but to perform this pilgrimage barefoot, with only sandals on his feet, was more than any one was prepared for. He was preceded by the poor

---

[1] Wiseman, *Recollections*, p. 284, who also gives a very interesting anecdote concerning it, too long to quote here.

[2] See above, p. 2.

surrounded and followed by them. Tears flowed on every side, and blessings were uttered deep and warm. His look was calm and devout, and abstracted from all around. It reminded everyone forcibly of St. Charles at Milan, humbling himself by a similar act of public devotion to appease the divine wrath manifested in the plague."[1]

---

[1] Wiseman, *Recollections of the Last Four Popes*, pp. 283, 284.

CHAPTER V

THE VISITS TO THE BASILICAS

THE Bull *Antiquorum* of Pope Boniface VIII., which was the foundation of all subsequent legislation regarding the Holy Year, prescribed only two conditions for the gaining of the great Indulgence. The first and more important was the reception in proper dispositions of the Sacrament of Penance; the second, the visits to be paid during a certain specified number of days to the Basilicas of the Apostles in Rome. In the fulfilment of this latter condition there was, of course, involved for all, except the actual residents in the city, a considerable amount of toil and fatigue, for such a pilgrimage to Rome under medieval conditions was usually by no means a pleasure jaunt. It was the *labor itinerationis*—the hardships of the journey—which seemed to Cardinal Joannes Monachus, the contemporary of Boniface and the glossator of his Bull, to constitute that adequate motive which was required for the valid granting of so ample an Indulgence.[1] Consequently, the inhabitants of Rome, who had no

[1] According to the generally received theory of the medieval canonists, the power of binding and loosing, in which was involved the right to dispense the "treasure" of the Church, was committed to the Roman Pontiff to use according to his discretion. None the less there was bound to be some proportion of congruity between the Indulgence granted and the good work to which it was annexed. If this proportion were altogether wanting, many authorities held that the Indulgence was, *ipso facto*, invalid. It may also be worth while to note in this place, though we shall have to return to the subject later, that when an Indulgence was granted for any good work, this always presupposed, whether confession were mentioned or not, the state of grace in the recipient. It was the *universal* teaching of medieval theologians that no one was capable of gaining any sort of Indulgence as long as there rested upon his soul the stain of grievous sin still unrepented of.

CENTRAL PORTION OF A PICTURE OF THE SEVEN CHURCHES; prepared for the Jubilee of 1575. The patron of each church is seen blessing the pilgrims.
From an engraving in the British Museum.

painful journey to undertake, were required to pay just twice as many visits to the Basilicas as those who came from a distance, an arrangement which, with slight modifications, has been maintained in principle down to the present time.

This is not the place to enter upon a discussion concerning the teaching of the Catholic Church with regard to pilgrimages. The practice is older than Christianity, and it is built upon an instinct which lies deep down in the human heart. There is no age of the Church in which we have not abundant evidence of its prevalence in all countries and amongst all classes. Such a detailed narrative as that of the *Peregrinatio Silviæ*[1] shows that it was as fully developed in the fourth century as in the fourteenth. Moreover, when the goal of the pilgrimage was not the shrine of any local saint, but the Mother Church of Christendom, the tombs of the great Apostles, the spot where the voice of the Vicar of Christ made itself heard, controlling the practice and confirming the faith of all true believers throughout the wide world, the most unfriendly critic will surely recognise that it was the legitimate and logical outcome of the system to regard such a journey to Rome as amongst the most meritorious of works of devotion. It was in this way that the outlying parts of Christendom were knit to their ecclesiastical centre; and under the conditions of life in the Middle Ages, when intelligence was diffused slowly and inaccurately, the very existence of the Church as one body Catholic and Apostolic depended upon such means of constant communication. Hence it is that in Bede and the early English chroniclers we find that to make a pilgrimage to Rome was the greatest ambition on this side of the grave of every earnest Christian. From powerful kings, like Alfred and Canute, down to the poorest of their subjects, there was a constant stream of visitors Romewards; and the practice, while it may have led to abuses in individual instances, wrought the greatest possible benefit to religious society as a whole.

There are writers who can find in any attempt to attract

[1] First printed from a MS. at Arezzo by Signor Gamurrini in the *Studi e Documenti di Storia e Diritto*, Rome, 1887.

pilgrims to Rome nothing but an unworthy cupidity on the part of the Roman Court, and ignorant superstition on the part of the deluded visitors; but surely this is a narrow and cynical view. It would be hardly more perverse to treat every parent as domineering or selfish who inculcates upon his children the duty of filial respect. Although there may be always a tendency in the ruler to insist unduly upon the merit of loyalty, docility, and devotion to constituted authority, such virtues, on the whole, undoubtedly make for the good of the body politic, and are not merely for the benefit of the ruler alone. Not to speak of such men as Charlemagne, or Alfred the Great, or St. Louis, even the humblest pilgrims who came to Rome in the spirit in which the Popes would have had them come, laying aside their strifes, confessing their sins, and, if you will, making their offerings at the tombs of the Apostles, would have furthered in their own degree the union and right government of the world, and would have helped to elevate the moral tone of Christian society. It must never be forgotten that during all that earlier epoch, when the Jubilee Indulgence was instituted and in a sense exploited by the Holy See, Christendom was face to face with one ever-present danger which threatened its very existence. We have grown so accustomed now to think of the Turkish power as effete and quiescent, that it is hard to recall the days when Mohammedanism, both from the south-east and the south-west at once, seemed about to engulf Christian Europe like an incoming tide. Nor, again, should there be left out of account the deep feelings of devotion which were evoked in the hearts of the pilgrims by the religious ceremonies and the sacred associations of Rome. Although we cannot escape the uncomfortable conviction that many of the objects of veneration, even those that called forth the greatest demonstrations of piety, were not the genuine memorials of antiquity which they professed to be, still clergy, people, and pilgrims alike believed in all good faith; and at least the glorious past of Rome, her sites, and her dignity, were real. She was truly the Head and the Mother of Churches; and it was here that the Apostles and martyrs had shed their blood for Christ, and that their tombs might still be visited. We could hardly find a better representative of the medieval spirit in its more cultured aspect than the poet Petrarch—"Fraunceys Petrark, the laureat poete,"

> Whos rethoryke sweete
> Enlumined al Itaille of poetrye,

in the phrase of his contemporary and admirer, Chaucer. Now, nothing can be more clearly proved than that the atmosphere of Rome during the jubilee tide of 1350 produced upon Petrarch a deep religious impression, which did not stop short at barren emotion, but which bore fruit in amendment of life. Speaking of certain vanities of his youth, the poet says in a letter to Boccaccio, of all people in the world—"So far as regards this part of human frailty, I trust that by the grace of Christ our Lord I am already entirely delivered from it. For many years past, and more particularly since the Jubilee, which is now seventeen years ago, although I am still hale in body, I am so free of that plague that I now loathe and detest it a thousand times more than I ever found satisfaction in it." And elsewhere in the same letter—"I went there in a spirit of fervour, because I wished to put an end to the sinfulness of my life, which overwhelmed me with shame."[1] Similarly, in an earlier letter to the same correspondent, written during the year of Jubilee itself, Petrarch was not ashamed to say—"So, now, this is my fifth journey to Rome, and who knows whether it may not be my last, as certainly it is the most happy of all, seeing that the care of the soul is a nobler work than the care of the body, and the glory of heaven is more worthy to fire our aspirations than all the glory of this world."[2] The eloquent scholar met with a serious accident on the way. His knee was badly injured by the kick of a horse, and he was laid up in bed for more than a fortnight. Still, he seems to have recovered sufficiently to make the visits and perform the other works of devotion enjoined on the pilgrims. He took his accident as supplementing the penance his confessor had imposed

[1] *Epistolæ Seniles*, bk. viii. ep. 1.
[2] *Epist. de Rebus Famil.*, xi. 1.

too leniently, and we find him telling a friend later on that it was providential they did not meet in Rome, "otherwise, instead of visiting the churches *devotione Catholica*—with Catholic devotion—they would, careless of their souls, have wandered about the city with the curiosity of poets—*curiositate poetica;* for, however delightful intellectual pursuits might be, they are as nothing unless they tend to the one great end."[1] And this, be it remembered, was Rome shorn of much of its glory by the long absence of its supreme ruler in Avignon—a city almost in ruins, with its inhabitants on the brink of rebellion. None the less Petrarch could write—

"How well it is for the Christian soul to behold the city which is like a heaven on earth, full of the sacred bones and relics of the martyrs, and bedewed with the precious blood of these witnesses for truth; to look upon the image of our Saviour, venerable to all the world,[2] to mark the footprints in the solid stone for ever worthy of the worship of the nations, wherein is verified to the letter and clearer than the day the word of Isaiah, 'And the children of them that afflict thee shall come bowing down to thee, and all that slandered thee shall worship the steps of thy feet;'[3] to roam from tomb to tomb rich with the memories of the saints, to wander at will through the Basilicas of the Apostles with no other company than good thoughts."[4]

So far from seeming sceptical about the many dubious relics preserved in the Holy City, the poet, in the verse-epistle to Clement VI. from which we have quoted on a previous page, compiles a long catalogue of these treasures elegantly and ingeniously worked into metre.

---

[1] *Epist. de Rebus Famil.*, xii. 7.

[2] This must be a reference to the *Volto Santo* or *Sudarium* of St. Veronica preserved at the Vatican. See above, p. 58.

[3] Isa. lx. 14. The writer refers most probably to the supposed impression of our Lord's feet left in the stone when He appeared to St. Peter near the little oratory known as the *Domine Quo Vadis?* It is now generally admitted by scholars, that the stone exhibited with the impression of the two feet is only a pagan votive tablet. See Armellini, *Chiese di Roma* (ed. 29), p. 892. In Petrarch's day the footprints were believed to be miraculous.

[4] Petrarch, *Epist. Famil.*, ii. 9.

But to turn to the more immediate subject of this chapter, it is interesting to find that the Bull of Boniface VIII., when prescribing the conditions of the Jubilee, makes no mention of the *Sudario* or *Scala Santa* or any other more or less doubtful relic as objects to be venerated during the pilgrimage—these were matters left to the pious devotion of the faithful; but it enjoins only a series of visits to the Basilicas of the Apostles, to wit, the Church of St. Peter at the Vatican, and the Church of St. Paul outside the walls. These were the true shrines of Rome, the glory of the city, and hence it had come that from an early age a pilgrimage thither had been described as a visit *ad limina apostolorum*—to the thresholds of the Apostles. That the bodies of St. Peter and St. Paul still repose in the Basilicas which bear their name there is, as a mere question of historical evidence, no good reason to doubt, and it was primarily beside their tombs that the Pontiff wished all faithful children of the Church to enkindle their fervour and to pray for the welfare of Christendom.

It has already been noticed in our review of past Jubilees that the number of the Basilicas to which a visit is obligatory was added to by the Popes who succeeded Boniface. A visit to St. John Lateran was prescribed, besides those to St. Peter's and St. Paul's, by Clement VI. in 1343, and the Church of St. Mary Major was included by Gregory XI., who, though he did not live to celebrate a Jubilee, issued a decretal on this subject in 1373. Let us turn now to consider the four Basilicas to which these visits have to be paid somewhat more in detail.

St. Peter's.

If there be one fact in the history of the early Christian centuries for which we have clearer and stronger evidence than for almost any other, it is the fact that St. Peter not only went to Rome, but that he was martyred and was buried there. Christian Rome is itself a standing witness to the truth of these events. "For the archæologist," says one of the most eminent of modern experts, not himself a Catholic, "the presence and execution of SS. Peter and Paul in Rome are facts established beyond a shadow of doubt by purely monumental evidence."[1]

The divine prophecy concerning the death of St. Peter was accomplished on the Vatican,[2] which was the scene of his crucifixion. He was buried near the same spot, at the foot of the hills. The author of the *Liber Pontificalis* says—"He was buried in the Via Aurelia, . . . near the place where he was crucified, near the palace of Nero.[3]

When the Apostles came to Rome in the reign of Nero, the topography of the Vatican[4] district was as follows:—On the left of the road was a circus, begun by Caligula and finished by Nero; on the right a line of tombs, built against the clay cliffs of the Vatican. The circus was the scene of the first sufferings of the Christians. St. Peter shared the same fate in the same place. He was affixed to a cross like the others, and we know exactly where. A tradition current in Rome from time immemorial says that Peter was executed *inter duas metas* (between the two metæ), that is, in the *spina* or middle line of Nero's

---

[1] Lanciani, *Pagan and Christian Rome*, p. 123. Signor Lanciani adds—"If my readers think that I am assuming as proved what they still consider subject for discussion, I beg to refer them to some of the standard works published on this subject by writers who are above suspicion of partiality." Whereupon he mentions Döllinger's *First Age of Christianity*, Lightfoot's *St. Clement of Rome*, and De Rossi's *Bullettino*, 1877.

[2] Armellini, *Storia delle Chiese di Roma*, p. 695—"*Il divino Vaticinio . . . si compì nel Vaticano.*" The play on the words is classical in writers on this subject.

[3] *Liber Pontificalis*, i. 118.

[4] The hollow of the Janiculum lying between S. Onofrio and Monte Mario is held to have been one of the sites of Etruscan divination. Hence the name, which, although now used only in regard to the papal palace and the Basilica of St. Peter, was at one time applied to the whole district between the foot of the hill and the Tiber near S. Angelo. (Hare, *Walks in Rome*, vol. ii. p. 293.) M. Elter, writing in *Bulletin Critique* for 1891, p. 210, concludes—"Que l'antiquité n'a pas connu de *Mons Vaticanus*, mais seulement un *ager Vaticanus;* les hauteurs qui bordent la rive droite du Tibre depuis la porte St. Pancrace, jusqu' à Monte Mario inclusivement s'appelaient le Mont Janicule. Comme elles se trouvaient dans *l'ager Vaticanus* on a pu les donner aussi le nom de *Vaticanus Mons*, *Vaticani Montes*, mais c'est seulement au moyen âge chrétien que l'on voit se produire l'adaptation précise et privative du terme *Mons Vaticanus* au lieu occupé par la basilique de St. Pierre et le palais pontifical."

Circus, at an equal distance from the two end goals; in other words, he was executed at the foot of the obelisk which now towers in front of his great church. For many centuries the exact spot was marked by a chapel called the "Chapel of the Crucifixion." This chapel disappeared seven or eight centuries ago.[1] In accordance with the liberty permitted by Roman law as to the burial even of criminals who had been executed, a monument was erected over the sacred remains. Anacletus, the second successor of St. Peter, who had been ordained priest by him, "built and adorned the sepulchral monument (*construxit memoriam*) of blessed Peter, . . . and other burial-places where the bishops might be laid."[2] The idea conveyed by the words *construxit memoriam* is that of a monument above ground according to the usual Roman custom; and such a monument, even though it covered the tomb of Christian bishops, would probably not have been disturbed at any time during the first or second centuries.[3]

We have incidental evidence of the existence of this monument to the holy Apostle in very early writings. For instance, towards the end of the second century a Roman priest named Caius, writing to the Phrygian Montanist Proclus, says—"If thou wilt go either to the Vatican or to the Ostian Way, I can show thee the *trophies* (τροπαῖα) of the founders of the Church." This letter of Caius is lost, but Eusebius has quoted from it in his "History."[4] Again, the earliest pilgrim's book that has come down to us places at the head of the holy places to be visited, "First, Peter, he rests on the western side of the city, in the Via Cornelia, near the first milestone. At the same place also rest his successors (*pontificalis ordo*), except a few, in their own tombs."[5]

This account, confirmed by other evidence which may be

---

[1] Condensed from Lanciani, *op. cit.* p. 127.

[2] *Liber Pont.*, i. 125.

[3] Northcote and Brownlow, *Roma Sotteranea.*

[4] Eusebius, *Hist. Eccl.*, ii. c. 25.

[5] *Itinerarium*, in De Rossi, *Roman Sotteranea*, i. 141, 182. Alcuin, *Opera*, ii. p. 600.

here neglected, shows that St. Peter's grave was surrounded by other tombs. During the excavations made when the "Confession" was being reconstructed under Paul V., the remains of this ancient burying-place were found. "Several bodies were discovered lying in coffins, tied with linen bands as we read of Lazarus in the Gospel—*ligatus pedes et manus institis.* Notwithstanding the absence of any inscriptions, we thought they were the graves of the ten bishops of Rome buried *in Vaticano.*"[1]

Torrigio, who also witnessed the exhumations, adds that the linen bands were from two to three inches wide, and that they must have been soaked in aromatics.[2]

One of the coffins bore the name of LINVS, who, according to the *Liber Pontificalis,* "was buried side by side with the remains of the Blessed Peter in the Vatican, October 24." De Rossi considers that the absence of the title of bishop—*episcopus*—is a convincing proof of the date of the interment. During the first century this designation (which was not of Christian coinage) was not always applied to the rulers of the Church, though this was the invariable custom in the second and third centuries.[3]

To return, however, to the earlier ages, we may note that during the persecutions which fell on the Church in the third century the remains both of St. Peter and St. Paul were temporarily transferred from their graves on the Via Cornelia and the Via Ostiensis to the catacombs in the Appian Way, for fear of desecration. This is not mere tradition. The fact is referred to by Pope Damasus in a metrical inscription published by De Rossi,[4] by the *Liber Pontificalis* under Cornelius, and by Pope Gregory in one of his epistles. A curious entry in the Philocalian calendar—otherwise called *Bucherianum*, from its first editor—seems to point to a second translation. The entry is dated June 29, A.D. 258.

---

1 Severano, *Le Sette Chiese di Roma* (Roma, 1629), p. 20.

2 *Le Sacre Grotte Vaticane* (Roma, 1639), p. 64.

3 Armellini, *Chiese*, p. 697.

4 *Inscriptiones Christianæ*, vol. ii. pp. 32 and 77. Armellini, p. 901 *seq.*

Tertio Kalendas Julias, Tusco et Basso Consulibus, Petri in Vaticano, Pauli in Via Ostiensi, utriusque in Catacumbas. "Since in early calendars the date is only appended in case of transferment of remains, archæologists have suggested the theory that the bodies of the Apostles may possibly have found shelter twice in the catacombs of the Appian Way—once shortly after their martyrdom, and again during the persecution of Valerian (A.D. 258)."[1] It has even been maintained that the frescoes in the crypt *ad Catacumbas* belong to two different epochs; though after carefully examining the paintings, etc., round the place of deposition, Lanciani came to the conclusion that they are by one hand and of one epoch—the epoch of Damasus.[2] However, whether these sacred remains were translated for safety's sake to the catacombs on one or on two occasions, there is no doubt that St. Peter's body was ultimately restored to the Vatican, and that it now rests in its brazen sarcophagus deep down below the crypt of the Basilica, where it has lain for more than sixteen hundred years.

The *Cella Memoriæ*, or oratory of Anacletus, remained the only monument to the Apostle till the beginning of the fourth century, when, at the request of Pope Sylvester, the Emperor Constantine built Basilicas both over the tomb of St. Peter at the Vatican and over that of his fellow-Apostle and martyr, St. Paul, in the Ostian Way. The building was begun in 306, the Emperor taking great interest in the work. He also adorned the sarcophagi of the Apostles with gold crosses, that on the sarcophagus of St. Peter weighing one hundred and fifty pounds,[3] and bearing an inscription on it in which the name of his mother, the Empress Helena, appears, together with his own. We may quote the quaint account of the founding of the Basilica by Constantine given in the *Mirabilia Romæ,* an early guide-book to

---

[1] *Op. cit.* p. 346. The entry above cited from the Philocalian calendar does not give the actual words we find there, but is a restoration of what De Rossi believes, on good evidence, to have been the original reading.

[2] Lanciani's investigations have since been rectified by Mgr. de Waal's.

[3] This cross seems to be still there, lying upon the tomb of St. Peter, below the "Confession," under the high altar. It was seen in 1594.

Pope Gregory XVI. Celebrating Pontifical High Mass at the High Altar of St. Peter's, over the body of the Prince of the Apostles.

Rome, the earliest extant copy of which appears to be found in a manuscript of the Vatican Library[1] attributed to the end of the twelfth century—

"He made also in the time of the said Pope (Sylvester) and after his prayer a Basilica for the Apostle Peter before Apollo's temple on the Vatican.[2] Whereof the emperor did himself first dig the foundation, and in reverence of the twelve Apostles did carry thereout twelve baskets full of earth.[3] The said Apostle's body is thus bestowed. He made a chest closed on all sides with brass and copper,[4] the which may not be moved, five feet of length at the head, five at the foot, on the right side five feet, and on the left side five feet, five feet above, and five feet below;[5] and so he enclosed the body of blessed Peter, and the altar above in the fashion of an arch he did adorn with bright gold.[6]

"And he made a civory[7] with pillars of porphyry and purest gold. And he set there before the altar twelve pillars of glass,[8] which he had brought out of Grecia, and which were of Apollo's Temple at Troy. Moreover, he did set above the Blessed Apostle Peter's body a cross of pure gold, having an hundred and fifty pounds of weight, whereon was written, 'Constantinus Augustus

---

[1] *Cod. Vat.* 3973.

[2] The remains of the Circus at the Vatican were called the palace of Nero, and near this, according to ecclesiastical tradition, was a temple of Apollo.

[3] Exuens se chlamyde, et accipiens bidentem, ipse primus terram aperuit, ad fundamenta basilicæ Sancti Petri construenda; deinde in numero duodecim apostolorum, duodecim cophinos plenos suis humeris superimpositos bajulans, de eo loco, ubi fundamenta Basilicæ Apostoli erant jacienda.

[4] Loculum ex omni parte ex ære et cupro conclusit.

[5] These measurements, taken from the *Liber Pontificalis*, have recently received an interesting new interpretation in Father A. S. Barnes' *St. Peter in Rome.* See below, p. 161 *seq.* His view, however, is open to objection; see *The Month*, April, 1900.

[6] Ornavit superius altari ex fulvo auro archam.

[7] *Ciborium*, a canopy of stone or marble over an altar. Hence the word *civery*, *civer*, or *severy* was used by English architects for the compartment of a vault. See Parker, *Glossary of Architecture.*

[8] Columpnas vitrineas. This is a curious corruption of the word originally found in the *Liber Pontificalis*, *i.e.*, *vitineas*, spiral columns either "covered with vines," as Lanciani translates, or perhaps twisting like vines.

et Helena Augusta.'"[1] When this old Basilica was demolished eleven hundred years later, many bricks were found bearing the inscription, *D.N. Constantinus Aug.*[2]

This early Basilica was 395 feet in length by 212 in width. The nave and aisles were divided by ninety-six marble columns of different sizes, in great part brought from the Septizonium of Severus. The wide atrium, surrounded by porticos, in front of the Basilica measured 212 feet by 235 feet. Here, among others, were buried Conrad, King of the Mercians, who came to remain as a monk; Offa, the Saxon; and Caedwalla, King of the West Saxons, who, "forsaking all for the love of God," as we read in the inscription placed on his tomb by Sergius I. (689), came to Rome for baptism and died there immediately afterwards—"*Candidus inter oves Christi.*"[3] A flight of thirty-five steps led up to the atrium from the piazza. The pious pilgrims used to ascend these steps on their knees; it is said that among those so ascending was Charlemagne, when he paid his first visit to Rome in 774. Symmachus enlarged these steps in 498, and added a covered portico at the sides for the convenience of pilgrims. The atrium was generally called the *paradisus*, paradise, or "parvis," because these *atria* or courts were, of old, ornamented with plants and flowers, which gave the place the appearance of a beautiful garden.

The practice of pilgrims ascending the steps of the atrium of St. Peter's on their knees lasted as long as the atrium itself lasted.

---

[1] *Mirabilia Urbis Romæ: The Marvels of Rome*, or *A Picture of the Golden City*. An English version of the medieval guide-book. Edited, with notes, by F. M. Nichols. London and Rome, 1889.

[2] *Dominus Noster Constantinus Augustus;* an illustration of these is given in Grisar, *Geschichte Roms*, etc., i. p. 238.

[3] Caedwalla's tomb was brought to light again in the sixteenth century, during the rebuilding of St. Peter's. It is doubtful whether his successor, King Ina, and his wife, Ethelburga, were buried in the same place, or in the Anglo-Saxon quarter by the Church of Sta. Maria in Saxia (now called S. Spirito in Sassia), which was founded by Ina for English pilgrims in 728. The English spread themselves over the district reaching from the portico of St. Peter down to the Tiber, which came to be known as the *Burgus Saxonum*. This district is still spoken of as *in Sassia*, while the Saxon word *Burg* (Borgo) has become the title of the whole region.—Lanciani, pp. 232, 233.

It was recommended to those who came to Rome for the Jubilee as almost the first duty to be performed. Moreover, rich Indulgences were supposed to be attached to this very fatiguing exercise of devotion, though it must be added that the authenticity of the innumerable Indulgences attached, according to popular tradition, to every possible shrine or church in Rome must be regarded as more than doubtful. A quaint old English Pilgrim's Guide-Book in verse—*The Stacions of Rome*—counts only twenty-nine steps leading up to the atrium—

At Seint Peter we schul biginne
To telle of pardoun, that slaketh sinne.
A feir mynstre men mai ther se
Niyene and twenti greces [steps] ther be;
As ofte as thou gost up or doun
Because of divocioun
Thou shall have at uche gre, [at each step],
Mon or wommon whether thou be,
Seven yer to pardoun
And therto Gode's benisoun.[1]

The beautiful fountain in the midst of the atrium was placed there by Pope Damasus, and was afterwards further embellished by Symmachus (498-514). The *Mirabilia Romæ* thus describes it—"In Saint Peter's Parvise[2] is a basin that was made by Pope Symmachus, and dight with pillars of porphyry that are joined together by marble tables with griffins, and covered with a costly sky of brass, with flowers and dolphins of brass gilt, pouring forth water. In the midst of the basin is a brazen pine cone, the which, with a roof of gilded brass, was the covering over the statue of Cybele, mother of the gods, in the opening of the Pantheon. Into this pine cone water out of the Sabbatine Aqueduct was supplied underground by a pipe of lead, the which, being always full, gave water through holes in the nut to all that wanted it; and by the pipe underground, some

[1] *The Stacions of Rome* (E.E.T.S.), ll. 17-26. This earlier text of the *Stacions* belongs to the fourteenth century. Paul II. increased the number of steps to thirty-six.

[2] The Parvise with the fountain of Symmachus are shown in an engraving of 1575, reproduced further on.

part thereof flowed to the Emperor's bath near the Needle."[1] The description here given accords, in its principal features, with that quoted by Lanciani. The pine cone is now in the Vatican garden.

A series of porticos or covered colonnades led from St. Peter's to the Ponte S. Angelo. Here another series began, which extended beyond the city to S. Paul's, thus connecting the two great Basilicas. We are told that an incessant procession of pilgrims poured through these covered ways, along which vendors of religious objects, formerly called in Rome *paternostrari*, sold their wares. A street near St. Peter's is still called the *Via dei Coronari* (of the Rosary-makers). But it was not only under the porticos that these things were sold, but on the steps, in the piazza, and in the atrium. As we learn from contemporary sources, a brisk traffic went on in all manner of objects. Vendors of food, gold ornaments, earthenware, etc., had their stalls there, and in a census of 1384 we find mentioned "the place of the fig-sellers in the paradise" (*loca vendentium ficus in paradiso*). There was even a Jew, who sold Syrian wares, who sat at his stall "under the image of the Saviour." In fact, the precincts of St. Peter's seem to have been the centre of the civil, mercantile, and social life of Rome in that day. In the Vatican archives are documents of John XXII. and Leo X. relative to these merchants and their stalls.[2]

From an early period Rome came to look upon St. Peter as the Romulus of the Christian dispensation. In the fourth century St. Peter's Day was to the Romans what Christmas Day is to us, both as regards public and private feasts and rejoicings. St.

---

[1] *Mirabilia Urbis Romæ* (The Marvels of Rome), pp. 73, 74. Dante compares the face of Nimrod, in the last circle of Hell, to this pine cone.

> *La faccia sua mi parea lunga e grossa*
> *Come la pina di San Pietro a Roma.*
> —*Inferno*, canto xxxi. ll. 58, 59.

His face appeared to me as long and big as the pine cone of St. Peter's at Rome. Philalethes gives the height of the cone at about 7½ English feet.

[2] These documents are quoted by Armellini, *Chiese*, p. 730 *seq.*, where exact references will be found.

Jerome writes to his friend, the virgin Eustochium, acknowledging a present of fruit and sweets in the shape of doves on one of these occasions, and recommends sobriety on this day more than on any other. "We must celebrate the birthday of Peter rather with exaltation of spirit than with abundance of food. It is absurd to glorify by the gratification of our appetites the memories of men who pleased God by mortifying theirs."[1] Solemn feasts and banquets were held under the porticos. At first they were meant to relieve the poor, but they degenerated into such excesses that St. Augustine in 395 complained that sad examples of drunkenness might be met with daily within the precincts of St. Peter's.[2]

We know that in the fourth century the Vatican was the chief place of resort for mendicants, and as they assembled there then, so they continued throughout the whole of the Middle Ages to solicit in this spot the alms of those who went into the church. According to Ammianus Marcellinus, Lampadius when he was Prætor caused the poor who frequented the Vatican to be fetched from that place. The Plebs had made an unreasonable demand for money from him to be spent in public games and similar purposes, but Lampadius wished it to be distributed to those who were in need. This incident must have occurred long before 354, for in that year Lampadius had passed the dignity of the Prætorship, and had already been promoted to that of Prefect of the Prætorium. This would set back the date of the occurrence almost to the time of Constantine.[3]

Five great doors, each of which had its own name in the Middle Ages, led into the five naves of the Basilica. The centre door was the so-called *Porta Argentea*, thus named from its silver metal work, dating from the sixth century. The names of the cities given by Charlemagne to the Pope were later inscribed upon these doors in silver letters. The two doors on the right of the *Porta Argentea* were the *Porta Romana* for women and the

---

[1] Epist. xxxi., *ad Eustoch*, ed. Vallarsi, t. i. p. 152.

[2] Epist. xxix., *ad Alypium*, sec. 10.

[3] Grisar, *Geschichte Roms und der Päpste.*

Porta Guidonea or Pilgrim's Gate, so called from the *guidones* or guides stationed within it who could speak the Lombard dialect, and who accompanied the pilgrims. On the left of the central entrance were the *Porta Ravegnana* or Ravenna entrance for the inhabitants of Trastevere, called *Ravennati* during the Middle Ages, and the *Porta del Giudizio*, or Gate of the Judgment, through which the bodies of the dead were carried for burial.[1]

"Near the *Porta Guidonea*," says a modern authority, "was a little door called the *Porta Santa Antica*, which was only opened once in the century at the termination of the Jubilee. It was small and narrow, to remind the faithful of the words of Christ respecting the gate of the kingdom of heaven, 'Strive to enter in by the narrow gate.' But Sixtus IV. (1471), on account of the serious accidents which occurred by the people crowding through this gate at Jubilee seasons, caused it to be disused, and opened a wider door, also called the *Porta Santa*."[2]

The late Signor Armellini, who is responsible for the foregoing statement, was so careful and exact an antiquary that one hesitates to impugn his accuracy without knowing the evidence upon which he was relying. This he does not indicate, though no doubt some evidence was before him. We have already shown in chapter ii. that at the Lateran a "golden gate," opened only during the Jubilee season, undoubtedly existed before the time of Alexander VI., and we know from Burchard himself that popular tradition spoke of a similar door at St. Peter's, in the Chapel of St. Veronica. At the same time it seems almost impossible to reconcile Burchard's narrative with the statement of Armellini just quoted. The place pointed out to Burchard proved on examination never to have been a doorway at all, and it is incredible that if Sixtus IV. had had the narrow door walled up only twenty-five years before, and a new and large

---

[1] Armellini, p. 722. The façade of the old Basilica is depicted in Raffaelle's fresco of the Incendio del Borgo, and its interior in that of the Coronation of Charlemagne.

[2] Armellini, *Chiese di Roma*, second edition, p. 722.

Porta Santa had been constructed in its place, the memory of all this should have been completely obliterated when Burchard came to make his inquiries.

Moreover, we are confronted by another difficulty in the shape of certain statements contained in a German block-book, a popular guide for pilgrims to Rome, which, for convenience sake, we may call, with Dr. Paulus, the *Rombüchlein*. This was printed at latest in 1475, and it is probably two or three years older. Now, in the description given of the principal altars of St. Peter's, the *Rombüchlein* speaks of the Chapel of St. Veronica, the same chapel as that which is mentioned by Burchard, and of the *Sudario* or *Volto Santo* which was enshrined there, and he proceeds—"Also beside the Veronica altar is the Golden Door, which is walled up, and it is forbidden under pain of excommunication ever to open it again."[1] Thereupon he goes on to tell the story of a man in Rome who murdered his father and mother and sister that he might have all their property for himself, and then went through the Golden Door, impiously saying aloud, "Be God lief or be God loath, this day He must needs forgive me my sin." Thereupon an angel's voice was heard saying, "This day and never more." As it happened, a cardinal was standing by while this was going on, and he straightway informed the Pope of what he had heard.

"Then the Pope had the door walled up, and he set his curse on all that should lend their aid in undoing it again. And when the Pope died he had himself buried in front of the door for a sign that the door should never be opened."[2]

All this goes to confirm Burchard's statement that no "golden door" was known in this place but one which had been walled

[1] "Item bey der Veronica altar ist die gulden phort, und ist vermaurt, und verpannt vorpotten auf zu thon." Muffel, who gives an account of a visit he paid to Rome in 1452, also speaks of the walled-up door in St. Veronica's Chapel, and tells about it a story very like that of the Rombüchlein. His narrative is printed in the *Bibliothek* of the Stuttgart Literarischer Verein, vol. cxxviii. p. 20.

[2] "Do liesse der pabst die phortten vermaueen (*sic*) und vermaledeiet alle dee hand anlegetten die phort aufzethon. Und der pabst dor er starb do liesse er sich fuer die phort begraben zu aynem zaychen das die port nich soldt geoffent werden." There were several Popes buried near the entrance of the Veronica Chapel. See De Rossi, *Inscriptiones Christianæ*, vol. ii.

up for many years, long before the time of Sixtus IV. It may be noticed that a somewhat similar story was told by a Spanish traveller[1] in connection with one of the doors of the Lateran nearly fifty years earlier, and it seems that the latter, being so much the older, is likely to be the original.

The Veronica Chapel of which we have just been speaking, which stood near the entrance of the church to the right, close to the *Porta Guidonea*, was originally constructed by John VII. about the year 705, and was then known as the Chapel of the Manger (*presepio*).[2] It was adorned with mosaics representing the Apostle preaching in the cities of Antioch, Jerusalem, and Rome. A few fragments of these decorations are still preserved in the crypt of St. Peter's and in the chapel of the Ricci family at St. Mark's in Florence. In this spot, close beside the entrance of St. Peter's, John VII. is said to have placed the ancient picture of Christ called the *Volto Santo* or *Veronica*. As we have already had occasion to notice, no relic was more famous in the Middle Ages, and none gave rise to such enthusiastic manifestations of devotion. The sonnet of Petrarch quoted on p. 58 represents the sight of the Volto Santo as the worthy crown of a long life, after which the aged pilgrim might fittingly sing his *Nunc dimittis*. So, too, in Dante we read—

Of one
Who haply from Croatia wends to see
Our Veronica, and the while 'tis shown,
Hangs over it with never sated gaze
And all that he has heard revolving, saith
Unto himself in thought: "And did'st thou look
E'en thus, O Jesus, my true Lord and God?
And was this semblance Thine?[3]—CARY.

---

[1] Tafur, *Andanças é Viajes*, p. 28.

[2] Armellini, *Le Chiese di Roma*, second edition, p. 722. Nothing in the mosaics suggests the least reference to the *Volto Santo*. See Müntz, *Revue Archéologique*, 1877, p. 145 *seq.*

[3] Quale è colui che di Croazia
Viene a veder la Veronica nostra,
Che per l'antica fama non si sazia,
Ma dice nel pensier, fin che si mostra
Signor mi Giesu' Christo Iddio verace
Or fu si fatta la sembianza vostra.—*Paradiso*, xxxi. ll. 103-108.

Dante's accentuation Veroníca is also that of the Greek Βερενίκη.

It would seem that the image is now almost effaced, and that the features can hardly be distinguished. That this Sudario is identical with the *Imago Salvatoris* of which we have evidence in the eleventh century, there seems no good reason to doubt; but the conscientious researches of Herr von Dobschütz, the most recent authority on the subject, have not succeeded in tracing it further back.[1] All that we can say of the legend of its earlier history is, that there is some reason for believing that Veronica, *i.e.*, Berenice (Βερονίκη—the medieval Greek pronunciation of this word is practically identical with Veronica), may really be an historical personage, though there is no sort of early authority for her meeting our Saviour on the way to Calvary. Evidence, however, may be quoted for believing that the woman healed by our Lord of an issue of blood was named Berenice, and that she erected a statue in honour of her heavenly Physician at Paneas, in Syria, representing the scene of her own cure. The widely diffused notion that the name Veronica has something to do with *vera ikon* (true image) is a fallacy.

That the devotion to the *Volto Santo* did not stop short with the Middle Ages may be proved by the vivid description of Montaigne, which we hope to quote further on, giving an account of the exposition of the relic during his visit to Rome. He was evidently much impressed by the scene, and he relates how the people "threw themselves down before it upon their faces, most of them with tears in their eyes and with lamentations and cries of compassion. No other relic," he adds, "has such veneration paid to it."

The nave of old St. Peter's terminated in a wide apse, with a throne at its extremity, and seats for the clergy on either hand. It was reached from the nave by seven porphyry steps, and with the remains of these steps were made the two by which we

---

[1] See Garrucci, *Storia del' Arte Cristiana*, vol. iii. p. 8; Kraus, *Geschichte der Christlichen Kunst*, vol. i. pp. 178, 179; Armellini, *Lezioni di Archeologia Cristiana*, p. 254. The extract from Methodius which refers to this *Volto Santo* is certainly apocryphal. It is said by Thilo that the Paris MS. 2034 in which it is quoted is itself of the ninth century; but Dobschütz, *Christusbilder* (p. 279 and p. 220), dates the passage conjecturally A.D. 1100.

ascend to the present apse or "*tribuna*." On the great arch of the chancel was formerly a mosaic, representing the Emperor Constantine being presented to the Saviour by Peter and offering Him a model of the Basilica. Professor Frothingham found this arch described in a book by Cardinal Jacobacci (1538), *De Concilio*. The arch, with the inscription on it, was destroyed in 1525.

The altars and chapels scattered through the vast Basilica were almost innumerable.[1] One of the most notable features was the very ancient baptistery, made by Pope Damasus, and supplied with water from the streams from the hills. The inscription he placed on it is still preserved in the crypt of the Vatican. In this baptistery was the famous chair of Peter; and Ennodius of Pavia, who lived at the end of the fifth century, speaking of the newly baptised who went from the font to be confirmed, says that the bishop was seated in the *sella gestatoria apostolicæ confessionis*,[2] whence it was written of Siricius, the successor of Damasus, in his epitaph—*Fonte Sacro Magnus Meruit Sedere Sacerdos.* The baptistery came itself to be known as *Cathedra Apostolica;* we find it thus designated by Prudentius. This chair, now enshrined in the beautiful altar by Bernini, at the extremity of the apse, was last shown in 1867, and was described by De Rossi.[3] The legs are of oak, and the seat and back of acacia wood of later date than the legs. The iron rings which stand out on either side, and through which poles were thrust, show that it was a *sedia gestatoria*, meant to be carried on the shoulders of four or more bearers, a custom introduced by the Roman senators in the time of Claudius.

Even Gregorovius speaks of this relic with becoming respect. From the second century, he says, it has been held to be the very seat used by the Apostle St. Peter. "This remarkable

---

[1] Lanciani says there were sixty-eight altars; Grimaldi says fifty-two; and the medieval *Reliquiæ Rhomanæ Urbis* states that there were ninety-nine.

[2] *Apolog. pro Synodo*, ed. Hartel, p. 328.

[3] *Bull. di Archæol. Crist*, June and July, 1867, pp. 38 *seq.*

IHS
IHS
INNOCENTIVS.IX.PON.OPT.MAX.CREATVS.XXVIIII.OCTOBER.MDL

THE SEDIA GESTATORIA USED IN THE SIXTEENTH CENTURY, WITH BEARERS AND SWISS GUARD.

From a contemporary print at the British Museum.

chair, the oldest throne in the world, upon which have sat first of all obscure bishops, and then mighty Popes, whose sway was felt through many lands and peoples, is still in existence." He mentions also that he himself examined it in the year 1867, when it was last exposed to public view.[1]

One other famous memorial of the great Apostle, which has for centuries attracted the veneration of Christians, must not be passed over without a word. The celebrated bronze statue in the nave of the Basilica, in which St. Peter is represented seated, his right hand raised in blessing and his left holding a key, has had the protruding foot saluted by the kisses of such countless multitudes that the toe has almost entirely disappeared. The statue is not, of course, a relic in any sense, except that it bears witness to the devotion of the faithful, and there is a curious diversity of opinion as to its age. As a matter of historical evidence we cannot trace it further back than the fifteenth century, and certain archæologists,—*e.g.*, Didron, more than fifty years ago, and Dr. F. X. Kraus at the present day—consider that it is a work of the Middle Ages imitating classical models, and very probably cast by Arnolfo di Cambio between the years 1250 and 1300.[2] On the other hand, other authorities, who differ as widely on most topics as Professor Gregorovius and Father Grisar, assign it to the fifth century after Christ, and this latter may be considered the more generally received opinion.

Even those who pronounce for an early date are inclined to consider the key a later restoration. Father Grisar,[3] however, defends its antiquity, citing both another statue of St. Peter in the crypt of the Basilica which is similarly distinguished, and also some early representations of keys of like shape to be found in the Lateran Museum. As early as the fourth century St. Optatus Milevitanus seems clearly to have recognised the keys as the personal prerogative of Peter, a symbol of unity as well as

[1] *Geschichte der Stadt Rom*, fourth edition, vol. i. pp. 93, 94.

[2] Kraus, *Geschichte der Christlichen Kunst*, i. p. 231.

[3] Grisar, *Geschichte Roms und der Päpste*, i. p. 445, and *Civiltà Cattolica*, 1898, ii. 459 *seq.* Cf. Lanciani, *Pagan and Christian Rome*, p. 142; Wickhoff, *Zft. f. bild. Kunst*, 1890, p. 109.

of the power of binding and loosing. "He alone received the keys," he writes, "that he might communicate them to the rest"; and again, "It was ordained that the sinner should open to the innocent, in order that the innocent might not shut the door in the face of sinners, and in order that in this way there might be no hindrance to the unity which is necessary."[1]

A beam went from one side of the chancel arch to the other, supporting a great cross between two keys, and beneath it hung a gigantic lamp, containing, it is said, 1300 lights, which is believed to have been stolen by the Saracens in 846. These lights were lit on great festivals—such as Christmas, Easter, and St. Peter's Day. It may be noted that the greater Roman Basilicas, from the time of their foundation, received endowments of lands expressly to defray the cost of lighting them. In the inventory of gifts made by the Emperor Constantine[2] to the Lateran Basilica this purpose is specially provided for. The expense of lighting was, of course, very great. The most precious oils (*e.g.*, balsam) were used in the sanctuaries, and the contents of the lamps were often rendered still more costly by the addition of fragrant perfumes.

At the end of eleven centuries the magnificent Basilica began to show signs of decay, and Nicholas V. conceived the idea of entirely rebuilding it. Little, however, was done before his death, and the work was only undertaken in earnest half a century later by Julius II. On 18th April, 1506, the operations commenced, and the cross on the summit of the dome was finished on 18th November, 1593. The following account of the construction of the dome, given by Lanciani,[3] may be of interest:—

"The construction of the dome was begun on Friday, 15th July, 1588, at 4 p.m. The first block of travertine was placed

---

[1] Optatus Milevitanus, Migne, P.L. XI., 1088.

[2] In the list of endowments to the Lateran we read—"Constituit (Constantinus) in servitio luminum massa Gargilana," etc.—*Liber Pont.* i. 173; Silvester, n. 36. Cf. Duchesne, *ibid. i.* cxiv.; Grisar, *Geschichte Roms und der Päpste*, p. 413; Gregorovius, *Geschichte der Stadt Rom*, ii. p. 387, fourth edition.

[3] *Pagan and Christian Rome*, pp. 146, 147.

in situ at 8 p.m. of the 30th. The cylindrical portion or drum (*tamburo*) which supports the dome proper was finished at midnight of 17th December of the same year—a marvellous feat to have accomplished. The dome itself was begun five days later, and finished in seventeen months. If we remember that the experts of the age had estimated ten years as the time required to accomplish the work, and one million gold scudi as the cost, we wonder at the power of will of Sixtus V., who did it in two years and spent only one-fifth of the sum. The lantern, however, was not completed by Sixtus (who died in 1590), the gilded cross being placed on its summit on 18th November, 1593. Six hundred skilled craftsmen were enlisted to push the work of the dome night and day; they were excused from attending divine service or feast days, Sunday excepted. We may form an idea of the haste felt by all concerned in the enterprise, and of their determination to sacrifice all other interests to speed, by the following anecdote: The masons, being once in need of another receptacle for water, laid their hands on the tomb of Pope Urban VI., dragged the marble sarcophagus under the dome on the edge of a lime-pit, and emptied it of its contents. The golden ring was given to Giacomo della Porta, the architect, the bones put aside in a corner of the building, and the coffin was used as a tank from 1588 to 1615.

When we consider that the building materials — stones, bricks, timber, cement, and water—had to be lifted to a height of 400 feet, it is no wonder that 500,000 pounds of rope should have been consumed, and fifteen tons of iron.

We do not propose to attempt a description of the present St. Peter's, which would require a chapter to itself, but the following figures may give some inadequate idea of its size:—

The Basilica is approached by a square 1256 feet in diameter. The nave is 613 feet long, 81 wide, 133 high; the transept, 449 feet long. The cornice and mosaic inscription of the frieze are 1943 feet long. The dome towers to a height of 448 feet above the pavement, with a diameter in the interior of 139 feet 9 inches—a trifle less than that of the Pantheon. The letters on the frieze are 4 feet 8 inches high. The church contains 46 altars—before which 121 lamps are burning day and night—and 748 columns of marble, stone, and bronze. The statues number 386, and the windows 290.

In the vestibule and facing the centre door is the celebrated mosaic called the *Navicella,* a piece of thirteenth-century work representing St. Peter navigating his ship through the troubled waters. The reason of its being placed here was, it is said, that for many generations the heathen custom prevailed, especially among the Christians from the East, of looking at the sun and venerating it before entering the Basilica. In order to afford them an object worthy of veneration, the mosaic was placed in the position it now occupies. It is related of Cardinal Baronius that for thirty years, when entering St. Peter's, he never failed to venerate the picture and to pray, *Domine ut erexisti Petrum a fluctibus ita eripe me a peccatorum undis*—"O Lord, who didst deliver Peter from the waters, so preserve me from the waves of sin."

Finally, we may note that an important contribution to the archæology of the Basilica of St. Peter's has recently been made by Father A. S. Barnes in his work entitled *St. Peter in Rome, and His Tomb on the Vatican Hill.*[1] The author believes, though perhaps more confidently than the evidence warrants, that he is able to rectify in several particulars the views commonly held, even by the most distinguished Roman archæologists, such as De Rossi, Armellini, Duchesne, Lanciani, and Grisar, with regard to the translations and final disposal of St. Peter's body. So far as concerns the translations, the key of Father Barnes' new theory is the suggestion that the entry about the restoration of St. Peter's remains to the tomb *in Monte Aureo in Vaticano,* which is inserted in the *Liber Pontificalis* under Pope Cornelius (251–252), really belongs to Pope Marcellus (306–308). This is not a mere arbitrary guess, but it finds curious support in the

[1] *St. Peter in Rome, and His Tomb on the Vatican Hill.* By the Rev. Arthur Stapylton Barnes, M.A., University College, Oxford. London: Sonnenschein, 1900. See a criticism by the present writer in *The Month,* April, 1900.

recurrence under Marcellus of the name of the matron Lucina, mentioned under Cornelius, and also in the prominence given to a certain Marcellus in the apocryphal Acts of Sts. Peter and Paul. Father Barnes is therefore led to pronounce in favour of a double translation of St. Peter's body to the Platonia "*ad Catacumbas*" on the Appian Way; the first immediately after the martyrdom, whence his remains were transferred a year or so later to a *cella memoriæ,* constructed near the place of the martyrdom on the Vatican Hill, the second in A.D. 258, on which occasion St. Peter's body remained *ad Catacumbas* until the time of Marcellus, who again restored it to the Vatican. There Constantine built a Basilica over it a score of years afterwards, and there it still lies deep down under the high altar of the present St. Peter's. With regard to the site and construction of this tomb, Father Barnes has also much that is new to say. He considers that the curious measurements of the *Liber Pontificalis* (quoted above, p. 146) afford an interesting record of the dimensions and shape of the sepulchral chamber. The sarcophagus was raised upon a pedestal 5 feet from the floor, and the containing walls and roof originally left a free space of 5 feet all around and above it, thus giving us a chamber about 17 feet long, 14 feet high, and 14 feet broad. This was underground, and would necessarily have been approached by a flight of steps from the road on the south side, the opening of which staircase Father Barnes believes to have been masked by a wall built across it at the time of the Saracen invasion in A.D. 846.[1] Over this chamber another storey was constructed above ground. This was the true *cella memoriæ,* a chapel in which an altar was erected vertically above the sarcophagus, and in which the Holy Sacrifice was offered for the handful of Christians who assembled there in the second and third centuries. When

[1] He considers that some cautious and tentative explorations undertaken in the chapel of S. Salvatorino in the crypt would easily decide the question as to the existence of this flight of steps. If Father Barnes is justified in his conclusions, it would thus be possible to descend to the actual sarcophagus in which the body of the saint reposes, and to view once more the golden cross laid upon the tomb by Constantine.

Constantine's Basilica was built over this chapel it would seem that the north and south walls of the chapel were left intact, while the east and the west walls and the roof were removed. The central part was almost filled up with fresh masonry, and upon this, still *bien entendu* vertically over St. Peter's body but at a considerably higher level, was built a new altar, which served as the high altar of the Basilica. Eastward of this the floor of the chapel was raised level with the pavement of the nave of Constantine's church, and this small portion of the old *cella memoriæ*, thus somewhat elevated, now remains to us as the "Confession." In the new St. Peter's, the pavement of which stands 11 feet higher than the floor of the old St. Peter's, we have to descend to the Confession by steps; but formerly, as we may see in Raphael's pictures, the grating of the Confession was on a level with the floor of the nave itself. The tiny western segment of the *cella memoriæ* was left at the same level, and even in Constantine's Basilica formed a subterranean chamber under the apse. In the new St. Peter's this is proportionately much deeper down. The space was enlarged by Paul V. and made into a chapel, in which is the altar used by all priests who obtain permission to say mass "over the body of St. Peter." The central portion of the *cella memoriæ* under the high altar has been so much built up that there is now left hardly more than a deep alcove or recess, which penetrates nearly but not quite through to the chapel on the western side. It will be noticed that both this underground chapel and the open well before the high altar, where the alcove is, have an equal claim to the title "Confession," since they formed originally the eastern and western extremities of the old *cella memoriæ.* This fact, in Father Barnes' opinion, is responsible for endless confusion in the authors who have written on the subject. The body of St. Peter, however, lies vertically under the space between them, *i.e.*, under the high altar itself. Father Barnes has also much to say on the subject of the "cataracts," the openings by which it was formerly possible to lower objects into the sepulchral chamber that they might touch the tomb, but the matter is too complicated to be discussed here. The cataracts are reached by a door in the floor of the alcove or recess, which opens, as we have said, into the Confession, more commonly so called, *i.e.*, that on the eastern side. In this alcove stands permanently the golden casket, in which are kept the *pallia*, the outward symbols of jurisdiction given by the Pope to archbishops, and said to be taken "from the body of Blessed Peter."

St. Paul's.

What gave its special sanctity to Rome, and what brought the pilgrims flocking thither, was not the fact that it was the sanctuary of half the relics of the world, but simply that it was the See of Peter and the resting-place of the two leaders of the Apostles. Even as early as the beginning of the sixth century we find Elpidia, the wife of Boethius, writing thus in a hymn which has been incorporated by the Catholic Church in her office for the great festival of Sts. Peter and Paul on 29th June:—

O happy Rome, made holy now
By these two martyrs' precious blood,
Earth's best and fairest cities bow,
By thy superior claims subdued.

For thou alone art worth them all,
City of martyrs! thou alone
Canst cheer our pilgrim hearts and call
The Saviour's sheep to Peter's throne.

—*Father Faber's Translation.*

Remembering, then, the provisions of the Bull of Boniface VIII. which enjoined visits to those two Basilicas only in which were entombed the bodies of the Apostles, it is natural that we should direct our attention, in the second place, to the Church of St. Paul fuori le Mure. The site of that edifice does not mark the spot where St. Paul was actually beheaded. Although the martyrdom was carried out on the Ostian Way, it seems clear that the place at which it occurred lay nearly a mile further along the road than that where now stands the Basilica which bears his name. When the worst of the persecution was over and the Christians felt that they could safely bring the remains of the Apostles from the catacombs, where they, no doubt, were concealed for a time, in order to inter them in a more accessible position, they were probably prevented by some accidental reason from obtaining any plot of ground near the place of St. Paul's martyrdom. They had therefore to be content with what circumstances permitted, and Anacletus would seem to have erected on the Ostian Way a sepulchral chamber, to contain the body of St. Paul, similar to that which he had built on the Vatican for the remains of his fellow-Apostle St. Peter. Such a "*memoria*" or "*cella memoriæ*" was probably a very tiny edifice, measuring, according to pagan analogies, some fourteen feet by eight or ten, and containing in the centre the sarcophagus in which the remains were deposited, with just reasonable space to move about it. Over this, in many cases, an upper chamber was constructed in which the Holy Sacrifice was offered immediately above the body of the martyr.

Two centuries and a half later, when peace was established in the Church, the Emperor Constantine transformed these *cellæ memoriæ* of the two Apostles into Basilicas. He also, according to the *Liber Pontificalis* (i. 178), placed the body of St. Paul in a coffin of solid bronze; but, says Lanciani, "no visible trace of it is left. I had the privilege of examining the actual grave, 1st December, 1891, lowering myself from the *fenestrella* under the altar. I found myself on a flat surface paved with slabs of marble, on one of which (placed negligently in a slanting direction) are engraved the words, Paulo Apostolo Mart. . . . This inscription belongs to the fourth century."[1]

The Basilica erected by Constantine was very small in size.

---

[1] *Pagan and Christian Rome*, p. 157. See also "Die Grabplatte des h. Paulus," etc., by Fr. H. Grisar, S.J., in the *Römische Quartalschrift* for 1892 and his *Analecta Romana*, i. p. 257, for illustration and further discussions concerning the tomb. There seems no reason at all to believe that the marble slab with the inscription is the cover of the actual sarcophagus. See Barnes, *St. Peter in Rome*, p. 220 *seq*.

It would seem to have been hardly more than 100 feet long. This was not due to any wish to disparage St. Paul at the expense of his fellow Apostle St. Peter, but it resulted from the position of the tomb relatively to the high road to Ostia. The traditions of church construction at that period inexorably required that the altar of the Basilica should stand at its western end, and that there the bishop or priest should offer the Holy Sacrifice, his face turned towards the people, the altar between him and them, and the whole length of the building stretching eastward before him. Now, as the Ostian Way ran close to St. Paul's tomb on its eastern side, and as the high altar had necessarily to be erected immediately over the tomb, there was no room to throw the nave of the Basilica out eastward. The only possible arrangement which occurred to the builders of that epoch was to construct a Basilica of very diminutive proportions, utilising for the length of its nave only just that narrow space which was left between the tomb and the road. At the end, however, of little more than half a century this building seemed so unworthy of the great Apostle that a bold innovation was decided upon. On the western side of the tomb the ground was free, and it was determined to reverse the direction of the church. The priest would still offer sacrifice with his face towards the east, but the people in the long nave stretching westward would now stand behind him facing the same way as he did. The new Basilica of St. Paul, begun in accordance with these plans by the Emperors Valentinian II., Theodosius, and Arcadius in the year 368, was probably the prototype of that arrangement of the altar and nave in church building which has now become universal. The imperial rescript to the Roman prefect Sallustius, ordering him to commence the rebuilding of the Ostian Basilica on a magnificent scale, is still extant. Valentinian died in 392, but the work was continued under Theodosius, Arcadius, and Honorius, being completed by the last-named emperor.

The celebrated Galla Placidia, daughter of Theodosius, and sister of Arcadius and Honorius, also contributed to the work later on. An inscription over the great arch of the Basilica recorded that

> *Theodosius cœpit, perfecit Honorius, aulam*
> *Doctoris mundi sacratam corpore Pauli*

And

> *Placidiæ pia mens operis decus omne paterni*
> *Gaudet pontificis studio splendere Leonis.*

At the beginning of the last century a very interesting little record of the early years[1] of the Basilica was brought to light in the shape of a bronze tablet pierced through on either side, and with an inscription engraved on it. Muratori edited this inscription, but could not explain it. De Rossi believes that this little tablet was hung round the neck of a watch-dog which belonged to the Basilica, and which was in charge of a shepherd called Felicissimus. The inscription runs, "*Ad basilicam Apostoli Pauli et DDD NNN* (*i.e., trium dominorum nostrorum*) *Felicissimi Pecor-* (*orarii*)"—"(I belong) to the Basilica of St. Paul the Apostle, rebuilt by our three sovereigns; I am in charge of Felicissimus the shepherd"; so we may construe the sentence.[2] Such inscriptions were often engraved on the collars of dogs and of slaves in order that their ownership might be known.

In the Breviary Office for the 18th November, on which day is commemorated the dedication of the Basilicas of SS. Peter and Paul, it is recorded that both these churches were consecrated on the same day, about 324, by Pope St. Silvester I. It was not, however, generally understood, before the discovery early in this century of an inscription on one of the columns, that the Basilica of Theodosius was consecrated anew on the same day of the same month by Pope Siricius in 390.

Round the top of this pillar run the words, SIRICIUS EPISCOPUS TOTA MENTE DEVOTUS, but this is further elucidated by the inscription at the base which contains, amongst other things, the date of the consecration, 18th November, 390, and the name of

[1] The date of this tablet is indicated by the triple D, which refers to the three emperors.

[2] Armellini, *Chiese di Roma*, p. 929.

the architect of the building, Flavius Philippus. This pillar was set up again in the north porch of the new Basilica, the base being preserved in one of the cloisters of the monastery.[1]

Two fragments also remain of another important inscription, which fragments are now also affixed to the walls of the monastery cloister. They tell us how one Eusebius, in the sixth century, restored the "*cemetery*," and relate how he rebuilt or repaired the porticos, the roof, the baths,[2] the seats, windows, pavement; how he mended the door hinges and provided the locks with keys, made conduits for the water, and repaired the *mensa* stones on the martyrs' tombs, etc.

Besides the great monastery attached to the building, many small oratories, lesser Basilicas, and houses grouped themselves round St. Paul's Church, which thus became the centre of a Christian village or township. This, being situated on the borders of the river, was exposed to the ravages of the Saracens, and, in fact, suffered greatly from their depredations in 846. About 880 Pope John VIII. fortified it, and the place was afterwards known as *Johannipolis*—John's town. Lanciani[3] says—"The construction of Johannipolis . . . is described by one document only, an inscription above the gate of the Castle, which was copied first by Cola di Rienzo, and later by Pietro Sabino, professor of rhetoric in the Roman archigymnasium towards the end of the fifteenth century. A few fragments of this remarkable document are still preserved in the cloisters of the adjacent monastery. It states that John VIII. raised a wall for the defence of the Basilica of St. Paul's and the surrounding buildings in imitation of that built by Leo IV. for the protection of the Vatican suburb." The anonymous *Magliabecchiano* mentions Johannipolis,[4] and says it was more than two miles in circumference. Further, a document of Pope Gregory VII.[5] (who was

[1] Grisar, *Geschichte Roms und der Päpste*, p. 283. See also De Rossi, *Musaici: S. Paolo, arco di Placidia*, fasc. 15, concerning the partly illegible inscription on the base.

[2] Baths were frequently attached to the old Basilicas.

[3] *Pagan and Christian Rome*, p. 153.

[4] An. Mag., xxviii. *cod.* 5.

[5] Bull, Cas. Cost. cxii.

cardinal arch-priest of St. Paul's before he ascended the Papal chair) confirms to this church *totum castellum S. Pauli quod vocatur Joannipolim cum mola juxta se.*

To return to the Basilica itself as it was in the fifth century. Its dimensions exceeded those of the old Vatican Basilica, the interior being composed of five broad aisles, divided by four rows of twenty pillars each, of various styles of architecture and of divers species of marbles, many of the pillars being taken from other buildings and adapted to their new position. The roof was of gilded or bronzed wood, and the internal walls were covered with marble. The centre nave terminated in the immense arch, supported by two imposing Ionic pillars of Greek marble, which Gallia Placidia had decorated with mosaics. Beneath this arch was the Confession, or tomb of the Apostle, whose body lay under it, enclosed, as we may assume, in a bronze sarcophagus within an outer one of marble.

Constantine had richly endowed this Basilica, and the poet Prudentius[1] describes it as being splendid with gold, silver, and precious stones, at the time when he saw it, during the reign of Honorius. On the wall, above the columns of the nave, was a series of portraits of the Popes from St. Peter onwards, but these had, many of them, suffered serious injury before the seventeenth century, and only those on the south wall still exist, this wall having been left comparatively unharmed by the conflagration of 1823. The great bronze gates, which were cast in Constantinople in 1070 by the order of the Abbot Hildebrand (Gregory VII.), were terribly damaged on this occasion. These doors were adorned with fifty-four scriptural compositions wrought in gold and silver lines or threads. The remains of these gates are now in the cloister. Almost the only ancient treasure left in the Basilica is the magnificent marble paschal candlestick, one of the most curious pieces of medieval sculpture in Rome. It is of twelfth-century work, and covered with carving in high relief representing the history of the Passion.

---

[1] Prud., *Hymn XII.*

Around it is the legend, "*Ego Nicolaus de Angelo cum Petro Bassalecto hoc opus complevi.*"[1]

The "great chalice" of Honorius mentioned in the little fourteenth-century tract *Mirabilia Romæ*[2] has disappeared. Of this we read, "In St. Paul . . . is the great chalice of Pope Honorius, where he has written verses to this purport—

"Paul, of high name, take this noble vessel,
Which I, Honorius, who preside in the Sacred Court, give in thine honour;
That thou, in answer to pious prayers, mayest give me thy realms of piety,
And that I may seek the rest of peace and be united with the blessed."

In the course of ages the Basilica was repeatedly restored and beautified, and in the first half of the thirteenth century the magnificent cloister was added. But in 1823, in one night, was destroyed by fire that vast Basilica, next in importance to the Vatican; and pictures, marbles, mosaics all perished. The work of rebuilding was at once begun, and contributions were sent from all the Catholic countries in Europe. It was completed and opened by Pius IX. in December, 1854. The dimensions of the Honorian Basilica have been adhered to, and the interior, with its eighty granite columns, is striking and magnificent. The baldachino over the high altar is supported by four pillars of Oriental alabaster, presented by Mehomet Ali, Viceroy of Egypt, to Gregory XVI.

MEDAL REPRESENTING THE RUINS OF ST. PAUL'S AFTER THE FIRE.

St. Ignatius of Loyola, when making the visits to the seven churches with his companions on the 22nd April, 1541, made his

[1] Armellini, *Chiese*, second edition, pp. 932-934.

[2] *The Marvels of Rome, or a Picture of the Golden City*, an English version of the medieval guide-book, *Mirabilia Urbis Romæ*, by F. N. Nichols. Rome, 1880.

solemn profession of vows before a picture of Our Lady, which was then kept at the altar of the Blessed Sacrament, and is now at that of the Crucifixion.[1] Attention is drawn to this picture in a little manual of Jubilee devotions which has in a special way attracted the interest and received the approbation of Leo XIII.

"Near the Chapel of the Blessed Sacrament is that of the Holy Crucifix, in which is venerated an ancient crucifix of carved wood, before which St. Bridget often prayed and obtained signal favours. At the foot of the crucifix there is a representation in mosaic of the Blessed Virgin with the Infant Jesus. This image is specially honoured as that before which St. Ignatius and his nine companions made their vows. The crucifix and image of our Lady were solemnly transferred from their former altar to this place by Benedict XIII. in the Jubilee year of 1725. The memory of this translation is preserved in an inscription carved in stone."[2]

In the little book we refer to, it is suggested that on visiting the Basilica of St. Paul a special prayer should be said before this crucifix.

It is stated that before the Reformation the kings of England took the Basilica of St. Paul under their special protection, as the kings of France acted as patrons of St. John Lateran, and the kings of Spain of St. Maria Maggiore. The device of the Order of the Garter may still be seen carved in marble near the side door of the church, and elsewhere.[3]

---

[1] *Ribadeneira*, cap. xiv., with the note of the Bollandists, 31st July, p. 701. The church was almost deserted, and St. Ignatius and his companions went there to be able to take their vows in privacy.

[2] *Le Jubilé de l'année Sainte, 1900*, etc., p. 53. Rome, 1900.

[3] Nicolai, *Della Basilica di S. Paolo* (Roma, 1815), pp. 308, 309—"Sull' architrave di questa porta, ci osserva scolpita in marmo la divisa dell' ordine della giarrettiera, poichè anticamente questa basilica era sotto la protezione del Re d'Inghilterra, come le altre erano, e sono; sotto quella di altri principali sovrani." It is further stated that as the kings of France were canons of the Lateran, and the kings of Spain canons of St. Mary Major, so the English kings were canons of St. Paul outside the walls. *Notes and Queries*, series vii. vol. 7, p. 483, and Barbier de Montault, *Description de la Basilique de St. Paul.*

When "James III." of England (better known as the Old Pretender) was living at Rome, he used to send an offering of a wax candle to St. Paul's for the Feast of the Purification.

The Lateran.

The Basilica which next claims our attention is that of the Lateran; not only because in point of time it was the third of the four churches to be named in the Jubilee Bulls, but also because it is the Cathedral of the Bishop of Rome, and in a certain sense takes precedence of all the rest. According to its own proud boast, it is OMNIUM URBIS ET ORBIS ECCLESIARUM MATER ET CAPUT (the Mother and Head of all the Churches of the City and the World); and even in the matter of architecture, its glories seem to have left the deepest impression upon the mind of the medieval pilgrim. Dante, in the *Paradiso*, tells how

> The grim brood from Arctic shores that roamed
> Stood in mute wonder 'mid the works of Rome,
> When to their view the Lateran arose
> In greatness more than earthly.[1]

The Lateran Basilica derives its name from the Laterani, an old Roman clan, whose palace was situated on this part of the Cœlian Hill. Their estates were confiscated when the head of the family, Plautius Lateranus, was discovered to have taken part in a plot against the life of Nero. At the beginning of the fourth century the palace became the property of Fausta, daughter of the Emperor Maximian and wife of Constantine. After the celebrated victory of the Milvian Bridge, Constantine took this palace for his own dwelling, but soon afterwards, in 312, gave it

---

[1] *Se i barbari venendo da tal plaga*
Veggendo Roma e l'ardua sua opra
Stupefaceansi quando Laterano
Alle cose mortali andò di sopra.
—*Paradiso*, canto xxxi. ll. 34-36.

It may be that the Lateran is here only substituted by metonymy for Rome in general, but the possibility of such metonymy is itself a tribute to the pre-eminence of the Lateran.

to Pope Miltiades, when it became the papal residence; and on the 2nd October, 313, Pope Miltiades presided at the first Council assembled against the Donatists, "*in domum Faustæ in Laterano.*"[1] Constantine built a Basilica in one part of the palace[2] (tradition states that he laboured at it with his own hands), which was dedicated to the Saviour by Pope Sylvester. From the beginning it was commonly known as the Constantine Basilica, and was the most favoured of all the buildings which the Emperor erected in Rome for the worship of the God of the Christians. We have still preserved in the *Liber Pontificalis* an authentic inventory of the rich endowment—both in revenues, in landed property, and in gold and silver vessels—bestowed by Constantine upon this, the principal church in the city. In later times it was known in popular parlance as *Basilica Aurea*, the Golden Basilica. This was probably due to the splendid decorations in marbles and mosaics and precious metals with which it was adorned; but the name of the old Roman family never quitted it, and has thus been perpetuated throughout all ages.[3] Down to the time of Gregory the Great, however, continual reference is made to the building as the *Constantine* Basilica, which establishes beyond doubt the fact that he was the founder. Probably the extravagant legend concerning Pope Sylvester and the emperor, as well as the famous forged "donation of Constantine," were originally developed out of this historical fact. The name "Lateran Basilica" is used by St. Jerome (*Ep.* 67, n. 4) and by Prudentius (*contra Symmachum*, bk. i. v. 586).

From this period the history of the Lateran becomes almost identified with the history of Christianity in Rome, for Constantine's Basilica, as a modern writer has said, may be truly regarded as the "glorious *Capitol* of the City of Peter and Paul."[4] As the Cathedral Church of the Roman Pontiff, it

[1] Optatus, *De Schismate Donatist*, i. c. 23.

[2] Or, more probably, adapted for use as a Christian church a hall already existing in the palace.

[3] Grisar, *Geschichte Roms und der Päpste*, i. p. 160.

[4] Armellini, *Chiese di Roma*, p. 263.

claimed a higher dignity even than the Vatican and Ostian Basilicas, which were hallowed by the relics of the Apostles. The chapter of the Lateran still takes precedence over that of St. Peter, and every Pope, as the final act of his installation, takes solemn possession of the Lateran.

The first church would seem to have been a comparatively small and unornamented building, the most conspicuous feature of which was a picture in mosaic of our Blessed Lord, to whom the Basilica was dedicated. In the course of time the names of SS. John the Baptist and the Evangelist were added to that of our Saviour in its dedication, probably from the fact of a neighbouring monastery being dedicated to these saints. The church suffered so much injury from Genseric and his vandals that Leo the Great restored it in the fifth century, and 300 years later Hadrian I. (771-795) again repaired, with great splendour, the ravages which time had made; but an earthquake having nearly destroyed the fabric in 896,[1] it was completely rebuilt by Sergius III. on the old foundations and in the old dimensions. This new Basilica was dedicated to St. John the Baptist, and is the building which Dante saw and commemorated in the words above quoted. Unfortunately, the Sergian Basilica was almost totally destroyed by fire in 1308. The rebuilding was commenced by Clement V., and completed by his successor, John XXII.; but in 1360 it was again burnt down, and remained in utter ruin for four years. Even at an earlier period Petrarch, in a letter to the Pope at Avignon, laments over the state of desolation in which he saw it.

The church was once more rebuilt by Urban V. (1362-1370), who entrusted the work to the Sienese architect Giovanni Stefani, and during the succeeding pontificates the magnificence of the Lateran Basilica suffered no diminution.

Martin V. in the fifteenth century, and after him Eugenius IV., restored Urban's Basilica, while the latter Pope also repaired the adjacent palace. But amongst all benefactors in recent

[1] "Hujus tempore ecclesia Lateranensis ab altari usque ad portas cecidit."—*Liber Pontificalis.*

times Pope Sixtus V. deserved especially well of the Lateran. He built the still-existing north front of the Basilica, then called the loggia of Sixtus V., because from it he gave his blessing, erected the obelisk in front of the loggia, cleared the piazza,

North Front of the Basilica and Palace of the Lateran, c. 1825.

rebuilt the great palace, and transferred the *Scala Santa* to a new and more convenient site.

The eastern facade of the church[1] at that period still maintained its original type, with three arched windows such as may

[1] During the seventeenth century it would seem, from the numerous engravings of the cavalcade of the "Possesso," that the northern approach to the Basilica under the loggia of Sixtus V. was used as the principal entrance.

still be seen at S. Maria in Trastevere. It was decorated with mosaics, the centre being a figure of Christ, and below the four prophets with other figures. On the walls of the nave the principal events of both the Old and New Testaments were set forth for the instruction of the faithful. This was the common practice in earlier ages when the walls of the church were the book from which the unlettered could read and learn the sacred story. A large portico with six columns stood in front of the building, with a fountain in the centre. But although from the time of Eugenius IV. there were few Popes who did not do something towards enriching and embellishing the Basilica, the fabric in the seventeenth century was again becoming ruinous, and Innocent X. began, and Clement XII. completed, a fifth restoration, the façade, as now seen, having been erected from the designs of Alessandro Galilei in 1734.

For our actual purpose two further points of special interest may be noted in connection with this Basilica. The first is the reputed presence at the high altar of the heads of SS. Peter and Paul. If we say the reputed presence, it is not that there exists any positive reason for doubting the authenticity of these *insignes reliquiæ,* but simply to mark the fact that the evidence in this case is quite of a different order from that which attests the preservation of the bodies of the Apostles beneath the high altars of their respective Basilicas. We have no certain record of the epoch at which the heads were separated from the bodies, nor of the circumstances of their removal to the Lateran; and there is nothing to bear witness to their presence at the latter church earlier than the eleventh century.[1] None the less, it seems

[1] The account of the Lateran, which is confidently assigned by De Rossi to about the year 1075, says of the Sancta Sanctorum, "In alio vero altari ejusdem oratorii sunt capita Apostolorum Petri et Pauli."—Georgi, *Liturgia Romani Pontificis,* vol. iii. p. 546. A similar reference has been found by M. Léopold Delisle in a Paris MS. of the twelfth century. See Rohault de Fleury, *Le Latran au Moyen Age.* The Bollandists, *Analecta Bollandiana,* xi. 188, seem to regard the authenticity of these relics as somewhat doubtful. So also does Père Mortier, O.P., *St. Pierre de Rome,* p. 155. Mgr. de Waal, in his article "Die Haüpter Petri und Pauli im Lateran," in the *Römische Quartalschrift,* 1891, is more confident.

probable that our authorities[1] are justified in conjecturing that the heads were removed before the final closing of the tombs, brought about by the invasion of the Saracens in 846. One thing seems quite certain, viz., that these relics had really been known at the Lateran long before they were lost and then found again by Pope Urban V. about the year 1373. However suspicious may seem the not infrequent discoveries of such objects of which we read in medieval history, it must not be forgotten that in reality reliquaries and their contents were constantly being secreted to rescue them from thieving and profane hands, when a descent of pirates, or of hostile mercenaries, or even a popular insurrection, were anticipated. And when holy things were so hidden, and the secret was necessarily confided only to a few, probably aged, persons, it may very easily have happened that the memory of the hiding-place was lost, and that the accidental re-discovery of the treasures was hailed as a most fortunate and marvellous occurrence. Moreover, while there was every reason for keeping silence when such relics were lost, there were equally good reasons for making the fact public when such relics were happily found again, even if it were only to contradict uneasy rumours about their disappearance.

During the fifteenth and succeeding centuries the heads of the Apostles, preserved in magnificent reliquaries at the papal altar of the Lateran, were held in the highest honour.[2] A fifteenth-century pilgrim, John of Tournai, tells us in 1487 how they were then shown to the people. We may omit the greater part of the long list of relics which, like other chroniclers of the same epoch, he set out in full detail. It must be confessed that the account of many of them is not only utterly incredible, but even offensive to the pious ears of this our more refined age. But the following passage may serve as a sufficient specimen of a class of works which, in the Middle Ages, formed quite a little literature of itself:—

---

[1] Cf. Barnes, *St. Peter in Rome*, p. 387, and De Waal, *loc. cit.*

[2] Cf. Barbier de Montault, *Œuvres*, vol. i. p. 415 and 472.

"There (at the Lateran), in an old chapel, may be seen the altar at which Monseigneur St. John Baptist, when he was in the desert, performed his devotions; the table upon which our Lord Jesus Christ made the Supper with His disciples on the day of White Thursday (Maundy Thursday); the two tables of Moses, upon which is written the law of the Old Testament; the rod of the said Moses, and of Aaron. And all these things Titus and Vespasian brought from the holy city of Jerusalem, with the four hollow pillars full of the soil of the said Holy Land. There also may be seen a portion of the golden gate. Under the said four columns there is an altar upon which rest the heads of the Apostles SS. Peter and Paul. And a little before the time comes for showing them a big bell is rung, and while they are actually being shown they sound a number of little bells. And when the Bishop and those who are to expose the relics have climbed up on high, they draw up the ladder and leave it suspended in the air for as long a time as they are showing them. And in the said church there are two cruets full of the blood and water that flowed from the side of Christ," etc.[1]

It seems clear that at an earlier period the heads of the Apostles were kept not at the high altar of the Basilica, but in the neighbouring *Sancta Sanctorum* or Chapel of St. Laurence,

---

[1] *Annales Archéologiques*, vol. xxii. p. 90. On the Lateran relics, see Nicoll's edition of the *Mirabilia Romæ* (Rome, 1889); G. Rohault de Fleury, *Le Latran au Moyen Age;* Barbier de Moutault, *Œuvres*, vol. i.; Urlichs, *Codex Topographicus*, etc. As regards the bronze columns referred to above, they are believed to be those which are now at the altar of the Blessed Sacrament. Urlichs cites the following extract from Vatican MS. 1984 (*ad hist. misc. f.* 54 *in margine*)—Augustus, conqueror of all Egypt, took from the sea fight many *rostra* or ships-beaks; therewith he made four molten pillars, that were afterwards set by Domitian in the Capitol, and which we see to this day, as they were at a later time well ordered by the Emperor Constantine the Great in the Basilica of St. Saviour. (Urlichs, *Codex*, 17.) The other tradition which says that these columns were brought from Jerusalem by Titus, and that they are hollow, and filled with earth from Palestine, seems to have been the version of the story told to the Jewish traveller Benjamin of Tudela about 1170. "I heard," he tells us further, "from Jews abiding in Rome that every year, on the ninth day of the month Abib, a sweat like unto water droppeth from these pillars."

of which we shall shortly have to speak. Even in the middle of the fourteenth century, to judge from that curious versified English Guide-Book known as the *Stacions of Rome,* this would seem to have been the case. Speaking of the chapel of the *Sancta Sanctorum,* the writer says—

Of Peter and Paul the heads be there
Well y-closed under the high autere,
And other relics many one
There be closed in a stone.
Whoso is there Pope of Rome
The keys with him he hath y-nome (taken),
That no man may them there ysee
But (unless) he himself present be.[1]

The last passage points plainly enough to the fact that during the absence of the Popes in Avignon the heads of the Apostles were not to be seen in Rome, which agrees very well with the story of their loss and with the rejoicing made over their discovery when Urban V. returned to Italy.

The other object at the Lateran which seems worthy of particular notice is the mosaic in the apse behind the high altar, in the centre of which is seen a bust of our Saviour. To what extent this mosaic can be regarded as work of the fourth century is matter of considerable uncertainty. It must in any case be admitted that it has been extensively restored. None the less, this image of Christ was to an extraordinary degree famous in medieval legend. It is commemorated in the lessons of the Divine Office for the 9th November on the feast of the "Dedication of the Basilica of our Saviour" (*i.e.*, the Lateran), wherein we read that on the occasion of the consecration of the Basilica of Constantine by Pope St. Sylvester, "the image of the Saviour appeared to the people of Rome painted upon the wall."

---

[1] The *Stacions of Rome* (Vernon MS.) E.E.T.S. ll. 357-364. In this extract the spelling has been modernised. In the Cotton MS. of the *Stacions* (*Political, Relig. and Love Poems,* E.E.T.S.), the heads are represented as having been moved to the Basilica.

This is the bust which, as we have already seen in chapter ii.,[1] is shown over the doorway in the spurious Jubilee medal of Boniface VIII., and which is frequently introduced in various ways into the shields and heraldic devices connected with the confraternities attached to the Basilica. This image in the ceiling of the apse immediately over the papal throne (which throne, according to the old Basilica arrangement in the first Christian churches, always occupied the western extremity of the building),[2] was, of course, believed to be miraculous. Thus in the fourteenth-century English poem, from which we have just been quoting, we read—

> In the roof over the Pope's see (seat)
> A Salvator there may thou see
> Never y-painted with hand of man,
> As men in Rome tellen can.
> When Sylvester hallowed that place,
> It appeared there through God's grace.

But not only was the "Salvator" or bust of the Saviour, which we still see in the ceiling of the apse, regarded as an achiropiïton (ἀχειροποίητον, never painted by human hand), but it was supposed miraculously to have survived all the injury done to the Basilica by fire and earthquake.[3] And what makes more for our immediate purpose, tradition in the fifteenth century declared that it had floated into the church through the "Golden Door" or Holy Door before it affixed itself to the vault of the apse, and that in its passage it had communicated to this door that special sanctity which was recognised in the Jubilee Indulgence. A

---

[1] P. 41. This mosaic was accounted a relic, and is thus described in the first entry of that semi-official list, which Mgr. Barbier de Montault calls "la grande Pancarte":—"In tribuna a Nicolao IV. instaurata est primo imago Salvatoris, parietibus depicta, quœ visibilis apparuit Populo Romano cum S. Sylvester dedicavit ecclesiam, quœ imago nec comburi potuit nec violari, quando ecclesia ab hereticis septies combusta fuit et transivit per portam sanctam quœ est in porticu sita, per quam si quis introierit in anno Jubilei, remissionem omnium peccatorum, per Papam Clementem concessam in forma ecclesiæ consueta consequetur."—Barbier de Montault, *Œuvres*, vol. i. p. 399.

[2] We have already called attention to this arrangement in speaking of St. Peter's chair, still preserved in the apse of the Vatican Basilica; see above, p. 155.

[3] This is stated in the *Rombüchlein* and other medieval authorities.

quotation from the account of the Florentine merchant Rucellai, to which reference has already been made in an earlier chapter, will illustrate how these ideas were brought into connection—

"It is said that the image of our Lord Jesus Christ passed through this door and then affixed itself to the apse of the high altar of the said church, and on account of this devout belief every one who goes to the pardon passes through the said door, the which is walled up again immediately the Jubilee is over. It is also said that the palace of the Emperor Constantine stood in the place where is now the said church, and that in the palace there was a door which possessed this privilege, that whatever person had committed murder or robbery or done any other kind of wickedness, if he passed through that door he was free from the crime which he had done; and that in the time of St. Sylvester, Pope, it was ordained that, as up to that time an offender had been released from his temporal transgressions, so in future whoever passed through that door should be released from his spiritual ones."[1]

This, in introducing the idea of sanctuary,[1] imports a new element into the analysis of the Holy Door tradition, and it is possible that it contains a germ of truth. It is, of course, out of the question to suppose that the idea of such plenary Indulgence could date from the time of Constantine, but in later ages a remission of spiritual penalties might easily be suggested by the thought of the protection which the place of sanctuary extended to temporal offenders. In several of the medieval versions of the story, notably in that of the *Rombüchlein*, Constantine is represented as asking for a plenary Indulgence, which St. Sylvester grants. Thereupon the Pope at once feels a scruple as though he had acted with too great temerity, but a voice from heaven reassures him.

---

[1] Rucellai, in *Archivio*, vol. iv. p. 570.

[2] It is stated that the doors of the Lateran were hung with curtains to afford readier entrance for those who sought sanctuary there. All who passed the threshold were secure from pursuit, however grievous their crimes. See Clausse, *Basiliques Chrétiennes*, vol. ii. p. 332.

According to another version of the story Constantine asked that sinners might be cleansed at the Basilica of their sins, just as he himself had been cleansed of his leprosy—

> Pope Sylvester then saide he
> Of Peter and Paul and of me
> They shall be clean of sin and pine (*culpa et pœna*)
> As Christ cleansed thee of thine ;
> And as the filth fell from thee,
> So clean of sin shall they be.[1]

A curious illustration of the utter confusion and entanglement which pervades all these stories is afforded by the reference which several of the accounts make to the three doors which apparently led out of the "hall" of Constantine adjoining the Basilica, and communicated with the palace and with the chapel of the Sancta Sanctorum or St. Laurence. These doors seemingly were taken, like the Scala Santa, to be part of Pilate's palace, and it was stated that Christ had passed through one of them. Naturally, this was regarded by some as the Holy Door, conferring a plenary Indulgence, and it was hopelessly mixed up with the "Golden Door" of the Basilica itself through which the image had passed. Thus in our German *Büchlein*—

"Also they open the Golden Door at St. John's only in the year of special pardon, but at all other times the golden door is walled up. People pass through all three doors in order that they may be sure to find the right one and may not miss it, for they stand side by side, and whoever passes through he is as completely cleansed from his sins as a man who is newly baptized; that is to say, if a man do it with contrition and devotion. People may also pass through the door for the holy souls."[2]

No one could tell from this statement where the three doors were, but the other descriptions make it clear. For instance,

---

[1] The *Stacions of Rome* (Vernon MS.), ll. 277-283.

[2] "Item man thuet dy gulden phort zu sand johanns nur in dem genaden reychen jare auf; sust zu andern zeitten so ist die gulden phort vermaurt. Man geet durch die phortten alle drey dorumb dass man die recht treffe und nicht verfele, sie sten pey aynander; wer dardurch get der ist ledig von seinen sunden als ayn mensch das erst getauft ist, wer das tuet mit rew und mit andacht; man mag auch fur die selle durch die phortten geen."—*Rombüchlein*, ff. 28 v°, 29 r°.

that of the *Stacions of Rome,* after coming to an end of the account of the Basilica and its relics, continues thus—

Here may we no longer be,
Into the Pope's hall must we.
In that hall three doors there be,
Each day open, you may them see.
As often as thou passest through any of them,
And entered through another then,
And passest through another of them three
Forty year is granted to thee.[1]

But even this is not so explicit as the account of John of Tournay, who himself undoubtedly visited the places he describes, and took notes of them. He says—

"In order to quit the said church there is a door on the left hand up three or four steps, and then a hall. There is a great marble erection in it, supported on columns. It is the height of Jesus Christ, and they pass underneath it going in procession. And to leave the said hall there are three exits, and they say that our Saviour passed through one of the three. And in as much as people do not know which of the three it is, when they go in procession they pass through all three of them."[2]

Before we follow John de Tournay's example and take our leave of the Basilica, one word ought to be said of the famous fresco of Giotto, which commemorates the institution of the Jubilee. The fresco is not very conspicuous, but will be found behind the first pier of the nave along the inner aisle commencing from the door. Beside it may be read the following inscription:—

Imago iconica A. Bonifacii VIII. Pontif. Max.
Jubileum primum in annum MDCCC indicentis
Pictura Giotti æqualis eorum temporum
Quam e veteri podio in claustra inde in templum translatam
Gens Gaietana ne avitum monumentum vetustate deleretur
Anno MDCCLXXXVI cristallo obtegendam curavit.[3]

---

[1] *Stacions of Rome* (Vernon MS.), ll. 341-348.

[2] Et en issant hors de lad. salle yl y a iii issues et dict-on que Notre Seigneur passa parmy l'une des iii. Et pour ce qu'on ne seuct par laquelle des iii, en allant en procession on passe parmy touttes les iii.—Jean de Tournay, in *Annales Archéologiques,* vol. xxii. p. 91.

[3] "The representation of the august Boniface VIII., Supreme Pontiff, proclaiming the first Jubilee for the year 1300; the painting of Giotto, a contemporary

M. Rohault de Fleury declares that, in spite of this inscription, the painting does not seem to him to be as old as the time of Giotto. From the drawing of the heads he would assign it to the fifteenth century. He also thinks that the capitals of the columns are not in the style of the early fourteenth. The work has therefore probably been very extensively restored. The same critic goes on to say that the fresco, in his opinion, is only a fragment of a much larger composition which were intended to be looked at from a considerable distance, such a fresco as might, for instance, have been destined for the loggia from which the papal blessing is given.[1]

Finally, let us note that in the Church of the Lateran is said to have taken place the first meeting between St. Dominic and St. Francis of Assisi; also, that the Lateran is under the spiritual protection of France, whose kings were *ex officio* canons of the Basilica. The portico contains a statue of Henri IV., by Cordier, erected to that monarch by his fellow-canons in gratitude for the gift which he had made to them of the revenues of the Abbey of Clarac.

It seems impossible to quit the precincts of the Lateran without saying at least a word about some of those buildings connected with it, which have helped to make the name familiar to all the Christian world.

In the first place, the "Pope's Hall," to which our rhymed *Stacions of Rome* has already introduced us, is none other than the famous council chamber in which five œcumenical councils have held their sittings.[2] The first council of the Lateran was convened in 1123 under Calixtus II., the fifth, in 1512, under Julius II. and Leo X. Of these five the third and fourth, in 1179 and 1215 respectively, were really momentous assemblies, which produced a profound impression upon the Christian

---

of that age. It was removed from the ancient tribune (or portico) first to the cloister and thence to the church. The family of the Gaietani, to prevent this monument of their ancestors from perishing by age, had it covered with glass in the year 1786." The family name of Boniface VIII. was Benedict Gaietano, which explains their interest in the picture.

[1] *Le Latran au Moyen Age*, p. 406.

[2] The "Pope's Hall" is plainly seen in the sketch of the Lateran on p. 135.

society of the Middle Ages by their measures of internal reform, and by the increased definiteness which they gave to the whole system of ecclesiastical law.

The baptistery of the Lateran is detached from the Basilica, and is an octagonal building with eight porphyry columns round the interior supporting a cornice, from which rise eight smaller marble columns to sustain the dome. These columns are said to have been the gift of Constantine, who, although the legend of his baptism by St. Sylvester at the Lateran must be rejected as quite unhistorical, was nevertheless the founder of the baptistery.[1] Sixtus III. (432-440) was the first restorer, and he placed an inscription on the marble architrave, which still remains, referring to the spiritual effects of baptism. As this took place just after the Pelagian controversy, it is not too much to say that the baptistery may be regarded as a monument to the triumph of the Christian faith over Pelagianism.[2]

In the centre of the building is the font of green marble, which is at a lower level than the entrance, and to which we descend by steps. In this font or basin Cola di Rienzo bathed the night before he summoned Clement VI. and the Electors of Germany to appear before him for judgment, 1st August, 1347, and before his coronation with seven crowns in the adjacent Basilica.[3]

The Lateran baptistery served as the model of all the ancient baptisteries in Italy, and was at first the only such building in Rome, that attached to the Vatican being a later addition. According to primitive ecclesiastical custom the baptisteries were always separate from the churches, though their dependence was fully recognised. Thus the Lateran baptistery was known as St. John *ad vestes* or *ad fontem*, both names

[1] Armellini, *Chiese di Roma*, second edition, p. 99.

[2] Grisar, *Geschichte Roms und der Päpste*, vol. i. p. 200.

[3] E prima per grandezza se bagnò a Laterano nella conca del paragone ch'è nella detta chiesa, ove si bagnò Costantino, imperadore, quando santo Sylvestro papa il guari della lebbra. (G. Villani, *Chroniche*, xii. 90.) Vagnaese nella conca de lo imperatore Costantino, la quale ene de pretiossime paraone. (*Vita di Rienzi.*)

referring to the ceremony of baptism—the first to the white robes of the neophytes, and the second to the water in which they were immersed. This baptistery was always used on Easter Eve, when it was the custom, down to modern times, for Jewish converts to be baptized there by a bishop.

The portico to the baptistery of the Lateran is called the chapel of SS. Rufina and Secunda. Anastasius IV. placed an altar there over the relics of these two saints. De Rossi conjectures that here the Pope made the sign of the cross with the chrism on the foreheads of the newly baptized, or, in other words, administered the Sacrament of Confirmation, which was formerly always conferred immediately after baptism. This conjecture De Rossi founded upon the prominence of the Latin cross in the ancient mosaic decorations of the chapel, considered in the light of the words of Prudentius—

Cœtibus aut magnis Lateranas currit ad ædes
Unde sacrum referat regali chrismate signum.

Or to the Lateran fane
They throng, that each may have the sacred sign
With royal chrism marked upon his brow.

Again, although a visit to the Sancta Sanctorum has at no time been prescribed as a necessary element of the Jubilee observances, still this sanctuary is so closely identified with the Lateran that it cannot well be passed over in silence. It was formerly best known as the chapel or Basilica of St. Laurence, and it formed part of the somewhat straggling edifice which then constituted the patriarchium or patriarchal palace. Since the time of Sixtus V. the portion of the building which it occupies has been isolated, and the so-called *Scala Santa*, which formerly stood at some little distance, has been moved to serve as an approach to Rome's most famous sanctuary of relics.

These Holy Stairs, or, as they were called in the Middle Ages, the *Scale di Pilato*, consist of twenty-eight marble steps, which tradition states to have been those of Pilate's palace, and to have been ascended and descended by Christ. They are said to have been brought from Jerusalem by St. Helen, mother of

Constantine the Great, and to have been regarded with great reverence for 1500 years. As already mentioned, this staircase, upon the demolition of the old Lateran palace, was removed by Fontana, the architect of Sixtus V., to its present site in the year 1589. Clement XII. caused a casing of wood to be made for the steps, which has had to be renewed more than once, being worn out by the knees of the ascending pilgrims.

The ascent of these stairs, which is usually made by pilgrims upon their knees, has always been regarded as one of the most suitable devotions for the Holy Year. Clement VIII., old and infirm as he was, is said to have visited the Scala Santa as many as seventy times during the Jubilee of 1600, and we are told of many other Popes, amongst them Urban VIII., Innocent X., and Clement IX., that they practised this devotion with the same humility of posture as the ordinary faithful. It is perhaps even more striking to read in the diary of the master of ceremonies of so magnificent a Pontiff as Leo X. that when this Pope slept at the Lateran he used to ascend to his apartments by the "Stairs of Pilate." "I remarked," says Paris de Grassis, "the devotion of the Pontiff as he mounted these sacred steps, which are ascended by women only on their knees. He uncovered his head and kept praying all the time, and when he reached the top he used, as it were, to beg pardon of God for not having climbed up kneeling."[1]

No one who has noticed the allusions to these stairs in contemporary literature, or still more, who has examined the manuals of devotion which have been compiled for the use of those who visited them,[2] can hesitate for a moment to believe that this penitential exercise of the Scala Santa has led many a man to think more tenderly of Christ's passion, and has been for the most part a source of true piety to the faithful. It is interesting to notice how simply and unaffectedly such practices of devotion entered into the everyday life of the Italian people.

---

[1] See Mgr. Barbier de Montault, *Œuvres*, vol. i. p. 506.

[2] See, for instance, the handbooks of Mazzucconi and Severano referred to by De Montault.

THE SCALA SANTA, c. 1825.

Thus an English traveller (Fynes Moryson), who visited Rome in 1593, tells us how he had joined a large company of gentlemen, men of the world apparently, and in no way more religious than their neighbours, who were to make the journey to Naples together for protection against the banditti.

"When we went out of Rome," he says, "our consorts suddenly, in a broad street, lighted from their horses and gave them to the *vetturini* to hold, and so went themselves to the Holy Stairs, vulgarly called *le Scale Sante*, that they might there pray for a happy journey; at which time myself and my [English] consort slipped into the next church [the Lateran, no doubt], and going in at one door and out of the other escaped the worshipping of those Holy Stairs, and at fit time came and took our horses with the rest." [1]

People will probably judge very differently the evidential value of the tradition that these twenty-eight marble steps really formed part of the prætorium of Pilate. To some, the devotion of the faithful and the sanction, both formal and informal, accorded to this devotion by many Popes will be a sufficient guarantee of authenticity. Others will wish to examine the historical evidence, and will ask for fuller proof. To discuss the matter adequately would take more space than can be afforded here. We must content ourselves with pointing out that the difficulties which exist have not been ignored by Catholic writers. A good example of the spirit in which such questions are approached is afforded by the well-known antiquary, Mgr. Barbier de Montault, who has written extensively upon the devotions of Rome, and who is open to no suspicion of liberalism. He pronounces it to be "*infiniment probable*" that the *Scala Santa* was brought to Rome by St. Helen in the fourth century, and he considers that any one who denied its authenticity would be lacking in respect towards the Holy See. None the less Mgr. Barbier de Montault does not hold himself debarred from challenging the rather dubious utterances of certain Popes, from Sergius I. (687-701) to Gregory IX. (1227-1241), which are cited by Benedict XIV. in

[1] Moryson, *Itinerary*, p. 103.

favour of the *Scala Santa*. "We do not," he continues, "suspect either the honesty or the erudition of this learned Pontiff, but for full assurance in a historical thesis like this, it would be much more satisfactory to have proofs instead of bare assertions." [1]

Mgr. de Montault is equally dissatisfied with the evidence of a certain Abbot Megistus,[2] supposed to be of the ninth century, and with the appeal to two passages of the *Liber Pontificalis*,[3] which he, like the Abbé Duchesne, considers to admit of a far simpler interpretation. In fact, he goes so far as to assert[4] that no authentic mention of the *Scala* is found before 1513. This, however, somewhat overstates the case, for after about 1450 there are frequent references to the stairs of Pilate, although before that date there seems to be absolute silence on the point. The earliest definite allusion that the present writer has been able to discover is to be found in the description of Rome by Rucellai, the Florentine merchant who came, as we have seen, for the Jubilee of 1450. He tells us[5] that in the Lateran were to be found the stairs of the palace of Pilate at Jerusalem upon which Jesus Christ stood when sentence was pronounced upon Him, and he adds that for more devotion those who came to the Jubilee, and more particularly the *oltramontani*, were accustomed to mount this staircase upon their knees (*la sagliono ginochioni*). Two years later Nicholas Muffel,[6] who formed one of the suite of

---

[1] *Œuvres*, vol. i. p. 505. note. The fact that Mgr. de Montault's instincts are all conservative, and that no one will suspect him of an excess of sympathy for modern critical methods, lends additional weight to his words.

[2] Quoted by Loresino, *De Scala Sancta*, p. 25 *seq.*

[3] Ed. Duchesne, i. p. 502, l. 10, and ii. p. 91, l. 14. There is no word in either of these passages to connect the steps spoken of with Pilate or our Saviour.

[4] The article to which reference is here made was originally published in the *Analecta Juris Pontificii*, but it has since been reprinted in the first volume of Mgr. de Montault's complete works, pp. 503-530. The learned author's criticisms are summed up in the words, "L'antiquité est donc complètement muette au sujet de l'origine, du transport et de l'installation de la *Scala Santa*. Le moyen âge est, sinon aussi silencieux, au moins fort obscur à cet endroit."—Barbier de Montault, *Œuvres*, i. p. 505.

[5] *Archivio di Storia Patria*, vol. iv. p. 571.

[6] Muffel's account of his travels has been published in the *Bibliothek* of the Stuttgart Literarischer Verein, vol. cxxviii.

the Emperor Frederick III. when he journeyed to Rome for his coronation, writes a still fuller description of the Holy Stairs. He tells us that they are of greyish-white marble and twenty-eight in number, that Christ our Lord stood on these stairs when the *Ecce Homo* was spoken, and that there He swooned and fell when judgment was passed upon Him. The place, he says, is marked by a little green cross, on the eighteenth stair from the top, and there is a grating over it. Moreover, he informs us, like Rucellai, that the people from devotion ascend it on their knees (die Leut phlegen von Andacht auf den Knyen hinauf zu gehen); a thousand years' Indulgence are gained at each step, and at each a Pater Noster is said. He adds that it is a common belief that by every ascent of the Holy Stairs a soul can be released from Purgatory. It would be tedious to quote further from the evidence which from this date meets us in every traveller's note-book.[1] Let it only be mentioned that in a map of Rome,[2] considered to have been designed between 1455 and 1464, the Holy Stairs are drawn, with the words written against them, *Scala hæc per quam Xtus ad Pilatum* (the staircase by which Christ was led to Pilate), and that John of Tournay, in 1487, asserts that there was a spot where the Precious Blood had fallen, which pilgrims could touch with their fingers through some kind of lattice.[3] It seems worth while to add that the approval of the Holy See, which may be accorded from time to time to such popular devotions as that of the *Scala Santa,* does not involve any infallible pronouncement upon a question of pure history. It implies that reasonable care has been taken to exclude fraud or the probability of error; but that such care is necessarily proportioned to the canons of historical criticism prevalent at the

[1] The stairs are mentioned in the *Rombüchlein* (1475) and in the *Reliquiæ Rhomanæ Urbis* (c. 1483). They seem to be referred to in connection with the Sancta Sanctorum. "Capella vero ista sita est in sancto lateranensi palatio, itaque fit ascensus per viginti (!) gradus et quilibet homo confessus et contritus ascendens istos gradus et in quolibet gradu dicat (*sic*) unum pater noster, et nonies ascenderit, penitus est solutus a pena et a culpa." See also the *Indulgentiæ Ecclesiarum* (Rome, 1513), where a different Indulgence is mentioned.

[2] De Rossi, *Piante Iconografiche di Roma*, tab. ii. 1, and iii.

[3] *Annales Archéologiques*, xxii. p. 92. Cf. the *Rombüchlein.*

period at which the approbation was first granted. Hence it may readily be allowed that the Pontiffs of the fourteenth and fifteenth centuries were often satisfied with evidence which would be considered far from conclusive in our own more sceptical age. Similarly the facts which are recounted in the Martyrologium or the Roman Breviary are not guaranteed free from all error, because these books are formally authorised by papal Bulls. All the world knows that corrections and emendations are occasionally made in statements which the progress of historical knowledge has shown to be no longer defensible. But where the disproof of an old tradition depends only upon negative evidence, which might be reversed by new discoveries, the Holy See is naturally slow to act.

The absence of evidence for the earlier veneration of the *Scala Santa*[1] may be contrasted not unprofitably with the abundant allusions we find at all periods of the Middle Ages to the sanctuary of the *Sancta Sanctorum*, to which the *Scala Santa* now forms a pendant. This chapel was formerly best known as the chapel of St Laurence,[2] and whether it be true that it was originally the Pope's private chapel or not, it was used at an early date as a sanctuary of precious relics. The

[1] We should more particularly expect to find some mention of the *Scala Santa* in the monograph which John the Deacon devoted to the glories of the Lateran. But he, and Petrarch, and Giraldus Cambrensis, and the *Mirabilia Romæ*, as well as the *Graphia* and the *Stacions of Rome* all remain silent. Even Pedro Tafur, who came to Rome between 1435 and 1439, and his contemporary Biondo, seem to have heard nothing of these Holy Stairs. One argument in favour of the *Scala Santa*, of which I am unable to gauge the value, consists in the assertion that they are made of a veined white marble (*marmor tyricum*), unknown in Italy, but largely used in Syria. *Guide à Rome* (Bleser Royer), ed. Marucchi, i. p. 137.

[2] The name *Sancta Sanctorum* dates at least from the end of the twelfth century. Cardinal Stefaneschi, the historian of the first Jubilee, writes in his verse narrative of the *possesso* of Pope Boniface VIII. :

Sublimis Apex Laurentia templa
Ingreditur, quæ jure sibi meruere capellæ
Præcipuum nomen, cleri populique relatu,
Sancta Sanctorum ;

but the name appears in Giraldus Cambrensis' *Speculum Ecclesiæ* (p. 278) a century earlier.

earliest detailed account seems to be that incorporated by John the Deacon in his memorial to Alexander III., but dating itself from the eleventh century, and assigned confidently by De Rossi to about 1075.[1] It mentions a considerable list of relics preserved in this chapel, and amongst them the heads of the Apostles Peter and Paul; and, like all the later catalogues, it assigns special prominence to "a certain image of the Saviour marvellously represented on a certain panel of wood (tabula) which Luke the Evangelist outlined, but which the power of the Lord (virtus Domini) completed through the ministry of angels."[2] While it would certainly be rash to accept the medieval account of the miraculous origin of this famous picture, we may gladly admit that its claim to high antiquity can easily be vindicated. We have an unquestionable reference to it in the *Liber Pontificalis*, under the reign of Pope Stephen II. (A.D. 754),[3] when, amid the panic caused by the Lombard invasion, the Pontiff instituted a solemn procession to the Basilica of Sta. Maria Maggiore, taking from the chapel of St. Laurence "the image of Jesus Christ, which is called acheropsita" (ἀχειροποίητος, not made by the hand of man). Pope Stephen himself bore the picture aloft, and the clergy and people followed him with ashes sprinkled upon their heads and chanting the litanies. It is sufficiently obvious from the whole narrative that even at that period the picture must have been regarded as ancient, and there is not the least reason to question its identity with the picture still preserved in the same place.

---

[1] De Rossi, *Inscriptiones Christianæ*, ii. p. 105.

[2] Georgi, *Liturgia Romani Pontificis*, iii. p. 546. Petrarch, strange to say, when referring to the miraculous images of our Lord, mentions the *Volto Santo* at the Vatican and the mosaic in the Lateran Basilica, but not the picture in the Sancta Sanctorum—

> . . . faciemque agnoscere Christi
> Vel quæ femineo servatur condita panno
> Vel populo quæ visa olim sub vertice templi
> Emicuit, perstatque minax in honore verendo.

[3] Duchesne, vol. i. p. 443. Cf. ii. p. 110, and i. 376 and 381 (n. 44); Dobschütz, *Christusbilder*, p. 136.

This supplication gave rise to an annual procession to St. Mary Major on the 14th of August, which is thus described by a liturgical writer of the twelfth century—

"In the Assumption of St. Mary my Lord Pope, with all the Curia, doeth vespers and vigils of nine lessons in the Church of St. Mary Major. When this is done he returneth to the Lateran, and the Cardinals and Deacons, with all the people, take the Image of Jesus Christ from the Basilica of St. Laurence (the Sancta Sanctorum) carrying it through the Lateran field. . . . And when the Image is come to St. Maria Novella, they put it down before the church and wash its feet with basil. Meantime in the church the choir do matins, to wit, of three lessons. And the people standing and blessing the Lord, take the image thence and carry it to St. Hadrian, where they again wash its feet,"[1] and go to St. Mary Major's.

The image was almost entirely covered over with silver, beautifully wrought and chased, in the pontificate of Innocent III.[2] Giraldus Cambrensis, who visited Rome more than once at this epoch, has left an interesting account of the most famous Roman achiropiïta, which is in some respects unique.

"We will therefore," he says, "speak first of the two images (iconiis) of the Saviour, to wit, the Uranica and the Veronica, the one of which is at the Lateran, the other is reputed amongst the more precious relics at St. Peter's.

"Now, the Evangelist Luke was a physician, exceeding skilful in tending alike body and soul, and a wonderful painter to boot. When, therefore, after the Ascension he had made his home with the Mother of Jesus, Mary said to him, 'Luke, why dost thou not paint my Son?' And so, under her guidance, he painted first His members one by one, and then, after many erasures and corrections, he joined them all together into one image. Which, when he had shown to the Mother, she, looking

---

[1] The *Politicus* of Benedict Canonicus in Mabillon's *Ordines Rom ni*, xi. cap. 72. *Mus. Ital.*, ii. 151.

[2] Dobschütz, *Christusbilder*, p. 66. Cf. G. Rohault de Fleury, *Le Latran*, whose account Herr von Dobschütz appears not to have seen.

intently upon the image, exclaimed, 'This is my Son!' Of such images he made two or three, one of which is preserved at Rome at the Lateran, that is to say, in the Sancta Sanctorum. And when a certain Pope presumed to scrutinise it, it is told that straightway he lost the sight of his eyes, and after that it was covered all over with gold and silver, excepting only the right knee,[1] from which oil trickles unceasingly. Now, this image is called the Uranica, that is, so to speak, *essential* (Hæc autem imago dicitur Uranica quasi essentialis).[2] But there is another image preserved at Rome, which is called *Veronica*, from a matron, Veronica, who had so long desired in her prayers to see the Lord, and in the end obtained her request. For once when she was going out of the Temple she met our Lord, who said to her, 'Veronica, behold Him whom thou didst desire to see.' And when she had looked upon Him, taking her cloak, He put it to His face, and He left the impression of His

---

[1] The MS. clearly reads genu, but I cannot help conjecturing that the word written by Giraldus was genam (cheek). M. G. Rohault de Fleury, who seemingly speaks from a careful personal examination, writes—"The oval of the face, as far as the point of the beard, is painted upon coarse canvas; but upon the *right cheek*, between this canvas and the silver nimbus which surrounds it, a little gap may be noticed (*on remarque un interstice*), and, on lifting the canvas with the point of a penknife, a painting may be seen made on the panel itself. No doubt this was the original painting which has been covered by a copy on canvas. In fact, Processi states that Alexander III. or Innocent III. had the face masked in this way in order to give it a more severe expression. I should prefer to believe that the restoration was necessitated by the decay of the painting underneath."—*Le Latran*, p. 383. Giraldus wrote in the time of Innocent III. or soon after. Perhaps the chink was left designedly that pilgrims might say that they had looked upon the real picture.

[2] In the two places in which this word occurs, the late Professor Brewer, in his edition of the *Speculum Ecclesiæ*, prints it *Uronica.* The Cotton MS., Tiberius B. xiii., the only manuscript which contains the *Speculum*, reads, in the first instance, *Uranica*, in the second *Uronica.* There seems no reasonable doubt that the former is the correct reading. *Uranius* or *uranicus* was not an uncommon word in medieval Latin. Ducange quotes from a Chartres Missal—"Uranicæ patriæ civibus nos interesse concede." It comes, of course, from the Greek *οὐράνιος*, heavenly. Giraldus, in explaining the word *quasi essentialis*, was clearly, by some confusion, thinking of *usia* (*οὐσία*), as though the word had been *usianica.* To judge from Dobschütz's copious quotations, no other writer seems to know the image at the Lateran by the name *Uranica.*

countenance depicted upon it. This image also being kept in like veneration is seen by no one except through the curtains which hang before it, and this is kept at St. Peter's.

"This woman, we read, was the same woman that touched the hem of the garment of Jesus, and was healed of an issue of blood. It is recorded also that this same woman, after Christ's Passion, was compelled to come from Jerusalem to Rome and to bring with her that image which she would fain have left behind her, but as soon as she was brought into the presence of Tiberius Cæsar he was healed of an incurable disease from which he had been suffering. And some maintain, playing upon the name that Veronica is so called from *vera iconia*, that is to say, 'true image.'"[1]

The name *Uranica* given to the picture in the *Sancta Sanctorum* seems peculiar to Giraldus, and his account of Veronica also differs in some respects from the later versions of the legend.[2] It will be noticed that he says nothing about her meeting our Saviour during the Passion and offering the handkerchief to wipe his Sacred Face. On the other hand, Peter Mallius, who wrote his description of the Vatican Basilica about thirty years earlier than Giraldus, uses the word Veronica simply as the name of the chapel in which the picture was kept, and he seems to know nothing of any holy woman so called. "In the oratory," he says, "of the Blessed Virgin, the Mother of God, at St. Peter's, which is called Veronica, there is preserved the napkin of Christ, on which before His Passion He wiped His face, when His sweat became as drops of blood flowing to the ground."[3]

But to return to our chapel of the Sancta Sanctorum. It is curious that more than one of the pilgrims who visited Rome in the fifteenth century describe the famous achiropiïton as a picture

---

[1] Giraldus Cambrensis, *Speculum Ecclesiæ*, *Opera* (Rolls Series), vol. iv. pp 278, 279.

[2] Cf. Dobschütz, *Christusbilder*, p. 197 *seq.*, and Karl Pearson, *Die Fronica* Neither of these authorities has noticed this passage of Giraldus.

[3] De Rossi, *Inscriptiones Christianæ*, II., p. 218; cf. p. 212.

of our Saviour when twelve years old.[1] On the other hand, modern accounts and representations exhibit the face as bearded. Armellini tells us that as far as the point of the beard it is painted on canvas, but that the lower portion of the painting is upon panel. This peculiarity, it seems, is also observed in the so called ἀχειροποίητος preserved at Genoa, which has led to the conjecture that both are copies of a common original, derived possibly from the Abgar portrait of Edessa. It is, however, admitted on all hands that absolutely nothing can be affirmed on this subject with certainty.

While the image of our Saviour[2] was the principal object of devotion at the *Sancta Sanctorum*, there were a multitude of other relics enshrined there which were believed to add to the holiness of the spot, and of which long catalogues were written out by medieval travellers.

NON EST IN TOTO SANCTIOR ORBE LOCVS

is the rather extravagant boast which for centuries has been inscribed there in letters of gold. It was, no doubt, the profound sense of this sanctity which in a remote age enacted the rigorous law that no woman's foot should cross the threshold. Similarly the principal altar of this chapel has been reserved for the Pope alone. "It is with very great fear," writes John of Tournay, "that a Pope says mass here once in all his life, for the very great holiness there is in the chapel"; but Rucellai, somewhat earlier, informs us that Nicholas V. in 1440 had a priest to say mass there for the first time for more than a century.

It is impossible to leave the Lateran without a reference to its beautiful cloister, formerly part of the Monastery of the Regular Canons, and to the Lateran Museum, which now occupies the chief apartments of the old papal palace. Both cloisters and museum owe much to the care and generosity of the present Pontiff, Leo XIII.

---

[1] So, for instance, John of Tournay, "Et là est l'ymage de Jhus en l'eaige de xii. ans et en forme de painture, et le paindit Mons. St. Luc," *op. cit.* p. 91.

[2] Armellini, *Chiese di Roma*, second edition, p. 111.

Sta. Maria Maggiore.

Although built after the death of Constantine the Basilica of Sta. Maria Maggiore may be considered as belonging to the same group as the other three churches to be visited by the Jubilee pilgrims. It must necessarily take a place in the first rank, both on account of its size—it is one of the largest religious edifices of the Christian world; on account of its antiquity—it is not a century younger than its rivals; and also as the most important church in Rome dedicated to our Blessed Lady. It is true that this was not its primitive dedication. The church was erected by Pope Liberius (352-366), and was at first known as the Liberian Basilica. But when Sixtus III. rebuilt it in the following century he dedicated it to the Holy Mother of God, and since that time it has been most commonly called the Basilica of St. Mary.[1]

A list of the revenues and treasures belonging to the church follows the brief account of its foundation in the *Liber Pontificalis,* a list which could only have been compiled by one who possessed an accurate knowledge of the archives of the church. It is to be noted that neither here nor in later records, not even in the long dedication poem inscribed in marble by Sixtus III.,[2] do we find any mention of the well-known medieval story of the miraculous fall of snow. According to this graceful but

[1] *Liber. Pont.* Duchesne, i. p. 208. The short but authentic record runs thus—Hic (Liberius) fecit Basilicam nomini suo juxta macellum Libiæ. The notice of reconsecration under *Xystus III.*, p. 232, is equally brief and matter of fact. "Hic (Xystus) fecit Basilicam Sanctæ Mariæ, quæ ab antiquis Liberii cognominabatur, juxta macellum Libiæ, ubi et obtulit hoc." (Grisar, *Geschichte Roms*, i. p. 152.)

[2] Given by De Rossi, *Inscr. Christ.*, ii. pp. 71 and 98. The suggestion was made by the congregation appointed by Benedict XIV. in the year 1741 to reform the Breviary, that the three lessons for the 5th August, in which this wonder is recounted, should be omitted, and that the Feast S. Mariæ ad Nives should return to its old appellation, *Dedicatio Sanctæ Mariæ.* However, nothing was done. The congregation admits that Baronius speaks of "vetera manuscripta ejus ecclesiæ," which make mention of the miracle, but adds that no one has ever seen them, and that it is scarcely possible that such a thing should have been passed over in silence for more than a thousand years. (Grisar, p. 153.)

apocryphal legend, the Basilica was built by Pope Liberius and John, a Roman patrician, to commemorate a miraculous fall of snow, which covered this spot of ground and no other, in the heat of summer, on the 5th of August, when our Blessed Lady, appearing in a vision both to the Pope and to John and his wife, showed them that she had appropriated in this way the site of a new temple to be erected in her honour.[1]

It is a pity to demolish so picturesque a legend, the more so that it is still retained in the Roman Breviary for the 5th August; but as Father Grisar, quite recently, and many others before him, have pointed out, it rests upon nothing which is worthy of the name of evidence.[2] Meanwhile, in the Borghese chapel, the story, it appears, is still commemorated every year when, during high mass, showers of white rose-leaves are allowed to fall continually from the ceiling, forming "a leafy mist between priests and worshippers."

St. Mary Major was at one time believed to be the second church ever dedicated to the Blessed Virgin, that at Ephesus being the first. De Rossi held that opinion, but Father Grisar considers that there is unquestionable evidence that the church now called Sta. Maria Liberatrice, formerly S. Maria Antiqua, in Rome was the first church known to have borne such a dedication, and that it was founded by Pope Sylvester on the site of the heathen temple of Vesta in the Forum.[3]

---

[1] The flat tombstone of John is said to be in the centre of the nave. Murillo has painted two beautiful pictures inspired by this legend. One represents the apparition of the Virgin to John and his wife; in the other they tell what they have seen to Pope Liberius. (Hare, *Walks in Rome*, vol. ii. p. 74.)

[2] Grisar, *Analecta Romana*, i. Diss. 14. The legend of our Lady of the Snow is told at great length in the *Reliquiæ Rhomanæ Urbis*, c. 1483.

[3] Cf. De Rossi, *Bull. Arch. Christ*, 1892, p. 54; Grisar, *Geschichte*, i. pp. 194, 297; Duchesne in *Melanges d'Archéologie*, etc., 1897, p. 13. A lively discussion is still being carried on over this question, which it is hoped that the demolition of Sta. Maria Liberatrice will set at rest. Of this demolition Professor Lanciani writes in a recent number of the *Athenæum*—"I am personally interested in the enterprise on account of the controversy about S. Maria Antiqua, in which Professor Grisar and myself have stood, and stand, against the illustrious editor of the *Liber Pontificalis*, Louis Duchesne. We contend that the church now being demolished is the modern representative of the once famous diaconia of S. Maria

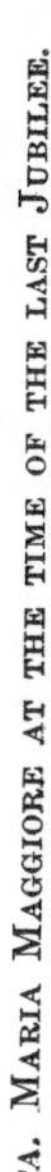

Sta. Maria Maggiore at the time of the last Jubilee.

It was just after the General Council at Ephesus which overthrew the Nestorian heresy and gave to Mary the title of *Theotokos, i.e.*, Mother of God, that Sixtus III. almost entirely rebuilt the Basilica on the Esquiline. He dedicated it to the Blessed Virgin, and adorned it with magnificent mosaics depicting the history of the Mother and the Child, making the Basilica of Sta. Maria Maggiore to be for long ages to come the most celebrated church of our Lady in the world.

Thus the series of mosaics above the great chancel arch, which terminates the majestic forest of pillars of white Parian marble in the nave, is a monument of the triumph of the faith over the heresy of Nestorius and of the honour won for Mary. As a theological record in stone and in marble it may be compared, though it is on a much grander scale, to the work of the same Pontiff, Sixtus III., in the baptistery of the Lateran, which commemorates the overthrow of Pelagianism. Over the arch is inscribed in gold letters, *Xystus Episcopus Plebi Dei* ("Bishop Xystus to the people of God") and above is seen the throne of the Lamb, as described in the Apocalypse, between the Apostles SS. Peter and Paul, and the symbols of the four evangelists. Then, on either hand are displayed representations of the Annunciation, the Massacre of the Innocents, the Presentation in the Temple, the Adoration of the Magi, etc., not forgetting the mystical cities of Jerusalem and Bethlehem, with a flock of sheep, type of the faithful, issuing from them.

It may be noticed that there is no picture of the Nativity included in the series. This omission has been accounted for [1] by

---

Antiqua, established here (in the inner hall of the Augusteum) at the end of the fourth century, and dedicated to the Virgin Mary in opposition to the worship of Vesta, the headquarters of which were on the opposite side of the street. Professor Duchesne, on the contrary, identifies the old diaconia with the present S. Maria Nuova (S. Francesca Romana), and says that the old church known to exist under S. Maria Liberatrice was dedicated to St. Antony, relying exclusively on the authority of the 'Mirabilia Urbis,' in which mention is made of an 'ecclesia S. Antoni juxta palatium Catilinæ (the Augusteum) et locum qui dicitur Infernus.' The disputed church is still in existence, although buried under thirty or forty feet of rubbish." —*The Athenæum*, Feb. 3, 1900, p. 154.

[1] See *Civiltà Cattolica*, series 16, vol. iv. pp. 473, 474 (1895).

the suggestion that in all probability the church even at that date possessed some relic or imitation of the Holy Cradle. If so, it may have been thought that the *Praesepium*, or Chapel of the Crib, near the high altar, rendered a pictorial representation of the mystery in mosaics superfluous and inadequate.

In the inner porch of the Basilica a mosaic was constructed representing the Blessed Virgin surrounded by martyrs, and it was accompanied by a metrical inscription, or rather invocation [1] beginning with the lines—

VIRGO MARIA TIBI SIXTUS NOVA TEMPLA DICAVIT
DIGNA SALUTIFERO MUNERA VENTRE TUO.[2]

Before this time, in the fourth century, St. Mary's was not unfrequently termed the *Basilica Sicinini*. Ammianus Marcellinus[3] thus names it when describing the tumult which took place in 366 between the followers of Ursinus, who had declared the election of Pope Damasus invalid, and set himself up as Pope, and those of the true Pope, Damasus. The schismatics barricaded themselves in the newly-erected Basilica, and the church had to be taken by assault like a fortified castle. A vivid if somewhat imaginary description of the struggle may be found in Mr. Crawford's recent work, *Ave Roma Immortalis*—

"The great doors are closed, and Orsino's followers gather round him as he stands at the steps of the altar; but these are few, and those for Damasus are many; down go the doors, burst inwards with battering rams, up shoot the flames to the roof, and the short, wild fray is over. Orsino and a hundred and thirty-six of his men lie dead on the pavement, the fire licks the rafters, the crowd presses outwards, and the great roof falls crashing down into wide pools of blood."[4]

---

[1] Cf. Grisar, Antichità, e significato della denominazione "*S. Maria ad Præsepe*" in *Civiltà Cattol.* 1895, iv. 470 *seq.*; and for the poem *Virgo Maria*, etc., Grisar, *Analecta Rom.*, i. 77. For illustrations of the mosaics see De Rossi, *Musaici*, sec. v., and Garrucci, *Arte Crist.*, tab. 211 *seq.*

[2] To thee, O Virgin Mary! Sixtus has dedicated this new fane, a gift not unworthy the womb that brought salvation to the world.

[3] *Hist.*, xxvii. 3, 13.

[4] *Ave Roma Immortalis*, vol. i. pp. 134-35.

De Rossi, some thirty years ago, made a discovery of considerable interest in the Vatican archives,[1] where he came upon certain authentic documents concerning this schism. Among them is the rescript of the Emperor Valentinian ordering the prefect of Rome to restore the church seized by the schismatics to the legitimate occupant of the see.[2]

In the number of tragic occurrences of which it has been the scene the record of Sta. Maria Maggiore seems to have been almost unique. Three hundred years later, in the seventh century, Pope St. Martin I. was celebrating mass in St. Mary's when a guard sent by the Exarch Olympius appeared on the threshold with orders to seize and put him to death. It is said that the soldier was stricken with blindness, a miracle which led to the conversion of Olympius and many other persons.

"Olympius, Exarch of Italy," to quote once more from Mr. Crawford, "had attempted again and again to destroy the brave bishop and make way for the impostor—an Anti-Pope. At last, says the greatest of Italian chroniclers, . . . he attempted to murder the Pope foully in hideous sacrilege. To that end he pretended penitence, and begged to be allowed to receive the Eucharist from the Pope himself at solemn high mass, secretly instructing one of his bodyguards to stab the Bishop at the very moment when he should give Olympius the consecrated bread. . . . The soldier looks, and little by little his thoughts wander, and he no longer sees Pope or altar, and is wrapt in a sort of waking sleep that is blindness. Olympius kneels at the steps within the rail, . . . he trembles, for the moment has come, and the blow must be struck then or never. . . . Not a breath, not a movement in the church, and the saint turns and ascends the altar steps once more unhurt. A miracle, says the chronicler. A miracle, says the amazed soldier, and repeats it on solemn oath. A miracle, says Olympius himself, penitent

[1] *Codex Vat.*, 4961.

[2] *Ubi redditur basilica Sicinini.* De Rossi, *Bull. d'arch crist*, 1871, pp. 20, 21.

and ready to save the Pope by all the means he has, as he was ready to save him before. But he only, and the hired assassin beside him, had known what was to be, and the people say that the Exarch and Pope were already reconciled and agreed against the Emperor."[1]

The great Basilica also witnessed another tragic scene when, on Christmas Eve, 1075, Pope St. Gregory VII., amid blows and bloodshed, was violently forced from the altar by Cencius and his fellow-conspirators,[2] but was brought back in triumph by the Roman populace and finished his interrupted mass. This church has also been called *S. Maria ad Præsepe,* from its possessing the relics of the Holy Cradle, in which it is said our Saviour was laid. In consequence of the presence of this relic the Basilica has the singular privilege of containing two papal altars—one in the grand nave, and another in the magnificent chapel *ad Præsepe,*[3] erected by Sixtus V. to receive the *Santa Culla,* which is there preserved in a reliquary six feet high, adorned with bas-reliefs and statuettes in silver. The cradle, which consists only of a few rough boards, is carried in procession through the church on the night of Christmas Eve, and is exposed

---

[1] *Ave Roma Immortalis,* vol. i. p. 138. The miracle is recorded in the Roman Breviary in the second lesson for Nov. 12, St. Martin's Feast.

[2] Armellini, *Chiese,* p. 289.

[3] The authenticity of this relic is considered by many to be sufficiently guaranteed by the antiquity of the name S. Maria ad Præsepe. The Basilica is found to bear this designation as early as the time of Pope Theodore (642-649). It has been conjectured that, in consequence of the invasion of Palestine by the Arabs, certain relics of our Lord's infancy were brought to Rome for greater security shortly before this date. See F. Liverani, *Del Nome di S. Maria ad Præsepe,* p. 67, etc. Unfortunately for this theory, the name can be shown to be older than the Arab invasion; for the record of the donations of Xanthippe, preserved in an exact copy of the ninth century, belongs itself to the sixth, and contains the designation, *Basilicæ S. Dei Genitricis quæ appellatur ad Præsepem.* In the last important monograph dealing with this subject, *Le Memorie Liberiane dell' Infanzia di N.S. Gesù Cristo,* Rome, 1894, Mgr. Cozza Luzi frankly avows that all positive evidence for the authenticity of the relics of the crib, etc., is wanting before the eleventh century. Strangely enough, an inscription in Greek uncials of the eighth century is found on one of the boards; the inscription has apparently nothing to do with the crib. It is hard to explain its presence on the supposition that the relic is authentic.

for veneration on the high altar on Christmas Day. Other relics, said to be of our Lord's infancy, are preserved in this Basilica.

In the metrical English guide-book, the *Stacions of Rome*, which we have more than once quoted, it is curious that, although the chapel of the Præsepe—"Præsepe men clepeth it"—is mentioned, nothing is said of the cradle itself, from which that name is derived. On the other hand, the minor relics are duly catalogued. They form an interesting record of the simplicity of medieval faith. Indeed, the list is moderate compared with many others that might be cited. We modernise the spelling:—

Above the stone a griddle is,
Of iron strong I wot it is;
And relics there be many a one,
In honour of our Lady and her Son.

The two relics first mentioned concern the infancy. They are the cloth that Christ was wrapped in when He was born (? the swaddling clothes), and a portion of the hay which served Him for a bed.

A little cloth there is thereto,
In which Christ's body was first in ydo,
Of His Mother when He was born
To save the world that was forlorn.
And of that hay more and lasse (less)
That Christ lay on before the ass.

The relics next mentioned have a special interest for English pilgrims, and are likely to have been quite authentic. They are still, we understand, preserved at St. Mary Major.

And an arm, men say, is there,
Of Saint Thomas, the holy martyr,
And a parte of the brain,
At Canterbury he was slain.
And a rochet that is good,
All besprinkled with his blood,
Which he had on, when he was take
For all Holy Church's sake.

The next treasure belongs to a different category. It is the supposed achiropiïtos picture of our Lady.

And an image surely,
Wonder fair, of our Lady,
Saint Luke, while he lived on land,
Would have painted it with his hand.
And when he had ordained so,
All colours that should thereto,
He found an image all apert (open to view),
None such there was middelert (on the earth below),
Made with angels' hands and not with his,
As men in Rome witnesseth this.
And written it is all there
On a table at the high altere.

The guide-book then goes on to catalogue the Indulgences, in which it would be tedious to follow it further. Perhaps, however, it will be remembered how from an early date the miraculous image of Christ in the Sancta Sanctorum, which Geraldus calls the *Uranica*, was brought in procession to St. Mary Major on the eve of the Assumption. The Assumption was naturally the great feast of that Basilica.

On our Lady's Assumption
Then is there great pardon,
Unto the day that she was born (her heavenly birthday),
Never a day shall be forlorn.
In that time, there is fourteen thousand year
To all that come to that minster.

As the Lateran Basilica has been taken under the special protection of the kings of France, and that of St. Paul's is said to have owned the English monarchs for its patrons, so the church of St. Mary Major was identified for centuries with his most Catholic Majesty of Spain. One visible sign of this connection with the Spanish throne may still be seen in the richly-panelled and ornamented roof. It is gilded, we are told, with the first gold brought from America and presented to Pope Alexander VI. by Ferdinand and Isabella.

We are not pretending to write a complete archæological description of the Basilicas (each of which would require a volume), but simply to give just so much of an outline of the history and features peculiar to each church as will afford our readers some slight knowledge of, and interest in, these great monuments of antiquity to which the visits of the Holy Year are paid. It is unnecessary therefore to attempt any description of the various restorations, embellishments (or the reverse) which St. Mary's and the other Basilicas have undergone at various periods of their history. In spite of many alterations, St. Mary Major is considered by some to be in many respects internally the most beautiful and harmonious building in Rome, and it still retains much of the character which it had in the fifth century. Before passing to another subject, however, a few words may be said about the fifth church, Sta. Maria in Trastevere, which, it may be remembered, was substituted for St. Paul on three occasions, when accidental circumstances rendered visits to the latter Basilica hazardous or impossible.[1]

Sta. Maria Trastevere.

This church has been regarded by some authorities as the most venerable of all the Christian buildings in Rome. To say that it was one of the twenty-five "titles" known to exist in the fourth century, in their view would be to say little. Its history extends very much further back than the time of Constantine. The historian Lampridius relates that during the pontificate of Callistus I. the Christians were in possession of a place of assembly in Trastevere, their right to which was, however, disputed by the corporation of the *popinarii* or tavern-keepers. The question was brought before the Emperor Alexander Severus, who decided in favour of the Christians, saying that it was better that God should be worshipped there, in whatever fashion it might be, than that the place should be given over to revelry.[2] No doubt some sort of

[1] In the Jubilees of Urban VIII., Clement XI., and Leo XII.

[2] *Quum Christiani quemdam locum qui publicus fuerat occupassent, contra popinarii dicerent sibi eum deberi, rescripsit melius esse ut quomodocumque illic deus colatur quam popinariis dedatur.*—Lamprid., *Alex. Severus*, 45.

oratory was erected, but not a church in the modern acceptation of the term, and the later compiler of the life of Callistus in the *Liber Pontificalis* was certainly in error when he said that that Pope built a church on that spot, and dedicated it to the Blessed Virgin. The churches in those days were little more than private houses set apart for worship, and the earliest dedications made to saints began with the fourth century, and were at first confined to the buildings erected over their tombs. Be that as it may, the absence of documents renders it impossible to distinguish truth from falsehood in regard to the supposed origin of this Basilica before the time of Constantine. It may be taken for granted that fable is legend mingled with history, and this is the best that can be said of the story of the fountain of oil, or rather naphtha, which is supposed to have sprung up in this place shortly before the birth of Christ, in the year of the city 753.[1] Eusebius was the first to relate the story, which was also recounted by Eutropius, Isorius, and other historians of that period. Possibly there may have been some foundation for the legend in a natural oil spring which burst forth here; but, if so, the fact, no doubt, was transformed and embellished in popular tradition.

The actual history of the church dates from 340, when Julius I.[2] rebuilt it from the foundations, and transformed the primitive guest house or title of the Christians of Trastevere into a Basilica constructed after the architectural style of the fourth century. This Basilica was known as the *Titulus Julii*,

---

[1] In the earlier recension of the *Stacions of Rome* (Vernon MS.) the story appears in this concise form—"At Seinte Marie, in Trismere, that ilke niht that Crist was boren, most of miht, sprong oyle of a welle." The legend of Sta. Maria Maggiore and that of Sta. Maria Trastevere are touched upon by Petrarch almost in the same breath—

> Condita quin etiam supremo mœnia monte
> Æstivæ nivis indicio, delubraque partu
> Obruta virgineo et fontes torrentis olivi
> Ac Tibridis commixta undis nova flumina cernes.

These lines occur in the poet's verse epistle to Clement VI. commemorating the glories of Rome, and inviting the Pontiff to shorten the interval of the Jubilee. See above p. 55.

[2] Grisar, *Geschichte*, i. p. 150, considers Julius to be the *founder* of the church.

and is described in the *Liber Pontificalis* as "Basilica Julia juxta Callistum." It is said that Pope Callistus, whose tomb was in the neighbouring Via Aurelia, was martyred in the vicinity, and this tradition receives confirmation from the fact that an inscription discovered on the collar of a fugitive slave of the period of Constantine shows that at that time this region was known as the *Area Callixti*. It appears uncertain when the Basilica received its present dedication to our Lady.

John VII., in the eighth century, was the first Pope who restored the Julian Basilica and adorned its walls with frescos. His example was followed by Popes Gregory II. and III. Adrian I. enlarged the church by adding two aisles. Gregory IV., in 828, built a monastery near, and raised the level of the "tribuna" or apse, under which, in a "confession," he placed the bodies of SS. Callistus and Calepodius. During some recent excavations the remains of a marble balustrade were found with which the same Pope had enclosed a choir or *schola cantorum*. The church has been repeatedly restored in more or less good taste, according to the epoch, but, nevertheless, it retains much of its primitive form. It is believed that the twenty-four red granite pillars, dividing the nave from the aisles, once belonged to a temple of Isis, since the volutes of the columns were decorated with heads of Isis and Serapis. These remarkable symbols were broken and destroyed during the restorations executed in the nave of the Basilica in 1870. The high altar is of the time of Innocent II., and underneath it is the confession, with the tombs of the martyrs. Near it is the spot—marked by the words, *Fons Olei*—where, according to legend, the oil gushed forth. To the right of the altar is a chapel built from designs by Domenichino, in which is venerated a picture of our Lady, taken from a street in Trastevere called the *Strada Cupa*, and removed to the church in the sixteenth century.[1] The Cardinal of York, the grandson of James II., who was Titular Cardinal of this church, completed the decoration of this chapel.[2]

[1] Armellini, *Chiese*, p. 644.

[2] Moroni, vol. xii. p. 108.

Different Roman Pontiffs, as was mentioned above, have substituted this church for that of St. Paul without the walls, both for the visits to the Seven Churches and for gaining the Jubilee Indulgence, when pestilence or inundations of the Tiber have rendered the latter Basilica difficult of access. At the last Jubilee, in 1825, when St. Paul's was in ruins, after the conflagration of 1823, Leo XII. appointed Cardinal Pacca, Sub-Dean of the Sacred College, to open the Holy Gate of Sta. Maria Trastevere. But by the Pope's desire the Holy Gate at St. Paul's, which had not been destroyed by the fire, was opened and afterwards built up again by the Father Abbot of St. Paul's as Sub-Legate of Cardinal Pacca. A special medal, reproduced on p. 169, was struck for the occasion, representing the Basilica in ruins, which medal was placed in the Holy Door of St. Paul's at its closing, and will there have been found, presumably, at the opening of the Jubilee of 1900.

Although the usual ceremonies were gone through at Sta. Maria Trastevere the door was not walled up, but closed with the ordinary wooden door, on which were placed two metal crosses. During extraordinary Jubilees also Sta. Maria in Trastevere has sometimes been designated as one of the churches to be visited, and on such occasions the Popes have gone there in solemn procession.

APPENDIX TO CHAPTER V

THE Roman Jubilees have produced quite a literature of their own, and besides the more learned treatises, mainly historical or theological in character, of which a bibliography may be found in Zaccaria or Manni, the *Anni Santi* of more recent times have usually been marked by the appearance of a shoal of ephemeral booklets intended to stimulate the devotion or instruct the inexperience of the pilgrims. In the seventeenth century such aids often took the form also of single sheets in which we find a plan of the city, with the route carefully marked, by which the visits to the churches may most conveniently be paid. Several such may be found bound up with plans and other prints in the library of the British Museum. One curious little booklet which was printed in 1675 seems of sufficient interest to be translated here. It is the record of a careful measurement of the distance which had to be traversed each day in making the round of the four Basilicas. The writer is one Carlo Padredio, who was assisted in his measurements by several other gentlemen, who all sign their names. It appears from their careful survey that the whole distance was more than eleven miles.

"*First Mile.*—On the evening of Monday, the 8th July of this year (1675), I and my companions met on the steps of St. Peter's, and taking with me a chain, such as is used in measuring distances, and which repeated 116 times equals a mile in length, we commenced our operations beneath the façade of the said Basilica, pursuing the way by the piazza of the same towards the Church of S. Michael, or rather oratory of the Confraternity of the Blessed Sacrament of St. Peter's, and continuing by the Borgo S. Spirito, and turning down the road which leads by the side of the Church of S. Spirito to the Via della Longara, we completed the first mile in this road at the carriage gate of granite of the Chigi (*i.e.*, the Farnesina) Palace, where is the famous *loggia* painted by Raphael Sancio di Urbino.

"*Second Mile.*—Pursuing our way and our measuring, having passed the Porta Settimana and keeping on by the direct road to the Madonna della Scala, and thence to Sta. Maria in Trastevere, we turned to the right by the way which leads to the Ponti de' Quattro Capi;[1] having passed these, and also the Sabelli Palace, we finished the second mile in front of the little side door of San Nicola in Carcere.

"*Third Mile.*—Continuing our way, and turning down the street which leads to the Piazza Montanara, we passed in front of the façade of San Nicola, following the road behind S. Giov. Decollato, and thence proceeding to Sta. Maria in Cosmedin, called the Scola Greca, to Sta. Anna (Dei Calzettari) on the Via Salaria, and by the ruins upon the Aventine. We completed the third mile under the shoulder of this hill at the first house, where there is a carriage gate with stone ornaments, where the trees join the road on the right-hand side.

"*Fourth Mile.*—Continuing our route under the trees, we left Rome by the principal road through S. Paul's gate, and ended the fourth mile at the end of the wall of the vineyard which belongs to the convent of St. Frances of Rome, called Tor de' Specchi, that is, two chain lengths beyond the end of the wall of the said vineyard, which is on the right-hand side going to St. Paul's Church.

"*Fifth Mile.*—Continuing on the same road, and then turning to the right to enter by the Holy Gate, thus measuring the length of the Basilica of St. Paul, we left it, and returning by the same road, finished the fifth mile at the door of the mill, which is on the right-hand side going towards Rome.

"*Sixth Mile.*—Then going on by the same road, and having entered Rome, taking the carriage route towards St. Gregory's,

[1] There were two bridges at this point, where the river is divided by an island in the centre.

we completed the sixth mile where the wall ends on the right-hand side, before reaching the railings of the cave of tufa and the tavolozze di Benedetto Sanctorum.

"*Seventh Mile.*—Proceeding to measure the seventh mile, and having passed the *maranœ* and crossed the Appian Way, we turned into the road leading to the Arch of Constantine, and having turned into the piazza in front of S. Gregory's, going under the arches which support and abut the church of SS. John and Paul, we pursued our route towards S. Thomas *in formis*, under the Claudian aqueduct, leaving S. Maria in Dominica, commonly called *La Navicella*, on one side, and having passed St. Stephen Rotondo by the road, where the aqueducts are, we finished the seventh mile before the railings of the vineyard of the Signori Fonsechi, where there are some large fir trees.

"*Eighth Mile.*—Following the same road, and having passed the Church of St. Andrea, belonging to the Hospital of the Lateran, leaving on one side the said Hospital in the Piazza of the Lateran, after passing the Pontifical Palace, we reached the Holy Gate of the Basilica of St. John Lateran, and having gone through the church, we came out by the door under the organ. We then directed our steps by the straight road towards St. Mary Major, and having passed the Church of St. Matthew in Merulana, we completed the eighth mile, four chains lower down, where are two little spiral columns attached on one side to the walls.

"*Ninth Mile.*—Still going on, and measuring, we arrived at the Piazza of S. Mary Major, and having entered by the Holy Gate, and taken the length of the church, we descended by the new flight of steps to the front of S. Lorenzo in Pane e Perna, and having passed the road called dei Serpenti, ascending towards the Church and Monastery of SS. Dominic and Sixtus, we ended our ninth mile at the extremity of the apse of the said church.

"*Tenth Mile.*—Continuing by the same road towards Trajan's Column, and under the archway of the Palace of St. Mark, we passed in front of the façade and piazza of St. Mark, and reached the Triumphal Way by the palace of the Astalli, skirting the

Professed House, and passing in front of the Church of the Gesù, leaving the Altieri Palace on the right. We then came to the Cesarini Palace, and turned down by that of the Signori Roberti, passing by the mansion of the Signori Della Valle, and leaving the Church of S. Andrea, also called Della Valle, on our left, thus reached '*Pasquino*,' and finished the tenth mile at the corner of the palace of the Signori Mignanelli, where at present stands the posting house for Milan.

"*Eleventh Mile.*—Following on our course by the Via di Parione, we passed in front of the palace of Monsignor the Governor of Rome, and pursuing the road from the Piazza de Monte Giordano towards the Banchi, we passed the bridge of the Castle S. Angelo, and going straight towards St. Peter's by the Borgo Nuovo, we completed the eleventh mile at the end of the railings of the palace of the Signori Accoramboni, just where it joins the shop of Signor Dominico Rosso, the barber.

"From this spot, where the eleventh mile ended, to the place whence we set out, at the façade of St. Peter's, was a distance of sixteen chains; and from thence to the centre altar, where are the bodies of the Holy Apostles, and back again to the façade, we measured twenty-two chains more, which, added to the sixteen just mentioned, amount to thirty-eight chains, or nearly a third of a mile.

"And this is a correct account of the expedition made by us, the undersigned, and the exact distance measured was eleven miles and one-third of a mile." (Then follow the names.)

CHAPTER VI

The Ceremonies of the Jubilee

In the still unpublished diary[1] of Francesco Mucanzio, papal master of ceremonies at the close of the sixteenth century, we find that distinguished rubrician in December, 1574, discussing at some length the ritual to be used in the unwalling of the Holy Door at the forthcoming celebration of the Jubilee.

He tells us that as the time for the ceremony drew near he went to his Holiness Pope Gregory XIII. and submitted to him a memorandum concerning the preparations to be made, and the things to be then observed. It appears, however, that his colleague in the office of master of ceremonies also went to the Pope with a similar programme, which he declared to be that which had been followed by Julius III. in the year 1550. "It differed very little from mine," says Mucanzio, "except in the versicles and responses. Those which I had set down were taken from an ancient roll (*a quodam rotulo antiquo*) used in the time of Clement VII., and of these versicles there was probably no accurate copy forthcoming in 1550 on account of the pillage and disasters to which the city had been subjected [he refers presumably to the sack of Rome in 1527]; hence they had been somewhat altered. My opinion was that out of the two sets which we had before us, a third more appropriate than either might have been drawn up, but when the matter was proposed in the Congregation of Cardinals appointed for the revision of ceremonies, they decided that as regards the versicles

[1] The copy here quoted is contained in MS. Addit. 26811 at the British Museum.

and prayers the precedent of Julius III.'s time should be adhered to in every particular. The fact is," adds Mucanzio, "we have nothing prescribed about this matter in the Book of Ceremonies,[1] and on this account I think that in printing the new *Ceremoniale* care should be taken that the ritual for opening the Holy Door be included in it."

Mucanzio's suggestion has, in one sense, never been carried out. Catalani, who revised and annotated the *Ceremoniale Romanum* in an edition dedicated to Benedict XIV. in 1750, does not include in his two stout folios any mention of the office for the opening of the Holy Door. Nevertheless, the rite now followed differs in hardly any respect from that which was agreed upon in the time of Julius III., and, indeed, to any one but a master of ceremonies the variations from the form originally devised by Burchard, and modified by Alexander VI., would appear matter of little moment. Mucanzio is at pains to copy out not only the ritual prescribed in his "ancient roll" of Clement VII., but also that of Julius III., and to these he appends a third form composed by a private friend of his, one Curzio Franco, Canon of St. Peter's. We cannot help regretting that this last was never examined by the Congregation of Sacred Ceremonies, for it certainly seems in many ways more appropriate and more full of apt symbolism than that actually in use.

Although the extracts previously quoted from Rucellai and other fifteenth century writers[2] prove incontestably that the ceremony of the building up and unwalling of the Holy Door is older than the time of Alexander VI., there is no reason to distrust Burchard's statement that he, as just mentioned, drew up the service which Alexander, with a few modifications, sanctioned and adopted for use. In any case, the account given

[1] The *Ceremoniale Romanum;* not to be confounded with the *Ceremoniale Episcoporum.* The former, which is concerned only with the ceremonies of the Papal Court, was the work of Agostino Patrizi Piccolomini, and was compiled in 1488. The latter, which deals with the ceremonial of all episcopal functions, is a work of much later date, and was printed for the first time in the year 1600.

[2] See above, chap. ii. p. 39.

by Burchard in his *Diario* appears to be the earliest description which we possess of the details of any such ceremony. It will be interesting, therefore, to have it before us in order to compare it with the observances of later times.

"On Wednesday, the 24th of December," says Burchard, "being Christmas Eve, before our most Holy Lord (the Pope) came down to the Basilica of St. Peter to sing Vespers, the marble doorway, with its ornaments, was all arranged in the spot where the 'Golden Door' was said to exist, the same marble framework being wider by two palms than the recess which had been supposed to be a door, but agreeing with it in height. The wall had had part of its thickness removed on the inner side, though not sufficiently, as far as the portion covered by the new marble door-posts placed on either hand. Moreover, near the centre, at the height of six palms from the ground, it had been completely perforated for the breadth of one palm, and had then been filled up again with loose bricks, without mortar, so that our Lord the Pope might strike his blows in that spot when he came to open it. Thereupon, on the Vigil of the Nativity, about the twentieth hour (*i.e.*, about two p.m.) before celebrating the Solemn Vespers of the Feast in the Vatican Basilica, the Pope, vested in cope and wearing the Tiara, holding a gilded candle lighted in nis hand, and accompanied by cardinals, bishops, and other prelates, each of whom carried lighted candles, and also by the clergy, both regular and secular, of the city, was carried in the *sedia gestatoria* in solemn procession to the portico of the Basilica.

"Having reached the door to be opened under the portico of St. Peter's, the choir commenced singing certain versicles proper to the occasion, and the Pontiff then said the following prayer:—

"Let us pray. O God, who through Moses, Thy servant, didst ordain for the people of Israel a fiftieth year of remission and Jubilee, graciously grant to us Thy servants that we may happily begin this hundredth year of Jubilee instituted by Thy authority, so that obtaining therein the pardon of a true indulgence and remission of all our sins, when the day of Thy summons

A SOLEMN FUNCTION IN THE SISTINE CHAPEL.
A sermon is being preached during High Mass in the presence of the Pope.
From an engraving, c. 1575, in the British Museum.

shall arrive, we may enjoy glory unspeakable and happiness without end. Through Christ our Lord. Amen.

"The Holy Father then proceeded on foot to the door which was to be opened, and having received from the hands of Master Thomas Mataracci, the master mason and foreman of the fabric, a hammer such as is commonly used by masons, he struck three or more blows upon the opening which had been made in the middle of the door, causing the loose bricks which filled it to fall to the ground. The Pope then returned to his seat, while the workmen proceeded to demolish the masonry on either side as far as had been indicated. This took about half an hour, our choir meanwhile singing antiphons and repeating them without intermission. The opening having been cleared, our Holy Father, descending from his seat, advanced to the door on foot, and upon reaching the threshold knelt down and prayed with uncovered head for the space of half a *miserere*, still keeping his lighted candle in his left hand. He then rose, and while I (Burchard) supported him on his left side by his arm and by the hand which held the candle, the Pope entered through the said door of the Basilica, myself with him; and a little bit in front of him, Master Bernard, my colleague, also along with us supporting the Pope on the right. Then closely following him came his cross with the sub-deacons, cardinals, and prelates in a great crush, in which order we all proceeded to the high altar of the Basilica."[1]

A few additions were made to this ceremonial by Clement VII. In the first place, this Pope decreed that the Blessed Sacrament should be exposed in the Sixtine Chapel, whence the procession started; and, secondly, the hammer made use of by the Pontiff in striking the Holy Gate was to be of silver gilt. Also when entering the door, while still holding the candle in the left hand, as did Alexander VI., Clement bore a long handled cross in his right. From an account of the ceremonies with which the Holy Gate was opened at a later date by Clement VIII. (in 1600), left to us in the diary of Paolo

[1] Burchard, *Diarium* (ed. Thuasne), vol. ii. p. 599.

Alaleona, a canon of the Vatican, and at that time master of the papal ceremonies, we also learn that as soon as the gate was opened, guns were immediately fired by the Swiss Guard in the Piazza of St. Peter's as well as from the Castle of St. Angelo. All these modifications are still retained in the ceremonial used for the opening of the Holy Door, and it may be interesting to set down here an account of the whole procedure, which was printed in English as far back as the year 1699. Although this translation of the Latin original cannot be commended for its elegance, it gives a substantially accurate description of what is still done, and it will be sufficient to interpolate here and there a few supplementary notes. The reader may feel an interest in remembering that this was the guide to the Jubilee which was in the hands of the fashionable young dandies of 1700 when Farquhar, as already described, produced his comedy of a *Trip to the Jubilee,* and when Protestant England devoted such an unusual amount of attention to the ceremonies of the Roman Court. The broadside from which it is taken is headed—

"A true and exact account of all the Ceremonies observed by the Church of Rome at the Opening, during the Progress, and at the Conclusion of the next approaching Jubilee in the year 1700. Taken and translated into English from the Latin Original, printed at Rome by Order from the Pope."[1]

We have already had occasion to quote the description given in this pamphlet of the promulgation of the Jubilee on the Ascension Day of the preceding year, and these introductory paragraphs may consequently be omitted.

"The solemnity of the jubilee itself," so the writer informs us, "begins upon Christmas Eve, just before the Vespers, by a ceremony which deserves particularly to be taken notice of,

---

[1] The whole of what is here given and more besides is printed on one side of a large single sheet almost the size of the *Daily Mail* newspaper. It is subscribed, "London, printed by D. Edwards in Fetter Lane 1699, Price twopence." A copy is in the British Museum. This broadside was reprinted in London in pamphlet form for the Jubilee of 1750. Since then it has been included also in Scott's edition of *Somers' Tracts,* vol. ix., 1813.

which is the opening of the Holy Gate. For the better understanding of which, it is to be known that this Holy Gate is one of the gates of St. Peter's Church in the Vatican, which is always shut, nay, even bricked up during the interval betwixt the jubilees, which always begin by the opening of this gate.

"On the 24th day, therefore, of December, which is the eve of the Nativity of Christ, all the gates of these four churches where there are any Holy Gates are shut up by his Holiness's order, so that nobody can pass through till such time as they are opened with the accustomed ceremonies.

"After dinner, about the time of the Vespers of this great eve, a most solemn procession is made, at which assist the ambassadors of foreign princes then residing in Rome, the magistrates of the city, all the penitentiaries and prelates abiding at Rome; all the chapters, fraternities, the Roman clergy, the College of Cardinals, and the Sovereign Pontiff in person, each according to his rank and quality.

"Thus they go in succession with a great cross before them to the chapel of the apostolic palace (*i.e.*, the Sistine), where the whole company being entered, the Holy Father, with all there present, fall upon their knees before the Sacrament; in the meantime that many officers are employed in lighting flambeaux for the cardinals to hold as a sign of joy. Then the Pope throws some incense upon a chafing-dish,[1] with a most profound reverence, before the altar; after which he begins the hymn *Veni Creator Spiritus*, which is continued to the end by a concert of music, and sung distinctly, to represent the holy fathers in

[1] The edition of 1699 and 1750 spell "chaving dish." To Catholic ears this translation will sound quaint enough, but a still more curious English rendering of the rite of thurification is to be met with in a brief account of the opening of the Jubilee of 1600, which was published in London in that year (not in 1660 as erroneously stated in the Museum Catalogue), by John Wolfe. "This done," we are there told, "our Holy Father, being still on his knees, poured incense upon the Holy Sacrament, after which they began to sing Veni Creator Spiritus." It would seem from such passages as these that the use of incense cannot have been very familiar to English churchmen in the seventeenth century.

Limbo (!)[1] From thence this procession goes on in the same order as before to St. Peter's Church, being followed by the Holy Father in person, who is carried in a chair to the Holy Gate, which, as well as all the rest, is kept close shut up. Everybody having taken his place, the Holy Father gets out of his chair, and with a lighted wax-taper in his hand walks up three steps to another chair, placed for that purpose just by the Holy Gate. After he has reposed a little he rises, and, turning himself towards the Holy Gate, he knocks with a silver hammer on the Holy Gate which is to be opened, and sings likewise three several times the following verses, unto which the musicians who compose the chorus answer at each time:—

V. Aperite mihi portas justitiæ.	*V.* Open unto me the gates of justice.
R. Ingressus in eas confitebor Domino.	*R.* When I am entered I will praise the Lord.
V. Introibo in Domum tuam Domine.	*V.* I will enter, O Lord, into Thy house.
R. Adorabo ad templum sanctum tuum, in timore tuo.	*R.* I will adore Thee in Thy fear in Thy temple.
V. Aperite portas quoniam nobiscum Deus.	*V.* Open the gates, because the Lord is with us.
R. Quia fecit virtutem in Israel.	*R.* Because He has made known His strength in Israel.

"Then the Pope sits down in the chair again and says—

V. Domine exaudi orationem meam.	*V.* O Lord, hear my prayer.
R. Et clamor meus ad te veniat.	*R.* Let my cry reach Thy ears, O Lord.

"At the same instant the Pope goes from the Holy Gate towards his chair, the masons begin to demolish the wall wherewith the Holy Gate had been bricked up, and as they are carrying off the materials the Pope goes on thus—

V. Dominus vobiscum.	*V.* The Lord be with you.
R. Et cum spiritu tuo.	*R.* And with thy spirit.

"OREMUS. *Actiones nostras quæsumus Domine,* etc.

---

[1] Our author's meaning in this passage is not very clear. Ricci (*Giubilei Universali,* p. 10) says that the versicle *Aperite mihi portas justitiæ* was said by the Pope in imitation of Christ, who, when entering Limbo to liberate the holy patriarchs, said *Attollite portas principes vestras.*

"Prevent, we beseech Thee, O Lord, our actions by Thy holy inspirations, and carry them on by Thy gracious assistance, that every prayer and work of ours may begin always from Thee and by Thee be happily ended. Through Christ our Lord. Amen.

"This prayer being done, the chorus sings the psalm *Jubilate Deo omnis terra, servite Domino in lœtitia*, etc., during which time the people crowd up as near as they can to the rails, and the penitentiaries, in their sacerdotal vestments, wash the head-piece, posts, and the threshold, and, in short, the Holy Gate, with holy water; which being done, the Pope, as he is approaching to enter the Holy Gate, says the following verses, and is answered by the chorus:—

V. Hœc dies quam fecit Dominus.	*V.* This is the day the Lord hath made.
R. Exultemus et lœtemur in ea.	*R.* Let us rejoice in it.
V. Beatus populus tuus Domine.	*V.* Happy is Thy people, O Lord.
R. Qui facit jubilationem.	*R.* Which enjoys this Jubilee.
V. Hœc est porta Domini.	*V.* This is the gate of the Lord.
R. Justi intrabunt per eam.	*R.* The righteous are to enter it.
V. Domine exandi orationem meam.	*V.* O Lord, hear my prayer.
R. Et clamor meus ad te veniat.	*R.* And let my crying come to Thee.
V. Dominus vobiscum.	*V.* The Lord be with you.
R. Et cum spiritu tuo.	*R.* And with thy spirit.

"Let us pray.

"O Lord, who by Thy servant Moses didst institute among the children of Israel the jubilee and year of remission, grant through Thy goodness to us, who have the honour to be called Thy servants, to commence happily this present jubilee, ordained by Thy authority; and in which it has been Thy will to set open to Thy people in a most solemn manner this gate through which to enter into Thy temple, to offer their prayers in the presence of Thy Divine Majesty; that thereby having obtained plenary and absolute remission of all our sins, we may, at the day of our departure out of this world, be conducted through Thy mercy to the enjoyment of the heavenly glory, through Jesus Christ. Amen.

"This prayer being ended, a cross is given into the Pope's hand, who, kneeling down in the Holy Gate, sings the *Te Deum*

Laudamus, etc., and afterwards, as he is entering through the gate, the chorus go on singing *Te Dominum*. He is no sooner entered through the gate into the body of the church but the chairmen, clothed in red, attending for that purpose, take him up in a chair and carry him straightways to the great altar of the Church of St. Peter, where, being set down, he arises out of the chair, and after some time spent in prayers before the Holy Sacrament he mounts to a throne, erected on purpose for this use, and begins the Vespers, which, according to custom, are sung for the Feast of the Nativity of our Saviour."

To interrupt here for a while the description of our narrator, it may be noted that even before the day of the function itself the master of ceremonies had a good deal to think about. Stands for distinguished visitors and for the more favoured of the nobility and clergy had to be erected in the portico; directions had to be given for the ringing of the bells in all the churches of the city on the three previous days at the same hour as that appointed for the opening; provision had to be made for keeping off the crowd and for maintaining order; holy water had to be blessed the day before,[1] and to be made ready in the portico, where it would be wanted by the penitentiaries in washing the door jambs; instructions had to be given to the cardinal legates who were to open the Holy Doors at the other three Basilicas; notifications of all kinds had to be served to the clergy of Rome whose presence was required at the ceremony; above all, the *Ceremoniarius* had to arrange with the masons and to make sure that the door would collapse, without too much noise and dust, at the proper moment. Obviously this could not be ensured without taking the masonry practically to pieces, and with this necessity the practice was introduced at a very early date of removing beforehand the receptacle full of medals, which was always buried by the Holy Father himself at the base of the wall when the Holy Door was bricked up at the end of the year of

[1] See the *Ragguaglio delle solenne Funzione e Ceremonie usate nell' apertura della Porta Santa, 1775.* This duty, however, primarily concerned the Monsignore Sagrista.

Jubilee. It seems an amiable weakness of the Italian character that such little perquisites should be coveted with an almost incredible keenness. Mucanzio has left us a lively description of the anxiety shown to obtain a share in the spoils even as early as the Jubilee of 1575.

Two days before Christmas, he tells us, when the brickwork of the walled-up door had to be loosened, there was great competition among the master masons as to who should be selected for the work, which was finally entrusted to the foreman of the San Pietrini, and to the chief mason of the papal palace. "Both were eager for the task, calculating that they would be able to carry off a prize of value in the shape of gold or silver medals from the demolition of the door. But in this expectation they were disappointed, for very few silver medals were found, in fact, only eleven in all, each of the weight of two crowns (*scudi*) or thereabouts, and the rest all bronze medals, few in number and small in size. Of these nearly all the silver medals came into the possession of the *Camerieri Segreti* of his Holiness, who had posted their servants there on the look-out on purpose to secure them. And I, who had been watching on the spot pretty well the whole night, that I might obtain some few for devotion's sake and for a souvenir, secured with the greatest difficulty a solitary medal of silver, which I afterwards gave to the illustrious Cardinal de Medicis, and a few other bronze ones which I divided with my colleague Louis."[1]

In the earlier days of the ceremony it would seem that the blows delivered upon the surface of the *Porta Santa* were not so entirely a formality as they afterwards became. Mucanzio records with zest how Gregory XIII. took the silver hammer with both hands from the Grand Penitentiary, and dealt the wall a vigorous blow[2] (*percutiendo viriliter ambabus manibus*) as he sang each versicle.

---

[1] MS. Addit. 26811, fol. 127 v°.

[2] In the diary of Blasio Baronio de Martinellis, who was papal master of ceremonies in 1525 at the Jubilee of Clement VII., we read that the Pope struck the door *fortiter et viriliter*, stoutly and manfully. Brit. Museum MS. Addit. 8445, fol. 59 v°.

In the first effort the handle broke, and it cut the Pope's finger, but what remained of the fractured implement was sufficient to allow the ceremony to proceed, and Mucanzio expressly notes that Gregory accomplished his purpose and broke a small hole right through the brickwork. After the Pontiff came the penitentiaries, standing on either side of the door, and provided with mallets of their own. They too struck vigorously (*fortiter percutiebant*), and being assisted by the workmen, who had arranged some ingenious expedient on the inner side, the door soon fell with a crash. The moment it was down there ensued, at least on this particular occasion, a general scramble—the workmen within, the soldiers outside, the populace crowding behind, all precipitated themselves upon the fragments of bricks and mortar. Nothing could stem the torrent, the guards were too busy in securing their own share to be of any use, and though, as Mucanzio tells us, he shouted to them at the top of his voice, they paid not the least attention. The result was, as we have already noted in a previous chapter, that a good two hundred had crowded and fought their way through the door before the Pontiff crossed the threshold. So great was the uproar during the whole scene that no one could hear the versicles and prayers sung by the Pope, or the responses made by the choir. The latter, as our master of ceremonies records, religiously went through the antiphons and psalms allotted to them, but their voices were completely drowned by the tumult. On the other hand, so great was the pressure of the crowd that it was absolutely impossible for the penitentiaries to sweep the threshold and wash the lintels with holy water, as custom and due order prescribed. More than half an hour elapsed before the service could be continued, but at last a way was cleared for the Pope, the remaining versicles were sung, the *Te Deum* intoned, and the artillery of St. Angelo burst forth in deafening peals. It was only after vespers were concluded that the Pope and his attendant prelates received the sad intelligence that six or eight of the crowd had been trampled to death in the tumult which they had just witnessed. It can well be understood that the incident threw a gloom over the whole city.[1]

One would have thought that this scene of confusion, with its disastrous sequel, would have served as a lesson for all time, but so great was the eagerness to obtain possession of the fragments of the Holy Door[2] that, even at the next Jubilee of 1600, the measures taken to secure the orderly performance of the ceremony were not entirely successful. This time it seems to have been the Pope's own *camerieri* who were the principal offenders.

"When the prayer (*actiones nostras*) was concluded," says the then master of ceremonies, Paolo Alaleona, "the Pontiff sat down, resumed his mitre, and took the candle again in his hand. In the meanwhile the choir sang the psalm *Jubilate*, and the penitentiaries sponged the threshold and door-posts with holy water and wiped them dry with linen cloths, but as soon as the door was open there were a number of people, especially among the papal camerieri, who darted through before the Pope, in defiance of the order that had been appointed. But it is always difficult on such occasions," adds Alaleona philosophically, "to carry out the order which has been arranged beforehand, and it was a consolation to think that this was the only mishap which occurred. It was due to the curiosity and eagerness of so many people to get fragments of the mortar of the Holy Door, but those that rushed in were not allowed to pass out again."[3]

While the main function is proceeding at St. Peter's, the Cardinal Legates are busy in opening the other Holy Door. Our account of 1700 goes on—

"On the same day, and at the same hour, his Holiness

---

[1] MS. Addit. 26811, fol. 128.

[2] It will be remembered that Rucellai expressly mentions this eccentric manifestation of popular devotion or superstition in 1450, in almost the earliest reference we have to the walled-up door. See above, p. 39. The English account of 1600 says—"In the meantime the said workmen and all the people, moved with devotion, tooke and bare away the stones and mortar of the said gate with great diligence and dexteritie, that all whatsoever was found (great or little) was voyded from thence, as it may be said, in the twinkling of an eye," p. 6.

[3] Diary of Paolo Alaleona, Brit. Museum, MS. Addit. 8454, fol. 141, v°.

deputes three cardinal legates to go and open the other Holy Gates of the churches, to wit, that of St. Paul, that of St. John Lateran, and that of St. Maria Maggiore, which is performed with the same ceremonies and prayers as have been mentioned just now. The choice falls commonly upon two archbishops and the dean, who go from thence with a most magnificent cavalcade to perform this function, which is like a proclamation to all the Christian world that the treasure of the church is set open, and distinguishes the true Catholics from the heretics and Jews."

It may be remarked upon this that, as a matter of fact, the cardinals appointed legates are usually the arch-priests of the Basilicas. But if neither the dean nor the sub-dean of the Sacred College are the arch-priests of either the Lateran or Liberian Basilicas, the former, or, in case he is unable, the latter, is delegated to open the gate of St. Paul's.[1]

The formula used by Clement X. when deputing the cardinals to open the Holy Gates ran as follows:—"We appoint your lordships legates *a latere* to open the golden gates of St. Paul, of St. John, and of St. Mary Major, granting you all the faculties requisite to enable you to grant the plenary Indulgence to all who shall enter in by them."

The legates formerly set out from St. Peter's, but were dispensed from so doing by Benedict XIII., and now each of them starts from his own palace to go to the Basilica he is deputed to open.[2]

Various slight modifications in the minor details of the function become evident when we compare the accounts of the different masters of ceremonies, but they are hardly of a nature to interest the general reader. It will be quite sufficient to say, by way of specimen, that the diary of Paolo Alaleona, from which we have just been quoting, lets us know incidentally that the Pope wore the *falda*[3] underneath his cope; that he no longer

---

[1] Moroni, vol. viii. p. 203.

[2] Zaccaria.

[3] This is a vestment peculiar to the Pope. It is a kind of long petticoat with a train, and is worn under the cope, or, more strictly, the *manto*.

used the tiara in this function, as Alexander VI. had done, but the mitre; that he was supported on either hand in crossing the Holy Door by two cardinal deacons; that two auditors of the Rota lifted the border of the *falda* and cope in front of him, and two chamberlains bore the train of the same vestments behind; and that with the two papal masters of ceremonies there was also in attendance the apostolic sub-deacon to receive from his Holiness the long-handled cross when he had passed into the Basilica and seated himself once more on the *Sedia Gestatoria*. The Jubilee medal of Leo XII.—the last struck before those of the present Pontiff—departs somewhat from the usual tradition,

JUBILEE MEDAL OF LEO XII., 1825. The Pope entering the Holy Door. In the exergue JANUAS · COELI · APERUIT.

and represents the Pope, as may be seen in the reproduction above, not striking the Holy Door with the hammer, but in the act of crossing the threshold. We may point out, as an illustration of the great difficulty of securing accurate representations of ceremonial, that, while the artist has correctly shown the lighted candle in the Pope's left hand and the long-handled cross in his right, he has erred in introducing the mitre at this stage of the function. The Pope, after intoning the *Te Deum* and kneeling for a few moments in prayer, passes through the Holy Door bareheaded.

The Swiss Guard, one of whose number appears so conspicuously on the left of the medal, were not only employed to keep off the crowd, but we are told that a detachment of them fired a salute in the piazza immediately the Pope had crossed the threshold of the *Porta Santa*, while the trumpets sounded, the drums rolled, the church bells were pealed, and the heavier guns were discharged from the Castle of St. Angelo. On the

Suizzero armato nelle Funzioni Solenni
149

SWISS GUARD IN ARMOUR ON A STATE OCCASION.

other hand, the Swiss were not responsible for the custody of the Holy Door throughout the year. This charge, at least in the last century, was specially entrusted by the Pope after the ceremony, with a suitable speech, to the Collegio of the Cavalieri of Sts. Peter and Paul.[1] The office was not wholly a sinecure,

[1] See the *Distinta Relazione delle Sagre Funzioni fatta della Santità di Nostro Signore Papa Benedetto XIV. nell' aperire la Porta Santa*. Rome, 1750. I am indebted for the use of a copy of this booklet to Mr. Hartwell D. Grissell.

for the Holy Doors in the four Basilicas had to be watched continuously night and day. It would appear, consequently, that those selected for the task were apt to regard it as a dubious privilege. As early as the Jubilee of Clement VII. (1525) we are told in the diary of Blasio Baronio de Martinelli—"After vespers had been sung the Pope summoned three or four of the knights of St. Peter, and entrusted to them the custody of the Holy Door, over which they were faithfully to keep watch and ward night and day, without intermission, in company with the canons of the Basilica. At this the said knights were not greatly pleased, neither was I on their account, but the matter had been so determined by his Lordship the Bishop of Pisa; and the three or four knights in question duly kissed the foot of the Pontiff and took their leave."[1]

From an interesting little manuscript volume of the eighteenth century, written seemingly for the use of the maestro of the papal choir, and formerly in the possession of the celebrated rubrician, Monsignore Pio Martinucci,[2] several further details may be gleaned. Perhaps the only point of any general importance is the fact that while the first set of versicles, *Aperite mihi*, etc., and the prayer, *Deus qui per famulum tuum Moysen*, etc., were *chanted* by the Pope, the second set, *Domine exandi*, etc., and the prayer, *Actiones nostras*, etc., were said without chanting on his return to the throne; for the choirmaster's booklet notes, "*e dice le sequenti versi non cantati.*" A characteristic note occurs at the end of the ceremony in the following terms:—"Let the Signor Maestro of the Choir remind the Master of Ceremonies to assign a suitable station to our College of Choristers,

---

[1] MS. Addit. 8445, fol. 59 v°.

[2] This also is in the possession of Mr. H. D. Grissell; as likewise a copy of the *Ragguaglio* of the ceremonies used in the Jubilee of Pius VI. (1775), *nell' apertura della Porta Santa*, which supplies further details. The knights of St. Peter and Paul were a body of mounted guards, founded by Leo X. in 1520 or 1521. It consisted of 400 horsemen. At the first foundation of the guard each member contributed 1000 gold florins to the papal treasury, which at that time was at a very low ebb. In return various privileges were granted them, and their eldest sons were declared nobles and counts of the Lateran. In 1825 the care of the Holy Door was entrusted to the confraternities.

that it may be possible to follow the ceremonies and sing the responses to his Holiness promptly"; or, as is mentioned on another similar occasion, let there be found "*buon sito per il nro. coll°, per sentire bene la voce di N.S.*"

But we shall now do well to return to the printed account of the Jubilee prepared for the English tourists of 1700. Some of the observations which immediately follow the passage last quoted have been anticipated and corrected by what was said about the opening of the Holy Door in our second chapter, and we may therefore pass on to the writer's comments upon the selection of St. Peter's for the principal ceremony.

"There being four several churches, which each have a Holy Gate, this has occasioned some dispute which of them ought to have the precedency in the performance of the ceremony. The Church of St. John Lateran is both the first in rank and enjoys some prerogatives before all the other churches of the city of Rome, as appears by the constitutions of Pope Gregory XI. and Pope Pius V. However, when any of these pontifical functions, which have a more strict relation to the Pope's authority, dignity, and majesty, are to be performed with the utmost splendour, such as the canonisation of saints, the coronations and benedictions of kings, the Church of St. Peter has always had the preference given her before all the rest. And it is upon this same score that this church claims the preference in this most just ceremony, both as to the time and other circumstances, the Holy Gate of St. Peter's Church being the first that is opened by the Pope's own hands. It has also been called in question by some whether any other person besides the Pope himself has any authority to open the Holy Gate; where it is to be observed that in case the Jubilee has already been published before by the deceased Pope, and the cardinals are not entered into the conclave in order to proceed to the election of a new Pope, it belongs to the Cardinal of Ostia, dean of the church, to open the first Holy Gate in the Pope's stead, as then their cardinals represent the Pope's person when they open the Holy Gates of the other three churches;[1] the reason is, that because this ceremony is not essential, but only an accidental part of the Jubilee, which might be celebrated without it, the same is not thought fit to be omitted, for fear of giving scandal to some who might, perhaps, look upon the Jubilee as imperfect without it. But many are of opinion that if the Jubilee be not promulgated before the death of the Sovereign Pontiff, the same cannot be published, and consequently the Holy Gate is not to be opened, the authority of giving plenary Indulgence to the whole church belonging only to the Pope and the general councils.

"However, it is to be observed that this Jubilee being established every twenty-five years by many preceding Popes, especially by Paul II., Sixtus IV., Alexander VI., Julius III., Gregory XIII., and Clement VIII.—this plenary Indulgence, I say, being so often published, confirmed, approved, and renewed by their authority, there is no question but that the cardinals, in case of a vacancy of the chair, may supply the Pope's place, and consequently also open the Holy Gate; and the dean of the church may send his circular letters throughout Christendom to notify that the Jubilee, established and confirmed by the authority of so many preceding Popes, being near at hand, they ought to prepare themselves to receive the benefit of it, and to invite them to undertake this holy pilgrimage, this being not to be accounted a new grant of Indulgences, but only the publication of what was granted before by a legal authority. Thus Pope Julius III. in his Constitution, *Si pastores*, etc., declares that without any further publication the Jubilee begins with the Feast of the Nativity of Christ in the Holy Year. And whereas his exaltation to the papal dignity did not happen till after Advent in the year 1549, when the Holy Year was actually begun, he published a Bull, dated the 23rd of February, 1550, in

---

[1] The meaning of this clumsily translated passage seems to be that, as the arch-priests of the Lateran and St. Mary Major have a prescriptive right to be named legates to open the Holy Door in those churches, so the Cardinal of Ostia, as dean of the Sacred College, has a claim to replace the Pope in opening the Holy Door of St. Peter's.

the first year of his pontificate, in which he declares that the Jubilee had actually commenced with the next preceding Feast of the Nativity of our Saviour.

"A few days before Christmas Eve, the last day of the Holy Year, proclamation is made that upon the next eve of the Nativity of Christ his Holiness intends to shut up the Holy Gate of the Church of the Vatican, which day being come, a procession is made from the apostolic palace to St. Peter's Church in the same manner as has been mentioned before, and, after some time spent in prayers before the Holy Sacrament, the vespers are sung, and three cardinals deputed to shut up the Holy Gates of the three other churches. No sooner have these three prelates and their company received the benediction from his Holiness, and are marching in a most splendid cavalcade to perform this function, but the Pope and cardinals who assist at the ceremony, being presented with lighted wax candles, they march in good order with the cross before them towards the Holy Gate which is to be shut up, the Pope being carried after them in a chair under a canopy, and as they pass by their chapel where the Holy Sacrament of the altar is deposited, he offers up his thanks to God for the happy conclusion of the Holy Year, which done, the Holy Pontiff begins the anthem, *Cum Jucunditate.* Whilst the chorus is singing this anthem or the psalm, *Nisi Dominus œdificaverit domum*, the procession moves from the chapel and towards the Holy Gate, where, after some prayers, the Pope, standing under his canopy, turns his face to the Holy Gate, without his mitre, and a wax candle in his hand, and thus imparts his benediction to the materials, which are ready at hand to close up the Holy Gate, in the following words:—

V. Adjutorium nostrum in nomine Domini.	*V.* Our help is in the name of the Lord.
R. Qui fecit cœlum et terram.	*R.* Who hath made heaven and earth.
V. Sit nomen Domini benedictum.	*V.* The name of the Lord be praised.
R. Ex hoc nunc, et usque in seculum.	*R.* Now and for ever.
V. Lapidem quem reprobaverunt œdificantes.	*V.* The stone which was refused by the artificers.

R. Hic factus est in caput anguli.
V. Domine exandi orationem meam.
R. Et clamor meus ad te veniat.
V. Dominus vobiscum.
R. Et cum spiritu tuo.

Oremus.

Summe Deus, qui Summa, Media, et Infima custodis, qui omnem creaturam intrinsecus ambiendo concludis, sanctifica, et benedie has creaturas lapidis, calcis, et sabuli, Per Christum, etc.

R. Is now become the corner stone.
V. O Lord, hear my prayer
R. And let my crying come before Thee.
V. The Lord be with you.
R. And with thy spirit.

Let us pray.

Great God, who protectest the highest, the middlemost, and the lowest, and who compassest internally all Thy creatures, bless these Thy creatures, the stones, the mortar, and the sand, through our Lord Jesus Christ. Amen.

"After which the High Pontiff, the clergy, and all the rest that assist at the ceremony, come out through the Holy Gate just before it is going to be closed up, and the Holy Father besprinkles the materials with holy water and some incense, and putting again his mitre upon his head, with a linen cloth round his middle, he gives thereby to understand that he professes himself to be the servant of the true servants of God, and that after the example of our Lord Jesus Christ, he is not exalted to the papal dignity and put in St. Peter's chair to be served, but to serve others. In this posture the grand penitentiary presents to him a silver trowel, gilt, wherewith he takes up three several times some mortar out of a basket, carried by the master of the ceremonies, which mortar he spreads and plasters all along the lower part upon the threshold of the Holy Gate, according to the vision of the prophet Amos, which saw the Lord with a mason's trowel in His hands. The threshold being thus covered all over with mortar, the Pope throws upon it, both to the right and the left,

The Bishop Laying the First Stone, in the Rite of the Dedication of a Church.
From the Giunta Pontificale of 1520.

as well as in the middle, several medals of gold and silver, representing the triumphant Jerusalem, the walls of which are described, Apocal, c. xxi., to be built of precious stones. The Pope after this covers the mortar and medals with three square stones, and whilst he is busy in performing this function, says, with a low but intelligible voice, these following words:—

In fide et virtute Jesu Christi Filii Dei Viri, qui Apostolorum Principi dixisti; Tu es Petrus, et super hanc Petram edificabo Ecclesiam meam, Collocamus lapidem istum primarium, ad claudendam hanc Portam Sanctam, singulo Jubilei anno reserandam. In nomine Patris, etc.

In the faith and by the authority of Jesus Christ, the only Son of the living God, who didst say to the chief of the apostles, "Thou beest Peter, and upon this rock I will found My Church," we lay this first stone towards the closing of the Holy Gate, which is not to be opened again till the next Jubilee. In the name of God the Father, etc.

"After the Pope has fastened these three square stones with mortar, and the master mason has drawn his line, the grand penitentiary, with a trowel in his hand, lays likewise a stone upon those laid by the Pope, being assisted by the other penitentiaries there present, to convince the world that they are the Pope's coadjutors in the administration of the Sacrament of Penitence. For each of them, in his due order, lays hand to the work, under the direction of his Holiness, and raises the wall which is to close up the Holy Gate to a considerable height, whilst the chorus sings the hymn, *Cœlestis urbs Jerusalem,*[1] etc.; which being ended, the

---

[1] Blessed City, Heavenly Salem,
Vision dear of peace and love,
Who, of living stones up-builded,
Art the joy of Heaven above,
And with angel cohorts circled,
As a Bride to earth dost move.

From celestial realms descending
Bridal glory round her shed,
To His presence, decked with jewels,
By her Lord shall she be led:
All her streets and all her bulwarks
Of pure gold are fashioned.

Sovereign Pontiff washes his hands and says these following words:—

V. *Salvum fac populum tuum Domine.*
R. *Et benedic hareditati tuæ.*
V. *Fiat Misericordia tua Domine super nos.*
R. *Quemadmodum speravimus in te.*

V. *Mitte nobis Domine auxilium de sancto.*
R. *Et de Sion tuere nos.*
V. *Domine exaudi orationem meam.*
R. *Et clamor meus ad te veniat.*
V. *Dominus vobiscum.*
R. *Et cum spirito tuo.*

Oremus.

Deus qui in omni loco dominationis tuæ clemens et benignus exauditor existis exaudi nos quæsumus et præsta, ut inviolabilis permaneat hujus loci sanctificatio et beneficia tui Muneris in hoc Jubilei anno Universitas Fidelium se impertrasse lætetur; per Dominum nostrum Jesum Christum, etc.

V. Lord, save Thy people.
R. And bless Thine inheritance.
V. Let Thy mercy, O Lord, appear unto us.
R. According as we have put our hopes in Thee.
V. Lord, send us help from Thy sanctuary.
R. And defend us from Sion.
V. O Lord, hear my prayer.
R. And let my crying come unto Thee.
V. The Lord be with you.
R. And with thy spirit.

Let us pray.

O God, who in every place where Thou rulest, givest to us innumerable proofs of Thy mercy and goodness, hearken unto our prayers, and grant that this place may always be sanctified before Thee, and that all faithful Christians may rejoice in having been partakers of Thy mercies in this Jubilee, through our Lord Jesus Christ.

Bright with pearls her portal glitters;
  It is open evermore;
And by virtue of His merits,
  Thither faithful souls may soar
Who for Christ's dear name in this world
  Pain and tribulation bore.

Many a blow and biting sculpture
  Polished well those stones elect,
In their places now compacted
  By the Heavenly Architect,
Who therewith hath willed for ever
  That His palace should be decked.

Laud and honour to the Father,
  Laud and honour to the Son;
Laud and honour to the Spirit,
  Ever Three and ever One:
Consubstantial, Co-eternal,
  While unending ages run. Amen.

(Dr. Neale's translation, one line altered.)

"This prayer being ended, the Holy Father sets himself upon the throne, and whilst twelve bricklayers—to wit, six on the right and as many on the left hand—are busy in closing up and raising the wall to the top of the Holy Gate, the chorus sings *Lauda Jerusalem Dominum*, etc., *Lœtatus sum in his*, etc., and other such like psalms. The wall being finished by the masons, the High Pontiff concludes the whole ceremony by imparting his benediction with a plenary Indulgence of the Jubilee to all there present, who are not sparing on their side in their acclamations of joy and making ten thousand vows for the prosperity and preservation of his Holiness. Which being done, the *Te Deum* is sung for a thanksgiving for the many mercies received by the people in this Jubilee, who, thus well satisfied and filled with spiritual joy, return to their respective homes as the Holy Father retreats to the apostolic palace."

The account which we find in this seventeenth-century tract coincides very nearly with the description of the last Jubilee, as given by Artaud de Montor in his *Histoire de Léon XII.*[1] For purposes of comparison a portion of his narrative may be quoted here:—

"On the morning of the 24th December the Pope read and approved the Bull for the extension of the Jubilee to the whole of Christendom, which document was to be signed the next day, Christmas Day. In the afternoon, after solemn first vespers of the feast had been sung in the Sixtine Chapel, the Holy Father, with his cardinals and prelates wearing their vestments of state, left the chapel and, descending by the private staircase leading to the Chapel of the Blessed Sacrament, went in procession to St. Peter's. Having venerated the relics there and adored the Blessed Sacrament, his Holiness, vested in cope and holding a lighted torch, intoned the Antiphon '*Cum Jucunditate exibitis, et cum gaudio deducemini; nunc montes et colles exilient expectantes vos in gaudio, Alleluia.*' Then walking with his retinue, he passed out through the Holy Door and ascended the throne prepared in the portico. When all had taken their places,

[1] Artaud de Montor, *Histoire du Pape Lèon XII.*, vol. ii. p. 137.

Pope Gregory XVI. vested in Chasuble, Fanon, and Pallium, receiving the Precious Blood through a reed in High Mass. See page 256.

the Pope proceeded to bless the tiles and mortar prepared to close the Holy Gate, which were placed on a Credence Table together with the tools to be employed. After reciting some prayers, the Pope was girded with an apron by the masters of the ceremonies, and, kneeling at the threshold of the door, he received from the Cardinal Penitentiary (Cardinal Castiglioni, afterwards Pius VIII.) the silver trowel and proceeded to lay a trowelful of mortar in the middle of the threshold, and two more to the right and left of it. On each of these he placed a brick, with various medals and pieces of gold and silver money coined during his pontificate. Amongst the medals was one struck to commemorate the Holy Father's restoration to health, and bearing the effigy of Minerva Hygeia, with S.P.Q.R. *Optimo Principi.* The Cardinal Penitentiary then placed three trowelsful of mortar and three bricks on those laid by the Pope, and the four penitentiaries of the Vatican did the same in their turn. While the masons inside the church were completing the closing of the gate, a canvas was drawn across it, depicting the Holy Gate walled-up."

De Montor informs us further that the trowel remained in the possession of the Grand Penitentiary, Cardinal Castiglioni, who presented it to his brother, Count Philip.

In the early days of the ceremony, when the device of the canvas screen had not been thought of and when they were contented to employ a much smaller number than twelve masons to close the aperture, the process of walling-up the door was a somewhat tedious operation. Mucanzio tells us that in the Jubilee of Gregory XIII. it occupied more than an hour. The Pope was urged to take his departure before the wall was completed, but he determined to sit it out, much to the dissatisfaction of the cardinals, two of whom could not even find seats, and, such was the crush of the throng standing around, that it was quite impossible to bring fresh benches or chairs to the spot Mucanzio himself, whose disappointment about the medals we have recorded above, put the delay to profit to do a stroke of business. The silver trowel used by the Pope to lay the first bricks of the door had been given into his keeping as master of ceremonies, and while all were seated waiting for the masons to finish their work Mucanzio took occasion to approach the Pope and whisper a petition that he might be permitted to retain the trowel as his own perquisite. He painted in such eloquent colours the additional labour and fatigue which had been entailed upon him by the celebration of the Jubilee, and the thanklessness of his official duties, that Gregory smiled good-naturedly and granted his request. Possibly he felt that, with an impatient crowd without and the cardinals in a bad humour within, the master of ceremonies for the moment had him at his mercy.

The silver-gilt hammer used in the opening ceremony is generally more remarkable as a work of art than the trowel which figures in the concluding function of the Jubilee. The hammer employed by his Holiness Pope Leo XIII. in the present year will be found figured on the cover of this volume. It has long been the custom to present the hammer after the function to some royal or distinguished personage. Leo XII., in 1825, gave it to the Duchesse d'Angoulême, daughter of Louis XVI. Clement VII., who seems to have been the first Pontiff to use a "golden" hammer made for the occasion, presented the implement to Cardinal Pucci, who subsequently added three little hammers to his coat-of-arms. That which broke in the hand of Gregory XIII. in 1575 was repaired and presented to the Prince of Bavaria. Formerly the silver hammers used by the cardinal legates at the other three Basilicas were made at the expense of the Pope, and were sent to the respective cardinals with his blessing. They usually bore the following inscription :—

Malleus a P.O.M. . . . pro Aperitione
Portæ Aureæ Apostolica Benedictione Munitus.

In the present year the hammers used by the cardinal delegates were subscribed for by the Catholics of the different European countries.[1]

[1] That used at the Lateran Basilica, for instance, in the present Holy Year by Cardinal Satolli was given by the Catholics of France, while Cardinal Vincent Vannutelli at St. Maria Maggiore was presented with the very beautiful silver hammer, which he employed, by the clergy and people of Italy.

After the Holy Gates are closed a marble tablet is placed over each inscribed with the dates of the opening and closing, and bearing the name of the Pope or cardinal who performed the ceremonies.

The legates at the other Basilicas are assisted by the penitentiaries attached to them, and the cardinals also place medals under the bricks, stamped with their own coats-of-arms or with some commemorative inscription, in the same manner as the Pope does at St. Peter's. One such medal, bearing the name of Cardinal Marefusco, who opened and closed the Lateran Holy Door in 1775, is depicted on the next page.

The penitentiaries are made prominent in the ceremonial both of the opening and closing of the Jubilee, because to them primarily are committed those extended faculties for reserved cases which constitute one of the chief objects of the Great Pardon, as it was formerly called. It is they who, in a more especial sense, are made the Pope's delegates in the work of the reconciliation of sinners. The wand or rod, which is still the emblem of their office, dates back to a time when the castigation of the offender invariably formed part of the ceremony of reconciliation. Even now, the form which stands printed in the official *Pontificale Romanum* for the public absolution of an excommunicated person, prescribes that the penitent is to kneel before the bishop while the *Miserere* is being said, the bishop to hold a rod in his hand, and to strike the offender lightly between the shoulders as each successive verse is pronounced. The picture accompanying the text of this rite in the Giunta *Pontificale* of 1520 is reproduced on this page. Another picture,

Absolution of an Excommunicated Person.
From the Giunta Pontificale of 1520.

taken from a Jubilee sheet of 1650, which will be found further on, represents the Roman penitentaries, with their rod of office, engaged in hearing the confessions of the pilgrims.

Before the opening of the *Porta Santa* of St. Mary Major in 1650, the question was raised whether the canons might not of their own authority and without permission from the Pope remove beforehand the medals which had been placed there at the previous Jubilee. The question was decided in the negative by the learned canonist Monsignor de Rossi. The right of opening and closing the door belonged to the Pope only, and to such cardinals as should be delegated by him. No other person might interfere with it. At this Jubilee (1650) a knock was accidentally given to the Holy Gate of St. Paul's before the arrival of the legate, Cardinal Lanti. The masons who were within the church awaiting the signal at once began to pull down the door. The crowd outside, to the number of two hundred or more, forced their way past the guards and rushed in, as at St. Peter's, to collect the fragments of stone and mortar. To remedy this accident the door was hastily rebuilt to about the height of a man, and the legate arriving in due course, the ceremony of opening was performed as if nothing had happened.

Medal Commemorating the Opening of the Holy Door at the Lateran Basilica in 1775.

At this Jubilee also it was debated whether a cardinal-deacon, not being in priest's orders, could be delegated to open and close the gates. Those who answered the question in the affirmative adduced the instances of Cardinal Orsini, deacon of Sta. Maria Nuova, who in 1500 opened the gate of St. Mary Major, and of Cardinal Sforza, deacon and archpriest of St. Eustachio, who also performed the same ceremony. The Congregation of Cardinals, however, decided that cardinal-deacons did not possess this right, since Clement VIII. in 1600, in the absence of

Cardinal Colonna, archpriest of St. John Lateran, passed over Cardinal Montalto because he was only a deacon, and elected Cardinal Tagliava to supply his place. Innocent X., notwithstanding, decided that holy orders were not requisite, and deputed Cardinal Maidalchini, nephew of his sister-in-law Olympia, to open the Liberian Holy Gate, in the absence of the archpriest of that Basilica.

The church of St. Peter *ad Aram* at Naples also possesses a *Porta Santa,* which, on the occasions of the extension of the Jubilee to other places than Rome, is opened by the archbishop with nearly the same ceremonial as that which is practised at the Roman Basilicas. Benedict XIII. also, at the request of the pious King of Portugal, John V., granted permission for four churches having holy gates to be built at Lisbon. At the Jubilee seasons one of these gates is opened by the patriarch, and the others by bishops whom he deputes for the purpose.

It was at one time popularly believed that the Holy Gates of the four Roman Basilicas were the doors of the palace of Pontius Pilate, and had thus been hallowed by our Saviour passing through them at the time of His Passion. But these doors were also, as we have seen, identified with the three which formerly led from "the Pope's Hall" to the *Scala Santa.*

Something has already been said of the symbolism which has been attached to the ceremonial of the *Porta Santa.* Despite its comparatively recent origin there has been no lack of mystical interpretations. Ricci, for instance, in his work on the Jubilee,[1] after first going off into a long digression about the door of the temple of Janus, which was open in time of war and shut in time of peace, with illustrative quotations from Virgil and Ovid, states that although these ceremonies are not really essential to the Jubilee, they are practised, in order to signify that in the Holy Year the Church opens the inexhaustible treasure which she has received through the Passion of Christ. The reason why Christmas Eve is the day chosen for the ceremony is that on that day the gates of heaven were opened wide to enable the Eternal

[1] *De' Giubilei Universali Celebrati negli Anni Santi*, etc. Roma, 1675. Pp. 5-15.

God to come down to earth, while the gates of hell were closed that the truly penitent and contrite might enter heaven.

Similarly, in the treatise on the Jubilee of Father Pientinus, we find quite an embarrassing choice of reasons why it is fitting that the Roman Pontiff should knock three times at the Holy Door. First, because by the opening of the door is signified the opening or communicating of the treasure of the Church to Christians in all quarters of the world, and as, according to ancient geographers, the world was divided into three parts, Europe, Asia, and Africa, so it was fitting that the gate should be struck not once but three times. Secondly, because the celebration of the Jubilee was an occasion of joy to the inhabitants of heaven, of earth, and also of purgatory, which fact was appropriately symbolised by the thrice repeated knocking. Thirdly, because it was also probably intended to teach that three things are necessary to all who desire to participate in the Indulgence, namely, faith, hope, and charity.[1]

The opening of the Holy Gate is further said to have been prefigured by the opening, on Sabbaths and Feasts, of the East Gate of the Temple at Jerusalem, which remained closed on other days.[2] In like manner, the Porta Santa is only open during the Feast of Jubilee. Again, the opening of the Holy Gates in four different churches signifies the calling of the faithful from the four quarters of the world, an explanation which hardly squares with F. Pientinus' first reason for the three knockings as quoted above. Moreover, as an angel opened the iron door and delivered St. Peter from prison, even so the opening of the Holy Gate symbolises our deliverance from the spiritual perils of this mortal life. Under the old law causes were heard and judgment given at the door of the Temple, thus also has Jesus Christ set up His divine tribunal in the Holy Gate, which is a figure of Him who said, "I am the door, if any man enter in by Me he shall be saved." So again the prophet Jeremiah,[3] by the command of

---

[1] Bonanni, *Numismata Pontificum Romanorum*. Rome, 1699. Vol. ii. p. 622.
[2] Ezechiel, ch. xlvi. v. 1.
[3] Chap. xvii. v. 21.

God, forbade the Jews to carry any burden through the Gate of Jerusalem on the Sabbath day; how careful then must the faithful be to leave behind them the burden of sin before entering the Holy Gate!

Such interpretations, devised with more or less of ingenuity by the writers of the seventeenth century, might be multiplied almost indefinitely. It should be added, however, that they did not overlook that explanation taken from the penitential discipline of the Church in earlier ages, which has historically the best claim to be considered. Upon this exclusion and re-admission of the penitents at the church door sufficient has already been said in an earlier chapter. The ritual of the Porta Santa reminds us that in the Jubilee Year the Church invites all to enter her doors in a spirit of contrition in order to receive pardon for their sins and to share more abundantly in her heavenly treasures.

The closing ceremonies of the Holy Year have also been provided with a mystical interpretation of their own. The three square bricks (*mattoni*) placed in position by the Pope or cardinal represent the stones spoken of by the prophet Isaiah when he said *Jerusalem shall be built of square stones.* The three bricks are also held to signify either faith, hope, and charity, or contrition, confession, and satisfaction. So, too, the soul when purified and embellished by grace and by the Indulgence of the Jubilee is as a stone set in the mystical building of the heavenly Jerusalem. For this reason the Antiphon, *Cum Jucunditate,* etc., is sung, and especially the hymn, *Celestis Urbs Jerusalem,* of which this thought may be said to form the principal theme, as in the lines:

Many a blow and biting sculpture
  Polished well those stones elect,
In their places now compacted
  By the Heavenly Architect,
Who therewith hath willed for ever
  That His palace should be decked.

There are, indeed, many points of resemblance between the walling-up ceremony of the Jubilee and the rite of the dedication of a church.

When the Holy Gate is closed the Cross of Christ, the standard of our salvation, is put on it in token of the victory won by the faithful over the evil one; and also to accomplish the precept of Daniel the prophet, chap. xiv., *Close the door and seal it with thy ring,* that is, with the Holy Cross, the seal of the King of kings, the High Priest Christ.[1]

POPE INNOCENT X. VISITING THE FOUR BASILICAS IN THE JUBILEE YEAR OF 1650.
From a contemporary print.

The ceremonial proper to the Holy Year may be said to be confined to the two functions which mark its opening and its close. The visits of the Sovereign Pontiffs to the four Basilicas or to the Scala Santa could hardly be regarded as belonging to the domain of ritual, even when they were attended with a certain amount of solemnity, which was not usually the case. Again, the exposition of relics, and more particularly of the *Volto Santo* at St. Peter's, though repeated with much greater frequency during the Jubilee years, was familiar enough at

[1] Ricci. p. 16. He does not seem to have been moved by a particularly happy inspiration in adding the following comparison:—"*Siccome appresso i Gentili erano conosciute le donne infame dall' iscrizione del nome e condizione loro, che tenevano sopra le Porte delle loro case, come dice Seneca, cosi i veri Cristiani saranno conosciuti dal segno e nome di Cristo scritto e portato sempre nelle fronti loro.*"

ordinary seasons to those who resided in Rome. Similarly the processions of the confraternities and the organised bands of pilgrims making their visits to the churches were at no time a strange and unwonted spectacle. Passing over these aspects of the Jubilee, we may pause to say a word about one feature which is in a sense more strictly connected with it, the making and blessing of Agnus Deis.

As in the case of the veneration of the Volto Santo, the devotion towards the little objects of piety called Agnus Deis seems in former ages to have occupied a much more conspicuous place in the estimation of the faithful than it does to-day. It is astonishing, for instance, how prominently the Agnus Deis are mentioned in the penal laws of Elizabeth and other English sovereigns directed against the importation of "Popish trumperies"; and it is equally striking to note how many references to them we come across in the diaries and correspondence of our Catholic forefathers. The use of these discs of blessed wax, stamped for the most part with the figure of a lamb, whence their name, has been traced by no less an authority than the Abbé Duchesne to the time of Pope Zosimus (417-418),[1] though others, with more probability, see in the passage of the *Liber Pontificalis* to which he appeals an allusion rather to the paschal candle.[2] But in any case it would seem that towards the end of the fifth century the remnants of the paschal candles were kept as objects of piety to serve as a protection against devastating tempests and the incursions of pirates;[3] and by the

[1] See *Liber Pontificalis*, vol. i. p. 225.

[2] Dom G. Morin in the *Revue Bénédictine*, vol. v. p. 108.

[3] *Ibid.* p. 115. Dom Morin bases this statement on the allusions of Ennodius (Migne, P. L. lxiii. pp. 259 and 262), who makes reference to this practice in both the forms of blessing the paschal candle composed by him. In the second of these, for instance, he concludes with the words—"Tu (Domine) resurrectionis tuæ tempore, quo vernat anni reviviscentis infantia, *sumptam ex hoc contra procellas vel omnes incursus fac dimicare particulam*, ut sacerdotis nostri votiva omnibus vel totius cleri ejus incolumitate concessa, *ubertatem terrarum* cum actuum innocentia et prosperitate concedas." Such language lends probability to the suggestion that has been made, that these specially blessed fragments of the paschal candle were intended by the Church to replace certain Pagan

time of Amalarius we have a definite reference to the blessing of wax "Agnus Deis" under the name by which they are now known. In one of the early Ordines Romani[1] the rite is thus described—"In the Catholic Church, within the city of Rome, at the Lateran, on Holy Saturday in the early morning, the archdeacon comes into the church and melts wax into a clean vessel of large size, and mixes it there with oil, and blesses the wax and moulds it into the figure of lambs, and keeps them in a clean place. And on the octave day of Easter, after Mass and Communion, these same lambs are given by the archdeacon to the people in the church, and they take them home with them and make incense[2] to burn for any necessity that may arise. And the same waxen lambs are made in the suburban churches." Amalarius, in the early part of the ninth century, quotes this passage, and adds the additional detail that these Agnus Deis ought to be made out of the remnants of the paschal candle itself.

The charge of making the Agnus Deis formerly devolved upon the pontifical sacristan. Panvinio says, *olim cera alba pura parata erat per Magistrum Ceræ Palatii Apostolici.* It was usual for the faithful who wished to have these consecrated tokens to make an offering of wax or money at the altar of St. Peter's. In the pontificate of Martin V. this offering was given to the apostolic subdeacon who made the Agnus Deis, a notice being attached to the gate of the Basilica to the effect that the Pope would consecrate Agnus Deis every seven years during his pontificate, and that all who wished to possess them must bring "pure, white, clean wax" to the subdeacon in good

---

amulets, spells, and incantations commonly used in the spring season by the peasantry to ensure the fertility of their fields. The blessing of houses, etc., on Holy Saturday with the newly-consecrated water is part of the same idea.

[1] Muratori, *Lit. Rom.*, ii. p. 1004.

[2] It seems to be clear from this and other passages that wax was one of the ingredients out of which incense was made. This fact helps to explain a very puzzling confusion by which the grains of incense have been introduced into the rite of the blessing of the paschal candle at the point where mention is made of *incensi hujus.* But the point is too complicated to admit of discussion here.

time.[1] Clement VIII., however, conferred the privilege of making the Agnus Deis on the Cistercian congregation established in Rome at the monastery of S. Pudenziana. This privilege was confirmed by his successor Leo XI., and afterward by Paul V. in a Bull dated 28th March, 1608.

For a long period the Agnus Deis only bore the impression of the lamb and flag, but in later times the images of the Blessed Virgin, of the Apostles, and of saints towards whom the reigning Pontiff may feel a special devotion have been added. Benedict XIV., *e.g.*, allowed the image of B. Imelda, who was of his own

THE POPE BLESSING AGNUS DEIS.
From a Jubilee print of 1650 in the British Museum.

family, to be stamped on them. Clement XI., besides the saints of the Latin Church, introduced the most noteworthy of the Greeks, as did also Pius VI. In the latter case the Pope, to show his affection for the Easterns, added inscriptions in Greek characters, with the year of his pontificate in which they had been blessed.

In the form of benediction of the Agnus Deis, printed by order of Benedict XIV. in 1752, the following mystic meanings are given to them. They are made of virgin wax, as symbolical of the human nature of Christ, who took flesh in the most pure

[1] Baldassari, *I Pontificii Agnus Dei Dilucidati.* Venezia, 1714, p. 35.

womb of His Blessed Mother without stain of sin. The figure of a lamb is printed on them, as a symbol of that Immaculate Lamb who was immolated on the cross for the salvation of the human race. They are immersed in holy water, God having made use of this element, both in the old and new dispensations, to work many miracles. They are mixed with balsam to signify the sweet savour of Christ. The chrism, which is another ingredient, is emblematic of charity.

The benediction of the Agnus Deis is performed publicly in the first year of the pontificate of each Pope, and every seventh year afterwards. This blessing takes place on the Wednesday, Thursday, or Friday of Easter week, and they are distributed to the cardinals and others on the following Saturday, known as *Sabbato in Albis*. They are also consecrated every Jubilee year, and are distributed to the pilgrims who visit Rome. If the Pope deems it necessary, he may also consecrate them privately at other times in the sacristy of the Church of Santa Croce.

The Agnus Deis, we are reminded, are included among the sacramentals of the Church. Due honour and veneration must therefore be paid to them; but they may be touched, worn on the person, especially when travelling, or be exposed in the house, which, as well as the persons who inhabit it, they are held to preserve from danger.

In virtue of the prayers which are said over them to that end the Agnus Deis are considered to possess special virtue against the fury of the elements. It is considered lawful to throw them into a burning house or into a swollen river. The Empress St. Helena, we are duly reminded, did not scruple to cast one of the holy nails, with which our Lord was crucified, into the Adriatic in order to appease the waves which threatened her with destruction. As a matter of fact, St. Pius V. had recourse to this expedient when the Tiber was in flood and seemed likely to submerge the city, and we are told that when an Agnus Dei had been thrown into the river the angry waters at once subsided.[1] On the other hand, it is considered super-

[1] Baldassari, *I Pontificii Agnus Dei Dilucidati.* Venezia, 1714, p. 137.

stitious to nail Agnus Deis to the top of church towers or lofty buildings as a protection against lightning, or to break them up into pieces to scatter them broadcast over the fields. This last custom, which is mentioned by Fra Vincentio Bonardo, O.P., in 1586, among practices to be reprobated, seems to be an interesting survival of what Ennodius tells us of the use made in the fifth century of the fragments of the paschal candle.[1]

From the seventeenth century, or perhaps earlier, it seems to have been the custom for the Popes in distributing Agnus Deis to the faithful to cause them to be accompanied by a leaflet[2] explaining the nature of these devotional objects and the special virtues attributed to them. The text of these leaflets has differed somewhat at different times, but they all agree in substance with the following enumeration, which is taken from an approved authority on the subject. The purport is to summarise the spiritual and corporal blessings bestowed through the Agnus Deis upon those who devoutly and confidently make use of them, as set forth by Popes Urban V., Paul II., Julius III., Sixtus V., and Benedict XIV.

The Agnus Deis augment sanctifying grace in the soul; they foster piety, banish tepidity, preserve from vice, and dispose to virtue.

They cancel venial sins, and purify from the stain left by grievous sin after it has been remitted in the sacrament of penance.

They put to flight evil spirits, deliver from temptations, and preserve from eternal ruin.

They are a protection against sudden and unprovided death. They drive away phantoms, and the fears occasioned by evil spirits.

They are a divine help against adversity, avert dangers, and are a cause of good fortune.

---

[1] *Discorso intorno all' Origine, Antichità et Virtù de' gli Agnus Dei di cera benedetti.* Rome, 1586, p. 32.

[2] Picart, in his *Cérémonies Religienses*, vol. i. part ii. p. 177, gives a facsimile of such a leaflet printed in French, and bearing date 1662, with the arms of Alexander VII.

They are a protection in combats, and have power to ensure victory.

They deliver from poison and from the snares of the wicked.

They are excellent preservatives against sickness, and also an efficacious remedy—especially in cases of epilepsy.

They hinder the ravages of pestilence, of epidemics, and of infectious diseases.

They quiet the winds, dissipate hurricanes, calm whirlwinds, and keep away tempests. They save from shipwreck, and the danger of lightning, and all kinds of inclement weather, floods, inundations, etc.

They extinguish fire and stop its ravages.

Lastly, they preserve mothers and babes from peril, and bring about a safe and easy delivery.

Pope Urban V., when sending ambassadors to the Emperor John Paleologus to endeavour to bring him back to the unity of the Church, also sent three Agnus Deis with some verses composed by Andrea Frari, which set forth in poetic diction the virtues we have just detailed—

Balsamus et munda cum cera chrismatis unda
Conficiunt Agnum, quod munus do tibi magnum.
Fulgura desursum depellit et omne malignum,
Peccatum frangit, ceu Christi sanguis, et angit,
Prægnans servatur, simul et partus liberatur,
Munera fert dignis, virtutem destruit ignis,
Portatus munde de fluctibus eripit undæ,
Morte repentina servat Satanæque ruina,
Si quis honorat eum retinet super hoste trophæum,
Parsque minor tantum tota valet integra quantum.
Agnus Dei, miserere mei,
Qui crimina tollis, miserere nobis.[1]

[1] These leonine hexameters are printed in the official *Ceremoniale Romanum* of 1582, at the end of the rite of the benediction of Agnus Deis. They are also cited in the brief directed by Pope Sixtus V. in 1586 to Pasquale Cicogna, Doge of Venice. Instead of an English translation, we may quote here the abbreviated version in French, which appears in the leaflet above referred to, distributed by Alexander VII., which Picart has reproduced in facsimile—

The Roman Pontiffs have more than once showed themselves jealous in guarding these objects of devotion from what they judged to be abuse or imposture. Nicolas V. in a Bull dated 7th December, 1452, imposed heavy penalties on John Urioch and Dionisius de Molinis, who issued false Bulls of Indulgences and counterfeit Agnus Deis. Paul II. in 1470 also decreed severe punishment against any person who should manufacture or sell Agnus Deis made of consecrated wax.

Gregory XIII. in 1572 forbade, under penalty of excommunication, that any one should venture to paint, or illuminate, or cover with gold or silver or any colour, or sell the consecrated Agnus Deis. This penalty was confirmed by Clement XI. in 1716.

It would give quite a disproportionate importance to a rite which is but slenderly connected with the Jubilee if we were to enter here at any length upon the description of the ceremonies with which the Agnus Deis are blessed. We have reproduced, however, a rare and interesting engraving in the Print Room of the British Museum of the time of St. Pius V., which gives a pictorial representation of the whole process in all its successive stages. We see the boxes full of the little discs of wax which have been already stamped with the image of the lamb and some other pious device.[1] We see the Pope first vested by his chaplains with stole and apron, and then engaged in blessing the water with specially-prescribed prayers, and pouring into it balsam and holy chrism. After the water is blessed it is distributed into four silver vessels, and the Pope himself and a

---

Il se lit que le Pape Urbain V. envoya à l'Empereur des Grecs trois Agnus Dei, avec ces vers et paroles :—

Les tonnerres il chasse
Les péchez il efface,
Sauve d'embrasement
Et de submergement,
Garde de mort subite,
Les Diables met en fuite,
Dompte les ennemis,
Hors de danger sont mis
Et l'enfant et la Mère
Qui travaille à le faire ;
Il donne maint pouvoir,
Aux dignes de l'avoir ;
La part quoy que petite,
Tant que la grande profite.

[1] With regard to the manufacture of these wax forms, some extremely interesting details, taken mostly from the diary of Paris de Grassis, are given by Catalani in his commentary on the *Ceremoniale Romanum*, vol. i. p. 283 *seq.*

The Blessing of Agnus Deis.
From a rare engraving of 1565 in the British Museum.

number of cardinals distributed in groups set to work to dip each individual Agnus Dei into the water, as a symbolical representation of the Baptism of Jesus Christ. The waxen discs are then carried off by the attendant chaplains, dried, and finally stored in boxes.

There is also a special rite provided in the *Ceremoniale Romanum* for the distribution of the Agnus Deis to the cardinals on the Saturday of Easter week.[1] The Mass is said by one of the cardinals, and after the Agnus Dei and the reception of the Pax, all the cardinals and prelates who are present put on white vestments. When the Communion has been sung the cardinal celebrant sits down, and the subdeacon, with incense and acolytes, goes to fetch the Agnus Deis, which are piled up upon a great silver charger covered with silken wrappings. On returning with his burden to the chapel the subdeacon says in distinct tones—"Holy Father, here are the new-born lambs which have announced to you the message of Alleluia. They come now to the fountains, they are filled with brightness." To which the choir answer—"Thanks be to God, Alleluia." This is thrice repeated as the subdeacon approaches nearer and nearer to the Pope. Finally the subdeacon stands beside the Pope with the Agnus Deis, and the Pope distributes them. Each cardinal advances holding his mitre with the points downwards, and the Pope puts into the mitre as many Agnus Deis as he thinks fit. The cardinals kiss the Pope's hand and his right knee, the prelates the Pope's knee only, the protonotaries and all others his foot. When this ceremony is concluded the celebrant says the post-communion prayers and finishes the Mass.

The oldest existing specimens of Agnus Deis seem to go back to the time of Gregory the Great. At any rate it is believed that one such disc of wax, sent by Gregory to Queen Theodelind, is preserved in the treasury of Monza.[2] Another early Agnus Dei was found in the tomb of Flavius Clemens, martyred under Domitian, but this specimen only dates from the time of the

[1] *Ceremoniale Romanum* (ed. 1582), fol. 178.

[2] Kraus, *Real. Encyclopädie der Christlichen Alterthumer*, vol. i. p. 29.

translation of the martyr in the seventh century. Some curious and ancient Agnus Deis are also extant, which have been attributed to the time of Charlemagne.

To give any elaborate description of the ceremonial of the papal High Mass, or of the other papal functions which were wont to be carried out with particular solemnity when Rome was thronged with pilgrims during the Jubilee years of the last and preceding centuries, would unreasonably occupy our space. We have included, however, amongst our illustrations an interesting engraving of the time of Sixtus V. representing a pontifical

A PAPAL "CHAPEL."
From a Jubilee print of 1650.

High Mass in the Sixtine, and showing the grouping of the cardinals and others during the sermon which is being preached before the Pope. Also there will be found on p. 238 a modern representation of what is probably the most curious and distinctive rite of the papal High Mass, that in which the Pontiff receives the Precious Blood through a tube or reed out of the chalice, which is brought by the deacon from the altar to the papal throne. The use of this fistula or silver reed in the reception of the Precious Blood was in the tenth and eleventh centuries almost general in the Church. It now survives in the papal Mass alone.

CHAPTER VII

Roma la Santa

Amongst the historical collections in the Print Room of the British Museum is an ill-executed but interesting engraving, reproduced on a later page, which was designed by a certain John Baptist de Caballeriis, to illustrate the spiritual glories of the Jubilee of 1575. At the head of the copious letterpress description which fills its lower margin may be read the following address:—"Thou hast here, Christian reader, a portraiture of the City of Rome, not that city which is constituted of hills and open spaces, and the magnificence of public buildings, but that which is spiritually built up of Christian virtues and grows into a 'Holy City, coming down out of heaven from God, and having the glory of God' (Apoc. xxi. 10, 11). If thou wouldst look upon the majesty thereof, then must thou diligently observe these few points which will disclose the meaning of this picture."

It would be a mistake to suppose that this and a good many similar pronouncements which appeared in the seventeenth and eighteenth centuries were prompted by a spirit of mere *réclame*, cynically indifferent to the true facts of the case. There was in reality a spiritual city, very different from the luxurious and sinful Rome of Alexander VI. and Leo X.; very different even from the temporal capital of the states of the Church, with its ecclesiastical magistracy and its petty intrigues and cabals. This spiritual Rome, the Rome of St. Philip Neri, of St. Ignatius Loyola, of St. Camillus de Lellis, of St. John Baptist de Rossi, and of countless hidden saints and holy religious, was that which was brought into prominence by the Jubilee, and which lent help and encouragement to the struggling souls of the pilgrims who flocked thither at such seasons. History, that is to say the type of history which is most in favour with reviewers and university examiners, tells us little of this spiritual city with its confraternities and hospices and religious houses, and

THE POPE WAITING ON THE PILGRIMS AT TABLE DURING THE JUBILEE.
From Picart's "Cérémonies Religieuses."

yet there is no aspect of pontifical Rome which is better worth chronicling. Those who have admired and wondered at the changeless endurance of the Catholic Church, in spite of all the forces arrayed against her from within and without, have not always attended sufficiently to that hidden life of Christian charity and Christian austerity which is the secret of all her strength.

We have said that this title of *Roma la Santa* was no

baseless fiction, and it is a striking thing how profoundly the truth seems to have come home to those who knew the city well, and who had sufficient experience of other lands to be able to draw comparisons. An interesting testimony, to take one amongst many, comes to hand in a letter of a rather famous Spaniard who settled in Rome as a vigorous old man with twenty years of life still before him. It was in 1567 that Dr. Martin de Azpilcueta, best known as the canonist Navarrus, a near relative of St. Francis Xavier, first came to Rome, and these were the terms in which, after three years' residence in the Eternal City, he wrote to his family in Spain—

"I ought to understand and realise better than anybody that we are only pilgrims upon the earth. It was in Navarre that I first saw the light; I was educated at Alcalà in New Castille; my early manhood was spent in France; Salamanca in Old Castille advanced me to preferment; then Portugal honoured me still further. It would, in fact, have exalted me far above my merits, if my good angel, so at least I believe, had not drawn me away from thence, but it is still Portugal that supplies my needs with the salary, an unheard-of generosity, which I draw from the professorial chair I once occupied at Coimbra. After leaving Portugal I passed nearly a dozen years either in Navarre or in the two Castilles. These three states welcomed me most kindly and sought my counsel in many matters. At one time during this period the king's sister took me for her confessor and asked me to direct the conscience of her two nephews, the Princes of Bohemia. At last, after a life so full of changes, I came to Italy, and here I have been at Rome for these three years past, in the seventy-eighth year of my age.[1]

"I now know how much honour is due to the inhabitants of Rome. They receive us well—all of us, whatever nation we belong to; they show us respect; they offer us affection. If any one comes to them who is unworthy of their favour they leave him alone, but they speak no evil of him unless he be himself the first to speak evil. I have seen devotion in other countries,

[1] Dr. Martin Azpilcueta died at Rome in 1586 at the age of ninety-five.

but as for that of the Romans I am never tired of admiring it. It fills me with stupefaction, for I cannot explain such fervour, such indefatigable piety on the part of all, great, middling, and little, men, women, and children, rich and poor. How keen they are in the pursuit of Indulgences, how they love to pay honour to our Lord, our Lady, the Saints, wherever any festival summons them! I see them come in on foot a distance of sixteen miles with extraordinary piety and modesty bent upon visiting, especially during Lent, as many as four, seven, or nine churches in a day, and in such crowds that, in order to assist at the Holy Sacrifice and the other offices of the Church, they almost imperil their lives. Assuredly, if one wishes to know what Rome really is in this respect as well as in many others, it is far better (I speak from experience) to see for one's self than to hear what others say. O princes and citizens of Rome, I pray that you guard very, very carefully this pearl of your piety!"[1]

It must not, of course, be forgotten that this letter was written during the pontificate of the most ascetic of all the occupants of the papal See in modern times, St. Pius V. The Romans, according to the testimony of all who know them best, are a very impressionable people. They catch with singular readiness the tone of those who rule them, and respond with enthusiasm to all good influences, though they are also sadly inconstant in their pious purposes when the examples before them are adverse. Naturally this type of character is easily worked upon by such devotional exercises as those of the Jubilee, where the contagious emotion of large crowds makes itself readily felt, but the piety is thoroughly sincere while it lasts, and there is no reason to distrust the accounts which we read of the extraordinary spectacles of charity and devotion which were exhibited on these occasions.

Turning then again to our Jubilee print of 1575, we find a huge allegorical device in which are more or less aptly symbolised the various works of charity and piety of which Rome was especially the home at such seasons. In the corners we

[1] L. J. M. Cros, *Documents Nouveaux sur St. François de Xavier*, i. p. 505.

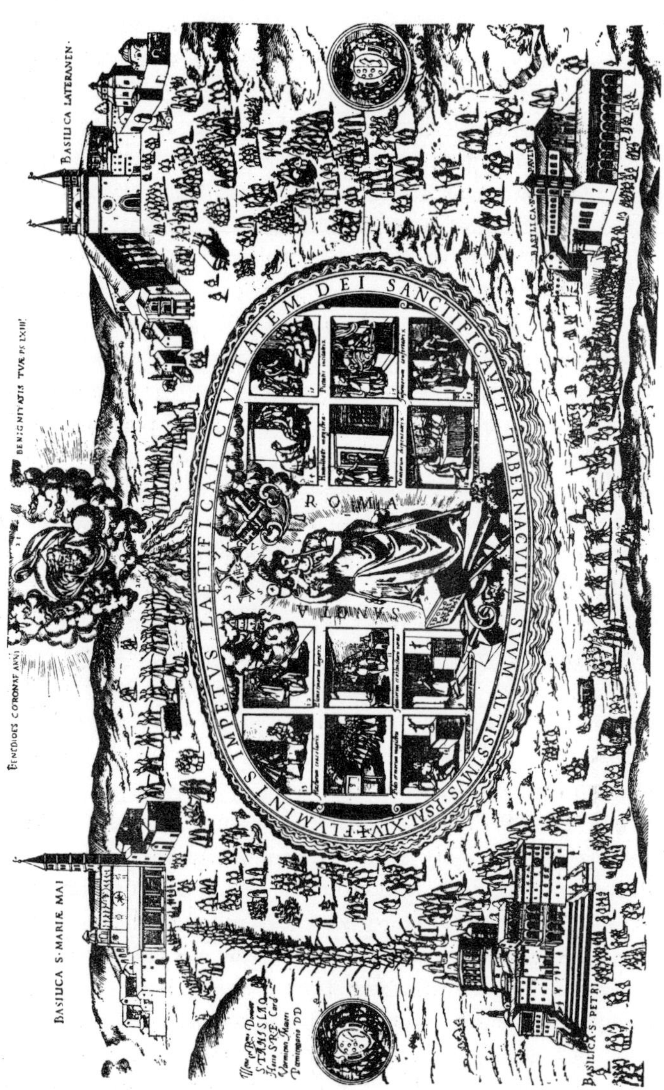

ROMA LA SANTA.
A Jubilee Print designed for the celebration of 1575 (considerably reduced). See page 262.

have representations of the four Basilicas, while along the margins are portrayed processions of pilgrims making their way from one to another, with the cardinals' coaches or ecclesiastics on horseback scattered at intervals here and there. In the centre we have an allegorical figure of *Roma la Santa* (Rome the Holy) trampling upon idolatry and inundated with streams of grace. Then grouped around this controlling impersonation we see twelve vignettes descriptive of those works of piety and charity to which we have referred, each of them representing the sanctity of Rome under a new aspect. Taking them in order, they run as follows:—I. *Mistress of faith and morals*—a preacher addressing a congregation. II. *Spur to devotion and prayer*—a figure praying before an altar. III. *Mirror of penance*—a penitent taking the discipline upon his bare shoulders. IV. *The norm of fasting and abstinence*—a man dining apparently upon bread and water. V. *The generous dispenser of alms*—money being put into a poor-box. VI. *Consoler of the sorrowful*—a visit being paid to some one in grief. VII. *Mistress of humility*—the washing of the feet. VIII. *Promoter of piety*—a figure teaching children, and apparently giving them rosaries. IX. *Channel of mercies*—a prisoner being set at liberty. X. *Comforter of the sick*—a visit paid to a sufferer in bed. XI. *The home of the pilgrim*—three pilgrims being waited on at table. XII. *The patroness of the needy*—a dole of food distributed to the poor.

We have already heard something of the work of the Arch-Confraternity of the Holy Trinity founded by the exertions of St. Philip Neri. It was undoubtedly by means of this association that the most extraordinary example of charity to the poorer class of pilgrims was shown. The statistics preserved to us of the enormous numbers that were assisted in various ways during the more frequented Holy Years seem almost incredible, but there is no reason to doubt that the books were carefully kept. Without going into unnecessary details, the following salient facts may be borrowed from a popular account of the institution, a broadside printed in Italian for distribution in the Jubilee of 1650, a copy of which is in the British Museum.

The Arch-Confraternity of the Holy Trinity is constantly occupied in the care of convalescents and in the lodging of pilgrims, and this more especially during the Holy Year, on account of the crowds that then come in from all parts. Since the last Jubilee, 1625,[1] they have tended 24,396 convalescents, giving them nourishing and substantial food; and afforded shelter and food for three, four, or more days to 588,633 pilgrims. It

DORMITORY FOR FEMALE PILGRIMS AT THE HOSPICE OF THE HOLY TRINITY.
From a Jubilee print of 1650.

seems as if during the present Holy Year the numbers would exceed those of any previous Jubilee.

On arriving in Rome, the pilgrims proceed to the Church of the Confraternity, where they are received by those deputed for the office and interrogated as to the place of their birth and as to their family. Inquiry is also made whether they be priests, in which case, as is fitting, they have a prior claim on the confraternity. The name, surname, and nationality of each is then noted in a book. The female pilgrims are in like manner received in their part of the hospice by women, among whom

[1] This was written at the beginning of February, 1650.

are often many princesses and ladies of rank, who do honour to their nobility by taking part in this holy service. After being admitted the pilgrims have every need supplied, and are waited on, and have their feet washed by princes, cardinals, and often by the Holy Father himself. Meanwhile their meal is prepared in the kitchen, and they are invited to seat themselves at tables laden with good cheer and wine, men and women being served in different dining-rooms. Supper being over, at which many Capuchins and other religious assist, besides the nobles, etc., already mentioned, the pilgrims are conducted to comfortable beds, and the more infirm of them assisted to undress. But this generous arch-confraternity is not content with caring for the bodies only of the pilgrims. A number of priests are specially retained to catechise and instruct them, that they may be induced to frequent the Sacraments, and, if need be, they preach to them in various languages in a way suited to their capacity. In their visits to the four churches the pilgrims are escorted by guides and instructed, Communion being given them at St. Paul's and the relics of the saints in all the churches being freely shown them. A collation is afterwards served to them in the courtyard of St. John Lateran, or in some other spacious place, and after having received the benediction of the Holy Father they are taken back to the hospice, where a paper is read to them explaining the nature and value of the Indulgence they have gained. "If space permitted," the account concludes, "we could have narrated in more detail the part played in all these proceedings by cardinals, princes, prelates, and nobles of all ranks. These vie with each other in generosity, spending liberally to supply all the needs of the pilgrims, providing lights for the hospice, and good food and entertainment of all kinds."

There seems to be absolutely no reason to believe that this account is in any way exaggerated. Indeed, we have abundant testimony from very different sources, some of which has already been quoted in our notice of the individual Jubilees, that the personal participation of the cardinals, prelates, noble ladies, and even of the Pope himself, in rendering the most humiliating services to the pilgrims was no flight of the imagination, but a sober reality. This admirable work was carried on by the arch-confraternity down to the Jubilee of 1825. Of this, Cardinal Wiseman, as already noted, has left us a singularly interesting account, and we cannot do better than retain his own words in giving some idea of the working of this medieval organisation under comparatively modern conditions.[1]

"The pilgrim on his arrival at the house had his papers of pilgrimage examined, and received his ticket of hospitality. In

THE INDULGENCE IS READ TO THE PILGRIMS.
From a Jubilee print of 1650.

the evening the new-comers were brought into a hall surrounded by raised seats, and provided with an abundant supply of hot and cold water. Then, after a short prayer, the brethren of the confraternity, or the sisters in their part of the house, washed their feet, way-worn and sore by days or weeks of travel. . . . Thus refreshed, the pilgrims joined the long procession to supper.

"A bench along the wall, and a table before it, railed off to prevent the pressure of curious multitudes, were simple arrangements enough, but the endless length of these, occupied by men of every hue and many languages, formed a striking spectacle.

---

[1] *Recollections of the Last Four Popes*, p. 279 *seq.*

Before each guest was his plate, knife, fork, and spoon, bread, wine, and dessert. A door in each refectory communicated with a roomy hall, in which huge cauldrons smoked with a supply of savoury soup sufficient for an army. . . . A cardinal or nobleman, in the coarse red gown and badge of the brotherhood, with a white apron over it, armed with a ladle, dispensed the steaming fluid into plates held ready; and a string of brothers, at arms' length from one another all round the refectory, handed forward

CONFRATERNITY ASSEMBLING IN THEIR CHAPEL TO WELCOME A PROCESSION OF PILGRIMS.
From a Jubilee broadside of 1650 at the British Museum.

the plates with the alacrity of bricklayers' labourers, and soon furnished each hungry recipient with his steaming portion. Two additional rations were served out in the same manner. . . . Opposite each guest stood a serving man who poured out his wine, cut his bread, etc., and chatted with him. Now, these were not hired servitors, but all brethren of the confraternity; sometimes a royal prince, generally some cardinals, always bishops, prelates, noblemen, priests, gentry, and artificers. Then, occasionally, a sudden commotion, a movement through the crowd . . . just as prayers were beginning. The Holy Father was coming without notice. Indeed, none was required: he came simply to do what every one else was going to do, only he had the first place. He knelt before the first line of pilgrims, taking his chance of who it might be. . . . Supper ended, and its baskets of fragments for the morrow's breakfast put by, the long file proceeded upstairs to bed, singing one of the short religious strains in which all Italians can join. During the day the pilgrims were conducted in bands from sanctuary to sanctuary; were instructed at stated times; were directed to the performance of their higher religious duties by frequenting the Sacraments; and at the close of the three days were dismissed in peace, and returned home, or remained in the city at their own charge. The Pope also, we may note, daily served in his own palace twelve pilgrims at table."

What Cardinal Wiseman describes from his own observation in 1825 is equally well attested by eye-witnesses at an earlier epoch. Take, for instance, this account of Mr. Richard Lassels, a seventeenth-century traveller, who, Catholic though he was, was no zealot, and who had more experience of foreign lands than almost any Englishman of his day.

"Here you shall find the Hospital of the Holy Trinity, which in the Jubilee year of Clement the VIII. is found to have treated at table in one day 15,000 pilgrims, and in the whole year 500,000. The last Jubilee year, 1650, I myself was present one day when the said hospital treated 9000 pilgrims that day, the Pope himself (Innocent the X.) and many of the cardinals having been there to wash the feet of the pilgrims and to serve them at table."[1]

The Maundy or washing of the feet of thirteen poor men is still performed every year by the Pope in person on Maundy Thursday, and this ceremony, commemorative of the action of

[1] R. Lassels, *The Voyage of Italy*, i. p. 8. The original owner of the Jubilee broadside of 1699, now in the British Museum, has copied out this passage on the margin of the sheet.

our Blessed Lord before the Passion, may be traced back as a quasi-ecclesiastical function to the earliest ages of the Church. The Catholic sovereigns of Europe have not even yet entirely discontinued the practice, and the rulers of Spain, and, I think, Austria are not content with the distribution of a mere dole or bounty, as the fashion is in our Protestant land, but themselves render this menial service in person to some of their poorer subjects as to the representatives of Christ. Can any one call this a superfluous or degrading rite and not rather see in it a singular and much-needed tribute to the truth of the Christian revelation? The more worthless or arrogant the character of the sovereign who renders such a service, the more perfunctory his discharge of the irksome task, so much the more forcible in some sense becomes the lesson thereby afforded that there is another kingdom, not of this world, in which some day all earthly precedence must be laid aside.

THE MAUNDY OR WASHING OF THE FEET.
From the Giunta Pontificale of 1520.

During the Jubilee years most of the Popes in the seventeenth and eighteenth centuries elected to discharge this and other like menial offices not once but many times. Clement X. in 1675, though eighty-five years of age and a martyr to the gout, visited the Hospital of the Holy Trinity twelve times during the year, washing the feet of the pilgrims on each occasion and giving an alms to each one of them.[1] Clement VIII. again insisted on performing the like office when one hand was crippled with the same complaint.[2] So, too, the last-named Pontiff, in order to impress upon the prelates and citizens of Rome that the season

[1] Novaes, *Storia de' Sommi Pontefici*, x. 244.
[2] *Ibid.* lx. 54.

of the Jubilee was one of humiliation and penance and not of festivity, went abroad with the slenderest of retinues and in the simplest of attire and persuaded the cardinals that during the greater part of the Anno Santo they should wear woollen and violet instead of their ordinary robes of scarlet silk.[1] Of the suspension of the carnival and the prohibition of theatrical performances during these seasons we have already spoken. This dominant note of penance and humiliation is also made prominent in the pictures of the various Jubilee sheets such as that referred to at the beginning of this chapter, and in nearly all the discourses of famous preachers which make reference to the Holy Year.

Although the Arch-Confraternity of the Holy Trinity was by far the most conspicuous organisation in Rome which undertook the work of providing for the bodily and spiritual needs of the Jubilee pilgrims, it must not be supposed that the burden fell upon this body alone. Italy was at that time, and had been for centuries, one vast network of confraternities, or, as we should call them, religious guilds.[2] Nearly all of these had some conspicuous central association or *arch*-confraternity in Rome, with which those in outlying parishes or in other districts were in some sort of relation of correspondence or dependence. Now, at the Jubilee time the arch-confraternities in Rome made it a part of their duty to welcome and assist in every way the bodies of similar denomination and scope with which they were in communication in the surrounding country. The brothers of the arch-confraternity of gardeners or stonemasons would render all kind offices to provincial confraternities of gardeners and stonemasons; or a more strictly religious arch-confraternity, such as that of the Blessed Sacrament, would give a welcome to the pilgrims of other confraternities of the Blessed Sacrament which, in their object, origin, or regulations, were similar to their own. One of those illustrated Jubilee sheets of 1650, to which we have more than once referred, gives a description of the work done by

[1] Diary of Alaleona, MS. Ad. 8454, fol. 140 r° *seq.*

[2] See Pastor, *Geschichte der Päpste*, third edition, vol. iii. pp. 43-52.

these Roman arch-confraternities to help the associated branches in other parts of Italy, and, despite a certain resemblance in its main features to the account of the institute of the Holy Trinity, it seems worth while to reproduce it here. It is headed—

An account of the way in which the Arch-Confraternities of Rome receive and entertain the Confraternities affiliated to them which come to Rome for the Jubilee.

"Letters of invitation are sent to the confraternities offering them hospitality, and a day before their arrival the latter send a messenger to the head of the arch-confraternity to give notice of their coming. The brethren are then bidden to meet at a certain hour in their oratory, and when all are assembled they sally forth in procession headed by their superiors, guardians, or priors, proceeded by the crucifix, with banners and lighted torches and a choir of musicians, making their way to the gate of the city by which the expected confraternity is to enter. On meeting them each stranger brother is placed between two of his Roman *confrères*, and when they reach the entrance of the city the strangers kneel and kiss the threshold of the gate, being assisted to rise by the Roman brothers who stand on either side. They usually proceed first to the church of the arch-confraternity, psalms and hymns being sung on the road thither by the musicians before named, while the people flock in crowds to see the sight. Having arrived at the church, the pilgrims are received with the usual religious ceremonies and then conducted to their lodging, where they are served and their feet washed by the most noble and distinguished members of the arch-confraternity, the women being in like manner cared for by noble ladies, no man being permitted to enter their quarters except a Capuchin or some other priest who goes to preach to them.

"The pilgrims are then entertained at a bountiful meal, during which some eloquent preacher discourses to them, and they are waited on and served by cardinals, prelates, and princes, who frequently provide the banquet at their own expense. If the arch-confraternity does not possess a sufficiently large house to lodge so many guests, an adjacent palace is hired and comfortably fitted up for the accommodation of the pilgrims, who are conducted thither and waited upon by the Roman brothers.

"The next day experienced priests are in attendance ready to instruct them, hear their confessions, etc., and when they are sufficiently rested physically, and prepared spiritually, the arch-confraternity obtains permission for them from the Holy Father

KISSING THE THRESHOLD OF THE GATES OF ROME.
From a Jubilee broadside of 1650.
N.B.—The whole drawing is ludicrously out of perspective.

to gain the Indulgence of the Jubilee by paying only one visit to the Basilicas. They are then taken in procession, with music and other spiritual consolations, to the four churches. They usually receive Communion at St. Paul's without the walls, where numerous priests are in readiness to give them Holy Communion. As the most sacred and celebrated relics are preserved at these four churches, the pilgrims have also the opportunity afforded them of seeing and venerating these relics.

About half-way, either in the courtyard of St. John Lateran or in some other commodious place, the arch-confraternity provides the customary collation, and at the end of the journey they are taken to the Apostolic Palace, where the Holy Father gives them his blessing. They are then conducted back to their own church or oratory, where, after returning thanks to God, the nature and value of the Indulgence they have gained is explained to them. The pilgrims' feet are again washed, and they are regaled with a bountiful supper, and comfortably rested. They are entertained thus for a few days longer, and at their departure from

PILGRIMS GOING IN PROCESSION TO VISIT THE FOUR CHURCHES.
From a Jubilee broadside of 1650 at the British Museum.

Rome are accompanied in procession by the arch-confraternity to the gate of the city, returning to their own country much edified and in great content.

"This is the usual order of proceedings as practised in the principal arch-confraternities, although they may be somewhat modified or altered according to the various regulations or customs of each in particular."[1]

[1] This broadside, with two others of similar purport from which we have already quoted, is bound up in a volume of miscellaneous religious engravings in the Printed Book Department of the British Museum.

It is obvious that the association of large masses of men joining together for a common religious purpose cannot have failed to enkindle their fervour in an unusual degree. Even at ordinary seasons the sights and associations of Rome seem to have called forth most striking manifestations of enthusiasm, especially at the time of the Holy Week processions and at the exhibition of the greater relics. We happen to possess a detailed account from the pen of the celebrated French essayist Michel de Montaigne of the spectacle which he witnessed in 1580 at the exposition of the Veronica or *Volto Santo* on Holy Thursday evening. This was not, of course, a Jubilee year, but his description will afford us an excellent idea of the spectacles which will have been renewed at such times with much greater frequency and upon an even grander scale.

It would not be easy to find a more satisfactory witness than this cynical old nobleman, who was in no danger of allowing his emotions to get the better of his judgment. Familiar as he was with the shows and the displays of the French capital, Montaigne seems to have been more struck by the procession of the confraternities which he witnessed at Rome in Holy Week in honour of the *Volto Santo,* than by any similar scene in his experience. "No relic," he says, "has such veneration paid to it. The people throw themselves on their faces on the ground, most of them with tears in their eyes, and with lamentations and cries of compassion." The exposition of the *Volto Santo,* as well as that of the Holy Lance, took place several times in the day, "with such an infinite concourse of people, that to a great distance from the church, at every point from which the eye could catch a glimpse of the platform from which the relics were shown, there was nothing but a dense mass of men and women." With regard to the procession in the evening he says—

"The confraternities during Lent perform at times their religious exercises in common, and on this occasion they all walk in procession draped with linen gowns, each company having a different colour, some black, some white, some red, some blue, some green, and so on. Nearly all have their faces covered. . . .

"The most impressive sight I ever saw here or elsewhere was the incredible number of people who thronged every square and street, all taking an earnest part in the devotions of the occasion. They were flocking to St. Peter's all through the day, and on the approach of night the whole city seemed in flames. Each religious confraternity came up in order, each man with a torch, almost all of white wax. I am persuaded that there passed before me not fewer than twelve thousand of these torches at the very least, for from eight o'clock in the evening till midnight the street was constantly full of this moving pageantry marshalled in such excellent order and all so well timed that, though the entire procession, as I have said, was composed of a great number of different societies coming from different parts, yet not for one moment did I observe stoppage or gap or interruption. Each company was preceded by a band of music" (p. 309).

The writer then goes on to describe other features in the procession, more especially the penitents, numbers of whom, with shoulders bared, scourged themselves until their backs streamed with blood. His account is perhaps a little too realistic to be reproduced here, but there are two observations particularly worthy of notice, confirmed as they are in every respect by the Dominican traveller, Father Labat, who visited Italy somewhat more than a century later.[1] In the first place, Montaigne was convinced of the entire genuineness of this severe penance which he witnessed, and he sets aside unhesitatingly the theory of some scoffers that the whole exhibition was but a stage trick performed to deceive the people. On the other hand, both he and Father Labat seem agreed that the contageous emotion and enthusiasm of the scene must have dulled to a very great extent the sense of pain and mitigated the suffering which this self-inflicted chastisement ought naturally to have produced. The flagellants in many cases laughed and jested as they moved

[1] Cf. also the Travels of the Protestant Sir John Reresby, who witnessed a similar procession in Venice in 1657.—*Travels, etc.*, third edition, p. 73.

along, and with merry Italian humour exchanged banter with the crowd of spectators. Neither would they seem to have been wholly indifferent to more worldly and mercenary considerations in deciding upon the particular confraternity whose banner they elected to follow. It is easy to sneer at the superstition and unreality of such penance as this, but it is precisely in matters of this sort that the average English Protestant goes so hopelessly astray. He can make no allowance for a national character which has never learned to dissociate cheerfulness from piety, the service of God from a practical and very matter-of-fact attention to temporal interests.[1]

The deep impression produced by such scenes and by the magnificent ritual of the Church, carried out as it can be carried out in Rome alone, was not confined to Catholics. Dr. John Moore, whose honest but somewhat irreverent comments on the papal ceremonial we have already quoted from, was present in 1775 at the closing ceremony of the Jubilee, and at the solemn benediction given by the Pope after High Mass the next day to the people in the Piazza of St. Peter's. He has left us an account of it in his very racy and interesting *View of Society and Manners in Italy*. We need make no apology for quoting this portion of his narrative without curtailment.

"After Mass, the Pope gave the benediction to the people assembled in the Grand Court before the Church of St. Peter's. It was a remarkably fine day. An immense multitude filled

[1] It should be noted that in the diaries of the papal masters of ceremonies the veneration of the *Volto Santo* is brought into some sort of formal connection with the Jubilee ceremonial. F. Mucanzio, for instance, tells us in his description of the closing rite that after vespers a procession is formed to the Holy Door *et ostenso vultu sancto* Papa stans sine mitra intonat antiphonam ex libro: *Cun jucunditate exibitis* (MS. Addit. 26811, fol. 169 r°). Again he tells us that the procession traversed the aisle of the *Volto Santo* (the northernmost aisle of the church), and there, with the Cardinals, the Pope venerated upon his knees the *Volto Santo* and the Holy Lance (fol. 177 r°). The Holy Lance was at this time preserved in the same chapel with the handkerchief of St. Veronica. It had been given to Pope Innocent VIII. less than a hundred years before by the Sultan Bajazet, not without an eye to certain political considerations, and the relic had been received in Rome with extraordinary enthusiasm. See Pastor, *Geschichte der Päpste*, third edition, vol. iii. p. 238.

that spacious and magnificent area. The horse and foot guards were drawn up in their most showy uniform. The Pope, seated in an open portable chair, in all the splendour which his wardrobe could give, with the tiara on his head, was carried out of a large window, which opens on a balcony in front of St. Peter's. The silk hangings and gold trappings with which the chair was embellished concealed the men who carried it, so that to those who viewed him from the area below, his Holiness seemed to sail forward from the window, self-balanced in the air, like a celestial being. The instant he appeared the music struck up, the bells rung from every church. and the cannon thundered from the castle of St. Angelo in repeated peals.

"During the intervals the Church of St. Peter's, the palace of the Vatican, and the banks of the Tiber re-echoed to the acclamations of the populace. At length his Holiness arose from his seat, and an immediate and awful silence ensued. The multitude fell upon their knees, with their hands and eyes raised towards his Holiness, as to a benign Deity. After a solemn pause he pronounced the benediction with great fervour, elevating his outstretched arms as high as he could, then closing them together and bringing them back to his breast with a slow motion as if he had got hold of the blessing and was drawing it gently from heaven. Finally he threw his arms open, waving them for some time as if his intention had been to scatter the benediction with impartiality among the people.

"No ceremony can be better calculated for striking the senses and imposing on the understanding than this of the Supreme Pontiff giving the blessing from the balcony of St. Peter's. For my own part, if I had not in my early youth received impressions highly unfavourable to the chief actor in this magnificent interlude, I should have been in danger of paying him a degree of respect very inconsistent with the religion in which I was educated."[1]

However much a certain element of emotional excitement

---

[1] *View of Society and Manners in Italy*, vol. ii. pp. 45-47. Dr. Moore was the son of a Scottish Episcopalian minister residing at Stirling.

The Papal Blessing given Urbi et Orbi from the Loggia of St. Peter's.

may have entered into scenes such as these, it would be very rash to infer that the impression produced was never permanent. The instance of such a man as the poet Petrarch, already referred to, is a striking testimony to the contrary, and in any case amendment of life, even if it be unstable and evanescent, is an object well worth striving for.

Before taking leave of the Jubilee pilgrims and the confraternities to pass to somewhat more general considerations, it may be worth while to say a word about the costume in which the old prints, from which several of our illustrations are taken, represent the pilgrims as attired. It will be noticed that they are clothed from head to foot in a long tunic or frock almost like the habit of a religious, while at their back hangs an object which, in the rude engravings here reproduced, looks almost like a tassel, but which must in reality be a sort of hood or cowl which could on occasion be drawn over the head. The following remarks of a native Italian, who wrote at the end of the seventeenth century, though referring primarily to the pilgrims at Loreto, are clearly applicable also to those who were received at Rome by the arch-confraternities during the Holy Year:—

"I saw a great number of persons coming into the town. . . . They were all pilgrims that came from Bononia, about threescore in number, all mounted on asses and accoutred in pilgrimage habits. These consist of a large linen gown of an ash-grey colour reaching down to the middle of the leg, with very wide sleeves coming down to the wrist. On the back of these gowns at the collar they have a kind of large cowl which they put over their heads, and being pulled down reacheth to the pit of the stomach, so that their faces are wholly covered with them. And to the end that in this posture they might have free sight and breathing, these cowls have openings in them answering to the eyes and mouth like masks. They never draw these cowls over their heads but when they come to places where they have no mind to be known, for otherwise they let them hang backward on their shoulders. They bind this gown about them with a girdle, and somewhat above the girdle, upon the breast, they have a scutcheon representing the arms of their society, confraternity, or company, which they call in Italian *scuola*. There are scarcely any Italians that do not belong to one or other of these confraternities. The pilgrims, moreover, have a long string of beads hanging at their girdles and a pilgrim's staff in their hands, which is the chief mark of their pilgrimage. These staves are about half a pike's length, with knots or protuberances at the top and middle of them. They carry them to the church to get them blessed by the parish priests before their setting forth. As soon as they have received them, it is not lawful for them to stay any longer than three days at the place of their residence, and they cannot be admitted to Communion until they have performed their pilgrimage unless it be commuted into a pecuniary mulct."[1]

Although this information comes from rather a tainted source (the author was an apostate who wrote in his exile a book to vilify the Church which he had scandalised and disgraced), it may probably be trusted as a record of customs with which its author was thoroughly familiar, and to which we have frequent allusions in other quarters. This friar-like costume of the confraternities was conspicuous in all processions, but most noticeable of all were the sombre habiliments of the brothers of the *Misericordia*, who performed the pious office of providing for the burial of the dead and who accompanied the body to the grave. Of the *Misericordia* we shall have to speak a little further on.

The great bulk of the Jubilee pilgrims no doubt performed their journey on foot, but even for those who could afford to ride, the undertaking must generally have been penitential enough. Two of our pictures, which have been taken from a collection of engravings by Bertellio, printed in the last decade of the sixteenth century, will serve to give the reader an idea of the appearance of the more wealthy and luxurious class of pilgrims as they travelled to Rome for the Jubilee in winter or summer as the case might be. They will also serve to illustrate

[1] D'Emiliane, *Frauds of the Romish Monks* (English edition), vol. ii. p. 112.

a note or two which we may borrow from the descriptions of contemporary English travellers. Take, for instance, the following from the famous Tom Coryat:—

After speaking of the prevalence of fans in Italy, which were used habitually by men as well as women, and which might be purchased very cheaply, he adds:—

"Also many of them doe carry other fine things of a far

TRAVELLING IN ITALY—SUMMER.
From a rare engraving by Bertellio in the British Museum, c. 1590.

greater price, that will cost at the least a ducket, which they commonly call in the Italian tongue *umbrellaes*, that is things that minister shadow unto them for shelter against the scorching heat of the sunne. These are made of leather, something answerable to the forme of a little cannopy and hooped in the inside with divers little wooden hoopes that extend the umbrella in a pretty large compasse. They are used especially by horsemen, who carry them in their hands when they ride, fastening the ende of the handle upon one of their thighes, and they impart so long a shadowe unto them, that it keepeth the heate of the sunne from the upper parts of their bodies."[1]

In this account Fynes Moryson, another English traveller, who recorded his experiences of Italy at the same epoch, entirely

TRAVELLING IN ITALY—WINTER.
Bertellio, c. 1590.

concurs, but he tells us of a danger from the use of these sunshades which we should not otherwise have suspected.

"On the contrary, in hot regions, to avoid the beames of the sunne, in some places (as in Italy) they carry umbrels, or things like a little canopy over their heads, but a learned physician

[1] Coryat, *Crudities* (originally published in 1611), vol. i. p. 135 (Edin. 1776).

told me that the use of these was dangerous, because they gather the heate into a pyramidall point, and thence cast it down perpendicularly upon the head, except they know how to carry them for avoyding that danger."[1]

In the winter portrait we may notice particularly the riding boots, about which we read much in all accounts of sixteenth-century travel, and the dispensing with which by St. Aloysius Gonzaga and other holy persons was accounted a great act of mortification.

To return to more important matters than those of costume, the apologists and panegyrists of the papal Jubilees were undoubtedly right in insisting that a pilgrimage to Rome was, ordinarily speaking, a means of moral education for those who undertook it in a spirit of devotion. No one can pretend to deny that abuses must have resulted at times from the gathering together of large bands of men and women, sometimes without adequate accommodation or suitable control. There was also in all probability a certain amount of extravagance or even superstition in these manifestations of popular devotion which can not be unreservedly commended. None the less, the impression which the pilgrimage left upon the bulk of the pilgrims must have made, on the whole, for edification, and for intellectual as well as moral improvement. During the four centuries with which we are more especially concerned, Italy and, in particular, Rome stood in the van of all civilising influences. In charitable organisations of all kinds, in her guilds and confraternities, in the treatment of the sick and the poor, in clemency towards the accused and towards convicted criminals, in the comparative moderation of her procedure against reputed sorcerers, at a time when northern nations almost without exception were dominated by the most extravagant witch-mania, in matters of cleanliness and politeness, as well as in the encouragement of the arts and sciences, Rome might bear comparison most favourably with any country of Europe, and, most of all, with any Protestant country. As we have already said, it was not

[1] Fynes Moryson, *Itinerary* (1617), part iii. p. 21.

without solid foundation that Rome was called *Roma la Santa.* The traveller, Richard Lassels, who had spent his life in visiting different European nations, not excepting Spain and the remoter parts of Germany, was giving expression to something more than mere partisanship when he wrote—

"And although Rome were anciently styled the head and mistress of the world, an earthly goddess, the eternal city . . . (while she was yet heathen), yet since her ladyship was baptised and became Christian, though she have had great eulogies made of her by the Holy Fathers, I find no title so honourable to her as that of *Roma la Santa*—Rome the Holy—which is given her by the common proverb, and common proverbs are nothing else but the observation of common sense, for whereas the other cities of Italy are proverbially called either fair, gentile, rich, proud, fatte, or great, as Florence, Naples, Venice, Genoa, Bologna, Milan; Rome only is styled the holy, and this deservedly for many reasons."

After some justification adduced from past history Mr. Lassels goes on—

"Besides these aforesaid reasons Rome may deservedly be called the holy for the many and singular acts of charity which are done there daily, more than in any other place. Charity is the queen of virtues; and if ever I saw this queen on her throne it was in Rome; for there I saw no evil, either of body or mind, but it had its remedy if curable, or at least its comforts if incurable.

"For the first—to wit, evils of the body—it has its hospitals, and those many, and many of those are hospitals in folio. Besides, no pilgrim comes to Rome but he finds Rome, as Adam did Paradise, with the table covered and the bed made ready for him. Poor young girls find portions either for husbands or nunneries, according to their choice. Infants whom cruel and unlawful mothers, like wolves, expose to death, Rome receives to life, and thinks it but a suitable *antipelargesis* to nourish wolves' children,[1] seeing a she-wolf nourished her founder being

[1] "Meretrices *lupas* vocabant, unde *lupanaria*," Augustine, *De Civit. Dei*, book xviii. c. 21.

exposed by men. Fools, too, and madmen, so much the more miserable, as not being so much as sensible of their condition (for *sæpe calamitatis solatium est nosse sortem suam*), have here those that take care of them. Poor men find hospitals when they are sick; and gentlemen whom nature hath not exempted from common miseries Rome exempts from common hospitals, and not being able to give them better health, she gives them at least better accommodation in their sickness. Here you shall find an apothecary's shop founded by Cardinal Francis Barberino, with a yearly revenue of twelve thousand crowns, and this for ever, to furnish the poor with physic gratis . . . Add to this that every nation hath here its several hospital and refuge, with church and churchmen to serve it. As the English College, once an hospital for the English; that of the Anima for the Germans; that of St. Louis for the French; that of St. Jacomo for the Spaniards; that of St. Antony of Padua for the Portuguese; that of St. Julian for the Flemings; that of St. Ambrose for the Lombards; that of St. Ivo for the Bretons; that of St. Jerome for the Illyrians; that of St. Mary of Egypt for the Armenians; that of St. Stephen for the Hungarians; that of St. Stanislaus for the Poles; besides a world of others. Nay, almost every corporation or body of artisans have their hospital among themselves which they maintain. In the Church of the Twelve Apostles they choose yearly twelve noblemen and one prelate who is called their prior; these go into every corner of Rome to seek out poor men who are ashamed to beg and yet are in great want. These bashful poor men put their names into a coffer well locked up and standing in a public place, by which means these charitable noblemen find them out and relieve them.

"What shall I say of the public charity of the Pope himself, well known to all; besides a world of private charities which he gives by his *Secreto Limosinero* to those that are ashamed to beg publicly? The like do many cardinals by their own hands; and in that high measure that Cardinal Montalto (to name no more) is found by his book of accounts to have given away above a hundred and seven thousand crowns to the poor.[1]

"As for those charities which concern the mind, if a great king of Egypt wrote over his library door *Medicina Animi* (physic for the mind), here in Rome I find store of such physic in libraries, colleges, monasteries, and devout companies."

After specifying some of the more famous of these libraries and colleges, the writer goes on—"Add to this the variety of monasteries and convents, both of men and women, where they may hide themselves securely *donec transeat iniquitas.* Then the taking away of young girls at ten or twelve years old from their poor suspected mothers, and the bringing them up virtuously under careful matrons of known virtue, till they either choose the nuptial *flammeum* or the sacred *velum.*

"Then the remedies for ill-married women whose unadvised choice (marriages being often made for interest) or incompatible humours force a corporal separation; and lest such unfortunate women should either live incontinently indeed, or give suspicion of it, they are provided here with a house where they live retiredly under lock and key till they either reconcile themselves again to their husbands, or, upon just occasions, leave them for ever. Over the door of this house is written, *Per le donne mal maritate.*"

Then after speaking of the house for penitent women, dedicated to St. Mary Magdalen, whose lives of voluntary penance often equalled in strictness that of the penitents of old, Mr. Lassels continues—

"What shall I say of the congregation of advocates and attornies instituted in Rome, where they meet once a week to examine poor men's law-suits, and either dehort them from proceeding in bad causes, or prosecute good causes for them at the cost of this congregation?

"What shall I say of several pious clergymen (especially the good priests of the Oratory, happy in this employment) who make it their task to reconcile disagreeing families, and with

[1] *A Voyage through Italy*, pp. 6, 7, part ii.

great zeal and piety exhort first the one and then the other of the parties, intervene between them, speak well of the one to the other, clear and take away jealous misunderstandings, and, in fine, piece again broken neighbours? What shall I say of the four sermons daily in the *Chiesa Nuova* by the most learned and good priests of the oratory, who being most of them learned men, as Baronius, Bosius, Justinianus, Renaldus, etc., and able to fly high, yet in their own sermons stoop to a low pitch and a popular facile way which aims rather at conversion than ostentation, and doth great good, though it make little noise, *Dominus in leni aura?*

"What shall I say of the weekly sermons to the Jews upon Saturday, where they are bound to be present to the number of 800; where the Pope entertains a learned preacher to convince them out of their own Scriptures; and those that are converted are provided for in the Hospital of the Catechumens till they be thoroughly instructed? I have seen divers of them baptized.

"What shall I say of the *scholæ piæ* in Rome, a company of good religious men who look like Jesuits, save only that they go barefoot in sandals? These good fathers make a profession to teach poor boys *gratis* their first grammar rudiments, and to make them fit to be sent to the Jesuits' schools, and having taught them thus in the schools, they accompany them home in the streets, lest they should either learn waggery as they go home or practise it. Nay, these humble men make it their profession not to teach higher schools where there might be some profit and honour, at least some satisfaction and pleasure, but they content themselves to go barefoot and teach only the lower schools and first rudiments, by which they neither grow wiser nor richer. A strange mortified trade, but *Beati pauperes spiritu.*

"What shall I say of the Fathers of the Agonizants, whose vocation is to be the *seconds* of those who fight against death itself; that is, whose profession is to assist those that are in the agony of death, and to help them to make then those pious acts which Christians should most of all then rouse themselves up to?

"What can be said more? Yes, Rome, not content to have fed, to have bred, to have converted, baptized, reconciled the living and assisted the dying, she extends her charity even beyond death itself, and hath instituted a pious confraternity called *La compagnia de' morti*, whose office is to bury the dead and to visit those who are condemned, and by praying with them, exhorting them, and accompanying them to the execution, help them to die penitently, and bury them, being dead, and pray for their souls, being buried; after which charity can do no more to man. And therefore I will conclude that, seeing such singular acts of charity, both for body and mind, are practised nowhere so much as in Rome, it is true, which I assumed above, that Rome deserves to be called the Holy."[1]

This quotation from our seventeenth-century traveller sums up so well the argument which is the subject of the present chapter that it seems unnecessary to apologise for its length. What remains for us now is to prove by the evidence of other more independent witnesses who were not of the same creed as Mr. Richard Lassels, that his eulogy is not extravagantly overdrawn. And first with regard to the general question of charity and charitable institutions.

Although in our own day a large measure of philanthropy is met with almost universally, and hospitals, orphanages, refuges are to be found all over the earth's surface, it is very important to remember that these works of charity have been of very slow growth in Protestant England. The books of John Howard, published very little more than a century ago, would alone suffice to let us see how wretchedly inadequate was the provision made in his day for the relief of the infirm and destitute of this country. There was hardly a hospital in London which received patients without fees, and the insanitary conditions under which lived prisoners in gaol, the insane in lunatic asylums, and even the sick in the infirmaries, were

[1] *A Voyage through Italy*, pp. 11-13.

appalling. No one who has looked into such original authorities as are available will consider the picture of the state of affairs which is given in the fourth and fifth volumes of *Social England* to be at all exaggerated. It falls, to our thinking, rather short than in excess of the facts.

"The public assistance of the poorer classes in time of sickness," writes Dr. Creighton, "so conspicuous as it is in modern life, was late in beginning, having made little progress until the great wave of philanthropic sentiment in the second half of the eighteenth century. There were indeed many almshouses, . . . and there were some 'hospitals' in the sense of asylums for the aged and infirm, which had survived the general alienation or decay of medieval charities. In London the two great monastic foundations of St. Bartholomew in Smithfield and St. Thomas in the Borough had been converted into surgical and medical infirmaries. The old royal palace of Bridewell adjoining Fleet Street has been used from time to time as a plague hospital, in addition to the two small pest-houses in Finsbury and Westminster. But the design of great hospitals for the sick, which makes one of the most characteristic socialist visions of More's "Utopia," had come to little in the London of half a million or more inhabitants; while in Bristol, Newcastle, and other large towns nothing had been done towards it except under the Poor Law." "It is not easy to name any hospitals," says Dr. Creighton further on, "existing at that time (1664) outside London."[1]

With regard to prisons a full century later, in the time of John Howard, Major Arthur Griffiths, Her Majesty's Inspector of Prisons at the present day, and the highest authority on the subject tells us—

"From one end of the kingdom to the other our prisons were a standing disgrace to civilisation. Imprisonment, from whatever cause it might be imposed, meant consignment to a living tomb, an existence of acute suffering. Gaols were pest-houses; a fell disease peculiar to them, but akin to our modern typhus, was bred within their foul limits, and flourished constantly,

[1] *Social England*, edited by H. D. Traill, vol. iv. pp. 589-91.

often in epidemic form. Pauper prisoners, by far the largest population, were nearly starved, for there was no regular allowance of food; their beds, of old littered straw, reeked with filthy exhalations; if they were ill the doctors feared to approach them; chaplains held aloof, and the dying were left to the ministrations of an occasional self-devoted layman. Worse even than the cruel neglect of the authorities was the

POLISH PILGRIMS JOURNEYING TO ROME.
From an engraving by Bertellio at the end of the sixteenth century.

active oppression exercised by the stronger over the weaker prisoners; there were gaol customs, such as that of 'garnish' or 'footing,' exacted from the new-comers who were called upon to 'pay or strip.' In default their clothes were torn off their backs, and they were left naked to eke out a wretched existence, forbidden to approach the fire, to lie on the straw, or share in the daily doles of food made by the charitable."[1]

As a mere matter of statistics, it may be asserted without fear of contradiction that at the end of the seventeenth century there were more charitable institutions and organisations in the one city of Rome, with a population of under 150,000 souls, than there were, exclusive of almshouses, in the whole of the United Kingdom, with a population of nearly 8,000,000.

In spite of the strong religious prejudice of the sixteenth, seventeenth, and eighteenth centuries, there is no lack of evidence from anti-papistical sources that the contrast between England and Rome in this respect forced itself upon the attention of all honest-minded observers. It is very instructive to note the reproaches which were addressed by Protestants themselves to their fellow-countrymen in Elizabeth's day on the ground of the little charity shown in England to the sick and the poor. "I have heard travellers of credit avouch," writes Thomas Nash, the friend of Marlowe and Greene, "that in London is not given the tenth part of that alms in a week which in the poorest besieged city of France is given in a day. What is our religion? all avarice and no good works. Because we may not build monasteries, or have Masses, Dirges, or Trentals sung for our souls, are there no deeds of mercy which God hath enjoined us?"[2]

Again, it is instructive to find an Englishman of Elizabeth's day speaking in such terms as the following. The man was seemingly half a pirate, who had been captured in Italy and was subsequently condemned to the galleys for what he maintains to have been a religious offence. In any case, his narrative of his sufferings was intended to make a direct appeal to the no-popery spirit of his countrymen. It was printed in London in 1592.

"Now, as I have spoken of the two deadly sins (murder,

---

[1] *Social England*, vol. v. pp. 483, 484.

[2] Nash, *Christ's Teares*, edition 1613, p. 172.

and the toleration of courtesans[1]) wherein they erred, so will I speak of one thing wherein some of them are to be commended, that is this: If there be any Christian, of what nation soever, poor and in distress, making his case known and asking for Christ's sake, he shall be relieved, with all those necessaries whereof he is destitute, as apparel, meat, and drink, and some money, though it be but little; if he is sick, then shall he be put into a hospital, where he shall be choicely attended upon, having good lodging, dainty diet, and comfortable physic for the restoring of his health, whether he be Papist or Protestant; but if he be a Papist he shall be better used, and if he be a Protestant they will use all means they can to convert him, but force him to nothing at all."[2]

Or let us take this description of one of the most famous Roman hospitals in 1644. It occurs in the well-known Diary of John Evelyn, who, needless to say, was no Papist.

"Hence we went to see Dr. Gibbs,[3] a famous poet and countryman of ours, who has some intendency in an hospital built on the Via Triumphalis, called Christ's Hospital, which he showed us. The Infirmatory, where the sick lay, was paved

---

[1] No better defence of the attitude of the Roman authorities in this matter could be found than that which is contained in the remarks of the Protestant traveller Keysler (*Travels*, vol. ii. pp. 40 *seq.*, 1756, English translation). His book was regarded at the beginning of the last century as a thoroughly reliable and authoritative work. It was translated from the original German into several foreign languages, and more than one edition appeared in English. Those who know anything of the dramatic and satirical literature of Elizabeth's reign, or who have studied such books as Cordy Jeaffreson's *Middlesex County Records*, will know how little the Englishmen of that day could afford to throw stones at other nations for their toleration of immorality.

[2] W. Davies, *A True Relation, etc.* A copy of this somewhat rare booklet is in the British Museum.

[3] This Dr. Gibbs was a St. Omers boy, the son of a convert. In recognition of his remarkable skill in Latin versification the Emperor presented him with a gold medal and the title of poet laureate. His fame as a physician further obtained for him the honorary degree of M.A. from Oxford University, a unique honour for a Catholic in those days. In his will he bequeathed the Emperor's gold medal to the University of Oxford, where it is still preserved, and a smaller facsimile of it, which he was accustomed to wear around his neck, was left by him to his old College of St. Omers.

with various coloured marbles, and the walls hung with noble pieces. The beds are very fair. In the middle is a stately cupola, under which is an altar decked with divers marble statues, all in sight of the sick, who may both see and hear Mass as they lie in their beds. The organs are very fine, and frequently played on to recreate the people in pain. To this joins an apartment destined for the orphans; and there is a school; the children wear blue, like ours in London, at an hospital of the same appellation. Here are forty nurses who give suck to such children who are accidentally found exposed and abandoned. In another quarter are children of bigger

THE ASSEMBLING OF THE PROCESSION OF PILGRIMS.
From a Jubilee print of 1560.

growth, 450 in number, who are taught letters. In another 500 girls, under the tuition of divers religious matrons, in a monastery, as it were, by itself. I was assured there were at least 2000 more maintained in other places. I think one apartment had in it near 1000 beds. Those are in a very long room, having an inner passage for those who attend, with as much care, sweetness, and conveniency as can be imagined, the Italians being generally very neat. Under the portico the sick may walk out and take the air. Opposite to this are other chambers for such as are sick of maladies of a more rare and difficult cure, and they have rooms apart. At the end of the long corridor is an apothecary's shop, fair and very well stored; near which are chambers for persons of better quality who are yet necessitous. Whatever the poor bring is, at their coming in, delivered to a treasurer, who makes an inventory and is accountable to them, or to their representatives if they die.

"To this building joins the house of the commendator, who, with his officers attending the sick, make up ninety persons, besides a convent and an ample church for the friars and priests who daily attend. The church is extremely neat and the sacrestia is very rich. Indeed it is altogether one of the most pious and worthy foundations I ever saw. Nor is the benefit small which divers young physicians and chirurgeons reap by the experience they learn here amongst the sick, to whom those students have free access."[1]

It would be tedious to quote at length from the multiplied testimonies of travellers to the charity displayed in Rome towards the poor and suffering. Even the scurrilous and filthy little volume, *A Pilgrimage to the Grand Jubilee*, owns grudgingly that "the Romans are very charitable towards the poor," though it at once proceeds to sneer at pecuniary gains the people were supposed to reap from the pilgrims who visited it. Keysler, the famous German traveller, to whom reference has been made in a previous footnote, and who was acquainted with France and England as well as Italy, tells us very honestly that "no country in the world equals Italy in the care of the poor and sick," and he gives a most attractive description of one or two famous hospitals which he had himself visited.[2] With

---

[1] *Evelyn's Diary*, vol. i. pp. 144, 145.

[2] The account which Keysler gives of the principal hospitals of Paris, which follows immediately on the above passage, is appalling, and the London hospitals were worse: "*La Charité* and *l'Hotel de Dieu*, at Paris, indeed receive a great number of patients; but nothing of the regularity and cleanliness of the Italian hospitals is to be seen there. Only the lower wards of the *Hotel de Dieu* have single beds for each patient, and these are but few in number, and are paid for; most of the other beds are for two persons, who also lie one at the head and the other at the feet, and in many of the beds four patients lie in the same manner. In such a situation, it must necessarily fall out that some patients who are on

regard to Howard's visits to Italy, although it would seem that he or his editors were not willing that he should become too directly the panegyrist of Italian institutions, it is at the same time obvious from incidental remarks that he regarded the state of things in Italy as far superior to the rest of the world. For instance, we find that he gives a very favourable account of the Hotel Dieu at Lyons as he saw it in 1783. In 1785 he visited the hospital again and was not so well satisfied, whereupon he remarks of his former impression—"Having not then seen the well-regulated hospitals of Italy and Spain, perhaps I was now too much struck with the difference, and perhaps also an allowance should be made for my seeing this hospital in the depth of winter."[1] So on going to Italy he remarks—"I entered Italy . . . with raised expectations of considerable information, from a careful attention to the prisons and hospitals in a country abounding with charitable institutions and public edifices." Though he is not satisfied with the condition of the Santo Spirito hospital in Rome, he lets us know that it had 1103 patients all in separate beds, and there were several other hospitals beside this. At the same period the largest hospital in London, with a population of over 1,000,000, was St. Thomas's, with 440 beds while St. Bartholomew's had 428. In nearly all the London hospitals entrance fees were charged, amounting to some four shillings for "clean" and twenty-five shillings for "foul" patients.[2]

Howard speaks well of the prison in Rome, and of the galleys for convicts belonging to the States of the Church. He considers that he had never seen any galleys that were better managed than these last, and he remarks further—"In visiting the prisons of Italy I observed that in general great attention was paid to the sick; but I could not avoid remarking that too little care was taken to *prevent* sickness. From the heat of the

the mending hand may be obliged to lie several hours with others who are in the agonies of death; and it is no very uncommon case for the dead to lie an hour or longer among the living; especially if it happens that the patient dies after ten of the clock at night."—Keysler's *Travels*, vol. ii. p. 345.

[1] Howard, *State of Prisons, etc.*, p. 179.

[2] Howard, *Prisons*, p. 106. *Lazarettos*, pp. 134, 136.

climate one might imagine the gaol fever would be very likely to prevail, but I did not find it in any of the prisons."[1]

There seems to have been an equally general agreement in commending the mercifulness of Roman punishments, as compared with the practice of the rest of Europe, England emphatically not excepted. Montaigne gives an interesting description of the execution of a criminal in Rome at which he was present, and of the assistance in their black hoods of the brethren of the *Misericordia*, including, as he avers, gentlemen of the best families of Rome. The tall crucifix with its black cover, the veiled faces and shadowy forms of the brethren, the two friars on either hand of the criminal holding a picture of our Saviour before his face, never leaving him until the very last moment; the rapid death by hanging; and the demeanour of the crowd, all impressed the cynical old essayist most favourably. He contrasted it with the practice, too often adopted in his own country, of inflicting such terrible torments upon the criminal that the very thought of them beforehand must destroy that composure of mind which seems requisite for a proper preparation for death. He adds that the deterrent effect of extreme severity is sufficiently secured by the outrages inflicted on the dead body. Indeed, as he goes on to remark in his present description—

"The spectators, who had not evinced the slightest commiseration when the living man was being strangled, broke out into piteous cries and groans at every blow that was given him when they were cutting up his dead body. As soon as the execution was over," he adds, "several Jesuits or other religious climbed into some elevated position at different points, and began exhorting the people to profit by the scene which they had witnessed."[2]

---

[1] Howard, *Prisons, etc.*, p. 117 note; cf. *Lazarettos*, p. 58.

[2] In his *Essays* Montaigne remarks—"All that exceeds a simple death appears to me pure cruelty. Our law cannot expect that he whom the fear of being executed by being beheaded or hanged will not restrain, should be any more awed by the imagination of a slow fire, burning pincers, or the wheel. And I know not in the meantime whether we do not throw them into despair; for in what condition can the soul of a man be who expects for four-and-twenty hours together to be broken on the wheel, or after the old way, to be nailed to a cross?" (ii. 27, cf. ii. 11).

Very similar was the impression produced just two centuries later upon the Dr. John Moore whose satirical but good-humoured comments we have previously quoted.

He was present at the execution of a criminal thoroughly feared and detested by the Roman populace, a man who had committed no less than five murders. Notwithstanding this, he found the people reverent and compassionate. He was much impressed by the attendance of the brothers of the Misericordia, and he approved the expeditiousness and decorum which marked the infliction of the death penalty. An old woman, he tells us, cried out when all was over, "*Adesso spero che l'anima sua sia in paradiso*" (Now I hope that his soul is in heaven), and the multitude around seemed inclined to hope the same. "The manner in which this man was put to death was, no doubt, uncommonly mild when compared with the atrocity of his guilt; yet I am convinced that the solemn circumstances which accompanied his execution made a greater impression on the minds of the populace, and would as effectually deter them from the crimes for which he was condemned, as if he had been broken alive on the wheel and the execution performed in a less solemn manner."

Full, probably, of the remembrance of the ghastly spectacle of an English execution in the old hanging days, and of the callous indifference of the mob that attended on such occasions, Dr. Moore adds—

"The procession described above, I plainly perceived, made a very deep impression. I thought I saw more people affected by it than I have formerly observed among a much greater crowd, who were gathered to see a dozen or fourteen of their fellow-creatures dragged to the same death for housebreaking or highway robbery, mere venial offences in comparison of what this Italian had perpetrated. The attendance of the Capuchins, the crucifixes, the society of the *Misericordia*, the ceremony of confession—all have a tendency to strike the mind with awe and keep up the belief in a future state; and when the multitude beheld so many people employed and so much pains taken to save the soul of one of the most worthless of mankind, they must think that the saving of a soul is a matter of great importance, and therefore naturally infer that the sooner they begin to take care of their own the better."[1]

Neither was the treatment of criminals the only matter in which the moderation of the Romans was displayed. Keysler remarks that a much greater tolerance was shown to Protestants in Rome than in the cities of France. In Rome, for instance, such non-Catholics were permitted to remain standing during the Elevation, whereas in France all who were present, of whatsoever creed they might be, were compelled to kneel. And this candid Protestant continues—

"Travellers who have the least taste for arts and sciences meet with so many things in Rome to attract their curiosity that they may pass their time away without having recourse to frivolous diversions, debaucheries, or idle company. The variety of objects daily to be seen here afford sufficient topics for conversation in coffee-houses and public places, so that ribaldry and *double entendres*, which are perhaps to young people more prejudicial than gross obscenity, do not so frequently offend the ear as in France."

After commenting severely on the libertinism of the French capital, Keysler remarks—"I can with great truth affirm that the general conversation at Rome is less offensive and more instructive than in most other great cities"; and again, further on—"I have often thought that the popish religion, by affecting such pomp and splendour in churches and convents, especially in Italy, greatly contributes to the improvement of painting, sculpture, and architecture."[2]

The same traveller gives the following attractive description of the work of the Oratorians at Genoa. Though he specifies Genoa, the same methods of attracting, refining, and supernaturalising were employed elsewhere.

"In the Church of St. Philip Neri, belonging to the fathers of the Oratory, is some fine painting in fresco, by Franceschino di

---

[1] Vol. i. p. 486.

[2] Keysler, vol. ii. p. 212, English translation, 1757.

Bologna, with other pictures by Biola. Here are besides some admirable marble sculptures, and the church is lined in many places with *Brocatello di Spagna,* a beautiful kind of marble. Every Sunday evening during the winter an oratorio or religious opera is performed in this church, which is founded on some scripture history, and is succeeded by a sermon of near half an hour long, then the service concludes with a piece of church music. As the design of this is to keep people from ill company, and at the same time to incite them by the most animated exhortations to sanctity of life, no great objection, I think, can lie against it; but the summer diversion, though with the like view, cannot be looked upon with equal indulgence. Near Prince Doria's palace, without St. Thomas's Gate, these fathers have a garden, with a beautiful edifice in it, where every Sunday, in the afternoon, they permit several kinds of games, as draughts, chess, billiards; dice and cards indeed are excepted. It is true they do not play here for money but for *Ave Marias, Paternosters,* and other prayers; and at the breaking up of a party the losers kneel before an image of the Virgin Mary and there, according to their losing, discharge them to her, or to God, by *Paternosters,* etc. In the evening they leave off playing and an oratorio is performed; next comes a spiritual exhortation, and at length this medley of levity and religion closes with a solemn piece of music. The intent, indeed, is far from culpable, being to divert the commonalty from riotous meetings, and an excessive fondness for gaming is gratified without prejudice to their substance and families; but how this abuse of God's name in these lost prayers can be justified, or such babbling, to which many have but little inclination, can be termed lawful or edifying, is a mystery to me. I asked our guide, 'What course was taken when they played so deep, or the loss was so great, that the conquered party could not go through with the multitude of prayers he had lost?' He answered 'that this could seldom or never happen, the fathers not allowing of any great ventures, so that most of them play only for trifles, such as repeating a few rosaries, prayers, etc.'"[1]

[1] **Keysler, vol. ii. pp. 385, 386, English translation, 1725.**

It may appear strange to us at the present day that the northern countries of Europe should look to Italy in the sixteenth and seventeenth centuries, not only for a code of manners, but even for an example of cleanliness, but yet this undoubtedly was the case. It would seem that almost all those little contrivances at table which assist cleanliness and comfort are of Italian origin. Sir Fynes Moryson remarks, in evident surprise, that the southern nations are "curious" in keeping their churches "in which it were no small trespass so much as to spit."[1] He

THE FLORENTINE GAME OF "CALCIA."
An illustration in the Pilgrim Book of Schottus, originally prepared for the Jubilee of 1600.

tells us more than once that the Italians "eat neatly and modestly," showing a singular refinement in the ordering of their tables,[2] or, as he explains rather more fully in the following passage:—

"In generall the Italians, and more especially the Florentines, are most neate at the Table, and in their Innes from morning to night the Tables are spread with white cloathes, strewed with flowers and figge leaves, with Ingestars or glasses of divers

[1] *Itinerary*, part iii. p. 44.
[2] *Ibid.* p. 113.

coloured wines set upon them, and delicate fruits which would invite a man to eat and drink, who otherwise hath no appetite, being all open to the sight of passengers as they ride by the highway, through their great unglased windows. At the Table they touch no meate with the hand, but with a forke of silver or other mettall, each man being served with his forke and spoone and glasse to drinke. And as they serve small pieces of flesh (not whole joints as with us), so these pieces are cut into small bits, to be taken up with the forke, and they seeth the flesh till it be very tender. In summer time they set a broad earthen vessel full of water upon the Table, wherein little glasses filled with wine doe swimme for coolenesse."[1]

The following passage is even more significant in its implication of what contemporary English manners must have been:—

"I observed a custome in all those Italian cities and townes through the which I passed that is not used in any other country that I saw in my travels, neither doe I thinke that any other nation of Christendome doth use it but only Italy. The Italian, and also most strangers that are commorant in Italy, doe alwaies at their meales use a little forke when they cut their meate. For while with their knife, which they hold in one hand, they cut the meate out of the dish, they fasten their forke, which they hold in their other hand, upon the same dish, so that whatsoever he be that sitting in the company of any others at meale should unadvisedly touch the dish of meate with his fingers from which all the table doe cut, he will give occasion of offence unto the company, as having transgressed the laws of good manners, in so much that for his error he shall be at the least brow-beaten, if not reprehended in wordes. This forme of feeding, I understand, is generally used in all places of Italy, their forkes being for the most part made of yron or steele, and some of silver, but those are used only by Gentlemen. The reason of this curiosity is because the Italian cannot by any means indure to have his dish touched with fingers, seeing all men's fingers are not alike cleane. Hereupon I myself thought

[1] *Itinerary*, part iii. p. 115.

good to imitate the Italian fashion by this forked cutting of meate, not only while I was in Italy, but also in Germany, and oftentimes in England since I came home. Being once quipped for that frequent using of my forke by a certain learned Gentleman, a familiar friend of mine, one Mr. Laurence Whitaker, who in his merry humour doubted not to call me at table *furcifer*, only for using a fork at feeding but for no other cause."[1]

Without wishing to lay undue stress upon the principle that cleanliness is next to godliness, it seems not altogether out of place to call attention even to such minor matters. They all serve in their measure to show that in inviting the Christians of other countries to visit the shrines of the Apostles in the Mother City of western Christendom, the Popes were really doing a service to the cause of civilisation. Whatever may be the case in our own day, it is a curious fact that during just that period when the Jubilee pilgrimages were most frequented, Italy, and more especially Rome, set the example to the world in matters of piety, education, and refinement.

As for the piety, we can only say that a perusal of the various narratives of travellers writing from different points of view leaves upon the mind a very profound impression of the religious atmosphere which pervaded the whole country. It may, conceivably, have been a religion of externals, it may have been mingled with a good deal of crime, or of licentiousness, or of superstition. With that we are not for the moment concerned. But their religion, such as it was, was an intimate part of the life of the people, and it cannot be said that its observances sat upon them lightly. Let us note, for instance, the attention paid to the daily hearing of Mass, and the practice of fasting. Sir Fynes Moryson, an English Protestant, writing at the end of the sixteenth century, may speak for both these points, and Montaigne's narrative also bears witness to his own personal observance in these matters, courtier and man of fashion as he was. Now by Moryson we find it fully recognised that if a

[1] T. Coryat's *Crudities*, vol. i. pp. 106, 107 (1611).

traveller in Italy sojourning at an inn is to avoid suspicion, it is necessary for him daily to go out of his chamber in a morning as if he went to Mass; "for the Italians generally think they are not safe till in the morning they have worshipped the *Hostia* at the Elevation thereof."[1] So too he writes of Loreto:—

"Myself and my consorts were all this day fasting, for it had been an unpardonable sin to have demanded meat in our inn before we had been in the church, and would have given open occasion to suspect our religion."[2]

Moryson complains that during the whole of Lent he had to abstain from meat, which could not have been procured even if he had been willing to risk the suspicion which its purchase would have excited. Montaigne appears to have heard Mass daily, and during Lent not merely to have observed the abstinence, but to have attended the Stations in the different Roman churches. Moreover, although he seems to believe that the upper classes among his own countrymen were really more sincere in their religion than the Italians, he was struck with the number of devotions and confraternities with which Rome abounded, and with the great external manifestations of piety of which they were the occasion. He speaks of them as carrying their observance of the forms of religion even to extravagance.[3] Coryat seems to have been not less impressed by some of the practices he witnessed; as, for instance, the *Ave Maria* or *Angelus,* still familiar as a note of time in the mouths of residents in Italy. He says—

"Also there is another very superstitious custom, used not only in Venice, but also in all cities, towns, and parishes whatsoever of all Italy, in which they differ, as I think, from all Christian nations, that at noon and the setting of the sun, all men, women, and children must kneel and say their *Ave Maria* bareheaded, wheresoever they are, either in their houses or in the streets, when the *Ave Maria* bell ringeth."[4]

---

[1] Moryson, *Itinerary*, pt. iii. pp. 31, 32.

[2] *Ibid.* l.c. p. 100, pt. i.

[3] Montaigne, *Voyage* (ed. d'Ancona), p. 264.

[4] Coryat, *Crudities*, ii. p. 28.

Coryat adds that Josias Simler wrote a learned dialogue upon the question "whether it were lawful to pray bareheaded either at noon, or the evening, at the ringing of this *Ave Maria* bell," pronouncing it to be foolish and superstitious, a judgment in which Coryat himself concurs.

To some extent this piety of Rome is a matter of statistics. The strictness with which the Paschal and Lenten observances were maintained was due largely to the energy of the priests and the action of the Government. Moryson records that he was visited by the local clergy in his lodgings, "who took our names in writing, to the end, as they told us, that we might receive the Sacrament with our host's family." And the results of these official visitations were embodied in an elaborate document which gave returns of the total population, the number of Easter Communions, the number of children who had not yet been admitted to their First Communion, the number of courtesans, etc. The tables drawn up from this ecclesiastical census in Rome for more than a hundred years have recently been published, and it is almost startling to find that for nearly the whole of this period, out of all the thousands who were bound to fulfil the Paschal obligation, the number of defaulters amounted to hardly one or two per cent.

It may be interesting to set down here a few of these tables as specimens.[1]

The tables pretty well explain themselves, although the connection of the fluctuations in the numbers with political events might afford matter for a whole article. In the paper from which these are copied they are given for every year from 1600 to 1739, but we have only been able to find room for a few specimens, taking for the purpose some Jubilee years, together with one average ordinary year, 1674, for purposes of comparison. Of course, in these statistics only the *permanent* population of Rome is dealt with, not the pilgrims, but in the Jubilee years even the permanent population was increased by a few thousands.

---

[1] From *Studi e Documenti di Storia e Diritto*, Anno xii. 1891, Fasc. 2; *Censimento della popolazione di Roma dall' anno* 1600 *al* 1739. F. Cerasoli, pp. 169-201.

The enumeration of *Concubinari* is found only in the early lists, that of the *Mori, Pinzoche* (women belonging to different third orders who did not live in community), and of births and deaths, was introduced later. The year 1739 alone contains a note

	1600.	1650.	1674.	1675.	1700.	1725.
Parish churches, - -	97	85	82	82	81	86
Households, - -	20,019	30,429	27,995	29,712	30,782	30,469
Bishops, - - -	68	50	60	69	102	83
Priests, - - -	1,401	2,206	2,623	2,950	3,016	3,064
Monks and friars, -	2,148	3,355	3,342	4,074	3,790	3,871
Nuns, - - - -	2,372	2,796	2,297	2,307	1,910	2,084
Students, - - -	1,222	767	1,104	1,131	1,495	1,857
Retinue of cardinals, -	5,297	3,542	3,232	3,312	1,751	1,959
Poor in homes, - -	1,798	1,068	1,301	1,629	3,216	932
Prisoners in gaol, -	256	542	242	249	277	144
Males of all ages, -	63,133	73,978	73,843	79,786	78,929	85,622
Females of all ages, -	46,596	52,214	48,883	52,126	60,518	62,523
Fit for Communion, -	91,452	95,003	93,373	100,721	111,894	116,927
Not fit, - - -	18,277	31,189	29,335	31,141	37,491	31,218
Communicated, - -	91,183	93,805	92,421	99,511	111,451	116,692
Not Communicated, -	269	49	455	368	—	145
Courtesans, - - -	604	1,148	927	889	497	179
Concubinari, - -	43	32	—	—	—	—
Moors (Mori), - -	—	13	13	21	14	16
Pinzoche, - - -	—	63	63	87	85	119
Births, - - -	—	—	—	—	—	4,521
Deaths, - - -	—	—	—	—	—	6,015
Heretics, - - -	—	—	—	—	—	—
Total population, -	109,729	126,192	122,726	131,912	149,447	148,155

of the number of heretics (85). Jews, whom Labat estimates at the beginning of the eighteenth century at some ten or twelve thousand, are not included in any way in the census. So that the total population of Rome was some thousands in excess of the numbers here set down. The preponderance of males, due, of course, largely to the clerical element in Rome, is very striking. It would seem that the figures in the document from which these tables have been taken (a MS. which formerly belonged to the Roman College) have not been copied very accurately. The Dominican traveller Father Labat, in his *Voyage en Espagne et en Italie dans les années* 1705 *et* 1707, vol. iii., gives the census of a single year, which in one or two items does not entirely accord with the figures found in this table. Moreover, it may be noticed that while in some cases, *e.g.*, the year 1650, the number given of those who ought to have communicated (95,003) is more than a thousand in excess of the number of actual communicants (93,805), the number registered as non-communicants is only 49. Probably the number of non-communicants was arrived at sometimes by a rather careless enumeration (no parish priest would have an interest in making very accurate returns of the non-communicants in his district), sometimes by subtracting the total of Paschal Communions from the numbers of those who were fit (*atti*) to receive. What was meant by this heading, "fit to receive," may be gathered from some interesting remarks of Father Labat—

"Every parish priest is careful to visit all the houses in his parish at the beginning of Lent. He makes an exact enumeration of them in order to know how many communicants there are, and how many who are not in a fit state to approach the sacraments, such as children and women of bad life. The former are excluded by defect of age, the others because they are unworthy.

"Those who have been to Communion receive a little printed ticket to attest the fact that they have satisfied their Paschal obligation for such and such a particular year. After the fortnight of Easter the priests go to the different houses to take up these tickets, and comparing them with their own lists, they satisfy themselves as to who have received Communion and who have not. As they cannot be imposed upon in the matter, they endeavour to bring defaulters back to their duty by earnest exhortations.

"At the same time, it must not be said that any compulsion is used. The consequences of an unworthy Communion are far too keenly felt for that. All that they insist upon is that the sinner should present himself at the sacred tribunal, and should fulfil the penance which his parish priest may think it advisable to impose upon him. This is a most just arrangement, and it were greatly to be desired that the same custom might be introduced everywhere."

Besides the pious practices, the devotional enthusiasm, the singular examples of charity, and the many other educative influences with which men become acquainted through their pilgrimage to Rome, the Jubilee would seem to have brought at least occasionally two other benefits in its train. In the first place, it was a force making for the peace of Christendom, and secondly, it lent a great stimulus to works of public utility—the erection of hospitals and hospices, the repair of bridges and roads, and the restoration of the ecclesiastical monuments of Rome itself. Upon both these heads a few words may here be said.

That the Jubilee afforded some check to the quarrels of Christian nations and commonwealths seems too obvious a fact to need much insisting on. It is possible that this restraining influence did not go very far, but the gathering of large bodies of men, unarmed and in pilgrims' garb, with princes and bishops and nobles at their head, was certainly calculated to promote the peace of Europe, and does not seem ever to have been the cause of international complications.

To put it upon no higher ground, it gave a very large number of people an interest in the maintenance of public tranquillity, and that in an age when the chances of sudden war were far greater than they are in our own. Even at the present day such another world's fair in the heart of Europe as the Paris Exhibition of 1900 is distinctly a guarantee for the influence of at least one powerful nation being used for a while in the cause of peace.

Obviously the power most interested in preserving order was the papacy; and we are not surprised to find that, in spite of many rebuffs and very indifferent success, the Popes made persistent efforts to secure peace and safe-conduct for those who visited Rome in the Jubilee years. Let us take, for instance, that of Clement VI. in 1350. This occurred midway between the battles of Crecy and Poitiers, and was almost the central

The Pope Washing the Feet of Thirteen Poor Men on Maundy Thursday.

point of the great struggle between England and France which marked the reign of Edward III. On the 21st of November, 1349, we find the Pope writing to the king of England "entreating him to consider the motives which make for peace, and how the absence of it hinders many from gaining the Indulgences of the Jubilee by visiting the Basilicas of St. Peter and St. Paul and St. John Lateran."[1] Then, under date of 8th of December, we find his instructions to the two papal nuntios bidding them to visit certain influential statesmen and to urge the same argument. Similarly we have letters in the same sense despatched to Henry, Earl of Lancaster, Sir Walter Manny, Count Gaston de Foix, and a dozen other prominent men, both on the English and French side, asking them to give a favourable hearing to the papal nuntios. There are, of course, similar letters to the king of France, and it is noteworthy that the Pope requires, even of this illustrious personage, a personal visit to the shrine of the Apostles if he wished to gain the Indulgences of the Jubilee. This fact is the more remarkable in that the Pope was then and had long been domiciled at Avignon, so that it is difficult to see that he had any immediate personal interest in enforcing such a condition. Although the negotiations for the peace proceeded very slowly, and the treaty was not actually signed until 1351, the Pope was nevertheless so far successful in his appeals as to secure the maintenance of an armistice during all the Holy Year. How persistent were his efforts in the cause can only be appreciated by those who have studied the papal documents for that year calendared by Mr. Bliss.

The incident does not stand alone. In almost every succeeding Jubilee the correspondence of the Popes reveals that an earnest attempt was made to win over the sovereign princes of Europe to the cause of peace.

With regard to the second indirect result of which we have just spoken, viz., the furtherance of works of public utility in the repairing of roads, the restoration of churches, the building

---

[1] See Bliss, *Calendar of Papal Documents Relating to England*, vol. iii. pp. 42-45.

of hospices, and the like, something has incidentally been said in the account already given of the individual Jubilees. Even in such evil times as those of Alexander VI. we read that in view of the Holy Year he set on foot public works on a large scale. "As early as November 26th, 1498, he directed Cardinal Riario to examine into the possibilities of widening the thoroughfares and securing the bridges; and in 1499 he gave orders for the construction of the road called the *Via Alessandrina* or the *Borgo Nuovo* which leads from the castle of Sant Angelo to the Basilica of St. Peter."[1]

It was, of course, the city of Rome itself which profited chiefly by such activity, but it is interesting to note that the benefit by no means stopped there, but that it extended to other Italian towns, sometimes at a considerable distance. The following passage from an important monograph on the charitable institutions of Viterbo must serve as a sufficient vindication of this point:—

"But if leprosy had been the cause of the increase in the number of hospitals, another institution of the Church, the Jubilee, shortly afterwards made them multiply in Italy in the most marvellous way.

"The scattered hospices attached to the monasteries, for the most part situated in solitary and inaccessible places, were not sufficient to lodge and feed the great crowds of indigent people set in movement by these pilgrimages. It was necessary to build new refuges, both within and without the cities, and indeed to provide some kind of lodging in almost every village.

"Private charity appeared disguised in many various forms. The natives of the same province, and, above all, the foreigners scattered throughout Italy, grouped themselves together, formed associations and religious sodalities, and erected hospices for their compatriots or fellow-townsmen. Rome naturally set the example. Hospices arose for Lombards, for Genoese, for Florentines, for the inhabitants of Bergamo, and also for

[1] Müntz, *Les Arts à la Cour des Papes, Alexandre VI.*, p. 185.

Germans, English, Scotch, Hungarians, French, Bohemians, and Armenians. And since these few remarks are to lead us to the history of Viterbo, we shall see that here also were founded, primarily through the exertions of native-born philanthropists, hospitals for Latins, English, Germans, and even for Armenians. Thus throughout Italy, and more particularly in the provinces nearest Rome, a vast network of hospices extended, which, as long as the period of pilgrimages continued, had a more or less prosperous existence."[1]

Finally, it may be stated here as the outcome of a not inconsiderable amount of attention paid to the history of the years of Jubilee in their many different aspects, that there is singularly little in the way of evidence to justify the imputation of mercenary motives so commonly made in this connection, both against the Popes and the people of Rome. Speaking, as we are doing, of the *ordinary* Jubilees recurring at stated intervals, there is hardly one of them, if we may except the two doubtful celebrations of Boniface IX.,[2] in which a colourable pretext can be found for taxing the Popes with selling their spiritual favours for money. We have the fullest information as to the first institution of the great Indulgence under Boniface VIII. It is certain that it was wholly unpremeditated, and, as explained in the first chapter of this work, if any motive is to be sought for the Pope's action besides a spiritual one, it is to be found rather in the political circumstances of the times than in any hope of pecuniary profit. The alms given were purely voluntary; they formed no part of the conditions of the Jubilee; and there is not the slightest suggestion of the duty of almsgiving either in the papal Bull of Boniface VIII. or in the semi-official exposition of that Bull which was drawn up by an official of the papal Chancery, Sylvester, "scriptor Domini Papæ," or in the works

---

[1] Pinzi, *Gli Ospizi Mediovali e l'Ospedal-Grande di Viterbo*, 1893, pp. 13-15.

[2] Of these two Jubilees—the very existence of the second is problematical—we know next to nothing. They occurred during the Great Schism, when all things were in disorder.

of the two cardinals, Joannes Monachus and Gaetano Stefaneschi, who wrote upon the subject.

Certainly a not inconsiderable sum was actually offered at the shrines of the Apostles, but it seems to have been made up of the offerings of the poor in the smallest copper coinage, and it is distinctly stated that no part of the proceeds found its way into the papal treasury. It was spent, as it was intended to be spent, upon the fabric of the Basilicas and upon those who served them. During the second Jubilee, that of Clement VI., the Pope was in Avignon. There is nothing whatever to suggest that he derived pecuniary benefit from it. Nicholas V. realised a moderately large sum[1] from the Jubilee. It was spent upon what the whole world is agreed in praising as a most worthy and magnificent scheme for the cultivation of the arts and the restoration of the city. But in none of these ordinary Jubilees which required a pilgrimage to Rome was any offering or alms imposed as a condition of gaining the Indulgence. What was given was given quite freely out of pure devotion, and even in the extension of the Jubilee to other countries after the year itself had expired, *e.g.*, that of 1501, in which a certain offering of money was prescribed in lieu of the pilgrimage, it was expressly provided that no fixed contribution should be asked from those whose incomes were less than £20 a year, representing at least £300 a year of our money. In other words, the poor and labouring classes were left free "to pay for self, wife, and children as it shall please them of their devotion." When we learn that even those whose incomes were above £20 were asked to offer no more than 12 pence for self, wife, and children, *i.e.*, one four-hundredth part of that income, it must be clear that no extravagant attempt was made to impoverish the people. As for the last twelve of the twenty ordinary Jubilees recorded in history, it seems to be confessed on all hands that the expenditure of the Holy See far exceeded any possible receipts.

[1] The sum was not inordinately great. In 1400 the amount of the offering at St. Paul's Church was estimated at 60,000 ducats. Rucellai says it was much less in 1450!

Take, for instance, the following passage from so unfriendly a witness as Mr. H. C. Lea:—

"It is scarce worth while to follow in detail the subsequent Jubilees of 1625, 1650, 1675, 1700, 1725, 1750, and 1775, which could teach us nothing except that, in their greater or less success, there was a gradual falling-off in numbers and zeal.[1] There was likewise a great reduction in the oblations of the pilgrims, and we may well believe Zaccaria's assertion that the proceeds were much less than the expenses. Every effort was made to lighten the burden of the pilgrims by offering them gratuitous shelter and food, no small share of which was necessarily contributed by the Pope and the cardinals. In 1600 Clement VIII. thus gave 300,000 scudi; in 1650 Innocent X. took off six giulj per measure of the tax on corn. Since the sixteenth century we may fairly assume that every Jubilee has been a not inconsiderable burden on the Holy See. A not unnatural concomitant of this was an increased development of the spiritual features of the solemnity, which finds apt expression in the exhortation to repentance by Clement XIV. in 1774."[2]

Not less explicit is the testimony of the Scotch Presbyterian, Dr. Moore, after his visit to the Jubilee of 1775—

"It is not likely that any future Pope will think of shortening this period; if any alteration were again to take place, it most probably would be to restore the ancient period of fifty or a hundred years; for instead of the wealthy pilgrims who flocked to Rome from every quarter of Christendom, ninety-nine in a hundred of those who come now are supported by alms during their journey or are barely able to defray their own expenses by the strictest economy; and his Holiness is supposed at present to derive no other advantage from the uncommon fatigue he is obliged to go through in the Jubilee year, except the satisfaction he feels in reflecting on the benefit his labours confer on the

[1] This statement, which is wholly unsupported by evidence, has already been commented upon, p. 118.

[2] Lea, *History of Confession, etc.*, vol. iii. p. 217.

souls of the beggars and other travellers who resort from all corners of Italy to Rome on this blessed occasion. The States which border on the Pope's dominions suffer many temporal inconveniences from the zeal of the peasants and manufacturers, the greater part of whom still make a point of visiting St. Peter's in the Jubilee year."

CHAPTER VIII

The Jubilee Indulgence

It would be impossible in a work like the present to enter into any lengthy discussion of the Catholic doctrine of Indulgences. Still, a few words may fittingly be said upon the general question of their nature and history before we turn our attention to the particular Indulgences of the Jubilee. The teaching of the Catholic Church in this matter proceeds upon the assumption that, when sin is committed, the justice of God requires some proportionate satisfaction to be offered to the Divine majesty in reparation for the offence which has been done, and that even though the sin itself be pardoned and the eternal punishment due to it be remitted, the debt of the sinner is not on that account entirely cancelled. Catholics are consequently instructed that, ordinarily speaking, atonement has still to be made for forgiven sin. This may be done either through the patient endurance of the tribulations which God sends to all, or through deeds of penance and works of devotion voluntarily undertaken in this life. But if the duty be neglected here below, the debt will still remain to be discharged through the sufferings of purgatory in the life to come.

For this view of the Divine economy of sin and pardon abundant scriptural analogies can be quoted, the most classical being the instance of David, to whom Nathan announced that, on account of his repentance, God had forgiven him his sins, but that, nevertheless, a temporal chastisement would still be inflicted upon him in the death of his child. The Council of Trent accordingly, in its fourteenth session, summed up the Catholic belief on this point in the words, "It is an entirely erroneous doctrine, and opposed to the Word of God, to assert that there can be no remission of the guilt of sin without the whole penalty of sin being completely cancelled." In accordance with this teaching the Church has at all times impressed upon the faithful the need of making satisfaction even for sin forgiven, and in earlier ages an elaborate system of public penance was enforced, in which almost every kind of transgression had allotted to it a penalty proportioned to its heinousness, by which reparation was to be offered to God's offended majesty for the evil which had been committed. Historically speaking, it is indisputable that the practice of Indulgences in the medieval Church arose out of the authoritative remission, in exceptional cases, of a certain proportion of this canonical penalty.[1] At the same time, according to Catholic teaching, such Indulgence was not a mere permission to omit or postpone payment, but was, in fact, a *discharge* from the debt of temporal punishment which the sinner owed. The authority to grant such discharge was conceived to be included in the power of binding and loosing committed by Christ to His Church, and when in the course of time the vaguer theological conceptions of the first ages of Christianity assumed scientific form and shape at the hands of the Schoolmen, the doctrine came to prevail that this discharge of the sinner's debt was made through an application to the offender of what was called the "Treasure" of the Church. The infinite merits of Christ our Redeemer, and the superabundant penance of the saints, who offered to God a greater atonement

[1] An interesting example of the old form of Indulgence is still preserved in the Temple Church, London. The inscription is a restoration, but it is, I understand, a faithful copy of the original. Here may be read how Heraclius, Patriarch of Jerusalem (a protector of the Knights Templars), at the dedication of the Church in 1185, granted "a remission (*indulgentiam*) of sixty days *from the penance imposed upon them*" to all who visited the church on the anniversary of this celebration.

ANNO AB INCARNATIONE DOMINI MCLXXXV DEDICATA EST HEC ECCLESIA IN HONORE BEATE MARIE A DOMINO ERACLIO, DEI GRATIA SANCTE RESURRECTIONIS ECCLESIE PATRIARCHA, IV IDUS FEBRUARII; QUI ANNUATIM PETENTIBUS DE INIUNCTA SIBI PENITENTIA LX DIES INDULSIT. Baylis, Temple Church, p. 11.

than was required for the expiation of their own sins, were conceived of as creating a fund of satisfactions which the Church dispenses at will, and which she applies to those offenders who seem specially to deserve her favour.

It is clear, however, that this communication of the "Treasure" can only be made by those who have authority to administer it, and herein lies the distinction between the act of a confessor commuting or remitting a sacramental penance, and the act of the Supreme Pontiff imparting a "true Indulgence."[1] The confessor may deal so leniently with his penitent that the satisfaction exacted bears no sort of proportion to the sins of which the penitent has accused himself. Indeed, we may say that the practice of assigning such inadequate penances has become universal in the Church; for the recitation of a few psalms or prayers, which is commonly enjoined as a penance even for grievous sins, bears no proportion at all to the offence, nor to the long periods of fasting and humiliation which were formerly exacted for the same transgression. Still, this complacence on the part of the confessor cannot, in any true sense, be said to be a gain to the sinner. God's justice is not satisfied by it, and the debt of temporal punishment is not cancelled, though the payment be deferred. The atonement which is not made in this world will still have some day to be offered to God through the involuntary and consequently unmeritorious suffering of purgatory.

In an Indulgence, on the other hand, the Church does not merely neglect to exact a prompt and adequate penalty, but in virtue of her Divine commission to bind and to loose, she concedes a discharge. The discharge may be partial or it may be entire, and in as much as the concession of this discharge is made to depend upon certain conditions, it will only take effect in so far as these conditions are accurately carried out. It is obvious also that the conditions being in all cases of the nature of moral acts, the fervour, purity of intention, etc., with which

[1] The phrase so many days of "true indulgence" still survives in the formula used by bishops and others in proclaiming such concessions.

such moral acts are performed must necessarily have much to do with the gaining of an Indulgence.

So far, it may be said, the Catholic teaching with regard to Indulgences is clear and positive enough. Whatever is written over and above this is mere matter of theological opinion. Nothing, for instance, has ever been defined as to the precise meaning of an Indulgence of so many days or years. Historically speaking, we know the genesis of this terminology. We know that it has arisen out of the remissions of the canonical penances which were imposed for periods of time: for instance, for so many years and so many quarantines (*i.e.*, lents). But there can be no certainty even about the theory most commonly propounded, that the gaining of an Indulgence of seven years would benefit the sinner to the same extent as the performance of seven years of the old canonical penance. We have no evidence to show that the old canonical penance can be taken as a constant and absolute standard. On the contrary, what we do know is that in other directions there has been continuous variation. If the Church has so far relaxed her discipline as now to impose a *Miserere* in the tribunal of penance for an offence which, according to the letter of the law down to the close of the Middle Ages, should have been visited with the penalty of a weekly fast continued for seven years, it is free to any one to argue that an Indulgence of seven years may now only represent a remission of the penalties of sin equivalent to that which would be gained by the devout recitation of the *Miserere*. But, obviously, all this is mere speculation.

There can, of course, be no doubt that the Church in the course of time has knowingly, and, so to speak, with her eyes open, become more and more prodigal in administering the treasure of her Indulgences. The possibility of full and complete remission, which in the days of Boniface VIII. was an almost unheard-of boon, has now been rendered so common through the numberless plenary Indulgences available at all seasons, that the Jubilee of the *Anno Santo* seems the reverse of a privilege, entailing, as it does, the suspension of all these ordinary graces during the time of its continuance. In imitation of the prodigality of her Divine Master, the Church has deliberately faced the risk of depreciation to which her treasure was exposed. *Compelle intrare*—"compel them to come in"—seems to have been her motto throughout the ages. She has tried stern warnings and severe penalties, but the growing effeminacy or corruption of mankind has found her censures unendurable, and has openly bidden them defiance. Even when these sterner measures have been relaxed, and when the poor and the feeble, the blind and the lame have been gathered in from the streets and lanes of the city, there has yet been room at the supper table of the Lamb, and the Church, going out into the highways and the hedges, has tried to entice men with the offer of generous Indulgence, that even so they might be brought to repent and confess their sins. Is there not also a very similar lesson to be drawn from the parable of the labourers in the market-place? The reward which was offered at the beginning to those who were willing to face the burden of the day and the heat, was offered as the end drew near, upon condition of only an hour's service. But that hour's service there must always be. With all the seeming prodigality of her grants of Indulgence, the Church holds firmly to the condition of true repentance. No Indulgence can, under any circumstances, be gained by one who is God's enemy, and if the robe of grace has been forfeited by grievous sin, then even the least and simplest of the Church's remissions requires, as its indispensable preliminary, that the sinner must be reconciled with God by sorrow for the past, and a firm purpose of amendment.

So much it seemed desirable to say here, in general terms, about the Indulgence system of the Catholic Church, but before passing on to discuss the so-called remission *a pœna et culpa*, which claims particular notice on account of its connection with the Jubilee, attention may be directed to the wording of the decree on Indulgences passed in the twenty-fifth session of the Council of Trent. It illustrates, on the one hand, the very moderate range of the definitions of faith in this matter, and on the other, the frank admission by the Council of the existence of abuses which it was determined to remedy, and which, as a matter of fact, it may be said to have entirely banished from the Church.

"Whereas," says the Council, "the power of conferring Indulgences was granted by Christ to the Church, and she has, even in the most ancient times, used this kind of power, delivered unto her of God; the Sacred Holy Synod teaches and enjoins that the use of Indulgences, for the Christian people most salutary, and approved of by the authority of Sacred Councils, is to be retained in the Church; and it condemns, with anathema, those who either assert that they are useless, or who deny that there is in the Church the power of granting them. In granting them, however, it desires that, in accordance with the ancient and approved custom in the Church, moderation be observed, lest by excessive facility ecclesiastical discipline be enervated. And being desirous that the abuses which have crept therein, and by occasion of which this honourable name of Indulgences is blasphemed by heretics, be amended and corrected; it ordains generally by this decree, that all evil gains for the obtaining thereof—whence a most prolific cause of abuses amongst the Christian people has been derived—be wholly abolished. But, as regards the other abuses which have proceeded from superstition, ignorance, irreverence, or from whatsoever other source, since by reason of the manifold corruptions in the places and provinces where the said abuses are committed, they cannot conveniently be specially prohibited, it commands all bishops diligently to collect, each in his own church, all abuses of this nature, and to report them in the first Provincial Synod; that after having been reviewed by the opinions of the other bishops also, they may forthwith be referred to the Sovereign Roman Pontiff, by whose authority and prudence that which may be expedient for the universal Church will be ordained; that thus the gift of holy Indulgences may be dispensed to all the faithful, piously, holily, and incorruptly."

It will be observed that nothing is affirmed in this decree

beyond the power of the Church to grant Indulgences, and the utility of the Indulgences so granted. Upon the nature and effect of these remissions the Council does not pronounce; and it is rather remarkable, considering the conspicuous part which the Indulgence question had played in bringing about the Reformation, that the *Catechismus Romanus*, the authoritative summary of popular instruction drawn up at the instance of the Council of Trent, says nothing whatever on the subject of Indulgences, not even citing or making any reference to the decree of the Council which has just been quoted.

Very noteworthy also is the moderation which marks the writings of the English clergy upon this subject, both before and during the progress of the Reformation. Of pre-Reformation writers it would be impossible to cite any one more typically English than the canonist William Lyndwood. He had long been the chief legal official of the Archbishop of Canterbury; he was one of the most prominent and active members of the Privy Council, and he was promoted, at the king's own request, to the bishopric of St. David's. Although he was a staunch supporter of papal supremacy, his famous gloss upon the *Provincial Constitutions* was addressed, under the patronage of the Archbishop of Canterbury, exclusively to the English clergy, and could have no possible interest or application outside of England. In this manual, which, down to the final breach with Rome, was frequently reprinted, and which may fairly be said to have been in the hands of every parish priest, we find embodied a tolerably full discussion of the question of Indulgences.

Lyndwood begins his little dissertation in proper scholastic form by putting fairly and forcibly the principal difficulties against his thesis. Then he states his conclusion in favour of the practice of Indulgences, appealing in particular to the power of binding and loosing entrusted to St. Peter, and to the remissions granted by the old law in the year of Jubilee, of which we read in the book of Exodus.

"Moreover," he says, "the most fundamental ground which establishes the validity of such Indulgences is the unity of the

Church, which is the mystical body of Christ, in which many holy men have performed [*supererogaverunt*] works of piety and mercy over and above the measure of their own transgressions, patiently enduring scorn and contumely and infinite sufferings and torments which they have not deserved. These do not cease

Inside View of the Porta Santa in St. Peter's.
The mosaic of St. Peter is by Ciro Ferri.

to pray for us, and the Church pours forth prayers to them that they may intercede for us, as we see in the Litanies. Moreover, leaving all these out of account, the merit of the Death and Passion and Bloodshedding of Christ worketh the remission of sins. For He offered Himself as a victim for sin, and that pain and martyrdom which He unjustly bore, nay, even the least drop of His blood was sufficient for the washing away of all our offences. Communicating, therefore, to us His merits and those of saints, He gave the power of binding and loosing to Peter and his successors. Accordingly this remission of the penalty to be inflicted for sins, granted to all who are truly penitent and who have made their confession, is a reward which was won for us by the holy martyrs, who, as thoroughly solvent debtors, by making satisfaction in our place, set us free also from our penalties. And the dispensing of these merits by which we may be set free from the penalties due to our sins, Christ, as I have said, entrusted to Peter and his successors, who also in turn committed such power to the bishops that have been called to share a portion of their solicitude."[1]

But however strongly Lyndwood may defend the practice of granting Indulgences, he insists upon the absolute need of contrition of heart in those who seek to profit by them.

"Those who are unrepentant," he teaches, "cannot profit by Indulgences, because pardon is granted only to him who amends. But to the repentant it is granted, or to him who is resolved upon amendment, and so, if there be contrition of heart, then the Indulgence will avail (even before confession), providing only this be contained in the form of Indulgence."[2] And again, in replying to the objection that Indulgences are destructive of piety, he remarks—"On the contrary, they provide a remedy against sin which has to be avoided on account of the contrition to which a man must bring himself in order to benefit by them. However, a man must beware that he do not abuse such favour by neglecting good works in future on account of the Indulgence he has gained."

The same moderation and common sense is conspicuous in the writings of one whom all parties acknowledge to have been amongst the noblest characters of the Reformation period, John Fisher, Bishop of Rochester. He had studied Luther's argu-

---

[1] *De Poenit.* cap. *Cum salubriter*, s.v. *clavibus.*

[2] *De Celeb. Missarum.* cap. *Altissimus*, s.v. *Indulgentia.*

ments, and in his *Confutatio* he speaks with his usual candour of the abuses of Indulgences, but his testimony to their good effects is only the more striking.

"Perchance some man will tell me," he says, "that the majority of mankind live more laxly on account of Indulgences. I will not say him nay. But they do the very same on account of God's boundless clemency and His unfailing readiness to show mercy. What follows? Are we to condemn this clemency in Almighty God? Heaven forbid. We condemn only the miserable and thankless sinners who abuse His so great clemency. And in this matter of Indulgences a man ought to proceed no otherwise. Most assuredly there is no good reason to put an end to Indulgences. What we should put an end to is the malice of those who sin and who, after the fashion of spiders, suck poison from that very source from which they ought to have drawn sweetness."

So again he says—"I most certainly make no doubt that there are many who have derived help from Indulgences towards gaining the fruits of the spirit. Indulgences are never granted save for some definite work which is ostensibly a work of piety. But whosoever, being penitent for his past misdeeds, performs such a work for God's sake, cannot but gain merit thereby, seeing that he is already founded in charity, and charity, as Augustine says, deserves to be increased. Remember, moreover, that in the hope of gaining Indulgences, many a man is moved to raise his mind to God, and prepares himself by fitting penance and confession to become a partaker thereof; and this, most assuredly, such men would never have done, unless they had been prompted to it by the concession of such Indulgences."[1]

At the very beginning of this volume we spoke of the vivid impression retained by the present Pontiff, Leo XIII., of the great spiritual revival effected by the Jubilee of 1825. "I wish you could have seen," writes Cardinal Wiseman, another eye-witness, "not merely the churches filled, but the public places and squares crowded to hear the word of God. I wish you could

[1] Fisher, *Assertionis Lutheranae Confutatio* (1526), fol. ci. r° and v°.

have seen the throng at every confessional, and the multitudes that pressed round the altar of God to partake of its heavenly gift." The Jubilee of 1825 was in no way exceptional. The same scenes of genuine repentance and devotion have been witnessed in every one of the twenty celebrations which have succeeded each other in due order since Boniface VIII. issued his famous Bull just six hundred years ago. But it is necessary to remind ourselves of the fact on account of the persistent effort which has been made to represent the Jubilee as a mere barter of pardon for pence, an event absolutely devoid of all spiritual significance.

It would be impossible to discuss in detail the various objections that have been urged by controversialists against Indulgences in general and the Jubilee Indulgence in particular. But there is one which, on account of the popular use in earlier centuries of a misleading phraseology, may cause a real difficulty. This argument has been much urged in recent years by writers whose reputation for original research lends an importance to their contention quite out of proportion to its intrinsic worth. Mr. H. C. Lea, for example, the author of *The History of Auricular Confession and Indulgences*,[1] has laid great stress upon the point. His view is in close agreement with the utterances of a number of German scholars, notably of Th. Brieger, Dieckhoff, and Adolf Harnack.[2] For the purpose which we have in view in this chapter it would be useless to attempt to distinguish the precise shades of opinion by which these various writers are differentiated.

We may note, then, that Mr. Lea, in the course of his third volume, repeatedly affirms that the Jubilee Indulgence was an Indulgence *a pœna et a culpa,* and that by this phrase was meant an Indulgence which of itself remitted the guilt as well as

[1] The present writer has dealt more exhaustively with the main subject of this chapter in an article in the *Dublin Review* for January, 1900, entitled "The Jubilee Indulgence *a pœna et a culpa.*"

[2] Th. Brieger, *Das Wesen des Ablasses am Ausgange des Mittelalters.* Leipzig, 1897. Dieckhoff, *Der Ablass streif Dogmengeschichtlich dargestellt*, 1886. Harnack, *Lehrbuch des Dogmengeschichte*, iii. 528 (third edition).

the punishment, and consequently dispensed with the necessity of either sorrow or confession. Mr. Lea introduces this conception into almost the first reference which he makes to the Jubilee—

"If any impulse was lacking to strengthen the popular belief that pardon of sin could be granted and gained irrespective of contrition and the sacraments, it was furnished by the

The Opening of the Jubilee of 1575 by Pope Gregory XIII.
Scene in the Atrium of St. Peter's.
From a rare engraving in the Print Room of the British Museum.

promises of Boniface VIII. in proclaiming the Jubilee of 1300. A contemporary writer who was there speaks of it as an Indulgence *a culpa et a pœna,* while others assume that it was gained by the simple visits to the Basilicas of St. Peter and St. Paul, without alluding to any conditions of contrition and confession."[1]

The writer distinctly means to convey, as the context and the footnotes show, that this first Jubilee Indulgence might be gained without either repentance or the reception of the sacraments, and it is somewhat astonishing to find him, on p. 199 of the same volume, calmly reciting the terms on which it was offered, in which contrition and confession are explicitly mentioned as indispensable conditions. Regardless of this and other inconsistencies, Mr. Lea returns to his point again and again. Thus, for instance, he declares—

"The power of the Indulgence to remit both the guilt and the penalty was gradually winning its way, and in view of the financial advantages of such a doctrine it would in all probability have established itself, and the sacrament of penitence would have grown obsolete had the Church been left to its own devices, and not been forced to a reform by the revolt which its degradation rendered inevitable."[2]

Or, again, we may take such a passage as the following—

"The subject of the efficiency of Indulgences cannot be dismissed without considering one aspect of it which has caused an immense amount of discussion—whether they have power to release from the *culpa* or guilt as well as from the *pœna* or penalty left after the pardon of the guilt. Theoretically, it would seem that there could be no question concerning it, for the pardon of guilt is effected in the sacrament, and the Indulgence only purports to remit the temporal penalty. Yet for ages there was a widespread popular belief that plenary Indulgences were *a culpa et a pœna*, and this belief was a considerable factor in contributing to the large revenues which the Holy See drew from their sale throughout Europe."[3]

Let it be remarked here *en passant*, that although there is one sense in which the power of Indulgences to remit sin may

---

[1] Vol. iii. p. 63.
[2] *Ibid.* vol. iii. p. 73.
[3] *Op. cit.* vol. iii. pp. 54, 55.

be said to have caused some discussion, this is certainly not the sense which Mr. Lea's readers would gather from his words. The subject, no doubt, has given rise to controversy between the Catholics and Reformers; but prior to the Reformation there is not a trace of any such discussion. The suggestion that Indulgences could remit the guilt of sin was regarded as too preposterous to admit of argument,[1] and if the question was raised at all it was dismissed by the medieval theologian or canonist in a couple of sentences.

To return, however, to our more immediate subject, we have two distinct questions before us. The first is the nature of the Jubilee Indulgence and the conditions prescribed for the gaining of it. The second is the true meaning of the phrase *a pœna et a culpa*, which was no doubt popularly applied to the Jubilee, as well as to certain other Indulgences, for more than two hundred years before the Reformation.

It has already been pointed out in the course of this work that, with regard to the institution of the Jubilee Indulgence under Boniface VIII., we are singularly well informed. Not only do we possess the text of the Bull[2] in which it was proclaimed to the world, but we have the semi-official exposition of that text by Master Silvester, "Scriptor Domini Papæ," the full history of the Jubilee by Cardinal Stefaneschi, and an elaborate commentary on the papal Bull by another contemporary, Cardinal John Le Moine (Joannes Monachus). Both these two last took part in the papal consistories held at the time, and Joannes Monachus wrote his gloss in the course of the Jubilee year itself. More direct and authoritative information as to the mind of the Pope in instituting this new form of Indulgence it would be impossible to have.

Now in all these documents the nature of the remission and the conditions for gaining it are made abundantly clear. The

[1] "Uno ore omnes theologi," says Maldonatus, "nemine excepto respondent Indulgentiam non esse remissionem culpœ sed pœnœ." As far as my reading enables me to judge, this is the literal truth.

[2] This is translated above, pp. 13, 14.

Pope promises *non solum plenam et largiorem imo plenissimam omnium suorum veniam poccatorum*—"not only full and more generous but the very fullest pardon of sins." It is what is now familiarly known as a "plenary Indulgence," with the added circumstance of increased facilities for absolution. The Pope, we learn from Cardinal Joannes Monachus, stated in consistory, in answer to a query about the meaning of this very phrase, that he wished to grant as much remission as it was in his power to grant—"to go to the utmost limit," to use his own words, "to which the authority of the keys extended."[1] It was the Pope's intention, therefore, to ensure, so far as it rested with him, that those who faithfully performed the conditions expressed in the Bull should be discharged entirely from all debt of temporal punishment. But the performance of the conditions was essential, and the first of these conditions was that the pilgrim should be penitent and confessed (*poenitens et confessus*). Cardinal Stefaneschi condensed into a short Latin poem of nine lines all that it was most essential to know about the Jubilee. It begins as follows:—

> Learn then that in the hundredth year all crimes
> Are cancelled: learn, I say, that this shall be
> If only contrite lips lay bare the sin,
> The heart's foul secret.[2]

But to understand how utterly Mr. Lea's idea that the Indulgence could be gained without confession and repentance is at variance with the facts, we must turn to the commentaries on the Bull.

It is probable that Cardinal Joannes Monachus wrote his gloss for the guidance of the confessors in the city, and for that of others who had appealed to him, as one of the most eminent

---

[1] See the gloss of Joannes Monachus *ad locum* in the *Corpus Juris Canonici* (Lyons, 1584), vol. iii. col. 344.

[2] Discite centeno detergi crimina Phoebo,
Discite, *si* latebras scabrosi criminis ora
Depromant *contrita* sinu.

La Bigne, *Bib. Pat.*, vol. xiii. p. 485. This poem is distinct from that quoted on p. 21.

canonists of the day, to determine what was precisely the meaning of this new institution. He was residing in Rome at the time, as appears from his more than once saying that he had heard the interpretation of this or the other point in the Bull from the Pope's own lips in consistory. What then, we may ask, would Cardinal Le Moine have said to Mr. Lea's suggestion? He tells us his opinion very clearly in touching upon the conditions which all such Indulgences necessarily pre-supposed.

"The second condition is proper dispositions in the recipient. For, according to the philosopher, the acts of the agent require a corresponding disposition in the thing acted upon. For the Treasure of the Church is only applicable to him who is a member of the Church. . . . And certain it is that, so long as the guilt remains, the punishment due to it is not remitted, because, as Augustine says, God does not remove the disfigurement of the sin without bestowing the robe of justice. But if the punishment were remitted while the guilt is still there, the disfigurement of the sin would cease [the texts read *esset*, but the argument requires *abesset* or *cessaret*] without the robe of justice being restored, and so there would be a violation of right order in the economy of the world, which the Divine wisdom does not tolerate. That a man, therefore, may be capable of gaining an Indulgence, it is necessary that he should be cleansed from guilt, and this is done in contrition, and so we may say that that man (only) is able to receive Indulgence who is truly penitent and has made his confession. And this is alluded to in the form of Indulgence [the Bull *Antiquorum* which the writer is glossing] when it is said that this Indulgence is granted to those who are truly repentant and who make their confession, and to no others."[1]

So strongly indeed is the cardinal impressed with the necessity of contrition that he takes up a more rigorous position than that which now finds favour with the majority of theologians. He considers that for the valid gaining of the Jubilee Indulgence *all* the works belonging to it must be performed in a state of

[1] *Corpus Juris Canonici* (Lyons, 1584), vol. iii. pt. 2, col. 345.

grace. Consequently the *labor itinerationis*, the fatigue of the journey to Rome, which is the principal work by which the pilgrim merits such Indulgence, must not be a dead work, but must be supernaturalised by sanctifying grace. It is not, indeed, necessary that the pilgrim should actually (*facto*) have made his confession before he starts, because contrition with the intention of confessing in due season is sufficient to remit the guilt of mortal sin, but he must be confessed *proposito*, that is, he must have the purpose of submitting himself for judgment to a confessor, who has power to absolve him, when the proper time comes.[1] It is now, as I have said, the common opinion that it is not necessary that all the conditions of the Jubilee should be fulfilled in a state of grace, providing only that there is the devout intention of confessing and amending one's life before the works undertaken for the Jubilee are completed.[2] But the pilgrim must necessarily be in a state of grace when the last conditions of the Jubilee are complied with, and consequently, if any one after making his confession should fall again into grievous sin before the visits to the Basilicas had all been made, it would be necessary for him to place himself once more in a state of grace by a good confession before he could derive any benefit from the Jubilee Indulgence.

But, besides the gloss of Cardinal Joannes Monachus, we possess, as already stated, the "declaratio" of the Bull *Antiquorum*, drawn up by an official of the papal chancery, one Master Silvester. Although this document is of no great intrinsic value, for it does little more than paraphrase the Bull,

---

[1] In the gloss upon the word *confessis* a little above, Joannes Monachus remarks again—"He who is truly penitent and confesses his sins obtains the pardon which God alone [and therefore no papal Indulgence] confers in the case of the contrite. This pardon is never given unless a man first amends his life." (*Hœc non datur nisi correcto.*) *Loco citato*, col. 344.

[2] See, *e.g.*, Amort, *De Indulgentiis in genere et specie prœsertim de Jubileo.* Questio 66ª, an requiratur devota visitatio ecclesiarum, et quid ea velit dicere? Respondeo, 2° Etiam eos qui sunt in peccato mortali, attamen cum proposito confitendi et se emendandi, posse habere devotionem sufficientem ad lucrandam postmodum completo opere in gratia indulgentiam. Cf. Hilgers, *Das goldene Jahr* (Kevelaer, 1899), pp. 54, 55.

its extrinsic importance is considerable. Supposing that Mr. Lea's views were correct, it is here that we should expect to find the Pope's covert designs revealing themselves. An appeal had evidently been made to Rome by those who sought to know more clearly what the new Bull of Indulgence precisely meant. To this a semi-official answer was returned, beginning in the following form:—

"Universis Christi fidelibus presentibus et futuris Silvester, Domini Papæ Scriptor, veram pacem corporum et salutem perpetuam."

But now, do we find, as Mr. Lea suggests, that the condition of confession, and the need of true repentance, have been suppressed or glossed over to make the invitation more attractive? Quite the contrary, the clause, "penitentibus et confessis, vel qui vere penitebunt et confitebuntur," appears just as conspicuously as before,[1] neither is there any mention of *a pœna et a culpa.* The tone of the document is profoundly religious. So far as it adds anything new over and above the contents of the Bull *Antiquorum*, it is in the way of earnest exhortations to put this time of grace to profit by shaking off sloth, by doing penance, and by redoubling watchfulness in prayer. Although those who wish to avail themselves of the Indulgence are reminded of the duty of gratitude to the Pope who has opened for them the Treasure of the Church, there is not a word or hint that their gratitude should take the form of money offerings, but they are bidden to pray to God to preserve the life of so clement a Pontiff. The benefit to the souls of the pilgrims is the only point upon which this *declaratio* insists.

Precisely the same atmosphere of devotion pervades the copious narrative of Cardinal Stefaneschi. One could understand a hostile critic describing it as exaggerated or even superstitious, but of its general piety there can be no question.

Take the following passage—

"Who can reckon the number and the gravity of the crimes

---

[1] See the document in the *Gesta Boemundi Archiepiscopi Trevirensis*, printed in Pertz' *Monumenta Germaniæ*, S.S. vol. xxiv. p. 487.

that sinners laid bare—wounds that would never otherwise have been shown to the priests? Full is our joy alike that the confessor should have probed the hurt and that the penitent should have acknowledged it. Surely this goes far beyond the art of any earthly physician, that the remedy with tender kindness should be brought to the patient by the Prince of physicians, not only before it was asked, but even before it was dreamed of. He takes it more to heart to tend the debtors who have done Him a wrong than the best of fathers does to foster and caress his children."[1]

It can hardly be necessary to insist further upon the prominence of sorrow and amendment of life as pre-requisites for the gaining of the first Jubilee Indulgence. Neither has the least real evidence been adduced that in this or any later celebration this condition was lost sight of. The whole argument of Mr. Lea and those who agree with him is made to rest upon the fact that sundry medieval writers do not explicitly refer to confession, but do chance to speak of an Indulgence *a culpa et pœna*. To this last phrase we may now turn our attention.

Those who study at all closely the works of Messrs. Lea, Brieger, and the rest, will soon perceive that, apart from their ineradicable determination to discover in the medieval Church evidence of greed and trickery, and to convict it of a cynical indifference to moral principle, the immediate source of their chief misrepresentations lies in a peculiar conception of the so-called Indulgence *a pœna et culpa*. Mr. Lea, in particular, is one of those gentlemen whose principle of historical investigation is to devise a theory first and to make the facts fit in with it afterwards. If they will not fit in with it, so much the worse for the facts, and, as the investigator who follows up Mr. Lea's trail soon begins to discover, they suffer a procrustean curtailment which alters their appearance very considerably. Now in this particular matter it is plain that Mr. Lea early arrived at a

[1] The text of this passage, as of many others in Stefaneschi's treatise, is terribly corrupt. But there can be no question as to the general meaning. La Bigne, *Bib. Patrum*, xiii. p. 483.

very definite idea of what was meant by an Indulgence *a pœna et culpa. Pœna,* he must have said to himself, means punishment, and *culpa* means guilt. An Indulgence *a pœna et culpa* is therefore one which remits both the punishment and the guilt. In other words, this variety of Indulgence, according to Mr. Lea, was a highly popular and lucrative spiritual commodity, which relieved the purchaser of all need of contrition, confession, or reformation of life, and in which the pardoners consequently drove a roaring trade. This is no travesty of this writer's views. He enunciates the theory—to him it is not theory, but a self-evident proposition—in a score of different passages, and makes it the backbone of his argument. We have already quoted the passage in which he states that such Indulgences were fast supplanting the sacrament of penance altogether, and that, but for the revolt of the reformers, confession would soon have become obsolete. Let me repeat that several German scholars—Brieger,[1] Harnack,[2] and, in a less extreme form, Dieckhoff[3]—have also recently adopted the same view, and they are loud in their denunciations of the utter degradation to which the moral and sacramental system of the Church, in the later Middle Ages, had been brought by such Indulgences.

Certainly, if what is alleged were even approximately true the strongest language of reprobation would be justified, but, in point of fact, as Dr. Nicolaus Paulus has lately shown in several most valuable articles[4] criticising Brieger, the whole theory lacks even the shadow of foundation. Whatever may have been said or done by a few unscrupulous pardoners in remote country districts, there is no evidence to show that one single theologian

---

[1] Th. Brieger, *Das Wesen des Ablasses am Ausgange des Mittelalters.* Leipzig, 1897.

[2] Harnack, *Lehrbuch des Dogmengeschichte,* iii³. 528.

[3] Dieckhoff, *Der Ablassstreif dogmengeschichtlich dargestellt,* 1886.

[4] See particularly his papers in the *Zeitschrift für Katholische Theologie,* 1899, p. 48 *seq.*, p. 423 *seq.*, p. 743 *seq.*, and in the same journal for 1900, pp. 1 *seq.* and 249 *seq.*, also to his monograph, *Johann Tetzel der Ablassprediger* (Mainz, 1899) with some articles in the *Katholik,* 1899, i. p. 97 *seq.*, etc. Brieger has attempted, but very lamely, to answer Paulus in the *Theologische Literaturzeitung,* 1900, Nos. 3 and 4.

or canonist of repute ever suggested that grievous sin could be forgiven by an Indulgence without the sacrament, and it is equally impossible to find any authority who maintains that a plenary Indulgence could be gained by the sinner without sorrow for the past and amendment of life. The one or two medieval writers who have been appealed to as countenancing any such view have been completely vindicated by Dr. Paulus in the articles referred to.

It would not be easy to determine the exact epoch at which the term *indulgentia a pœna et culpa* first made its appearance. It certainly was used in the thirteenth century, and it is possibly older. As far as this form of words raises any difficulty against the Catholic doctrine of Indulgences, the trouble lies precisely in this, that we can affirm nothing positively about its origin. The writers who were confronted with it a few centuries later, and who tried to explain it, were reduced to conjectures, and their conjectures do not altogether agree. With regard, however, to the general attitude of the Church and her teachers, two facts can be overwhelmingly proved. The first is that theologians and canonists repudiated the phrase. They characterised it as unscientific, inaccurate, and calculated to produce a fundamentally false impression about Indulgences—that same false impression, in fact, which Mr. Lea so obstinately adheres to. Secondly, it is clear that this terminology—untheological as it was—was in familiar use among clergy and laity, but that it was universally understood to signify vaguely the most ample form of plenary Indulgence which it was in the Pope's power to grant. By what process of development it came to mean this is a doubtful question, but that it did mean this and nothing else, the citations in Mr. Lea's own pages would suffice to prove abundantly.

As a pure conjecture made with all reserves it may be suggested that the phrase originated with the confessional letters which were wont from a tolerably early period to be conceded by the Popes to favoured applicants. These conferred the privilege of choosing a confessor once or at most twice in a lifetime, who would have for that particular occasion, in virtue of this privilege, the special powers of absolving from reserved cases, and also of remitting all the punishment of sin—in other words, of applying to the penitent a plenary Indulgence. I think that such an absolution was called an absolution *a pœna et culpa*.[1] An ordinary absolution, of course, was from guilt (*a culpa*) only. This special absolution, including as it did a plenary Indulgence, was from punishment (*a pœna*) also. It was known then as an absolution from punishment as well as from guilt. Once such a locution had established itself, it would have been the easiest thing in the world to extend the phrase from the absolution itself to the papal grant which conceded it, and to talk not only of an *a pœna et culpa* absolution, which was quite correct, but also of an *a pœna et culpa Indulgence*, a terminology which cannot strictly be defended.

A passage of Thomas of Cantimpré, who died in 1263, illustrates admirably the transition stage of this development—"With regard," he says, "to the Indulgence which is promised to crusaders, no true Christian can doubt that those who are sincerely contrite and who make their confession receive in its entirety (*integraliter*) the Indulgence of all their sins; and in virtue of those dispositions of heart, by which, if occasion should offer, they welcome even death for the faith of Christ, they are absolved completely from punishment as well as from guilt" (*totaliter a pœna simul absolvuntur et culpa*). Again, a little lower down, he speaks of the confessional or crusading letters from Rome obtained in return for a money payment (to be applied to the purposes of the Crusade) in commutation of actual service: "O, what blessed letters are these which render the soul secure and purified from all guilt and penalty!" In the first of these cases the phrase *a culpa et pœna* is used in a way quite free from objection, for the priest's absolution given in virtue of these special Roman faculties released from both guilt and penalty. In the second case we find this formula associated with the letters of Indulgence rather than the priest's absolution,

[1] The idea seems to have been familiar to St. Thomas Aquinas, *Summa*, iii. 68, 2, 2.

and to this extent it is loosely employed, for the letters cannot be said to remit the guilt, though the priest's absolution can.

These letters were much prized, and we cannot wonder that the less instructed began to talk familiarly of an *a pœna et culpa* Indulgence as being the very highest spiritual favour the Pope could confer. They did not analyse the phrase, it was to them *a mere name*[1] for a much-valued type of privilege which implied power to absolve from almost any sins however grievous, and to remit the temporal punishment as well. We constantly meet illustrations of how the ignorant vulgar are caught by a name, and use it regardless of etymology and logic. With Mr. Weller, senior, the one effective form of argument in legal proceedings was an *alibi*, and until he had obtained or had been promised his *alibi*, he would probably in such a case have considered all efforts futile.

But whatever may be thought of this conjectural origin of the phrase, one thing is quite certain, that an Indulgence *a pœna et culpa* was not understood to remit the guilt of sin without confession and contrition. We need not deny that unscrupulous pardoners here and there may sometimes have abused the credulity of the vulgar in this sense. There is uncommonly little evidence of anything of the sort, and the extravagant statements of those who were more or less openly in revolt against ecclesiastical authority are always open to suspicion, and cannot be tested or controlled by any sort of statistics. But what we can test is the theological literature of the period,

---

[1] The author of *Piers Plowman* used *a pœna et culpa* in this loose sense, and obviously contradistinguished such an Indulgence, which was plenary, against a partial Indulgence for a term of years; as for instance in the following passage:—

> "Marchantz in the margyne · hadden many yeres,
> Ac none *a pena et a culpa* · the Pope nolde hem graunte,
> For thei holde nougt her halidayes · as holy churche techeth
> And for thei swere by her soule · and 'so god most hem helpe'
> Agein clene conscience · her catel to selle."
> (*Piers Plowman*, B. Text, Pass. vii. ll. 18-22.)

i.e., The Pope would grant to merchants an Indulgence of a good many years, but never a plenary, on account of their cheating and false oaths.

the writings of those who taught with authority, whose utterances were echoed in every theological school, and passed on by all faithful pastors in their instructions to their people.

One would have thought that the very passages quoted by Mr. Lea would have convinced him that his conception of the Indulgence *a pœna et a culpa* was an erroneous one. He admits that Thomas à Cantimpré required that those who gained such an Indulgence should be repentant and confessed. He admits that in another such grant made by Celestine V., the condition of confession, etc., was formally insisted on. He mentions that when Agostino da Ancona and Durandus a S. Porciano assert that the Pope can grant Indulgences *a pœna et culpa,* the context shows that a state of grace is assumed to be necessary. He quotes, as well-known examples of Indulgences so described, the Jubilees of 1300, 1350, etc., in which the Bull of promulgation requires contrition and confession in the most formal terms. He even cites the absolution form provided for the Indulgence of 1412 in the crusade against Ladislas of Naples, in which the priest first says, "I absolve thee from all thy sins truly confessed and repented of before God and myself," and then almost immediately afterwards continues, "and I further give and accord to thee that fullest remission of all thy sins which is *a pena et culpa.*" If the Indulgence alone was considered to remit all guilt, what could be the object of insisting on confession and sacramental absolution? These are by no means all the materials contained in Mr. Lea's own pages which serve to refute his interpretation of *a pœna et culpa,* but the only effect they produce upon him is to make him marvel at the "curious confusion" of mind and the hopeless inconsistency of these medieval writers. It never seems to occur to him that the meaning he affixes to the phrase is fundamentally wrong, and that the perversity lies not with the medieval theologians but with himself.

If evidence were forthcoming to support this view, the attitude we are speaking of would be more comprehensible, but there is hardly any pretence of producing evidence. When some chronicler mentions an Indulgence *a pœna et culpa*, and does not explicitly record that those who gained it made their confession, it is assumed that there was no confession.[1] When it appears that in some plenary Indulgences of Leo X. there is express mention of confession and communion, and in others not, instead of understanding, as every Catholic theologian would have done, that all such Indulgences were issued *in forma consueta ecclesiæ* and required of necessity the state of grace in the recipient, Mr. Lea concludes, without, of course, producing any evidence for his contention, that "the natural explanation of the distinction is that he charged more for one form of grant than for the other, and that the church applying for the concession took its choice."

Of anything like proof which goes to the root of the matter there is no trace. Yet such proof ought to be easy to obtain. There are in existence in the libraries of Europe hundreds of manuscripts of medieval sermons, numbers of which also are accessible in print. If any one wished to establish the fact that the people were taught that their sins could be forgiven by an Indulgence *a pœna et culpa* without any need of confession or contrition, such a writer should show us what preachers have said so, and where, and in what words. He should produce some passages affirming this doctrine from the Bulls of Popes, or from the scores of theological writers or canonists[2] who discussed the question of Indulgences before the Reformation. Of all such real evidence not a trace is forthcoming, while nothing is said

[1] It would be easy to quote hundreds of examples to show that however much the Indulgence was described as *a pœna et a culpa*, confession and sorrow were required all the same. One instance occurs in the extension of Alexander VI.'s Jubilee to England: "And the said confessor shall have power to give and grant to all the said persons *confessed and contrite*, clean and full remission, which is called *a pœna et culpa*."

[2] In the one or two cases in which Mr. Lea has attempted something of the sort, his perversion of the authors' meaning is simply indefensible. On p. 77 he refers to Catharinus in such a context that every reader would infer that that theologian asserted the Pope's power to remit guilt as well as punishment without the sacrament. All that Catharinus maintained was that the Pope's power was not limited to the remission of canonical penalties, but extended to the whole debt of temporal punishment in this life and in purgatory.

of the citations of writers like Dr. Janssen[1] and Dr. Pastor, who have shown that the preachers of the later Middle Ages were earnest in requiring confession and true repentance as a condition for the gaining of Indulgences.

As for the theologians, it is worth while to quote a few illustrations of the tone which they adopted and the attitude they took up. To give any idea of their unanimity, which is in one sense the most important point, is not easy. The present writer can only state that he is speaking from a first-hand examination, not of one or two, but of very many different books written in all parts of Europe, and in almost every decade between the time of St. Thomas Aquinas and the time of Luther. Upon three different points their verdict is, practically speaking, unanimous, first, that the phrase *indulgentia a pœna et culpa* is a popular locution, and not one chosen by theologians; secondly, that while various explanations may be offered of the term, they all agree in this, that an *indulgentia a pœna et culpa* does not pretend to remit guilt; thirdly, that to gain any Indulgence whatever, the state of grace is necessary. Let us take these points in order.

And, first, the impropriety of the locution *indulgentia a pœna et culpa,* if not suggested in the text of the canon law itself,[2] is clearly stated at the beginning of the fourteenth century by the Franciscan F. Mayron,[3] who was then Professor of Theology in Paris. "There can be no Indulgence given," he says, "*a pena et culpa*—the Church never uses such a form of words." This assertion, perhaps, is a little too sweeping, for one such Indulgence in these terms is still extant, granted by the hermit Pope St. Celestine V., who resigned the papacy. But, as Dr. N. Paulus has pointed out, the use of this form without qualification in a papal document is almost unique, and it

---

[1] In his *Geschichte des deutschen Volkes* and in his pamphlets *An meine Kritiker.*

[2] Clementine, bk. v. Tit. 9 de Pen. et Remiss. cap. ii. § 2. An extract from the decrees of the Council of Vienne.

[3] Mayron, *Sermones de Sanctis* (Basle, 1498), fol. xcii. *In quatour libris sententiarum* (Venetiis, 1519), fol. 215 a.

appears that the Bull was drafted by a layman, while the Pope himself was so completely ignorant of the forms and usages of papal documents that he signed whatever was submitted to him.[1] So again St. Antoninus of Florence equally rejects the phrase, though he pleads that it is capable of explanation.[2] Again, Nicholas Weigel, whom Mr. Lea and others have attempted to represent as giving a hopelessly involved account of the *indulgentia a pœna et culpa*, has been shown by Dr. Paulus to be perfectly clear and consistent. The citations from Weigel supplied by Mr. Lea and Brieger are taken either from Weigel's summary called *Clavicula Indulgentialis*, or the abstract of it in Amort. Brieger is even rash enough to suggest that it will only be possible to understand Weigel's real meaning when his bulky original work has been examined. Dr. Paulus has been able to discover and to study it in the original manuscript, and he shows by copious extracts how unfounded are the statements which have been made concerning him. Weigel begins by saying that "this manner of speaking *a pœna et culpa* is contrary to the form commonly used in the Church. For the Church commonly concedes Indulgences to those who are confessed and contrite, . . . and so she pre-supposes the guilt already pardoned by contrition or confession, granting Indulgences for the punishment which remains."[3] But leaving aside a quantity of similar passages which might be quoted, I will content myself with this extract from the work of W. Hane, printed, as Mr. Proctor thinks, at Hamburg in 1491:—

"In the likeness of that Jubilee of old there has been instituted, under the new law for mankind repeatedly falling into sin, a year of full forgiveness, *plenariæ remissionis*, as it is called, not of forgiveness *a pena et a culpa* as some erroneously

[1] Paulus, in the *Katholik*, 1899, i. p. 122.

[2] He repeats this both in his *Summa Theologiæ* and in his *Chronicon*. In the latter, for instance, he says, "Quæ indulgentia *vulgo* dicitur 'culpœ et pœnœ' sed culpam solus Deus remittit secundum illud Isaiæ 'ego solus deleo iniquitates tuas,'" part iii. p. 257 (ed. Lyons, 1580).

[3] The Latin is quoted by Paulus at length in *Zeitschrift für Kath. Theologie*, 1899, p. 748.

say, but only *a pena*, for the *culpa*—the guilt—is not remitted in virtue of the Indulgence, but the Indulgence supposes the guilt already remitted in virtue of sacramental contrition and confession, either actually made or at least purposed to be made. Hence, when it is said that there is conferred at such a time the remission of all sins, we must understand that this means the remission of all the punishment due for all our sins." [1]

With regard to the second point mentioned, there might at first sight seem to be a certain divergence among theological writers, but the divergence is only apparent, not real, and it is due to the attempt to find some logical explanation for a phrase, the popular use of which, as a mere name, all admitted and understood. In the passage where the phrase *a pœna et culpa* is mentioned in the Clementines, the glossator, Joannes Andreas, says, "*a pena et culpa:* this is that fullest remission of sins which is granted to Crusaders, and which is offered also in the hundredth year (*i.e.*, the Jubilee), which the Pope alone can grant." As W. Hane has just told us, the remission of sins [2] is simply the remission of the penalties due to sin, and we infer that the Indulgence *a culpa et pena* was nothing more than an ordinary plenary Indulgence, with the added circumstance that the confessor received full faculties. On the phrase *plenissimam peccatorum veniam* which occurs in the Jubilee Bull of Boniface, Cardinal Joannes Monachus, as we have noticed, remarks that he heard Boniface in consistory himself explain the words to mean that he wished to give the fullest Indulgence it was possible to give, so far, in fact, as the power of the keys extended. This, then, was the idea which remained consistently attached to the

[1] W. Hane, *Collecta ex diversis super Indulgentias Plenariæ Remissionis pro animabus in Purgatorio*, sig. c. vii. f. 7.

[2] A whole treatise might be written on this phrase. It still survives in its primitive sense in the concluding words of the prayer said by the priest after the form of absolution—"Sint tibi in remissionem peccatorum, augmentum gratiæ et præmium vitæ eternæ." It came quite naturally to the medieval theologian in this meaning of the cancelling of temporal punishment, and as late as 1500 we find ex Nottis writing—"Est ergo quolibet anno centesimo plenissima omnium peccatorum concessa venia quæ *secundum vulgare* a pœna et culpa absolutio appellatur," sig. b. ii. v°.

phrase in the popular mind. The laity cared little about the analysis of it, but they knew that the *a culpa et pœna* was the name for the biggest thing in the nature of an Indulgence which it was possible to get. They also probably realised vaguely that there were two elements in it—the remission of penalty and the increased facility of absolution—while it mattered little to them that these two concessions belong to quite different categories, that the Pope remitted the penalty directly (ut causa efficiens) and the guilt very indirectly (ut causa ne instrumentalis quidem sed velut dispositiva). This last inconsistency worried the theologians, and some tried to accommodate themselves to it by one explanation and others by another, though all were perfectly agreed that under no possible circumstance could an Indulgence in any proper sense be said to remit the guilt of sin. The most common explanation, and that which seemingly was historically nearest the truth, is the one first advanced that the *culpa* referred to the extraordinary faculties for confession, the *pœna* to the remission of temporal punishment. This, for instance, is the account given at some length in the *Celifodina* of Johannes von Paltz, who, after he has stated in the plainest terms that "no one in virtue of an Indulgence is, properly speaking, released from guilt and punishment but only from punishment,"[1] puts to himself the so-called Jubilee Indulgence *a pœna et culpa* as a difficulty, and explains it as just stated. We may take Paltz alone for mention out of the score of similar writers ready to hand, because he was himself a preacher of Indulgences, and his work and its supplements were widely circulated. "When the Pope grants a Jubilee," he says, "he does not grant a mere Indulgence, but he also gives faculties to hear confessions and absolve from all sins even as regards the guilt. And *in this way* the guilt is remitted through the sacrament of penance which is thus introduced."

Perhaps, however, the clearest proof that could be given to show that the phrase *a culpa et pœna* was often regarded as

[1] Sequitur quod virtute indulgentiæ proprie loquendo nullus absolvitur a pœna et culpa sed solum a pœna. *Celifodina* xl. r°

a mere synonym for a plenary Indulgence, and without any reference whatever to the guilt of sin, is supplied by the fact that Pope Pius IV. granted an Indulgence *a culpa et pœna* to any soul in purgatory for whom a certain alms should be offered.[1] Obviously there could be no question in such a case of remitting the *guilt* of sin in a soul upon which Almighty God had already passed judgment.

Finally, it would be easy to accumulate passages to show the universal opinion of theologians that Indulgences could profit none but those in a state of grace, and consequently that for those who have lost God's grace, confession, or at least contrition, with the intention of confessing at a suitable opportunity, are indispensably necessary. Something has already been said upon the point, and the plain language of the English canonist Lyndwood has been quoted, and we may now turn almost at random, for every theologian uses the same or similar expressions, to a treatise on Indulgences by Louis de Bologninis, printed in 1489, and dedicated to Cardinal Jerome Rovere After explaining the doctrine of the treasure, he continues—

"The Pope, in granting a plenary Indulgence, intends to communicate to us the treasure of the Church, and by its means that whole time of punishment is remitted which we owe for all our sins. The guilt, indeed, is remitted through contrition, joined with the intention of confessing, but the punishment, (even though) eternal, is remitted entirely by a plenary Indulgence. But one thing mark carefully—that unless there were that contrition by which the guilt is washed away, the plenary Indulgence would avail us nothing, as I shall explain more fully later on."

In returning to the point, the author states that one reason why Indulgences are seen to be useless to those who are not truly contrite, is that "Indulgences are always granted to those only who are truly penitent and who have made their confession (*vere penitentibus et confessis*), and this clause is included in

[1] I accept this statement on the authority of Dr. Lea. I have not had the opportunity of verifying it.

the form of grant, and in the case in which it should not be inserted—suppose, for instance, an Indulgence were granted by word of mouth—such Indulgences are still presumed to have been conceded in the accustomed form (*in forma consueta*)."[1]

But no one, perhaps, has summed up the essential facts more concisely and clearly than Jerome de Zanettis in his treatise *de Foro Conscientiæ*. "In the definition of an Indulgence," he remarks, "nothing is said about guilt (*culpa*), because an Indulgence does not remove the guilt; this has been already removed by contrition and confession, and although in popular parlance (*in communi locutione*) it be styled *a culpa et pœna*, still this manner of speaking is inaccurate (*non est propria*), because it is God alone who remits the guilt of sin."[2] He adds, however, that St. Antoninus of Florence considers that the phrase may perhaps be defended on the ground that the guilt is taken away by contrition and confession, which are the necessary prerequisites for the gaining of an Indulgence, and are thus in a sense bound up with it.

It will be noticed that all the writers quoted are earlier than the time of Luther, and that their evidence, consequently, belongs to the period during which the greatest corruption is supposed to have prevailed in this matter, before the Church was put upon her guard, as it were, by the criticism of the reformers. Moreover, there is abundant testimony forthcoming from the same epoch that the teaching of the theologians and canonists in their professorial chairs was faithfully transmitted to the people, and that, apart from exceptional cases of extreme ignorance, the laity were well instructed in all that was most essential in the doctrine of Indulgences. The late Dr. Janssen, in his *Geschichte des deutschen Volkes*,[3] has supplied abundant evidence of this, which he has drawn almost entirely from extant sermons and instructions delivered by medieval preachers in the vernacular.

---

[1] L. de Bologninis, *Tractatus de Indulgentiis* (1489), sig. c. i. v°.

[2] Jerome de Zanettis, printed in *Tractatus Tractatuum*, vol. iii. part i. fol. 408 v°.

[3] Cf. also Janssen's pamphlet *An meine Kritiker*, pp. 66-81.

"An Indulgence," explains Geiler of Kaisersberg,[1] "is the remission of a debt. But of what debt? Not that of mortal sin, since for the gaining of an Indulgence the condition is first required that the soul should be free from mortal sin; not the debt of eternal punishment, for in hell there is no redemption; but the debt of temporal punishment, which a man, after sorrow and penance, through which the eternal pain is converted into that which is temporal, has still to undergo." "Be it known to thee," says the *Guide of Souls*,[2] "that an Indulgence does not forgive sin, but only remits the punishment that thou hast deserved. Be it known to thee, that thou canst have no Indulgence if thou beest in thy sins and hast not confessed and truly repented and art not sincerely desirous to amend, otherwise all else profiteth thee nothing. God is gracious and merciful, and giveth power to Holy Church to absolve from sins, and puts into her hands the great treasure of salvation, but this is not for him who feigns in outward show (*einem usserlichen menschen*), and who thinks to gain heaven by merely outward works."

With regard to the understanding of the Jubilee Indulgence in particular, we have an interesting testimony (one only among many such) left in the note-book of a devout layman, Giovanni Rucellai, a merchant of Florence, who came to Rome for the Holy Year of 1450. He wrote an account of what he saw there, which he headed "Che vuole dire Giubileo" (What the Jubilee means), the beginning of which runs as follows:—

"By the Jubilee, which takes place once in fifty years, is meant just this: it is the plenary remission of all your sins, obtained by going to Rome in the said year of Jubilee and remaining there for at least fifteen days, making every day a visit to each of the four churches, to wit, St. Peter, St. Paul, St. John Lateran, and St. Mary Major. It is understood that you go there with confession, contrition, and satisfaction

[1] Lindenmnn, *Johannes Geiler von Kaisersberg*, p. 81. Apud Janssen *op. cit.* (fifteenth edition), i. p. 50.

[2] *Der Selenfürer, ein nutzberlich buch für yeglichen cristenmenschen zum frumen leben und seligen sterben.* Mainz, bei Peter Scheffer, 1498, fol. 21.

(*confesso et contrito et sadisfatto*), and having a true sorrow and true repentance and true detestation of all the sins that you have ever committed; and also that you have performed the penance which your confessor may have imposed, so that the visits which you have to make each day to the end of the fifteen days may be made with a clean heart, purified from all the filth of sin."[1]

Before turning to set down in his notes some account of the wonderful things he witnessed in Rome, Rucellai adds—

"The aforesaid confession delivers you from the pains of hell, but not from those of purgatory; but the plenary Indulgence, which is gained by means of the said Jubilee, is to deliver you from the pains of purgatory, where, it is said, for every mortal sin one must remain ten years."[2]

To illustrate the popular understanding of the phrase *a pœna et culpa*, and to make it clear how very far such an Indulgence was from being considered to exempt a man from confession, an interesting passage may be quoted from the narrative of the pilgrimage of Georges Lengherand, who came to Rome from Mons, in Hainault, in the year 1847. As he came at a season which was not one of Jubilee, the Indulgence *a pœna et culpa* had to be obtained from the Pope as a special and personal favour.

"I reached Rome about eight o'clock in the morning, and proceeded to visit St. Peter's Church, and to pay my respects to Monsignor the Bishop of Tournai, several of my fellow-countrymen being there also, who received me hospitably and made me welcome. I requested the said bishop that he would obtain for me the papal bènediction, and to kiss the Pope's feet; also that he would get leave for me and my three companions to make the journey to Jerusalem, and to St. Catherine on Mount Sinai; and to choose a confessor at Rome who would have power to absolve me *a pœna et culpa*, seeing that it was not then an

---

[1] *Relazione di Giovanni Rucellai* regarding the Jubilee of 1450. *Archivio di Storia Patria*, iv. p. 563.

[2] *Ibid.* p. 564.

ordinary season of Indulgence at Rome, and also that I might do the same at Jerusalem. To which requests my Lord Bishop of Tournai replied that he would do all in his power, and that on the following morning I might assist at the Pope's mass with him.

"Wednesday, the 12th of April, I was at the levée of my Lord Bishop of Tournai, who has his lodging in the papal palace, being the Pope's *maître d'hôtel*. He conducted me to the Pope's

PENITENTIARIES WITH THEIR WANDS OF OFFICE HEARING THE CONFESSIONS OF JUBILEE PILGRIMS.
From a print of 1650.

apartment and went to hear mass. At the conclusion of mass he got the Pope to sign the permit for me and my companions to make the journey to Jerusalem and St. Catherine; when giving it to me, he said that I could not receive the Pope's benediction till after his dinner; after which the said Lord Bishop of Tournai, who had dined with the Holy Father, invited me to enter the room, in company with an ecclesiastic from Burgundy, named Monsieur Guillaume du Fort, a priest living at Dijon; and we two together made our reverence to the Holy Father to the best of our ability, kneeling three times. And the Holy Father being seated in a gilt chair, and we kneeling before him, my Lord of Tournai introduced us, and he put out his foot, and we each kissed it; then raising us, the Holy Father kissed us both, and then gave us his blessing. He also gave leave for me and my three companions to make the aforesaid journeys, and granted the request I had made, by permitting me to choose a priest at Rome, and another at Jerusalem, as my confessors, giving them faculties to absolve me *a pena et culpa.* He again allowed me to kiss his foot, and kissing me a second time, he also a second time gave me his blessing, and ordered Monseigneur de Tournai to give me some *Agnus Deis*, which he accordingly did. The interview being ended, and reverence made on taking leave, I repaired to the chaplain of the Cardinal de Racanart, nominated by the Pope to be Penitenciary in St. Peter's Church, who was called Monsieur François, to enquire at what hour on the following morning he would hear my confession and examine my conscience, according to the favour granted me by our Holy Father. He had already received intelligence of the faculty granted him by the said Pope to absolve me *a pena et culpa*, and directed me to come to him at four o'clock the next morning.

"On Thursday, the 13th of April, following the above direction, I found myself at four o'clock in the morning before the said Monsieur François, who heard me carefully and at length. After confession and absolution, I was anxious immediately to make the pilgrimages (*i.e.*, the visits) and gain the Indulgences of the seven principal churches in Rome and the environs; but I could not make them then, as I could not get any one to bear me company, and it would be very dangerous to make them alone without trusty companions. So I waited till the next day to go in company with two good men from Ronerges in France, one of whom was a priest."[1]

[1] *Voyage de Georges Lengherand*, Mayeur de Mons en Haynaut, 1485-86, p. 57-59.

It is interesting to notice that this conception of the Jubilee Indulgence, *i.e.*, that it is in a legitimate sense a remission both of guilt and penalty, the former, however, only through the medium of the sacrament of penance, was taught by Pope Leo XIII. himself in the days when he was Bishop of Perugia, and before his elevation to the papal chair. At the beginning of the year 1875 he wrote, in a pastoral letter addressed to his flock—

"The Jubilee Year is a year of *plenary and entire remission of all sins,* however grievous, even of those ordinarily reserved to the Holy See. Every penitent, animated by the requisite dispositions for receiving the sacrament of penance, and having fulfilled the prescribed works, can obtain this remission, and, together with *the absolution from all sin,* the remission *of all penalties* for sin, due to the Divine Justice. It can be gathered from this general idea that with regard to *sin considered in itself,* in so far as it is a defilement of the soul, the Jubilee puts *the most extensive powers* into the hands of approved confessors in order that they may efface every stain from the hearts of well-disposed penitents, and may re-admit into the pale of the Church even those who lie under ecclesiastical censure. As regards the *penalty* due to sins, the Jubilee opens wide the treasures of the Church, supplied by the infinite merits of Jesus Christ, and the superabundant merits of our Blessed Lady and the Saints, and imparts them in the greatest possible abundance to all the faithful, in order that they may satisfy the Divine Justice, and extinguish the debt incurred by their sins."[1]

In this limited sense the Jubilee Indulgence may with strict accuracy be described as a remission *a pœna et a culpa,* and in this sense alone have Catholic theologians admitted the use of the phrase from the fourteenth century down to our own day.

---

[1] Quoted in the *Zeitschrift für Katholische Theologie*, ii. Quartalheft, 1900, pp. 391, 392.

CHAPTER IX

THE CONDITIONS OF THE JUBILEE

ALTHOUGH the aim of this book is historical rather than devotional, completeness seems to require that the more practical aspects of the Jubilee should not be entirely passed over. With this view, the present chapter has been compiled to provide a summary account of the conditions upon which the privileges of the Holy Year are offered to the faithful. The valuable little treatise of Father Joseph Hilgers, S.J., *Das Goldene Jahr*, which, owing to the facilities afforded to the writer in Rome, is of exceptional authority,[1] has been followed in the main.[2] It has, however, been supplemented by an enumeration of practical directions for pilgrims translated from an Italian Jubilee sheet, *Vera Roma*, published for the present year, which many will find convenient.

There is one important distinction to which it seems desirable to call attention at the outset, seeing that it is very generally overlooked, and is, consequently, productive of much misunderstanding. This is the distinction between the Jubilee properly so called, which is limited to the Holy Year itself, and the *extension* of the Jubilee, which follows immediately upon the Jubilee proper, and renders the gaining of the Indulgence easy

---

[1] I am much indebted to the author for his kind permission to make use of his book so far as it would serve the purposes of the present work.

[2] Some important moot points connected with the Jubilee Indulgence are discussed by his Grace the Archbishop of Dublin in the *Irish Eccles. Record* for March, 1900. This valuable article has also been consulted, together with the important work on Indulgences of Fr. Beringer, S.J., which exists both in French and in German.

for the faithful in every part of the world. *The Jubilee proper* can only be gained by ordinary Christians on condition of a pilgrimage to Rome; though here again there are exceptions made for nuns, prisoners, hermits, etc., and for the aged and infirm. *The extended Jubilee* does not entail any visit to Rome, and while it offers the same privileges as were conceded in the Jubilee proper, it offers them upon conditions which can be complied with by any one of the faithful without quitting the place in which he resides. As already stated, *the Jubilee proper* is limited to the Holy Year itself, and is available only during the year 1900, or, more accurately, during the twelve months which extend from 24th December, 1899, to 24th December, 1900. The privileges of *the extended Jubilee* may be expected to begin with the commencement of the year 1901, and will be available for such time as the Pope may determine. On the last three occasions when a Holy Year, duly celebrated in Rome, has been followed by an extension of the Indulgence to the rest of Christendom, to wit, in 1751, 1776, and 1826, the extended Jubilee has been conceded for a period of six months. Something more will be said of the extension of the Jubilee in connection with the *extraordinary Jubilees,* which will form the subject of the next chapter.

The conditions prescribed for the gaining of the Jubilee Indulgence proper are outlined in the Bull of promulgation *Properante ad exitum*, published by Leo XIII on the Ascension Day of last year. In this document the Pope proclaims that—

"During this year of Jubilee We grant and concede mercifully in the Lord a plenary Indulgence, remission, and pardon for sin to all the faithful of either sex who, truly penitent and having confessed and communicated, shall piously visit the Basilicas of the Blessed Peter and Paul, also of St. John Lateran and St. Mary Major, at least once a day for twenty days, consecutively or at intervals, according to natural or ecclesiastical computation, *i.e.*, reckoning from the first vespers of one day till nightfall on the following day. These are the conditions for those who are living in Rome, whether they are citizens or visitors. But those who come from a distance shall devoutly visit the same Basilicas on at least ten days, reckoned as above, and shall there pour forth their pious prayers to God for the exaltation of the Church, the extirpation of heresies, concord among Catholic princes, and the salvation of Christian people.

"Since, however, it may happen that some, in spite of the best of intentions, may be unable to fulfil the conditions above laid, down either in whole or in part, being prevented by sickness or other legitimate cause whilst in the city or on the way hither, We, in consideration of their good will, as far as We may in the Lord, grant that, provided they be truly contrite, purified by confession and strengthened by the Holy Communion, they shall share in the above-mentioned Indulgence and pardon as if they had actually visited the Basilicas on the days appointed by Us."

We may therefore consider these conditions under four heads—(1) true repentance, (2) confession and communion, (3) visits to the Churches, (4) prayers for the Pope's intentions.

I.—True Repentance

With regard to the first of these, it will have been understood from the citations in the last chapter that sorrow for sin is the indispensable condition of gaining any Indulgence whatever, great or small. Of course, this sorrow for sin need not necessarily extend to every venial transgression which stains the soul. Only that sorrow is here contemplated which is essential to a state of grace, and which consists in the detestation of all past grievous offences against God, with the firm resolution of avoiding in future anything that might forfeit His friendship. None the less, the more intense is that sorrow, and the more completely it extends not only to every transgression which kills, but even to those that stain and disfigure the soul, the greater may be the pilgrim's confidence of gaining in full measure the remission of guilt and penalties offered by the Jubilee.

It may be noticed, too, as already pointed out in the previous chapter, p. 330, that, according to the more common teaching of theologians, it is not indispensably necessary that this sorrow for past sin should accompany the performance of all and each of the conditions of the Jubilee. It is indispensable, of course, for the valid reception of the sacraments of Penance and the Holy Eucharist. Moreover, in the case that some of the other prescribed conditions yet remain to be performed, it is also indispensable for the final discharge of these obligations, for the Indulgence cannot be granted to one who has not yet fulfilled the conditions, and it cannot be granted to one who is out of the grace of God.[1] For this reason it is usually recommended that the special Jubilee confession and communion should be made to follow rather than to precede the visits to the churches.

II.—Confession and Communion

The second condition is the worthy reception of the sacraments of Penance and the Eucharist.[2] This is a usual though not an invariable condition for gaining a plenary Indulgence. Wherever the reception of the holy sacrament of Penance is formally prescribed, it is not sufficient that a man be already in a state of grace—the state in which holy confession places him—nor that he be restored to a state of grace by an act of perfect contrition; it is rather the actual confession itself which is necessary. It would not therefore suffice for the Jubilee Indulgence that the sacraments have been received at Easter. The sacraments of Penance and the Eucharist must be received expressly for the purpose of gaining the Indulgence.

During the Jubilee season the members of religious orders of men may confess to any secular or regular priest, approved

[1] Father Hilgers pronounces that if, after making the Jubilee Confession and Communion, the pilgrim should unfortunately lose the grace of God by grievous sin before completing the series of visits, a mere act of perfect contrition, even though it restores God's friendship and enables the pilgrim to perform the last conditions in a state of grace, is not sufficient for the gaining of the Jubilee Indulgence. A second confession is necessary. *Das Goldene Jahr*, p. 55. So also Beringer, *Les Indulgences*, i. pp. 484, 485.

[2] The reception of Holy Communion was first imposed as a necessary condition for gaining the Jubilee Indulgence by Benedict XIV. in 1750.

by the bishop of the diocese, without permission from their superiors.[1] Nuns can also choose their confessor during the Jubilee, but only from among those priests who have faculties to hear the confessions of religious women.

With the extension of the Jubilee to the whole world some explicit pronouncement is usually made as to how children who have not yet made their first communion can gain the Indulgence. These must be instructed on the point by their parents or others who are responsible for them. Benedict XIV. empowered confessors to impose some other good work on such children in place of Holy Communion, and as long as nothing is determined to the contrary this rule holds good for the present Jubilee and its extension.

It is not stated in the Bull that pilgrims to Rome must make their confession and communion there. This is optional, and the confession and communion need not even immediately precede or follow the visits to the churches, but this reception of the two sacraments must be distinct from that which is performed in discharge of the annual Easter obligation, and it must take place, like the other Jubilee observances, within the twelve months for which the Jubilee is granted.

A general confession is not prescribed, unless on account of previous invalid confessions such a confession is necessary. Seeing, however, that for most people a general confession—whether it be a complete review of their whole life past or be confined to a partial repetition of the matter of former confessions—is to be recommended on special occasions; the occasion of the Jubilee, the Holy Year, the first of the new century, seems a peculiarly fitting time for it. It should be made as devoutly as possible, after earnest preparation, with true contrition and firm purpose of amendment, so that it may be truly said of this work of God in our souls, "Behold I make all things new."

[1] If, as in the Jubilee of 1886, it is said that any approved secular or regular priest may be chosen, and this seems to be the case from the constitution *Æterni Pastoris*, the faculties granted by the superiors of religious orders suffice.

Inasmuch as the great work of the Jubilee, the remission of sin and of the punishments of sin, is accomplished primarily through the sacramental absolution, it is the invariable practice of the Pope to grant special powers at this season for the absolving of those more grievous offences which are usually reserved to the bishops or to himself.

The granting of these plenary faculties, and, in fact, the power of priests to remit sins at all, depends upon the absolute power of the keys given to St. Peter. The same is true of the power to absolve from the punishment of sin, or in other words to grant an Indulgence. But these faculties, so far as the *guilt* of sin is concerned, can only be exercised in the sacrament. Hence it follows that the plenary absolution which the Pope, in virtue of his apostolic authority, promises and imparts to those who truly fulfil the prescribed conditions, includes the pardon of all, even the worst sins, with all their guilt, and the remission of all punishments which these sins have merited. This is the sense and meaning of the words in the Jubilee Bulls, "plenissimam peccatorum indulgentiam remissionem et veniam," which we may freely translate, "fullest remission of all sins, and all the penalties of sin, together with pardon and favour."

III.—Visits to the Basilicas

The next condition for gaining the Jubilee Indulgence consists in the visits to be paid to the four chief Basilicas of Rome. Of course, the making these visits, except for those who reside in Rome, involves a pilgrimage to the Holy City, in whatever way the journey may be made. The four Basilicas, as we have already seen, are the Cathedral and tomb of St. Peter, beside the Vatican Hill on the right bank of the Tiber, and the Church of St. Paul, without the walls of the city, on the left bank of the Tiber, where is the resting-place of the Apostle of the Gentiles. To these are added the Basilica of St. John Lateran, dedicated to the Saviour of the world, as being the oldest, and also the mother of all churches; and that of Sta. Maria Maggiore, as being the largest and most important of the churches in Rome dedicated to our Lady.

Visits to these four churches of Rome are generally enjoined at ordinary Jubilees. But whereas formerly the number of visits to be paid was thirty for dwellers in Rome and fifteen for pilgrims, Leo XIII. has reduced this number to twenty days for Catholics living in Rome and ten days for those who come from a distance. Even this number is commonly considerably reduced in practice, the Jubilee confessors in Rome having powers for the purpose.

These days and visits need not be consecutive; it suffices that the days on which they are paid all fall within the Holy Year. Also, either the civil day, from midnight to midnight, or the ecclesiastical day, which is reckoned from the first vespers of one day to the close of evening of the next, may be chosen as the space of time within which the visits of that one day are paid. But during this time, whether it be a civil or an ecclesiastical day, each of the four churches must be visited, and there may not be two visits out of the twenty or ten requisite, paid on the same day.[1] Twenty such visits are prescribed, both for those who always live in Rome and also for those who have a domicile there during the Holy Year. For those pilgrims who come in from the suburbs merely to gain the

---

[1] Except in so far as the civil and ecclesiastical day overlap. Thus a person arriving in Rome on Monday at nine in the morning might visit the four churches before two p.m., and supposing him to have ended with the Basilica of St. Paul outside the walls, he might again, after a brief interval, visit the church of St. Paul, seeing that after two the first vespers of the next ecclesiastical day may be considered to have begun. In this way eight visits might be lawfully paid between sunrise and sunset, but it would not be possible for him to pay eight visits on the next day, Tuesday, but only those belonging to the ecclesiastical day, which begins at two p.m. It would seem that dispensations are commonly given to those who cannot make a long stay in Rome, allowing them to perform two or more sets of visits on the same day. Thus, supposing that a pilgrim be dispensed and required to make only four visits to each church, it would, with this relaxation, be sufficient for him to pay two distinct visits to each church, with the shortest of intervals between, on the first day and some one other day, leaving himself quite free for the rest of his stay in Rome.

Jubilee Indulgence, ten visits only are requisite. It should also be mentioned that these visits to the churches, as well as the journey to Rome, need not be made on foot.

When the Holy Year is over and the Jubilee is extended to the rest of the world, the bishop of each diocese is commissioned by the Holy Father to determine what church or churches are to be visited, and how often, by those who, through this extension, are enabled to gain the Indulgence without travelling to Rome; and, in general, all the conditions necessary for gaining the Indulgence are left to the decision of the bishops, particularly as regards the modification of any observance which the Holy Father may have laid down as of universal obligation, for those who gain the Jubilee Indulgence in Rome. The principal church in each locality must always be included in the number of those which the bishop designates to be visited. Thus in an episcopal city it will be the cathedral, in other places of the diocese the parish church.

If more than one visit to the same church is permitted on the same day, the visits must really be distinct. After each visit the church must be left, at least for a few minutes.

If a church be so full that it is impossible to enter, it suffices for the fulfilling the condition to recite the prescribed prayers at the church door near the rest of the faithful who may be standing there.

Members of religious orders will also be instructed by the bishops as to the churches to which their visits must be paid, unless they possess special privileges. For those religious who are legitimately hindered from fulfilling these conditions their confessor can, as a rule, substitute another good work.

IV.—Prayer for the Pope's Intention

The last observance to be spoken of, viz., the saying of prayers for a prescribed intention, is closely connected with the preceding, in so far as these prayers are to be recited during the visits paid to the churches.

The intention with which they are to be said is that which,

in the case of other Indulgences, is commonly known as "The Intention of the Holy Father," which, in particular, is interpreted to mean the exaltation of the Church, the uprooting of heresy, concord between Catholic Sovereigns, and the wellbeing of all Christian peoples.

As with other Indulgences, so also with that of the Jubilee, it is not necessary, although it is always a laudable practice, to direct the intention explicitly to each of these four objects in particular. Whoever makes the visits as prescribed, and prays devoutly each time in order to gain the Jubilee Indulgence, is really praying for the Intention of the Holy Father, even although he may not have each of these four objects explicitly before his mind. The same thing holds good with regard to the intention with which all the prescribed works are performed. It is quite true that each and every one of the observances enjoined must be performed with the intention of gaining the Indulgence, or of sharing in the pardon of the Jubilee. But it is evident that he who honestly desires to comply with all needful conditions also has the necessary purpose of gaining the Indulgence. The formal renewal of this good intention is not requisite before each work.

As regards the prayers to be recited, their purport and length, nothing is added to the general rule which holds in all indulgenced prayers said for the intention of the Holy Father. It is sufficient to pray orally, although this does not mean to pray with the lips alone, for in any good prayer the heart must be raised to God. Whoever makes his prayer mentally must add at least one vocal prayer thereto. It is generally considered that five Our Fathers and Hail Marys, or any other devotions of similar length, suffice for the purpose, and this opinion may be safely followed. Other prayers, according to the needs and judgment of each, can, of course, be recited in addition.

Plenary Powers of Confessors during the Jubilee time

During the Holy Year, and also during the time of the extension of the Jubilee to the rest of Christendom, the Holy Father grants extraordinary powers to confessors, but only for

Pontifical Blessing given from St. Peter's in the Jubilee of 1575.
From a rare engraving in the Print Room of the British Museum.

the benefit of those who intend to comply with the requisite conditions with a view to gaining the Jubilee Indulgence.

These powers are set forth in detail and published, and each confessor is bound to act in strict accordance with the regulations laid down by the Pope, or his own diocesan. It is therefore unnecessary to go into details, but a few words may be said on certain general principles which govern the use of these plenary powers. These principles were established by Benedict XIV. for his Jubilee in 1750, and they still hold good both for ordinary and extraordinary Jubilees, unless the contrary is intimated in the Jubilee Bull. This was expressly decided by Pius IX. in 1852.

The plenary powers above referred to are of three kinds. The first consists in this, that the confessor may commute the prescribed works for others. Of course this does not extend to the contrite dispositions required in the penitent, a condition from which no one, not even the Pope himself, can exempt. Neither does it extend to the conditions of confession and communion. Even the prayer for the Pope's intention, in so far as this may be made without visiting the churches, cannot be entirely dispensed with. It is supposed that all, even the sick, can fulfil these conditions. In commuting the other prescribed works the provisions of the Jubilee Bull must always be taken into account, and we may note that in the Bull *Properante ad exitum* for the present year it is laid down that for all pilgrims to Rome who, through sickness, are hindered from fulfilling the other conditions, the reception of the sacraments alone suffices to gain the Indulgences.[1] But this only has reference to the Holy Year itself, and to the pilgrims whose illness has come upon them after they have actually started on their journey to Rome.

It may happen that, through no fault of his own, a person may not be able to communicate during the Jubilee time. The

[1] The later constitution *Æterni Pastoris* of 1st November, 1899, determines that the infirm and aged who are resident in Rome shall, in lieu of the visits to the Basilicas, have other works assigned to them by the Cardinal Vicar. The same holds for nuns, cloistered orders of men, and prisoners within the city.

confessor cannot prolong the Jubilee season in such a case without further powers. This privilege must be granted to him in express terms.

The confessor cannot modify either wholly or in part any of the prescribed Jubilee observances without reasonable and lawful cause. Moreover, the good works imposed by the confessor must be in some sense the equivalent of those enjoined in the Jubilee Bull, unless the condition of the penitent, *e.g.*, in the case of illness, renders him incapable of performing such. It is to be noted, however, that in practice the Jubilee confessors in Rome seem to show themselves very benignant in the matter of reducing the number of visits to the Basilicas. If pilgrims are pressed for time, they are commonly let off with four or five days' stay in the city, while in the case of those who take part in the great Jubilee pilgrimages even this number is further reduced.

If the Jubilee Indulgence can be gained more than once, so also can the requisite conditions be commuted each time. The confessor can, however, only do this (as indeed he can only exercise all his extraordinary powers) in the confessional, *i.e.*, only at confession, in the tribunal of Penance, unless some particular constitution prescribes otherwise.

The second special privilege granted to confessors in the Jubilee Year is the power of absolving from all sins, however grievous, and from ecclesiastical censures. And this holds good of all sins, whether they have been specially reserved by bishops or by the Pope, or from whatever motive they may have been committed. The three sins only are excepted which are always reserved to the Pope alone, even when he grants the fullest faculties in regard to all other sins. This exception, however, is duly notified to the confessor in the same document which confers upon him these fuller faculties.

This second power can be exercised but once in favour of each penitent, even although the Jubilee Indulgence may be gained more often, and then, as we have seen, only in the confessional (*in foro conscientiæ*).

The same rule holds good also of a further power, that of dispensing from any irregularity. Upon this matter it is unnecessary to dwell further; first, because it may be considered as of like nature with the powers already explained, and, secondly, because it must be expressly mentioned in the papal faculties if the confessor wishes to use it. The terms used in the form of the grant must therefore be carefully consulted.

The third plenary power is concerned with vows made by the penitent. The confessor is generally authorised to dispense from any simple vow, even if confirmed by oath, and from vows to undertake pilgrimages, usually reserved to the Pope himself, by substituting other pious and holy works in their stead.

Certain exceptions, however, are always made in this matter, and, besides the three essential vows of religious, these exceptions include, first, the vow of perpetual chastity in the strict sense of the word; secondly, the vow to enter one of the religious orders approved by the Church; thirdly, vows made for the benefit of others, and accepted by them; and fourthly, vows taken as a protection against sin (the so-called *vota pœnalia*). The confessor, however, can always exchange this last class of vows, the penal vows, for some other work which, in his judgment, is likely to be equally efficacious as a protection against sin.

Since the confessor, in virtue of this power, not merely dispenses, but commutes, he must impose upon the penitent, in lieu of the vow, a work which is equivalent to it, or, at least, not wholly disproportionate. On the other hand, no special reason is required for this commutation, unless the papal grant expressly demands such. This power can only be exercised once during the Jubilee in favour of each penitent, even although the Jubilee Indulgence can be gained more often.

If any one knowingly and wilfully makes a bad confession, such a person naturally cannot gain the Jubilee Indulgence, neither has he any share in the privileges named. On the other hand, he who in good faith makes a Jubilee confession, having at the time the intention of performing the other conditions, is, and remains, freed from all reserved sins and ecclesiastical censures, and is released from any vows which may have been commuted for him, even if, from any reason, the confession was not entire, or if the penitent does not afterwards fulfil the remaining conditions, and consequently does not gain the Indulgence. Indeed, the reservation of a sin is equally cancelled in the Jubilee confession, even if the penitent forgot expressly to mention these reserved sins, provided only that the confession was made in good faith, and he intended to fulfil all the Jubilee works. It will be sufficient for him to accuse himself of the forgotten sin in his next confession, to any confessor, even after the expiration of the Jubilee season.

The confessor can then and there release a penitent from the reservation of sins, and from censures, and also commute a vow for other works, even if for good reasons he defers giving him absolution. The penitent must only be willing to follow the directions of the confessor and to fulfil the remaining Jubilee observances. Moreover, the confessor can absolve such a penitent even after the expiration of the Jubilee, provided no hindrance then exists to his so doing.

Further Jubilee Regulations

It may be seen how desirous the Pope is that the faithful should make the pilgrimage to Rome in order to gain there the Jubilee Indulgence, from the fact that during the time of its duration in Rome, *i.e.*, from the first vespers of Christmas, 1899, to the vespers of Christmas Eve, 1900, all other Indulgences, either plenary or partial, for the benefit of the living are suspended. This does not apply to the period of the *extension* of the Jubilee to the rest of the world after the Jubilee year itself is over.

The Indulgences of privileged altars, and in general all Indulgences granted only for the benefit of the dead, are not withdrawn. Moreover, what is still more important, during the Jubilee year all Indulgences (even those granted for the benefit of the living and suspended so far as these are concerned), may be gained for the dead, even although they may not have been specially declared to be applicable to the souls in purgatory.

Lastly, a certain number of Indulgences have not been suspended, and can be gained by the living for their own benefit. The most important of these are—(1) The plenary Indulgence at the hour of death; (2) the Indulgence for saying the *Angelus;* (3) the Indulgence for the Quarant' Ore; (4) the Portiuncula Indulgence;[1] (5) the Indulgences which are granted by cardinal legates, nuntios, and bishops. This does not, however, apply to the Indulgence attached to the papal benediction which the bishops are accustomed to give twice a year. On the same grounds as those upon which the majority of Indulgences are withdrawn during the Holy Year, the Popes during the same period suspend most of the extraordinary powers granted to bishops and to confessors outside of Rome. The wording of the Papal Constitution,[2] however, explains this matter in detail, and confessors must be guided by its provisions.

In view of this wholesale suspension of the ordinary Indulgences the question is not infrequently asked, in what respect is the Jubilee to be regarded as a privilege? Except for certain extended powers given to confessors, of which probably not one person in a hundred of those who make the Jubilee has any occasion to avail himself, the Holy Year offers no greater privileges or remissions than an ordinary plenary Indulgence; and whereas, during ordinary years, such plenary Indulgences are open to the faithful every time they choose to approach the sacraments, in the Jubilee year they can gain the same, practically speaking, but once, and then only at the cost of a long journey and of numerous visits to the churches, involving several days' residence in Rome.

The objection is certainly a formidable one, and we can only answer that the common opinion, while it seems to regard the

---

[1] This applies only to the Portiuncula as gained in the church of Sta. Maria degli Angeli near Assisi.

[2] The Constitution suspending Indulgences and faculties for the present Jubilee of 1900 was issued on 30th September, 1899, and begins *Quod Pontificum.*

gaining of an ordinary plenary Indulgence as an extremely difficult task, rarely accomplished even by the holiest, looks upon the complete remission of the Jubilee as much more easy of attainment by all who honestly do their best to comply with the conditions. After all, we know little or nothing, as was pointed out in the last chapter, about the manner in which Indulgences take effect. It is quite conceivable that, besides the dispositions of the penitent, something also depends upon the greater or less intensity of the Pope's desire to communicate them. We know that since the time of Boniface VIII. it has been the Pope's will to grant "not only full and more generous, but the fullest, pardon of sins," or, again in his own words, to bestow remission "as far as ever the power of the keys extended." We know, moreover, that in the Jubilee the pilgrims are engaged not so much in a private work of devotion as in an act of public homage to St. Peter and the Holy See, in which they are supported and borne along by the prayers of the Universal Church. It is noteworthy also that in that same Bull of Boniface VIII. the Pope lays it down, seemingly as a principle, that "each one will merit more, and gain the Indulgence more efficaciously, the more frequent and devout are his visits to the Basilicas."[1] This clearly suggests that the more arduous are the conditions of an Indulgence the more likely it is to be gained in full by those who generously comply with these conditions.

However, when all this has been said, it seems useless and unnecessary to deny that the lavish bestowal of Indulgences by the Popes, eager by every means in their power to attract to the King's supper even "the poor and the feeble, the blind and the lame," has involved them in certain inconsistencies. When the Jubilee was first proclaimed in 1300, a plenary Indulgence was accounted a stupendous and almost unheard-of thing, and for long years afterwards this great pardon seemed to swallow up all lesser pardons, and it was conceived to be only reasonable that at the season of such prodigal expenditure of the "treasure"

[1] "Unusquisque tamen plus merebitur et indulgentiam efficacius consequetur quo basilicas ipsas amplius et devotius frequentabit."

of the Church in this one magnificent grant, a certain economy should be exercised in other directions. Moreover, it is obvious that the Popes suspended the local and other Indulgences in order that no conflicting attractions in the spiritual order might divert men from that journey to Rome which the Holy See had so much at heart. It is easy to suggest sordid motives for the creation of this temporary monopoly, and we need not even scruple to admit that, human nature being human nature, the Popes were not entirely blind to the temporal advantages which, in this earlier age, the multitude of pilgrims might bring; but we have also seen that this intimate intercourse between the outlying members and the mother city, the centre of Catholic life, was not only beneficial to both, but almost a necessary condition of the unity of the Church. The Popes could hardly render a more real service to distant countries than by using every legitimate means to secure a vast concourse of all nations to the Eternal City during the Jubilee season. Rome is essentially conservative and faithful to old traditions, and so the old suspension of Indulgences is still maintained, and the faithful are still summoned to Rome by this kind of pious coercion, even now when the Jubilee seems to take away more spiritual favours than it bestows, and when, on the other hand, the crowds flocking to Rome have been for centuries past much more of a burden than of a benefit to the papal finances.

Repetition and Application of the Jubilee Indulgence

"There can be no doubt," writes the Archbishop of Dublin, "that the Jubilee Indulgence of the Holy Year can be gained *toties quoties, i.e.,* as often as the good works prescribed in the Bull of promulgation are repeated." This fact, though not formally stated in the Bull, seems to follow from one of the Jubilee *monita* of Benedict XIV., which have been published by order of the present Holy Father. On the other hand, it seems probable that the pilgrims can avail themselves but once of the special faculties granted to confessors. In the last ordinary Jubilee, that of 1825, it was provided that the Indulgence could be gained once for one's self and once for the souls in purgatory. Although nothing is explicitly said on the subject, either in the Bull of 11th May or in the Constitution of 1st November, it seems safe to assume that the present Jubilee Indulgence is applicable to the Holy Souls.

The Classes of Persons who can gain the Jubilee this Year (1900) without visiting Rome

After the promulgation of the Jubilee on Ascension Day, and before the opening of the Holy Year, the Pope published another Constitution on 1st November, beginning *Æterni Pastoris infinitam charitatem,* in which he concedes to certain classes of persons for whom a pilgrimage to Rome is, morally speaking, impossible, the privilege of gaining the Jubilee in this present year. The Holy Father supposes throughout that the persons so favoured would have wished to make the pilgrimage to Rome for the Jubilee, had it been in their power to do so.

The classes of persons specified in the Constitution are the following[1]:—

1. Nuns and, generally speaking, women or girls resident in convents or in similar institutions.
2. Cloistered anchorets and hermits, including members of certain religious orders of men, as, for instance, the Carthusians and some of the Cistercians.
3. Those who are in prison or captivity.
4. Those whose condition of health permanently hinders them from travelling to Rome, including under this head all persons who have completed their seventieth year.

It should be particularly noted that, with the exceptions specified in clause 2, religious orders of men derive no benefit from this Constitution. They are not considered to be incapacitated from making a pilgrimage to Rome, and consequently

[1] The summary of the Archbishop of Dublin (*Irish Ecclesiastical Record,* March, 1900, p. 242) has here been followed.

they can only gain the Jubilee during the Holy Year itself on condition that they travel to Rome and perform the visits to the four Basilicas.

But, for the classes of persons mentioned, the Jubilee Indulgence can be gained before it is extended to the whole world in the year 1901. The conditions are the same as those required from pilgrims who make the Jubilee in Rome, with the exception that the visits to the four Basilicas are, of course, dispensed with, but the bishops are empowered, each in his own diocese, to appoint other equivalent good works which may be performed in their place.

The inmates of convents, therefore, the aged and the others who wish to avail themselves of this privilege besides the confession, communion, and prayer for the Pope's intention, obligatory on all, must make inquiry what commutation has been appointed for the visits to the Basilicas by the bishop of the diocese in which they reside, and they must punctually carry out the good works which he has prescribed for this purpose.

Finally, it may be useful, as stated at the beginning of this chapter, to translate from an Italian Jubilee sheet, now circulated in Rome, a compendium of practical directions for the gaining of the Indulgence of the Holy Year.[1] It will serve to summarise and, in some cases, to supplement the information more discursively given above.

The works enjoined for the gaining of the Jubilee Indulgence

1. The requisite conditions are three — confession, communion, and visits to the four Basilicas.

2. It is not necessary that the confession and communion should precede the visits, but these two sacraments may be received either during the visits or at the termination of them.

3. It is necessary that the last of the works enjoined be

[1] It is entitled *Ricordo ai Pellegrini*, Anno Santo 1900, Numero Unico della VERA ROMA.

performed in a state of grace, hence it is recommended that confession and communion should be made after the visits.

4. Pilgrims who have fallen ill on the road, and are not able to continue the journey to Rome, as well as those who, having arrived there, are prevented by illness from beginning or completing the visits, are dispensed from them without asking for a commutation.

5. Enclosed nuns, lay sisters, women and girls who are inmates of convents, hermits or religious men belonging to strictly inclosed orders, and prisoners, are dispensed from the visits, provided they substitute for them acts of piety and charity which shall be imposed by the Cardinal Vicar,[1] or by confessors deputed by him.

6. Pilgrims who, from poverty or other grave reason, cannot remain long in Rome, Romans who, from illness or other legitimate reasons, may be hindered from making the visits, can obtain a commutation of the said visits for other pious works from confessors deputed for this purpose.

Confession and the Jubilee

7. The confession must be made with the express intention of gaining the Jubilee Indulgence, and the yearly Easter confession of obligation is not sufficient.

8. The confession must be valid, and the Jubilee is not gained by a sacrilegious confession; a general confession is not requisite.

9. He who is guilty of venial sins only is bound to confess them, and to perform the penance assigned him.

10. If any one has forgotten to accuse himself of some grievous sin, he is recommended to confess this sin before completing the Jubilee conditions, to obtain "direct" absolution for it.

11. Whoever should fall into grievous sin after having made his confession, should confess again, before fulfilling the rest of the works enjoined. Those, however, already performed need not be repeated.

---

[1] This, of course, applies only to residents in Rome.

12. The confession may be made in any place, and not necessarily in Rome.

13. In order to facilitate the gaining of the Indulgence, and absolution from censures, all the parish priests of Rome and other penitentiaries, besides those of the four Basilicas, are given the fullest faculties.

14. For the gaining of the plenary Indulgence of the Jubilee, any approved confessor may be chosen by the penitent.

15. To obtain absolution, however, from censures, and in reserved cases, recourse must be had to one of the appointed penitentiaries.

16. The penitentiaries attached to the churches of Rome, and the other appointed confessors, have faculties to dispense from, or to reduce the number of visits in the case of pilgrims who come to Rome for the Holy Year.

Communion and the Jubilee

17. The communion must be sacramental and valid, distinct from the Easter communion, and made with the intention of gaining the Jubilee Indulgence.

18. Children not yet admitted to Holy Communion can obtain a dispensation from that condition from their own parish priest or their confessor, as the case may be, at the confession made for gaining the Jubilee.

19. The communion may be made in any church, and consequently need not be made in Rome.

The Visits of the Holy Jubilee

20. The Basilicas appointed for the performance of the Jubilee visits are—St. John Lateran, St. Peter's, St. Paul's, and St. Mary Major; and these Basilicas must all be visited the same day, either civil or ecclesiastical.

21. The natural day extends from one midnight to the next. The ecclesiastical day from the first vespers of one day to sunset on the day following. First vespers may be reckoned as beginning at two o'clock p.m., and sunset about one hour after the Angelus.

22. Those who have a permanent domicile in Rome, whether Romans or not, and those who live within five miles of the walls of Rome, must pay these visits to the Basilicas for twenty days, either consecutively or with interruptions.

23. Those who have no permanent domicile in Rome must visit the four Basilicas on the same day, for ten days, either consecutively or intermittently.

24. It is not requisite that the visits should be made in a state of grace, although that is desirable; it suffices to perform the last of the requisite conditions in a state of grace.

25. It is not necessary to go on foot to pay the visits. Any means of performing the journey may be made use of.

26. It is enjoined that in order to gain the Holy Jubilee, visits must be paid to the four Basilicas, and prayers offered in them, but it is not necessary to enter or go out by the Holy Doors.

27. If, on account of an unusual crowd of people, it is impossible to gain admittance to the Basilica, the obligation is satisfied by praying outside. Should the Basilicas be closed at the time, the visit can be made on the steps of the church.

28. The Holy Father wishes that at the visit prayers should be devoutly offered for the exaltation of the Church, the extirpation of heresy, concord between Christian princes, and the welfare of Christian peoples.

29. Some kind of vocal prayer is prescribed; but each one may say what prayers he chooses, or what he knows by heart.

30. It is sufficient to recite five *Paters, Aves,* and *Glorias,* or other prayers of equal length.

31. If pilgrims who come in bands to Rome desire a reduction in the number of visits, they can make petition to that effect, addressing themselves to the Cardinal Prefect of the Holy Congregation of the Apostolic Penitentiary—*Palazzo della Cancelleria—Rome.*

CHAPTER X

EXTENDED AND EXTRAORDINARY JUBILEES

WE have already spoken of the *extension* of the Jubilee, in virtue of which the Pope, after the close of the *Anno Santo*, concedes, upon certain conditions, to the faithful throughout the world, the same Indulgences and privileges as were offered during the Holy Year to those who made the pilgrimage to Rome. Since the time of Alexander VI. the practice of extending the Jubilee to the whole of Christendom has been uniformly observed; although there has been some diversity of usage as to the conditions laid down, and as to the length of time during which the privilege has been available. Some brief extracts have already been given in a previous chapter[1] from the letters of Alexander VI., by which the Indulgence was extended to the people of England. The motive of the extension was stated to be that the Pope, "as well considering the infinite number of Christian people, both spiritual and temporal, which was desirous to have had the said remission and grace, and would have visited the said court of Rome, save only that they were let either by sickness, feebleness, poverty, long distance and great jeopardy of ways, or business and charge of spiritual or temporal occupation, or at that time purposed not to obtain and purchase[2] the said grace but now be in will to have the same, as willing and effectually desiring to provide (against) and

[1] See pp. 78, 79.

[2] Students of early English will be aware that the word *purchase* did not at that period bear so exclusively the meaning of obtaining in exchange for money which applies to it now.

withstand the most cruel purpose and infinite malices of the most cruel enemy of our Christian faith, the Turk," etc. Over and above the invariable condition of contrition and confession, which was clearly expressed, and, in any case, would have been taken for granted, the Pope prescribed visits to certain churches to be determined by his commissary, Jasper Pon, and the offering of an alms according to a fixed scale as a contribution towards the expenses of the war against the Turks. This offer of Jubilee privileges was to remain open from the time of promulgation, which must have been early in the year, until the Saturday in Easter week. At the beginning of the seventeenth century it seems to have been usual to limit the time during which the extended Jubilee could be gained to a fortnight.[1] Upon the two last occasions when an ordinary Jubilee has been extended, *i.e.*, in 1776 and 1826, six months have been allowed wherein to perform the conditions.

But besides the extension of the ordinary Jubilee the practice has prevailed, from an early period, of proclaiming special Indulgences on certain occasions, which were described as granted *ad instar Jubilei*—after the model of the Jubilee. These were conceded sometimes within a limited area, being attached to a particular cathedral or diocese, sometimes universally to the Church at large as a means of promoting some important object or to commemorate a passing event. Thus, from the time of Sixtus V., it has been the custom for each Pontiff to celebrate his accession to the papacy by proclaiming an extraordinary Jubilee, and on such occasions as the convening of a general council or the sacerdotal Jubilee of the reigning Pope a similar grant of Indulgence is commonly made. In the later Middle Ages these Indulgences *ad instar Jubilei* were used to promote a desired end in a double way, which undoubtedly led to abuse. Not only were the faithful exhorted to approach the sacraments, and by offering earnest prayers to God at this season of grace to implore the Divine clemency to grant to His

[1] A. Santarelli, *Tractatus de Jubileo Anni Magni Piacularis et aliis præterea Jubileis et eorum adjunctis.* Moguntiæ, 1626, p. 81.

Church some definite favour, but an attempt was also made to secure by the same spiritual concessions the earthly means of accomplishing the end in view. As in the extended Jubilee of Alexander VI. just referred to, so it was commonly prescribed as a necessary condition of gaining the Indulgence that a money offering should be made, which was to be applied to the purpose specified in the grant. Several crusading Indulgences were published in the fourteenth and fifteenth centuries, the object of which was to raise money for the war against the Turks. Others were issued—some less ample in their offer of remission, but some, again, *ad instar Jubilei*, conferring practically all Jubilee privileges—to those who, as the phrase then ran, *vellent porrigere manus adjutrices*, were willing to lend a helping hand [1] towards the building of a particular cathedral, or towards some other specified object for which funds were needed. Though the purposes for which the Pope was supplicated to grant such Indulgences were, for the most part, excellent in themselves, there can be no doubt that the practice soon led to serious abuses. The peculation of officials, the necessity of having recourse to underhand means to conciliate the representatives of the secular power, who often had an interest in preventing coin from leaving the country, the temptation to promote material ends at the expense of those that were spiritual, the jealousies and contentions between the preachers of rival Indulgences and other like causes must all have had a tendency to lower and degrade the administrators of the system, and, in the end, to bring discredit both upon the priestly office and upon the doctrine of Indulgences itself. The Council of Trent frankly says as much in the decree quoted in the last chapter, and from that time forward no Indulgences have ever been granted with the object of collecting money for any purpose whatever, however pious and laudable. The change, indeed, began much earlier, and the famous Indulgence for the re-building of St. Peter's, which was preached by Tetzel, and was the occasion

[1] There seems no reason to doubt that this English idiom, *to lend a helping hand*, is borrowed from the Latin of the canonists.

of Luther's theses, was followed by few others of similar character.

One extraordinary Indulgence *ad instar Jubilei* is of special interest to Englishmen. Reference has already been made to the action of Martin V. who, in 1423, addressed to the Archbishop of Canterbury, Henry Chicheley, a severe reproof for assuming to himself the powers belonging to the Holy See alone and proclaiming a Jubilee after the Roman model. This strange conduct of the English primate has a readier explanation than would at first sight have been deemed possible. It might even be contended, with some show of probability, that the English

Opening of the Holy Door by Clement X. in 1675.
From the bas-relief upon his tomb in St. Peter's.

Jubilee, so to style it, had, in point of time, preceded the Roman, though so far as it implied any concession of Indulgences it admittedly depended in the last resort upon the authorisation of the Holy See.

The facts of the case are these. St. Thomas Becket, Archbishop of Canterbury, was martyred in the year 1170. Despite his early canonisation, in 1173, and the injunction that his remains should be removed to a more worthy shrine, the disturbed condition of England during the reigns of Richard and John stood in the way of any such solemn translation, which was not effected until 1220. It seems to have been quite by accident that this event took place in the fiftieth year after the martyrdom; but the fact was noted at the time by Cardinal Stephen Langton and others, and a sermon, which must have been preached on the anniversary of the translation, a year or two later, refers to it in the following terms. After commenting upon a number of other coincidences about the translation, which seemed to him remarkable, the preacher continues—

"We testify in the Lord that it came to pass, by the disposition of the Divine favour and not through the intervention of any human design, that his venerable remains received the honour of translation in the fiftieth year from his martyrdom. And what is intimated to us by this fact? Surely the mystical virtue of the number fifty, which, as every reader of the sacred page is aware, is the number of remission. Seeing, then, that it was the Saint's will to be translated in the fiftieth year, he bestowed upon us a certain hope that, unless we ourselves shall put obstacles in the way, he will assuredly obtain for us the grace of pardon" (*spem certam nobis tribuit, quod, nisi per nos steterit, remissionis nobis gratiam obtinebit*).[1]

These words, spoken nearly eighty years before the proclamation of the first Jubilee by Boniface VIII., are certainly noteworthy, and the Archbishops of Canterbury of a somewhat later date may be pardoned if they drew from them a larger inference than the facts quite warranted. It would seem that in 1470 it was believed that Archbishop Langton had "asked and obtained, from Pope Honorius III., a Bull of Indulgence, by which special pardons and privileges were granted to all true penitents, who, after confession and a profession of contrition

[1] Migne, P. L. vol. 190, col. 421. This sermon or tractate was first published by Christian Lupus, *Epistolæ et Vita D. Thomæ Martyris et Archiepiscopi Cantuariensis* (vol. ii. p. 885, *seq.*), in 1682, and it has since been reprinted by Giles and Migne. Lupus entitles it "Tractatus Domini Stephani Cantuariensis Archiepiscopi de Translatione Beati Thomæ Martyris," a heading which he has presumably taken from some manuscript at the Vatican. Seeing that the very passage quoted above is cited in the petition addressed by the Christ Church monks to Paul II. in 1469, and is there also attributed to Cardinal Stephen Langton, there seems to be foundation for the belief that this discourse is really his.

for their past sins, should visit and make their offerings at the shrine during a period limited by the terms of the Bull."[1]

How early this belief became current it is not quite easy to determine, but something of the sort is certainly insinuated in the lessons of the Sarum Breviary for the feast of the Translation of St. Thomas (July 7th), and these same lessons are cited in the petition of the Christ Church monks to Paul II. in 1469. I translate the text of the Sarum Breviary from the edition of the Cambridge University Press—

"Let us ponder, dearest brethren, the mysteries of the fiftieth year. The fiftieth year is the jubilee year, and the jubilee is interpreted the year of remission. For just as under the law remissions took place in the jubilee year, so also in the jubilee year of the translation of the martyr the burdens of penitents are lightened.

"Hence the Holy Father, Pope Honorius III., in commemoration of the year of Jubilee, granted annually to those who should come to the solemnity of the translation of Blessed Thomas the Martyr such remission of penance imposed, as we cannot call to mind that the Roman Pontiffs anywhere gave to any others in ages gone by.[2] So that the Blessed Martyr may say not inappropriately what was said by our Redeemer Himself: 'O all ye that labour and are heavy-laden come hither to Me and I will refresh you.' And in order that property, as in the law of old, might return to its former owners the aforesaid Holy Father appointed that the churches (*i.e.*, benefices) in England, to which Romans or foreigners had been collated, should be restored after their death to their true patrons. Let us say, therefore, with the prophet—'The sun has arisen and the moon in its course has stood still"—*Tu Autem Domine*, etc.[3]

---

[1] Dr. J. B. Sheppard in preface to *Literæ Cantuarienses* (Rolls Series), vol. iii. p. xxxiv.

[2] Unde pius pater Honorius papa Tertius in Signum anno jubileo accessuris ad Translationis Solemnitatem beatissimi Thomæ Martyris annuatum de injunctis pœnitentiis remissionem talem indulsit, qualem retroactis temporibus nusquam meminimus Romanos pontifices aliquibus indulvisse.

[3] Sarum Breviary, Cambridge University Press, iii. 446, 447.

The petitioners of 1469 assume that these lessons also were either written by Cardinal Stephen Langton himself or were at any rate drawn up under his direction. No Bull is forthcoming in the extant Regesta of Honorius III. which in any way bears out the statement that he granted a remission *ad instar Jubilei* to the Canterbury pilgrims. At any rate, the very moderate Indulgence [1] of a year and forty days which was granted by him on the occasion of the translation does not answer the description, and is inconsistent with any privilege recurring at long intervals. Moreover, it is plain from the document still preserved that the Archbishop and monks of Canterbury recognised that the privilege required on each occasion a new and special grant. No evidence, save the very dubious assertions made in subsequent petitions to the Pope, exists that any sort of Jubilee celebration was held at Canterbury in the year 1270, but the chronicler, Thorn,[2] is

[1] The Bull is printed by Robertson, *Materials for the History of Thomas Becket* (Rolls Series), vii. 584. It appears also in Bliss, *Calendar of Papal Documents relating to England*, and in Pressuti, *Regesta Honorii III.* I am myself inclined to believe that even though the Breviary lessons describe the Indulgence granted by the Pope at the translation as one of quite unprecedented amplitude, they nevertheless only refer to that granted in the Bull just mentioned. In any case, from the words "accessuris ad Translationis Solemnitatem *annuatim* . . . indulsit," it is obvious that no great Indulgence can be in question which was to recur only at intervals of fifty years. But in 1220 an annual Indulgence of one year and forty days would have been esteemed a very great Indulgence indeed.

[2] An entry in the *Chronicle of St. Augustine's* shows that the Jubilee was not forgotten in 1320, though there is no mention of the Indulgence. "Anno Domini MCCCXX, et anno Sancti Thomæ martyris tunc jubeleo, Dominus Radulfus, Abbas, per seniores ecclesiæ Sanctæ Trinitatis effective requisitus missam et cetera solemnia inter ipsos in magno honore celebravit."—*Chronica*, W. Thorn, apud Twysden *decem Scriptores*, col. 2036, l. 17. That this visit of the Abbot of St. Augustine's to Holy Trinity (*i.e.*, Christ Church) was directly connected with the celebration of the Jubilee may be shown from Thorn's entry for the next celebration in 1370. "Anno Domini MCCCLXX die translacionis S. Thomæ martyris, dominus Thomas abbas hujus loci invitatus et a senioribus monachorum S. Trinitatis specialiter requisitus inter illos divina solempniter celebravit anno beati Thomæ tunc jubeleo, populo pro indulgentia quasi infinito congregato. Et nota quod durante ista solempnitate prædictus abbas a sacrista S. Trinitatis tam in vigilia quam in die sicut foret archiepiscopus illorum fuit obviatus et ad revestiendum reductus, *ib.* 2145, l. 43.

explicit about its being kept in 1370,[1] and in 1420 we have the still stronger evidence of the Pope's vigorous protest addressed to Chicheley, or, more accurately speaking, addressed to two papal nuntios in England, bidding them examine into and report upon the occurrence.

"It has come to our ears," writes the Pope, "through many different informants, that Henry, the Archbishop, and the Prior and Chapter of the Church of Canterbury, with unheard-of presumption and sacrilegious audacity, have introduced and caused to be publicly proclaimed, in the year of our Lord 1420, a general Jubilee for the remission of sins, in certain seasons, places, manners, and forms, after the style appointed by ancient fathers and by our predecessors the Roman Pontiffs, promising that all and sundry who visited the said Church of Canterbury should gain the same plenary remission of all their sins which those persons gain who visit the thresholds of the Apostles when a Jubilee has been duly proclaimed by the Roman Pontiff in his mother city; and, furthermore, that, with no less temerity, they appointed penitentiaries to absolve generally from all kinds of sin, or, more truly, to ensnare simple souls and extort from them a vulgar payment in money, to the incredible injury of the collectors' own consciences and the deceiving of other simple-minded persons."

The Pontiff goes on to condemn in very strong terms the iniquity of this practice, and to claim for the Holy See alone the power of the keys, bidding his nuntios make report to him and, if necessary, proceed to punish the offenders. It must be

---

[1] Wharton, in the *Anglia Sacra*, quotes a narrative which tells how Simon Sudbury, then Bishop of London, incurred unpopularity by discouraging pilgrims who were on their way to the celebration of 1370, warning them not to trust to the efficacy of the promised Indulgences; but no mention of the festival occurs in the registers of the monastery. Wharton, pars. i. p. 49. *Vita Simonis Sudbury.* Ex *Speculo Parvulorum*, lib. 5, cap. 27. The author of this account professes to regard the violent death of Archbishop Sudbury as a punishment for the dishonour he had done to St. Thomas. A Knight of Kent told him at the time: "Domine Episcope quod fecisti hanc rem seditiosam contra S. Thomam, morte nephandissima finies vitam tuam. Ad hoc autem succlamabant omnis populus: Amen, Amen."

remembered that this occurred at a time when the impressions of the Great Schism had not yet been effaced, and just when the Council of Siena was claiming to grant Indulgences of the most sweeping kind quite independently of the Pope. No doubt Martin V. saw in this act of the Archbishop of Canterbury another deliberate attempt to exalt the authority of a General Council at the expense of that of the Holy See. We have no means of following the matter further, but it appears probable that when the true state of the case was explained to him, and he understood that the Archbishop only claimed the right to act so in virtue of a grant of one of his predecessors, the Pope was pacified and was content to accept the promise of the accused that no such scandal should occur a second time.

However this may have been, we possess the text of the petition addressed to the Pope for the celebration of 1470, the next Jubilee of St. Thomas, and nothing could be more submissive than the language in which it was couched. No attempt was made to question the unique prerogative of the Holy See as the source of all jurisdiction in the granting of Indulgences.

As for the condemned Jubilee of 1420 it was, according to an entry in a contemporary record belonging to the City of Canterbury, "a most successful celebration, and attracted a hundred thousand pilgrims to the shrine, all of whom were, by the foresight of the municipal authorities, lodged and fed without any increase in the ordinary price of provisions. In this year the oblations at the shrine amounted to more than £600, say, in modern currency, at least £8000."[1]

The severe censure of Martin V. seems to have made the monks of Canterbury anxious about their privileges, and as early as 1454 Tiptoft, Earl of Worcester, approached the Sovereign Pontiff in their behoof. Furthermore, two of the most distinguished of the monks were sent to Rome. In answer to these representations Pope Paul II. seems to have conceded the Indulgence *ad instar Jubilei* without any difficulty. It proved

[1] Dr. Sheppard in *Literæ Cantuarienses*, vol. iii. p. xxxv.

to be the last occasion on which the Jubilee of St. Thomas was celebrated.

In the Bull issued for this purpose Paul II., after setting forth the motives and causes for attaching particular Indulgences to the Metropolitan Church of Canterbury on account of the martyrdom of St. Thomas, etc., proceeds to grant plenary Indulgence to all the faithful who, being confessed and contrite, should visit the cathedral on the Festivals of the Assumption, of the Nativity, of the Blessed Virgin Mary, and of St. Michael the Archangel,[1] from the first to the second vespers of the feast inclusive. And for the more convenient gaining of this Indulgence he gives to the Cardinal Archbishop, and in his absence to the Prior of the Cathedral. His power to depute a sufficient number of priests, regular or secular, approved by them with faculties to hear confessions, and to absolve even in cases usually reserved to the Pope alone, and to release from all vows (those of visiting the *limina apostolorum,* St. James at Compostella, and vows of religion excepted), commuting them for other works of piety, this faculty to hold good for two years from the date of the Bull. After which period any one proclaiming this Indulgence, or making use of it, would incur sentence of excommunication. Given at Rome, at St. Peter's, Anno Domini, 1470, the 4th of June, in the sixth year of the pontificate of Paul II.[2]

At the next occurrence of the Jubilee of St. Thomas, in 1520, application was duly made to the Pope that he would concede an Indulgence according to the usual forms. Leo X., however, as the letters show which were written home by the English advocates at the Curia, insisted upon requiring that half the offerings to be made at Canterbury by the pilgrims should be

---

[1] It will be noticed that the feast of the translation of St. Thomas (July 7th) is not assigned as one of the days to which the Indulgence is attached. It would have been too late that year for the news to reach England in time. Consequently three autumn feasts are named instead. In winter such Indulgences could not be held because the roads were impassable, hence the feast of St. Thomas, on December 29th, is also excluded.

[2] *Literæ Cantuarienses,* Rolls Series, iii. 253.

handed over to him for the building of St. Peter's. Upon this point the Archbishop and the Chapter were unable to come to terms with his Holiness. "As the registers," writes Dr. Sheppard, "contain no reference to any actual celebration of this festival, it may be concluded that neither Rome nor Canterbury made the required concessions, and that, therefore, no celebration took place. At the next recurring period of fifty years, in 1570, Jubilees, the monastery of Christ Church, and the cultus of St. Thomas in the Cathedral, had all become matters of ancient history."[1]

As an illustration of the negotiations carried on in 1520 the following letter from Thomas Bedyll, one of the English envoys, will be read with interest:—

"My very good Lord Prior, in my right hearty wise I commend me to your Lordship, doing you to understand that yesterday my Lord's Grace received letters from Rome which I send unto you with a certain suggestion conceived by Dr. Grig and his counsel concerning the Jubilee. *Item*, seeing that so great a difficulty is made at Rome for the obtaining of our purpose, which is like to be granted but for a few days as my Lord of Worcester hath written, a new way is devised for the obtaining thereof, with the which in a manner we be forced to be contented if we would have the great thing of our desire. It is this: the Pope hath desired to have half of the oblations in this year of Jubilee if it should go forth; the which if he have not, his mind is we shall not have the thing we would have: wherefore long and serious communication hath been had with the Pope's orator, *Auditor Camere Apostolice*, in this matter by Master Parr, the King's Grace's Secretary, at my Lord's request; upon the which communication the said *Auditor Camere Apostolice* wrote special letters to the Cardinal *Sanctorum IV.*[or] and also to the Pope's Holiness, for the short expedition thereof, showing to the Pope's Holiness that he should have half the oblations of this year of Jubilee, only if he would grant it *in perpetuum*, so that after this year the whole oblations may be

[1] *Literæ Cantuarienses*, vol. iii. p. xxxvi.

only to the church of Canterbury. Of the which effect my Lord hath written to my Lord Cardinal *Sanctorum IV.*[or] and to Cardinal Campeggio, and to my Lord of Worcester and to his Procurator Dr. Grig, to whom he hath specially written, that out of the Pope's half should be deducted the charges that we shall be at now for the expedition thereof and that it be granted in *amplissima forma*, for else, seeing the manifold and great pardons which have been and be in England, little advantage would arise to the Pope's Holiness. And therefore my Lord hath written to Dr. Grig that he should surely seek to have the pardon granted according to the Minute sent him by my Lord, the which if it be obtained will be a great treasure for ever after. And my Lord hath written to Dr. Grig that if any other way can be taken for the obtaining thereof he should not take this way, but that this should be the last refugie. In the which it is to be thought that the Pope will liberally grant to the said Indulgence, considering that partly it shall be his own cause and profit if it be granted in most ample form, which I trust shall be done. News here be none worthy writing but such as I dare not write. When I have next any messenger I will send to your Lordship how the world goes with us, which now suffer not a little disease and pain, etc., etc. *At Calais the IVth day of Juny.*

"THOMAS BEDYLL."[1]

We learn from another letter that the Roman authorities were keen enough to see the improbability that any Jubilee Indulgence had been granted to Canterbury as early as 1220. For the other envoy, Dr. Grig, who has obviously got rather mixed up as to dates, writes to the Archbishop:—

"I desired my Lord Campeggio to speak with *Sancti IIII.*, and then afterwards with the Pope *in publico consistorio*, and so he did. And to this the Pope made a plain answer, If it could be proved that it (the Jubilee) is in use, he would be glad to confirm it; or else to grant the said Jubiley *in festo S. Thomæ Martiris* and three days afterwards following, to have clean

[1] Somner, *Antiquities of Canterbury*, Appendix, pp. 47, 48, corrected by Dr. Sheppard's transcript.

remission, and also *in translatione* and three days following clean remission; and of such oblations as there were made half should go to the building of the church at Rome. Unto the which I would not incline, without consent of your Grace, in no manner of wise. *Item,* Where your Grace wrote unto the Pope that this Jubilee was granted in Honorius' days, the 3rd, he showed me there was then no such things granted. The first Jubilee that was granted in Rome was *in tempore Bonifacius the VIIIth,* the which was in the year of our Lord 1285(!). But Honorius was in the year of our Lord 1214, long before, and said it was not likely no such things to be granted not in his days."

The Indulgence *in amplissima forma,* spoken of in Bedyll's letter, was probably that which is commonly described as *ad instar Jubilei.* With regard to the remission of penalty, as already stated, it seems impossible to establish any valid distinction between the ordinary plenary Indulgence, the Jubilee, and the Indulgence *ad instar Jubilei.*[1] But with regard to the circumstances under which they are granted, the conditions commonly imposed, and the amplitude of the faculties enjoyed by confessors, it is convenient to adhere to these different designations, although in many cases they shade imperceptibly into one another. From a practical point of view, the chief distinction between the extended and extraordinary Jubilees, which we are discussing in the present chapter, lies in this, that in the latter fasting and alms-deeds are usually enjoined as part of the conditions, while in the former the visits to a certain assigned church or churches are alone required over and above the confession and communion common to all such Indulgences. But these details, of course, must always depend ultimately on the terms of the papal Bull or Constitution conceding them, and it is

---

[1] The question whether the Jubilee Indulgence was distinct from that *ad instar* or from the ordinary plenary was warmly debated in the sixteenth century. Bellarmine, for instance, pronounced them to be identical, but others, *e.g.*, R. Benzoni, *De Anno Sancto Jubilei*, Venice, 1599 (Bk. iv., ch. 2, pp. 403-411), strongly protested against this view.

impossible to pronounce upon them beforehand with absolute confidence. We may certainly take it for granted that the present Jubilee will be extended in the year 1901 to the whole of Christendom, and it seems probable, if we look to the analogy of previous concessions, that beyond confession and communion no other condition will be required than the making of a certain specified number of visits. What has been said in the last chapter with regard to the visits to the Basilicas in Rome and the prayers for the Pope's intention is applicable also to the visits of the extended Jubilee.

In the case, however, of an extraordinary Jubilee, such as is commonly granted at the accession of each new Pontiff and on other special occasions, the conditions for gaining the Indulgence usually include both fasting and the giving of alms. The number of such fasts, their nature and the time for performing them, are usually determined by the papal Constitution proclaiming the Jubilee in question, although it may be left to the bishops of each diocese to adapt these more general prescriptions to the circumstances of the faithful under their jurisdiction. The fast enjoined is a strict fast, excluding not only meat but also the use of *lacticinia* (milk, butter, eggs, cheese, etc.). In the Jubilee proclaimed for the Vatican Council three days of fast were required; in the Jubilees of 1879 and 1881 one day only was appointed, but in 1886 there were two. It may also be said in general with regard to the fast of the Jubilee that the dispensations which the faithful may enjoy at ordinary times must not be taken for granted in fulfilling the conditions of the Jubilee. A person who cannot fast is not debarred from gaining the Indulgence, and may obtain from his confessor a commutation of this condition; but he is not free, of his own authority, to omit the day of fasting or to substitute something else of his own accord. This seems even to apply to those who, on account of their age, are altogether exempt from the law of fasting at ordinary seasons.

With regard to the giving of alms it is no longer usual to specify anything as to the amount, or even as to the object of the charity. Those who are so destitute as to be unable to give anything may have this condition commuted by their confessor to some other good work, and the father of a family, or the superior of a religious community, may discharge this obligation for all those under his care.

It is difficult to distinguish at all accurately between an extraordinary Jubilee and an Indulgence *ad instar*, especially in the earlier centuries, and for this reason no very definite term can be assigned for the introduction of extraordinary Jubilees. Perhaps it would be a more convenient arrangement if the term *extraordinary Jubilee* were strictly confined to an Indulgence in Jubilee form offered to the whole Church, thus excluding the various local Indulgences *ad instar*, of which the Jubilee of St. Thomas at Canterbury supplies a convenient specimen. During the seventeenth and eighteenth centuries even these extraordinary Jubilees were generally inaugurated at Rome with a certain amount of ceremony. The Pope went in procession to the Church of Sta. Maria degli Angeli, near the Baths of Diocletian, and after celebrating a low Mass there moved on to Sta. Maria Maggiore. On the way the Litanies of the Saints were sung; and after the concluding prayers had been chanted at the Basilica the Pope dismissed the assembly with his blessing. In an extraordinary Jubilee proclaimed by Pope Leo XII. some such ceremonial seems last to have been observed. In this case a solemn novena was made to St. Michael the Archangel as protector of the Church, and for three days a station was held at the chapel of St. Lawrence, near the *Sancta Sanctorum*, for another three days' prayer was offered at Sta. Maria Maggiore, and for the last three at St. Peter's. The Pope himself on each occasion gave benediction with the Blessed Sacrament. It would not seem, however, that these or any similar processions were ever regarded as constituting an essential part of the proclamation of an extraordinary Jubilee.

On account of the above-mentioned difficulty in distinguishing between Indulgences *ad instar Jubilei* and extraordinary Jubilees more properly so called, it is almost impossible to compile any satisfactory list of the latter celebrations. But to give some indication of the frequency with which, during the last few centuries, the treasures of the Church have been opened to her faithful children we may condense from Noethen's *Geschichte aller Jubeljahre* a brief account of the Jubilees of which he has thought well to take notice. His point of departure seems somewhat arbitrary, and there is no very apparent reason why the Polish Indulgence of 1518 should be accounted the first celebration of the kind. Moreover, the list might no doubt be considerably enlarged, but the responsibility of the selection must rest with the compiler, and it will serve sufficiently for our present purpose.

The first instance, says Dr. Noethen, of an extraordinary Jubilee occurs in 1518, when Leo X. proclaimed the Jubilee Indulgence in Poland to obtain the Divine assistance against the Turks, at the same time prescribing that the Jubilee offerings should be principally applied to the arming and fortifying of the important town of Kaminiek, and that only a small part of the money should be devoted to the restoring of the churches. We are told, however, that either from a slackening in fervour, or because the Jubilee Indulgence was not understood, but few offerings were brought.

In 1545, when the principles of the Reformation were not only dominant in Germany, but had also spread to other lands, Paul III. ordered solemn processions and prayers to be offered throughout Christendom against this new danger. He himself, together with his cardinals, prelates, and the Roman clergy, went in penitential procession from the pontifical palace through the Leonine quarter of the city to St. Peter's, and proclaimed on the 11th December of the same year a Jubilee Indulgence to be gained by all who should pray for union among princes, and peace between the nations.

On the 13th December of the same year, 1545, the Pope authorised another Jubilee Indulgence on the occasion of the opening of the Council of Trent, granting a plenary Indulgence proclaimed by the cardinal legate, John Maria del Monte, to all those who were present at the first session. After the two principal prorogations of the Council, a similar Jubilee was again celebrated at the reopening of the same in 1551 and 1560.

The divisions in Christendom increasing, Paul III. proclaimed the fourth extraordinary Jubilee in Rome in 1546 to implore God's mercy and to check the spread of those heretical opinions by which so many men were drawn away from the Catholic faith.

The Council of Trent had suspended its sittings in 1547, partly on account of the differences between the Pope and the Emperor, and partly by reason of the pestilence which prevailed. The Pope died in 1549. His successor, Julius III., had sworn during the conclave to reopen the Council immediately, this being also the earnest desire of the Emperor. On the 1st of May the twelfth session was inaugurated, and the Pope ordered public prayers to to be offered on that day for its happy continuance, granting to all who took part in them the privilege of a Jubilee Indulgence.

The sixth extraordinary Jubilee was proclaimed by Julius III. in 1554, the object being the restoration of England to the Catholic faith, since the accession of Mary to the throne in 1553 raised hopes of this happy consummation.

The seventh of these Jubilees was held in 1560. Pope Pius IV. reassembled the Council of Trent, which had been suspended during the reigns of his predecessors, Marcellus II. and Paul IV. On the 2nd July, 1560, as well as on the 15th November, he proclaimed a general Jubilee. This he opened himself on the following Sunday by going in solemn procession from St. Peter's to the Sta. Maria Sopra Minervam, in order to obtain, through the prayers of all Christendom, the illumination of the Holy Ghost for the newly-assembled Council.

The eighth Jubilee was also held in 1560, being proclaimed by Pius IV. on the 31st May. The Indulgence was granted to all who should assist Philip II. of Spain with money for the equipment of a fleet against the Turks, and should offer prayers for the success of his arms and for the redemption of those held in captivity by the Moors.

The year 1566 saw two extraordinary Jubilees. On the 8th March St. Pius V., who had succeeded Pius IV., proclaimed a universal Jubilee Indulgence in behalf of the Maltese who were then being attacked by the Turkish navy, and on the 20th July, another to encourage the Emperor Ferdinand in his struggle with the Turkish land forces. Both these Indulgences might be gained by all who aided these objects by prayer, fasting, and alms-giving.

The eleventh Jubilee was in 1571. Its object was to implore the blessing of Heaven on the arms of Don John of Austria, half-brother of Philip II., who had sailed against the Turks at the head of the combined fleet of Spain, Venice, and the States of the Church. It was on the occasion of his victory in the famous battle of Lepanto, on October the 7th, that Pope Pius V. instituted the feast of the Rosary, the Rosary confraternity having gone in solemn procession to pray for the success of the allies on that day.

In 1572 Gregory XIII. proclaimed an universal Jubilee, first, as a thanksgiving to Almighty God for the victory over the Turks at Lepanto; in the next place, to implore the Divine blessing upon Alba's rule in the Netherlands; and lastly, to obtain the election of a good king in Poland.

Sixtus V., on his accession to the papal throne, was the first Pope to proclaim a Jubilee which had for its express object the begging of God's help and protection during the ensuing pontificate. To this end Sixtus, on the 23rd May, 1585, proclaimed an extraordinary Jubilee of fourteen days, first for the City of Rome, and afterwards for the rest of Christendom. His example has been followed by numerous[1] Pontiffs since that date, among

---

[1] No such Jubilee, however, is known to have been celebrated on the accession of Clement XII. in 1730, of Benedict XIV. in 1740, of Clement XIII. in 1758, or of Clement XIV. in 1769. At the election of Pius VI. in 1775 the ordinary Jubilee was already in progress. The state of Europe prevented the celebration at the beginning of the pontificate of Pius VII. Even as early as the election of Alexander IV. in 1251, and of St. Celestine V. at the end of the same century, special Indulgences seem to have been granted on the occasion of the Pope's inthronization.

others by Pius VIII., Gregory XVI., Pius IX., and Leo XIII. The conditions laid down by Sixtus V. for gaining the Indulgence have been those required on all similar occasions subsequently.

The fourteenth Jubilee was granted to the Society of Jesus by Sixtus V. in 1586, at the request of the General of the Order, to obtain the blessing of God upon the missionary labours of the society in China.

Sixtus V. proclaimed the fifteenth Jubilee in 1588 as a remedy against the evils and dangers then threatening the Church, and the sixteenth extraordinary Jubilee in 1589 to obtain peace in Germany, long torn asunder by civil wars.

Pope Clement VIII. celebrated the seventeenth Jubilee in 1592, on occasion of his elevation to the papacy, to implore the Divine aid in ruling the Church.

Clement also proclaimed the eighteenth and nineteenth Jubilees in 1595—one in Hungary in thanksgiving for the deliverance of that country from the Turks, and the other in Germany in thanksgiving for the preservation of the Catholic faith and restoration of peace.

The twentieth Jubilee was proclaimed by Clement VIII. in Rome in 1598, to implore God's pity on the miseries and want caused in the city by the overflowing of the Tiber.

The twenty-first extraordinary Jubilee was celebrated by Paul V. on his ascending the papal chair in 1605.

Paul V. also proclaimed four more Jubilees in the years 1606, 1608, 1617, and 1620, to implore God's mercy and aid in averting the evils and dangers which threatened and surrounded the Church.

The twenty-sixth and twenty-seventh Jubilees were proclaimed by Gregory XV. in 1621 and Urban VIII. in 1623, at the beginning of their pontificates, to ask God's blessing and guidance.

The twenty-eighth extraordinary Jubilee was proclaimed by Urban VIII. on 8th April, 1628, to obtain aid for the Church in the dangers and troubles which surrounded her on all sides. The twenty-ninth took place in 1629 on account of the war, famine, and threatened pestilence.

The thirtieth, thirty-first, and thirty-second extraordinary Jubilees were held in 1630 and 1631. The first of these was proclaimed by the same Pope (Urban VIII.), in thanksgiving for the cessation of famine and pestilence in Rome, on the 6th July, 1630. It was extended to the whole of Italy from the 25th September to the 26th December of the same year, and was renewed in March, 1631, for two months. Since the plague still prevailed in some places in Italy another Jubilee celebration was announced, beginning with the 15th of July, 1631, and resembling that of the 22nd October, 1629.

The next three Jubilees, in 1631, 1634, and 1636, were all celebrated on account of the constant recurrence of the plague.

Innocent X. celebrated his accession to the papacy by proclaiming the thirty-sixth extraordinary Jubilee in 1644; he also proclaimed the thirty-seventh in 1648 to obtain the Divine assistance for the Church in her necessities.

Alexander VII. ordered a Jubilee in 1655 on being elected Pope. The attacks of the Turks, the wars between Catholic princes, and the ravages of the plague were the causes which prompted the celebration of a thirty-ninth Jubilee in 1656, and the wish to obtain God's help against the Turks gave occasion for those of 1661 and 1664.

At the beginning of the pontificate of Clement IX. the forty-second Jubilee was published on the 18th July, 1667.

The wars between the Italian States and the Turks were also responsible for the two next Jubilees, that of September, 1668, which was first conceded for the States of the Church, and by a Bull of the 3rd October in the same year extended to Venice, and that of April, 1669, when prayers for a happy issue of the election of the new king of Poland were joined to those for help against the Turks.

Clement X. celebrated the forty-fifth Jubilee on being elected Pope in June, 1670. He also proclaimed the forty-sixth on the 5th November, 1672, again with the object of imploring God's aid against the Turks.

Innocent XI. inaugurated his papacy by celebrating the

forty-seventh Jubilee in 1677. This Pope also proclaimed an extraordinary Jubilee in 1681, to obtain unity between Christian princes and aid against the Turks. Innocent, besides this, proclaimed another Jubilee on the 11th of August, 1683, when the Turks were besieging Vienna.

Alexander VIII. in 1689, and Innocent XII. in 1691, each celebrated a Jubilee at the commencement of their reigns. Innocent XII. also proclaimed the fifty-second Jubilee in 1694, to implore aid against heretical teachers and the old enemy, the Turks. The next, that of 1696, had for its object peace between Christian princes, and again, deliverance from the Turks.

The elevation of Clement XI. to the papacy was marked by the celebration of the fifty-fourth extraordinary Jubilee in 1701. The two next, in 1703 and 1706 respectively, were proclaimed by the same Pontiff; the first of them, prompted by the pressing needs of the Church in the German Empire, was celebrated in Italy only, but the second, which also aimed at securing peace between the princes of Christendom, especially in Germany, was offered to the faithful throughout the world. Clement XI. lastly published another universal Jubilee in 1715 to frustrate the efforts which were then again being made against Christendom by the Turks.

Innocent XIII. published the fifty-eighth Jubilee in 1721 on his accession, and Benedict XIII. the fifty-ninth on the like occasion in 1724.

The sixtieth extraordinary Jubilee was proclaimed by Cardinal Caprara on the 9th April, 1802, for three days, on the occasion of the Concordat, when the people flocked in crowds to the churches to gain the graces and benefits there to be obtained.

The next two Jubilees were held on the accession to the papacy respectively of Pius VIII. in 1829, and Gregory XVI. in 1832. The sixty-third was proclaimed by Gregory XVI. on the 22nd February, 1842, and was offered to all the faithful to implore the mercy of God upon the clergy who were being cruelly oppressed in Spain.

Pius IX. celebrated the sixty-fourth on his accession in 1846.

He also proclaimed two extraordinary Jubilees in 1851 and in 1857, for the various needs of the Church. The definition of the doctrine of the Immaculate Conception was the occasion of the Jubilee of 1865, and the Vatican Council that of the sixty-eighth in 1870. This last was unprecedented in its duration, for after the adjournment of the Council the Jubilee was continued until all hope of its reassembling had vanished.

Dr. Noethen, in his enumeration, does not seem to have taken account of the Jubilee proclaimed in 1850, in lieu of the ordinary Jubilee which, owing to the political conditions of the times, could not be held in Rome. For similar reasons no ordinary Jubilee was proclaimed in 1875, but an equivalent Indulgence was offered to the faithful in all parts of the world. The present Pontiff, Leo XIII., has celebrated extraordinary Jubilees in 1879, 1881, and 1886, being moved in each case to ask his faithful children to join him in imploring God's special aid in the grievous difficulties of our times. The last of these, which was continued through the whole of the year 1886, was directed more particularly to the honour of our Lady of the Rosary.

THE POPE CLOSING THE HOLY DOOR AT THE END OF THE YEAR OF JUBILEE.
From a Jubilee broadside of 1650.

APPENDIX A

THE following little treatise on the Jubilee was compiled by the great leader of the Catholic reaction in Germany, the Jesuit, Blessed Peter Canisius. He seems to have thrown his thoughts together in this form to provide material for a sermon which was apparently delivered at Innsbruck on the 5th of January, 1575. The pregnant conciseness of this dissertation, the authority of the writer, and circumstances under which it was produced, seem to afford sufficient reason for printing a translation of it here in an appendix. The Latin has recently been published for the first time by Th. Mönnichs in the *Zeitschrift für Katholische Theologie*, ii. Quartalheft, 1900, pp. 373 *seq.* The text of the original manuscript seems to have been written by an amanuensis, but Blessed Canisius has occasionally interpolated clauses, sometimes in Latin and sometimes in German, with his own hand.

TRACTATE OF BLESSED PETER CANISIUS, S.J., ON THE JUBILEE YEAR

I.—Type and Origin of the Jubilee

It is founded in Leviticus xxv., "Thou shalt sanctify the fiftieth year, and proclaim a remission to all the inhabitants of thy land. For it is the Jubilee. Every man shall go back to his possessions, and each one shall return to his former estate." In the Jubilee year all were to return to their possessions. Jubilee is a Hebrew word; the Jews call it Jobel, and according to Theodoret it signifies remission and liberty. This year was full of gladness, having its trumpeters who stimulated the people to public rejoicings, because the slaves, afflicted, and exiles were restored to their pristine state and liberty. This was the figure of the clemency which was to be preached and announced by Christ and His trumpeters, the Apostles, to miserable sinners in the New Testament. Wherefore Christ (Luke iv.) testified of Himself in the Synagogue of Nazareth that now the prophecy of Isaiah (lxi.) was fulfilled, "The spirit of the Lord is upon me, therefore He hath anointed me; He hath sent me to p each the gospel to the poor, to heal those who are contrite of heart, to preach remission to the captives, and sight to the blind, to lift up those who are fallen, to preach the acceptable year of the Lord."

[The founder of the Jubilee.] It is manifest, then, who is the author of the Jubilee in the New Testament, no other than Christ Himself, who appointed the acceptable time and the day of salvation. Isaiah lxi., 2 Cor. vi. From Him proceeds this year of mercy according to Psalm lxiv.—Thou shalt bless the crown of the year of Thy goodness. Therefore, as the Jews by Moses, so we through Christ, have a year of Jubilee, *i.e.*, of liberty in which slaves and those oppressed by debt are redeemed and restored to perfect liberty, as the same Christ gave to Matthew (Mark ii.), to the paralytic (Matt. ix.), to Magdalene (Luke vii.), to the adulteress (John viii.), to the thief (Luke xxiii.). Upon these and upon many others did Christ bestow plenary Indulgence without imposing penance.

And not only by Himself, but also through His Vicar, Christ would show Himself liberal in granting a Jubilee, giving to Peter and his successors plenary powers to dispense the merits of Christ and of the Saints as from an immense treasury; for the consolation and salvation of those who, after lapsing into sin, wish to be reconciled to God and to the Church, not only freeing them from sins committed however grievous, but also from the penalties due to their sins. Notwithstanding, then, that Christ gave to the Apostles great power not only to preach the gospel, but also to instruct the faithful, to judge, to absolve, and to administer consolation, both in life and at death; yet He willed to bestow and confer the keys of the Church, especially on the Apostle Peter, in order that it might be in his power to open heaven to them, or to close it. Hence He committed the keys to Peter alone, and also entrusted to him the power of granting Indulgences and Jubilee at certain times and in certain places according as he should consider them to tend to the greater benefit of the flock and the edification of the Church.

[The Pontiffs have not the power of remitting sins so fully as does Christ.] But observe that there is a great difference between the Jubilee instituted by Christ and that granted by His Vicar. Only Christ could and would deal with sinners unrestrictedly and without appointed forms, as a lord, in fact, not having his authority embodied in sacraments or in any other means, who also knew how to search the hearts of the impenitent, and to judge and absolve them. But His

Vicar has not this Divine wisdom and power and must act as the minister of Christ, employing human means and using his power to edification. Hence the old canons prescribe the rule in what times and ways sinners are to be reconciled to the Church, what penance is to be enjoined them as a pure grace, and sometimes relaxed according to the judgment of the bishops and especially of the Sovereign Pontiff. In particular, public sinners were reconciled and admitted to the sacraments on Maundy Thursday. The first to dispute this power of the Church were the Waldenses and the Wycliffites, but these were justly condemned by the Church as enemies, her own custom having always been contrary to what they alleged.

[Why the later Pontiffs granted Indulgences and proclaimed Jubilees more frequently.] Since by degrees the pristine fervour of the faithful waxed cold in the Church, and few could bear the severity of the penance imposed for more grievous sins, as required by the old canons and confessors, it came to pass, not without the will and guidance of the Holy Ghost, that later Pontiffs were more clement and liberal both in granting Indulgences and in promulgating Jubilees. For they considered that some concession must be made to the weakness of the faithful, who dreaded rather than sought the more bitter medicine, and who were in such need of good and salutary punishment that they quitted this world with all their faults and misdeeds upon them and appeared before the tribunal of Christ quite unprepared. Therefore the chief pastors, moved by pity, acted as did the Samaritan towards the sufferer who had been so severely maltreated that he was unable to aid himself and needed oil no less than wine to recover his health.

As regards the present Jubilee no one can complain that anything new is announced to us, since the old and approved custom of the Church is observed, that at fixed times Christians should have their Jubilee, in which each and all may receive a plenary Indulgence of their sins to the health of their souls, and may have a sure proof that, in virtue of the merits of Christ and of the Apostolic power, they are absolved from all sins, on account of which, not only by the ancient canons, but also according to the justice of God, they were liable to undergo many and grievous penalties both in this world and in the world to come. For what greater consolation can a Christian have in life and in death than a good conscience, and a firm confidence that the gospel promise made by Christ to His successors, "Whatsoever thou shalt loose on earth," applies also to them.

II.—Why no one ought to complain of going to Rome to obtain the Jubilee

The principal thing required to obtain the Jubilee Indulgence is to go to Rome, in order that certain churches there may be visited for a few days with true devotion. In order, therefore, that we may not complain, but the more willingly undertake this labour, I will set forth some motives which moved our pious ancestors, and which can still justly move the good, that they may not suffer themselves to be deterred from such a journey.

[The special work of the Patriarchs and sons of Abraham.]

(1) There is the example of the Fathers of the Old Testament, whom God willed to be tried in a long pilgrimage, and to remain pilgrims upon earth. Such were Abraham, Isaac, Jacob, the most illustrious of the Patriarchs, and their descendants, who afterwards under Moses were pilgrims for forty years, until they came to the promised land.[1] (2) God willed that the Israelites should go to Jerusalem every year and celebrate three feasts there (Exod. xxiii.; Deut. xvi.). This custom continued until the time of Christ, who also

---

[1] In the first book of Moses it is written that the holy Rebecca, Isaac's wife, after she had conceived, went that she might consult the Lord at the altar of Abraham, that is, where prayers were offered; as Caleb also journeyed to the same place and prayed (Num. xiii.). Absolom, David's son, also had a devotion for this place, and wished to perform his worship there, thus he says, I will go and perform my vows, which I vowed to my Lord in Hebron (2 Kings xv.). In Hebron were the sepulchres of the prophets, and there the faithful more willingly worshipped, and God more peculiarly manifested Himself. . . . Not only the Jews, but the Gentiles also were accustomed to make pilgrimages to the Holy City from far-off places. Hence John (xxii.) writes of the *Gentiles*, who came up that they might worship at the feast day. Acts viii. The Ethiopian Eunuch was journeying to worship at Jerusalem. The shepherds of Bethlehem are praised in the gospel because they journeyed and specially sought Christ in the place of His nativity, and there adored Him. Still greater praise have the Magi, coming from afar, and journeying at so much expense, that they may worship the Messiah and honour Him with royal gifts. So also praise is given to the Maries, in that they visited the sepulchre of Christ, and gave example to the rest of the faithful, who afterwards always had that place in great honour, and visited it from all parts of the world, that the saying of Isaiah might be fulfilled, "And His sepulchre shall be glorious."

Himself came up to Jerusalem with His parents according to the custom of the feast (Luke ii.). (3) [The example of Christ.] Christ came eight times to Jerusalem, and there celebrated the feasts of Tabernacles, of the Encenium, and of the Pasch, that He might give us also an example of willingly making pilgrimages to holy places. (4) It is believed that Peter, after he had received the Holy Ghost, came at least five times to Jerusalem, as also Simon Metaphrastes observes. (5) Paul, after his conversion, came gladly and frequently to Jerusalem, desiring to celebrate there the feast of Pentecost, as the Acts of the Apostles teach us. (6) The example of the Saints. Great Saints were accustomed to journey from various places to the Holy Land, thus princes and kings went to great expense on that account, and led powerful armies there with them. So also St. Jerome was a pilgrim, and before him the Empress Helena, so, too, were St. Paula of Rome, the Emperor Heraclitus, Epiphanius, Nicholas.

III.—On Pilgrimage to the Tombs of the Apostles

Is it, indeed, a new thing to go on pilgrimage to the tombs of the Apostles Peter and Paul, who are the princes of the Apostles, and have a more honoured sepulchre than all kings and Cæsars?[1]

[The excellence of Rome.] There is the multitude of relics of martyrs of every condition, who have sanctified Rome with their blood. There is the Apostolic Seat, which Christ exalted above the chair of Moses, and to which He subjected all Christian kings and princes. Rome is the head of the world, the queen of the nations, the place chosen by God above every place to the supreme rule, first in the secular, now in the spiritual dominion. The Church of Rome is the mother and mistress of all churches, which, in particular, gave to us Germans our first Apostles or bishops, and which transferred the Roman empire from the Greeks to the Germans. She is a city exalted above every city of the East and West.

Objection I.—It is not every one who has the leisure or who is able to go to Rome.—That is certainly true and evident; and the Jubilee is

[1] In the German version it continues—"It has always been held by the Church that it is a praiseworthy and most Christian act to visit Rome. Origen bound himself by vow to visit the tomb of the Apostle Peter. And Eusebius writes that he faithfully discharged this vow. Chrysostomus says (Hom. 5 de S. Job)—If I were strong and free from cares I would make a toilsome journey to visit Peter's chains."

not recommended to any except those who can undertake the journey and have no grave hindrances. So that it is enjoined on no man as a duty to go to Rome, but men are enjoined not to condemn or hinder others from going, but rather to praise and help those who are ready and free to perform this good work.

Objection II.—Many abuses attended, and still attend, these pilgrimages, either from the ignorance or wickedness of man.—But surely there is nothing, however good and holy, which the wicked do not abuse. Is wine to be done away with because it leads to riotous living? Is the Word of God to be treated with contempt because to many the text of scripture is poison and death? Was not Christ set for the fall of many, and for a sign that shall be contradicted? The true use of the Jubilee is not for any desire of seeing Rome or any greed of gain, but it is to make the journey to Rome from devotion, and in order to gain the spiritual fruit which is promised to all who come devoutly and visit the temples. [It is not praiseworthy to have been at Jerusalem, but to have lived well at Jerusalem.] By so doing one is made a participator of the grace which God gives in so holy a place more largely than elsewhere, and one bears witness to the Catholic belief, together with so many others of the faithful.

IV.—What Profit there is in the Jubilee which we gain at Rome

1. It is profitable to the Christian as an act of profession of the true and Catholic faith which the Church, particularly at this time, requires of her sons, and wishes them to maintain against the Wycliffites and Waldenses and all false Christians, who do not heed but condemn pilgrimages, Indulgences, and all the grace attached to the Jubilee.

2. It is an act not only of faith, but also of reverence which the true faithful show towards the holy Apostolic See, and towards the mother of all the churches, exalted by Christ above all churches. There the Christian shows himself (*a*) to be a sheep of that universal shepherd to whom Christ committed His flock. (*b*) To belong to the faith of Peter, for which Christ prayed that it should not fail. (*c*) To be founded on that rock which has the promise that the gates of hell shall not prevail against it [into which treachery cannot effect an entrance, being, as she is, the mother and nurse of all churches].[1] (*d*) To be a citizen of that Church whose faith is made known to the whole world (Rom. 2). (*e*) To

[1] This clause is interpolated in the handwriting of B. Canisius himself.

confide in the grace of Christ, which He promised to Peter and to his successors, to whom He delivered the keys of the kingdom of heaven for the remitting of sins.

3. It is a work of real and voluntary penance, undertaken from a good motive, for sins committed, and whether a man suffers much or little by the way, whether he watches or whether he sleeps, all the journey and toil and expense is singularly meritorious, and is profitable to the eternal salvation of his soul.

4. Such a pilgrimage affords a great occasion for reminding ourselves of the true characteristics of the good Christian pilgrim, namely, that he should withdraw the mind from earthly and temporal goods, because we have here no abiding city, but as pilgrims we seek one to come, and we are, as it were, in a foreign land, and ought to hasten to our true country. It warns the pilgrim that he should lay aside heavy burdens, and be content with few and necessary things, lest he be hindered on his way; therefore he must avoid drunkenness, feastings, pleasure, and the cares of this life. He should habituate himself to patience, and care for nothing, but gladly suffer vexations, hunger, thirst, heat, cold, praise, or blame. He knows how to console himself with the hope of a good inn and honest entertainment at supper and at night. Such a pilgrim was David. "I shall be satisfied," he said, "when Thy glory shall appear" (Psalm xvi. 15).

5. It is a work of great prudence to make ready the soul for the grace of God and to set out to journey so far for God's sake that we may more fully attain the plenary Indulgence, and partake more largely of the merits of Christ and of His Saints. On which account many formerly travelled to Jerusalem, Compostella, Rome, and other sacred places. Not that they doubted that God and the grace of God were everywhere, and to be found everywhere when rightly sought and invoked, but because they knew that God often manifests Himself and shows forth His power and His grace more in one place than in another; as also He wills during this life to deal with men in divers manners through the agency of His Saints. They knew by experience also that both they themselves and other good men were often, by reason of the places they dwell in, aroused to greater devotion and to pray more diligently and effectually; nor, indeed, can it be doubted that God imparts His grace more abundantly to those who more diligently and earnestly labour, pray, beg, importune, and knock to obtain it.

6. [The city of Rome instructs the faithful.] As far as regards the place itself the pilgrim can confirm his faith and excite his devotion more at Rome than elsewhere. He sees there before his eyes the city in which the first and principal Apostles preached with their lips the gospel of Christ, and where many books of the New Testament were written, as the Gospel of Mark, the Epistles of Peter, the Acts of the Apostles set down by Luke, and some of the Epistles of Paul. He sees the city, the streets of which all the holy martyrs trod and consecrated by their blood, and adorn and protect with their relics. Who would not be moved at seeing the place where Peter was fastened to the cross, Paul beheaded with the sword, John cast into a vessel of boiling oil, where Peter said to Christ, "Lord, whither goest Thou?"—the place, I say, where Lawrence was roasted on the gridiron, Sebastian was shot with arrows? The house of St. Agnes, of St. Cecilia, the staircase of St. Alexis. Yes, the holy steps which were in Pilate's house, up which staircase Christ went at the time of His bitter passion, and which He sprinkled with His blood. [The title of the cross, the column to which He was bound.[1]] I pass over the seven principal churches known to all the world, and enriched by many privileges and precious relics of the Saints. I omit the many learned excellent Pontiffs, conspicuous for various gifts, who, after Peter, have shown themselves to the whole of Christendom as perfect pastors and rulers, and have preserved the Church in truth and obedience during so many centuries. I leave out also the distinguished clergy and the admirable people, who jointly exhibit such an example of all virtues that many strangers are justly astonished at beholding such piety towards God and devotion in the churches, such charity for the poor, such holy eagerness in the worship of God and the reception of the sacraments.

7. This year affords great consolation to men both during life and at death, if any one, out of devotion, desires to gain the Indulgence at Rome and receives it. For he has then a sure token that those sins are remitted by God, for which, according to Divine justice, and in accordance with the ancient canons, he ought to suffer long and severe penance from God and the Church, being bound to perform seven years' public penance for one sin. For what can oppress and sadden the conscience of a man more deeply both in life and death than the memory of grievous sins for which he has done or suffered nothing, nor ever

[1] Interpolated in the handwriting of Blessed Canisius.

perfectly reconciled himself to God and the Church, nor by the Apostolic power freed himself from the sin and the penalty due to it? Is it not terrible to fall into the hands of the living God, and to receive in vain the grace offered, through which participation in the passion of Christ and the merits of the Saints is conferred upon us, so that we may pass out of this life free from anxiety and cleansed from our sins? Oh what a blessed confidence! which Christ confirms in the word spoken to Peter, "Whatever thou shalt loose on earth"! The time will come when we must render an account of our debts to the uttermost farthing, and what we have not paid here we shall be compelled to pay in unspeakable suffering in another world? We shall be sorry for our negligence then.

8. It is becoming and efficacious and helpful to the Christian to offer worship to God in such a place and season, when so many thousands of the faithful of Christ turn towards God in one spirit, one faith, and with similar devotion, together praying and seeking the grace and blessing by which they may gain the true Jubilee in this life and in that which is to come. So much the more efficacious, without doubt, will be the contrition, confession, and prayer of those who in Christ's name and in true faith unite themselves with their chief pastor, in whom Christ wills to be recognised and honoured, by whom also He dispenses to-day the treasure of His merits to all those who are obedient and penitent. And are we better than so many Saints—so many righteous and pious of both sexes—who hasten to Rome for this end and visit those holy places, that like true Israelites they may be freed from ancient bondage, that they may be no longer bondmen to sin, and may be cleansed from all their guilt in this joyful year of Jubilee?

APPENDIX B

Giotto's Fresco of the Proclamation of the First Jubilee by Pope Boniface VIII

Comments of M. Eugène Müntz

The interior of the *loggia* was adorned with frescos, which tradition attributes to Giotto, and a fragment of which, representing Boniface VIII. standing between two members of the pontifical court and proclaiming the Jubilee, is still preserved in the Lateran Basilica. Modern critics all seem to believe that the original composition only comprised these three figures. But a drawing which I discovered several years ago in the Ambrosian library at Milan shows that the picture intended to represent the institution of the Jubilee was in reality much more important. This sketch to which I refer reproduces the style of the original in the most imperfect manner, but everything would lead us to believe that, from a material point of view at least, it is scrupulously exact. We see there the Pope standing under a baldachino which is supported by pillars of porphyry or serpentine marble; Boniface VIII., wearing the tiara, rests his left hand on a rich oriental carpet laid on the balustrade of the loggia, while with the right hand raised he announces to the faithful, *urbi et orbi*, the opening of that Jubilee of 1300 which has played so large a part in the annals of the Eternal City. On the Pope's right is an individual who, judging from the absence of the tonsure, appears to be a lay functionary; on his left stands a cleric holding a parchment roll on which we read, BONIFATIUS EP. SERVUS SERVORUM DEI, AD PERPETUAM REI MEMORIAM. Farther off, on both sides of the baldachino, stand prelates, soldiers of the pontifical guard, and courtiers. The arms of the Church, alternating with those of the Gaetani family, form the decoration of that part of the loggia. The pontifical umbrella may be specially noted; it is one of the oldest examples of this emblem known. Below is seen the crowd listening with surprise and delight to the promulgation of the Bull. Such was the composition, at once graphic and imposing, of which the sketch in the Ambrosian library is the only memorial now left to us.

A passage from the valuable treatise of Onofrio Panvinio on the churches of Rome, a passage which seems to have escaped the notice of modern archæologists, proves that the decoration of the loggia of Boniface VIII. was not confined to this fresco only. The *Institution of the Jubilee* formed part of a scheme, comprising, as well, the *Baptism of Constantine* and the *Building of the Lateran Basilica.* Here are the words of Panvinio—"De pulpito Bonifacii VIII. Papæ.—Inter aulam quam Salam Concilii vocant, et hanc quam supra descripsi porticum, est alia porticus oblonga, et de novo restituta, qua ad palatium ex basilica Constantiniana et Sala Concilii iter est; in cuius fine occidentem versus est pulpitum marmoreum a Bonifacio VIII. factum, totum fere depictum et emblematibus ornatum. Pulpitum extra Concilii aulam porrectum est, totum e lateribus et marmore factum. Picturæ pro temporum conditione elegantissimæ existimantur, Cimabonis egregii pictoris manu factæ, qui primus Italiæ picturam post antiquos restituit. In his pictus Bonifacius VIII. populo ex eo maeniano benedicens, Constantini baptismus, et basilicæ Lateranensis exædificatio: multis in locis sunt familiæ Caietanæ, ex qua Bonifacius fuit, insignia, cum hoc elogio: DOMINUS BONIFACIUS PAPA VIII. FECIT TOTUM OPUS PRÆSENTIS THALAMI. ANNO DOMINI MCCC."[1]

Cardinal Rasponi, whose work[2] is hardly more than an abstract from Panvinio, adds no new information beyond that afforded by the illustrious Veronese monk. He confines himself to telling us that in his time several amateurs attributed the frescos of the loggia of Boniface VIII., not to Cimabue, but to Giotto. "Pictura quoque eximia decoratum erat Cimaboti per ea tempora celeberrimi artificis opera, utpote qui multis a sœculis ejus artis restituendæ princeps in Italia fuisse dicitur, quamvis non desint qui picturas eas potius Giotti fuisse putent. In iis pictus cernebatur Pontifex ipse Bonifacius, Populo Romano ex eo pulpito seu pegmate apostolicam benedictionem more majorum impertiens. Constantini quoque Magni baptismus visebatur, ac præterea ædificatio Lateranensis Basilicæ cum hoc epigrammate: *Dominus Bonifacius Papa octavus fecit totum opus præsentis thalami. Anno Domini Millesimo trecentesimo.* Superest etiam hodieque picturæ hujus nonnihil et præcipue Bonifacii octavi quam diximus effigies, eamque cum pariete, in quo erat expressa, in claustrum Basilicæ Lateranensis translatam nunc intuemur."

After remaining for a long time exposed in the cloister of the Lateran, the fragment representing Boniface VIII. standing between his two followers was transferred to the nave of the Basilica, through the care of the Gaetani family, and attached to one of the pillars, where it still remains. It was restored on this occasion, and the restorer saw fit to substitute a magnificent arcade, supported by two columns, for the flat-roofed baldachino. The latest historian of the Lateran Basilica, M. Rohault de Fleury,[3] was not wrong in doubting the authenticity of this arcade and in saying that it singularly resembles that which in

---

[1] *De præcipuis Romæ sanctioribusque Basilicis quas septem Ecclesias vulgo vocant Liber*, p. 182.

[2] *De Basilica et Patriarchio Lateranensi libri quatuor.* Rome, 1656, in folio, p. 327.

[3] *Le Latran au Moyen-âge*, Atlas, p. 23, 24. Cf. the text, 201 and 373.

Raphael's *Burning of the Borgo* surmounts the loggia of Benediction at the Vatican (this loggia never existed save in Raphael's imagination, who was perhaps prompted to paint it by a design of Bramante). The Ambrosian drawing proves that in the original painting there was not the least trace of an arcade. Giotto's fragment has been subjected to a fresh restoration during the course of this century, as may be seen by comparing it with the engraving published by Agincourt.[1]

APPENDIX C

The Porta Santa and the Golden Gate of Jerusalem

Since the earlier chapters of this work were in type some fresh details have come to the writer's notice which seem to throw further light on the history of the unwalling ceremony.

In the first place, it may be noticed that the evidence for the existence of a walled-up door, both at St. Peter's and at the Lateran, long before the time of Alexander VI., is overwhelming. Beside the authorities already quoted in chapter ii., we may note the testimony of an English traveller, William Wey, one of the original fellows of Eton College. He seems to have visited Rome on his return from Palestine in 1458 or 1462, and informs us that "in the vestibule of the church of St. Peter's are six doors, one of which is closed, and this is the true Golden Door."[2] Without taking account, then, of the *aperi ostium* of the supposed vision of Clement VI., we have the following explicit testimonies—First, that of Pedro Tafur, c. 1437; he connects the Jubilee Indulgence with the right of sanctuary, which, he maintains, existed in pagan times for all who crossed the threshold of the "puerta tarpea" upon the site of the Lateran. At the request of Constantine, Pope Sylvester published a Bull proclaiming the same immunity from punishment for Christian sinners who took sanctuary there. The privilege, however, was grossly abused, and the Popes consequently ordered the door to be walled-up at all seasons save certain times of

---

[1] *Etudes sur l'histoire des Arts à Rome*, par E. Müntz. In *Mélanges d'Archéologie et d'Histoire*, vol. for 1881, pp. 128-132.

[2] "Item in introitu dicte ecclesie sunt sex porte, de quibus una est clausa, et hec est vera porta aurea."—W. Wey, *Itinerarium* (Roxburghe Club), p. 144.

special grace. Formerly the door was only unwalled once in a hundred years; this was afterwards reduced to fifty, and now, says Tafur, it is opened at the will of the Pope.[1] Then in 1450 we have the testimony both of Hämmerlein and of Giovanni Rucellai, already sufficiently detailed. Again, in 1452, we have the narrative of Nicholas Muffel, who travelled to Rome in the train of Frederick, King of the Romans. This pilgrim gives a tolerably full account of the "Golden Gate" (*porta aurea*) at St. Peter's,[2] it will be remembered that this is also the term used by both the witnesses last named. "Behind the altar," says Muffel, "on the right hand as one enters the chapel where the Holy Veronica is preserved, is to be found the *Golden Gate* which is made of costly marble.[3] Through this Christ our Lord bore His holy cross, but it was brought to Rome by the Emperors Titus and Vespasian." Muffel then proceeds to tell the story of the murderer, already related in the text, whose presumption caused the door to be walled-up. He adds that the stone which was rolled before the holy sepulchre when our Lord was buried there was also built up in the Golden Door. The same story is told in the Rombüchlein of c. 1475, which speaks at some length of the "Golden Gate" (*gulden phort*) both at St. Peter's and at the Lateran. Of this last guide-book six editions were printed prior to the year 1500, and in that year itself the demand was so great, no doubt on account of the Jubilee, that six other editions were issued in German by Roman printers within the twelvemonth. This persistent recurrence of the name "Golden Gate," when taken more particularly in connection with Muffel's story that the gate was that through which Christ our Lord passed with His cross, points unmistakably to some lingering echo of the traditions brought back by pilgrims to the Holy Land concerning the Golden Gate of Jerusalem. It is true that our Saviour is believed to have passed through this, not during the time of His passion, but on Palm Sunday; but a slight confusion as to such a detail is easily understood, neither can we ever hope, in the growth

---

[1] El Papa mandó çerrar é que no se abriese si non de çiento á çiento años, é despues abaxó á çinquenta años; é agora como el Papa lo quiere disponer.—*Andanças é Viajes de Pero Tafur*, p. 37.

[2] N. Muffel's *Beschreibung der Stadt Rom*, 128te Publication des Literarischen Vereins in Stuttgart, p. 20.

[3] To this day a particular kind of precious marble is known as *Porta Santa* marble. It may well be that the name is considerably older than the sixteenth century.

and development of these popular traditions, to unravel the tangle completely.

It seems worth while therefore to set down here something of what we find recorded in the narratives of pilgrims prior to 1500 regarding the Golden Gate of Jerusalem.

About the year 1171, during the period of Latin domination, Theodorich, in his account of the Holy Land, tells us of Jerusalem. "The city has seven gates, whereof they firmly lock six every night until after sunrise. The seventh is closed by a wall, and is only opened on Palm Sunday and on the day of the Exaltation of the Cross."

Again, when speaking of the ceremonies of Palm Sunday, he tells us of a tradition of our Saviour. "He (our Lord) went on beyond the valley of Josaphat and the brook Cedron until He arrived at the Golden Gate, which is twofold. As He approached one of the doors opened of itself, for the bolt fell out, and violently drawing out its ring, made the other fly open with a loud noise, wherefore a chapel has been consecrated in honour of it, wherein this ring, which is covered with gilding, is regarded with great reverence. The gate itself is never opened except on Palm Sunday and on the day of the Exaltation of the Cross, because the Emperor Heraclius passed through it with a large piece of the wood of the cross, which had been brought from Persia."[1]

Slightly later than this, c. 1181, we have another description in a French treatise upon the Holy Land.

"At the end of this pavement, towards the rising sun, one goes down some steps to get to the Golden Gate. After descending them is found a broad space reaching to the gate itself. This is the court which Soliman made. No one passed through these gates, which were walled-up, except twice a year, when the walling was removed, viz., on Palm Sunday, when they went in procession, because Jesus Christ passed through on this day and was received in procession, and on the day of the feast of the Holy Cross in September, because the Holy Cross was brought into Jerusalem through those gates when Heraclius, the Emperor of Rome, made his conquests in Persia, and brought it back through this gate into the city, being met by a procession. And because no one ever went out of the city through this gate, there was a postern at the side called the gate of Josaphat. Those who wished to get out

[1] I have borrowed this translation from that of the Palestine Pilgrims' Text Society, p. 35.

of the city from this quarter went through the postern, the postern being on the left hand of the Golden Gate."[1]

It would be easy to multiply such testimonies, but not to be too tedious it will be sufficient to quote the full account of the traveller Felix Fabri, who wrote about two hundred years later, *i.e*, 1480. He does not say much of the walling-up of the gate, but he adds other details even more interesting for the analogies they suggest with the *Porta Santa.*

"When we came to the corner of the wall where the northern wall joins the eastern one, we turned our faces away from the east, and looked along the wall towards the south, where we saw another great city gate on the east side, whose lofty tower had been thrown down and ruined. This gate is termed the Golden Gate, and through it the Lord Jesus entered the city on Palm Sunday, sitting upon an ass, while beneath it Joachim and Anna met together in obedience to a former command, because they had been told by a divine oracle that of them the Virgin Mary should be born. Moreover, it was here also that the following glorious miracle was took place: When the Emperor Heraclius, having conquered his enemies, and regained the cross which had been taken by the Persians, wanted to ride on horseback through this gate in imperial state, he no sooner came up to the gate than the stones joined themselves together, and became a closed, solid wall; nor could he enter until he had laid aside all worldly pomp, when at last, barefooted and humbled, he was permitted to enter with all his army, bearing the Lord's cross.

"Up to this gate the Lord was led in triumph from the Mount (of Olives) to the temple, with palms and green boughs, as also we read in the thirteenth chapter of the First Book of Maccabees that Simon entered it; and in the Second Book of Maccabees, and the tenth chapter, we read of the green boughs and palms. The Saracins will not allow us to come near this gate, and we could by no means obtain leave to go thither, because without it is the Saracen burying-ground, over which they will not suffer Christians to walk. However, we knelt looking towards it from afar off, and after worshipping God received plenary Indulgences. These Indulgences are given to every one who stands opposite this gate afar off and worships it, as many times as he does it.

"It is believed that the ruinous walls which now stand there are indeed the ruins of the true Golden Gate, through which the Lord

[1] Michelant and Raynaud, *Itinéraires*, p. 151.

entered sitting on an ass; because Titus, when he destroyed Jerusalem, left some towers standing for fortresses and watch-towers, whereof the tower of the Golden Gate was one, and was left standing, together with its woodwork. This woodwork is at the present day covered with plates of gilded copper. The Saracens cut off pieces and scraps of these plates and nails, and sell them to the Christians, because many Christians take great pains to get a piece of this gate, and often risk their lives by going thither at night and tearing little pieces off it. Some lavish their money instead, and bribe some Saracen to pluck morsels off the gate, and to give them copper or wood in return for gold and silver. The reason why relics from this gate are so dear is because it is said (whether it be a vain superstition or not I cannot tell) that whosoever carries about a morsel of that gate with him will be proof against apoplexy, falling sickness, and plague. In days of old, when the Christians possessed Jerusalem, a great feast was celebrated at this gate on Palm Sunday. On the previous Saturday, or Vigil of Palm Sunday, all the clergy went forth to Bethany, and kept the vigil all night in the Church of St. Lazarus. In the early dawn they went forth in procession from Bethany to Bethphage, where they set one of the great bishops, dressed in his priestly vestments, upon an ass, and went in procession towards the holy city. As they came down from the Mount of Olives the rest of the clergy and religious orders, with all the populace of the city, came in procession to meet them, carrying boughs of palm; and, after the fashion spoken of in the Gospel, they cut boughs from the olive trees and strewed them in the way, and spread out their garments in the way, crying 'Hosanna!' etc. When they came up from the valley towards the gate, the gate used to be shut, and young men stood upon the tower thereof singing *Gloria, laus*, etc. When they had done singing this hymn, they brought the bishop into the temple with great rejoicings. After the loss of the holy city, and the driving out of the Latins from thence, the Armenians continued to celebrate this festival with their bishop for many years until, at the instigation of the devil, they (the Saracens) began to bury their damned dead here, after which they blocked up the gate. Nowadays, therefore, they hurry through Palm Sunday in the following manner:—On that day itself, after divine service and the eating of food, the brethren of Mount Zion go out to Bethany, thence walk in singing procession up to Bethphage, where they set one of the brethren in his priestly vestments upon an ass, and accompany him towards the city singing praises. As they descend the Mount of Olives the other Eastern Christians run to meet them with boughs of palm and olive, and with strewing of garments in the way, and lead him as far as the brook Cedron, where the procession ends, for they dare not mount up towards the city singing praises in this fashion, lest the Saracens should break up their procession by pelting it with stones. It is wonder enough that they suffer them to do thus much, for a hundred or even fifty years ago they would not have permitted it, and as little as twenty years ago the Christians had not as much liberty as they now have. May God make it still greater, for His own praise's sake, that the mouths of those who sing of Him in these most holy places may not be for ever shut." [1]

To those who have noted the eagerness shown by the Romans down to our own day, and attested as early as 1450, to acquire fragments of the Holy Door, the analogy presented by the Golden Gate of Jerusalem will offer many points of interest. Our Appendix may be brought to a close with another brief statement of an Italian pilgrim.

"On the other side, in the walls of the city (which has been elsewhere rebuilt, but in this part has been only repaired), is seen the old Golden Gate, through which our Lord Jesus Christ (after having raised Lazarus from the dead), seated on the ass, made His glorious and solemn entry into Jerusalem, and was received with great honour and rejoicing by the people (who had come to the feast) three days before His bitter and cruel passion; crying Hosanna, son of David, blessed is He that cometh in the name of the Lord, etc.

"The gate is so called from having been gilded, and it was double, having its cornices in carved work resembling foliage, and by the inscrutable providence of God (after the city was in the hands of the Infidels), it has been closed and walled-up.

"Some suppose that they have done this because it is near the temple, in order that the court of the latter (by the entering of the people who passed through it) might not be profaned.

"On this account the great Soliman has caused the Sheep Gate, now called St. Stephen's Gate, to be widened in this vicinity, on the two sides of which, contrary to the laws of the Turks, are carved two lions, who look at each other, and similar carving is over the entrance to a mosque on the other side of the city, of which we made mention when speaking of our arrival." [2]

---

[1] Wanderings of Brother Felix Fabri (P.P.T.S.), pp. 458-461.

[2] *Viaggio di Gierusalemme*, pp. 159, 160.

APPENDIX D

The following brief account of the solemn exposition of the heads of St. Peter and Paul at the Lateran in 1580, which was accidentally omitted in its proper place, may be inserted here. Montaigne seems to have had a clear view and was evidently of opinion that what he saw was the actual flesh of the holy apostles. Presumably the skulls at this period had been enclosed in some kind of mask, preserving the semblance of human features; for such a shrewd observer as Montaigne could hardly have been so misled by an ordinary silver reliquary.

"On Easter Eve I went to see, at St. John Lateran, the heads of St. Paul and St. Peter, which are exhibited here on that day. The heads are entire, with the hair, flesh, colour, and beard, as though they still lived; St. Peter has a long, pale face, with a brilliant complexion approaching the sanguine, with grey peaked beard, and a papal mitre on his head; St. Paul is of a dark complexion, with a broader, fuller face, a large head, and thick grey beard. These heads stand in a recess some way above you. When they are shown, the people are called together by the ringing of a bell, and a curtain is then slowly pulled down, behind which you see the heads, placed side by side. The time allowed for viewing them is that in which you can repeat an *Ave Maria*, and then the curtain is again raised; shortly after the curtain descends, and once more ascends, and this is repeated thrice, so as to afford every one present an opportunity of seeing. This exhibition takes place four or five times in the course of the day. The recess is about a pike's length above you, and there is a thick iron grating before the heads. Several lighted tapers are placed in front of them, outside the recess, but still you cannot very well distinguish the particular features. At least I could not, and I saw them two or three times. There was a bright polish over the faces which made them look something like our masks."[1]

---

[1] *Montaigne's Journey into Italy*, p. 582.

INDEX